Antonio Rosmini

The origin of ideas

Vol. I

Antonio Rosmini

The origin of ideas
Vol. I

ISBN/EAN: 9783742861481

Manufactured in Europe, USA, Canada, Australia, Japa

Cover: Foto ©Thomas Meinert / pixelio.de

Manufactured and distributed by brebook publishing software
(www.brebook.com)

Antonio Rosmini

The origin of ideas

[*Formal sanction to the first edition of this work given at Rome in* 1830.]

NIHIL OBSTAT.
Fr. Antonius Franc. Orioli Or. Min. Conv.
Censor TheoL

NIHIL OBSTAT.
J. B. Pianciani S. J. Cens. Philos.

IMPRIMATUR.
Fr. Jos. Maria Velzi Sac. Pal. Apost. Magister.

IMPRIMATUR.
J. Della Porta Patr. Constantinop.
Vicesg.

THE

ORIGIN OF IDEAS

BY

ANTONIO ROSMINI SERBATI

TRANSLATED FROM THE FIFTH ITALIAN EDITION OF THE

NUOVO SAGGIO

SULL' ORIGINE DELLE IDEE

VOL. I.

ARBOR SCIENTIÆ
ARBOR VITÆ

LONDON

KEGAN PAUL, TRENCH, & CO., 1 PATERNOSTER SQUARE

1883

PREFACE.

---

1. ROSMINI'S *Nuovo Saggio, or Treatise on the Origin of Ideas*, was first published by Salviucci of Rome, in 1830, during the pontificate, and under the auspices, of Pope Pius VIII. It may be claimed that this work had the sanction, directly or indirectly, of five Popes. Pius VII., in 1823, urged Rosmini to apply himself diligently to the studies which led him to plan and begin it in 1825. Leo XII. encouraged him to proceed with those studies. Pius VIII. stimulated him to the same end, and lived to see the first edition published with the *imprimatur* of the Master of the Sacred Apostolic Palace. Gregory XVI. (a warm personal friend of the author) welcomed a new edition of it in 1836-8 ; and three other editions appeared, with full ecclesiastical approval, during the pontificate of Pius IX. To meet the wishes of many in our own country, where philosophical studies are steadily gaining ground, the present translation has been made from the fifth Italian edition, which appeared in 1851, carefully revised by the author.

No sooner had the first edition of the *Nuovo Saggio* been published than it produced a deep impression on the minds of Italian thinkers, who were not slow to acknowledge that its author had established a right to be deemed a great philosopher, many of them going so far as to proclaim him the greatest philosopher of the age. His subsequent works confirmed the high reputation he had thus won—and which he continues to win, from all who seriously face and are capable of overcoming the difficulties of his system.

But, though Rosmini's title to the rank of a great philosopher was promptly and generally allowed, the system he expounded did not pass unchallenged. Indeed, it would have been a marvel if the *Nuovo Saggio* had met with no opposition when it first appeared. The author struck at the root of many of the philosophical systems then dominant ; he laid bare the unsound assumptions on which they were based, and assailed them with all the force of a keen, searching and unsparing logic. It was very natural that the teachers and disciples of the systems thus exposed should set themselves against a work which threatened the destruction of their most cherished theories. In battling for these theories, they made use of every available weapon to maintain their own position and obscure the new light which Rosmini threw on all philosophy, ancient and modern.

Unfortunately many of those who thus felt themselves obliged to enter the lists against Rosmini, too often conducted the controversy as mere partisans. The triumph of their own theories appearing to them to be all-important, they did not hesitate to try and secure victory by misrepresenting the system they opposed. Probably they misunderstood it ; for it requires close study and clear heads to master it. Possibly the bitterest of its assailants acted in good faith while misjudging or misstating its principles. Be that as it may, its opponents have succeeded in throwing a misty atmosphere around it and producing some serious misconceptions as to the meaning of its author. Hence the necessity of a Preface dealing with the main objections that have been persistently urged against Rosmini's system.

In order to keep within the proper bounds of a Preface we must state these main objections briefly and content ourselves with indicating the answers to them.

2. Rosmini has been charged with holding and defending the most opposite opinions. At one time he is styled a sensist and subjectivist; at another, an idealist. Now he is called a pantheist, now a rationalist, and now an ontologist. Sometimes he is regarded as only an inaccurate interpreter of Kant; at other times he is classed as a Hegelian. In short, all or most of the main and clashing errors of modern philosophy are at times, in some form or other, attributed to him. And this happens, in spite of the fact that in his numerous philosophical works he resolutely attacks each and all of the errors contained in the systems he is accused of approving. A careful study of the *Nuovo Saggio* will, of itself, enable anyone to see that he not only repudiates the false views gratuitously attributed to him, but that he demonstrates their unsoundness with a vigour of argument and a cogency of logic that have never been surpassed.

How then does it come about that he is so egregiously misrepresented? Is it that, notwithstanding his extraordinary intellectual gifts and his vast philosophical erudition, he was such a careless writer as to express himself, frequently, in vague, ambiguous phrases which left his meaning at the mercy of every captious critic? No; for anyone who studies his works will soon be convinced that he was a most painstaking author, and this fact is nowhere more evident than in his philosophical productions. Some of the ablest literary and scientific critics of Italy maintain that he possessed a grasp of mind, an insight into the most hidden springs of thought, an analytical and critical discrimination, a clearness of expression, a logical consistency of reasoning and language, which it would be difficult to find united in any other writer. The severely minute examination which he often made of the thoughts and expressions of others was but a result of the continued and intense watchfulness he kept over the workings of his own mind, and over the best way of clothing his ideas in accurate phraseology. We do not mean to say that his style was faultless, but that it was vigorous, and so perspicuous as to leave his opponents no excuse on that ground.

3. To account for the misconceptions and misrepresentations that have been made to surround Rosmini's system, we have but to take up the *Nuovo Saggio* and consider how very abstruse and difficult of solution are the questions it discusses. The author seeks nothing less than to penetrate to the very source of all thought and of every kind of knowledge, to discover the true nature of human reason, to shew not merely whence our cognitions take their rise, but to demonstrate their truth, validity, and certitude. His investigations were therefore of the deepest and most extensive kind, and he found an answer to all his inquiries in the *Light of Reason.* He had then to describe what this light is, to prove how it enters into every act of thought, to point out how it gives fundamental principles, and order, and place to each of the sciences. The better to do all this he had to consider the Light of Reason in a great variety of relations, and to give to each of these relations its appropriate name ; he had to present the entire *scibile humanum,* both natural and supernatural, as forming but one great and magnificent whole.

If we but reflect on the abstract nature of the subjects Rosmini undertook to treat, and on the many and different aspects in which he had to contemplate this nature for presentation to others, we shall easily understand how diverse and even contradictory opinions could be attributed to him by many readers, according to their respective mental constitution, education, habit of thought, method of reasoning, ignorance, or prejudice. Some, already wedded to a system or to doctrines impugned by him, would, in consequence, be biassed against him. Others, too superficial to comprehend his real meaning and precise distinctions, or too impatient to

study it diligently, would, for all that, presume to think that
they understood him quite as well as those who had fathomed
the depths of his philosophy and entered fully into all his
views. Moreover, there are many readers of philosophical
works who, though confident of their own capacity to master
the subject, lack that clearness of mental vision so necessary
for distinguishing an object in itself from the multitudinous and
seemingly contradictory forms under which it may be viewed
—so necessary even for keeping it in sight amid the manifold
and often perplexing phrases in which it may have to be
clothed. Such readers are so apt to mistake and misrepresent the author, that Rosmini repeatedly gives them whole-
some warnings and examples in different parts of the *Nuovo
Saggio*, as he does, indeed, in nearly all his scientific works.
When these warnings and examples are neglected or fail of
their effect, grave misconceptions are the natural result ; but
the fault is in the reader, not in the writer.

4. From his earliest years Rosmini exhibited all the qualities which are usually taken to denote the perfect philosopher.
The testimony of those under whom or with whom he studied,
and whose opinions have value, may be thus summed up:
He received from nature the true philosophic spirit and
cultivated it to the utmost. He combined in a high degree
the keenness and accuracy of observation, the searching
analytic power of Aristotle, with the comprehensive mental
grasp and lofty aspirations of Plato. With him education had
been, and ever was, a true 'discipline in accuracy of mind.' He
bestowed more attention to the strengthening and developing
of his intellectual faculties, and to the distinct and clear
expression of his thoughts, than to the accumulation of
knowledge, or to elegance of language. He placed far more
value in the discovery and understanding of principles, and
seeing them in the order of their logical connection, and in the
power of rightly applying them, than in the possession of a

multitude of particular and unconnected truths. Not that he
neglected to store his mind and memory with the philosophic
treasures of the past. Even while yet very young he had
studied and mastered the greatest thinkers the world has ever
seen. He devoted himself with a special ardour to the works
of Plato, Aristotle, St. Augustine, St. Thomas of Aquin,
St. Bonaventure, Leibnitz and Kant. Nor did he neglect
either the English, the French or the Scottish schools. His
philosophic essays and letters prove how intelligently he
studied, and how justly he judged all the great authors he had
thus read.

The *Nuovo Saggio* alone is enough to confirm the testimony
just recorded. This work shows that Rosmini was not only a
man of extraordinary mental capacity, but also that, whilst
yet young, he had amassed a more vast and accurate knowledge of various philosophic systems, ancient, mediæval and
modern, than some of the most distinguished thinkers could
be justly credited with, even after a long life of extensive
reading and the closest application. It is almost needless to
add that Rosmini went on continually increasing his materials ;
and it may well be claimed that a philosophical erudition as
extensive, as deep, and as precise, as is contained in his published works, would be sought for in vain in any other writer.
We may then conclude that both nature and art combined to
make him almost as perfect a pattern for students of philosophy
as it is possible to set before them.

5. When we turn to Rosmini's other works in order to
gather from his own words what a philosopher ought to be,
and what he was ever striving to realise in himself, the conclusion just stated is more than sustained. In his *Introduction
to Philosophy*, after telling us with what youthful ardour he
first dedicated himself to metaphysical studies—how he gave
himself up daily to studying the acknowledged masters of
human thought, how resolutely he applied himself to the

investigation of the most baffling problems, how he never allowed difficulties of any kind to check his perseverance, and how every night he summed up the result of the labours of the day—he goes on to enumerate the chief qualifications of the philosophic inquirer.   In the first place, he lays much stress on the absolute necessity of seeking truth and truth alone, firmly persuaded that, in itself and in its consequences, it must lead to good.   Next, he reminds us that whoever would devote his time to philosophy, must cast aside every form of prejudice likely in the least to hinder him from discovering and possessing truth in all its fulness and distinctness.   Thirdly, he dwells with especial emphasis on what he terms the *liberty of philosophising*.   He declares that he always sought to contemplate and consider every problem, as it came before him, from all possible points of view, to deduce from it all sorts of consequences, and then to compare the conclusions thus arrived at with the truths already found and appropriated, and with the reasonings of other thinkers.   He insists that we must be prepared to sacrifice generously whatever would put the slightest obstacle in the way of truth.   'I have always considered,' he says, 'this generous disposition as being the first and most important duty, in fact the great *sine qua non* for everyone who means to devote himself in earnest to philosophy.   In this belief, I have invariably made it a point to push each of my investigations on from question to question, even to the very last ; and to accept unreservedly the results I found in my hands, whatever they might be ; then to do my best in verifying whether those results were really the best possible to be obtained, and why were they so ; and finally to draw from them legitimate and ultimate conclusions, and to gather up with exultation every one of these conclusions whatever it might be.   Next, I did my very best to discover if such conclusions were really the last, and if so, why they were so.   But all this was merely the first step. Conclusions thus obtained do not as yet deserve a full assent.

They must be regarded as little more than possibly true, till the whole process by which they have been obtained has been demonstrated to be logically correct. This demonstration is the second step, and it consists in attentively examining whether the results we have reached contradict any truth already known as certain, or any probable opinion, or finally, any prejudice, even though gratuitous. For, as truth is ever consistent with itself, if it can be shown that any conclusion whatever, or any necessary consequence from it, is in contradiction with even the least particle of truth, it must undoubtedly be rejected as false; and the whole process will have to be repeated till we discover where the mistake began. If a conclusion conflicts with a probable opinion, this opinion must be thoroughly examined and its meaning made clear before we can take another step. The same is to be said of prejudices generally received. We must not at once refuse to accept them, even when merely gratuitous; but submit them to careful examination in order to learn whether they rest on any ground of reason, or whether there be a reason which will demonstrate them to be baseless or erroneous. In this way the philosopher may by his researches either change opinions and prejudices into well ascertained truths, or detect their erroneousness; and according to the result, he avails himself of them as of a sure sign of some mistake or oversight in his first reasoning, or, leaving them behind, advances courageously on his path.'[1]

6. An accurate knowledge of preceding philosophic systems, respect for the opinions of their authors, and a spirit of conciliation, which seeks rather to harmonise seemingly discordant doctrines than to detect and widen differences of views, may be added to the qualifications already enumerated, and deemed by Rosmini essential to the student of philosophy. A passage in the *Introduction to Philosophy*, tersely sets

[1] *Introduzione alla Filosofia*, p. 53 (Casale, 1851).

before us the chief of these qualifications. Luigi Bonelli having asked him the best way of classifying philosophical systems, and the best dispositions for discovering the truth, Rosmini answered the first question by shewing that systems can be known, not from the names of their authors, but only by a profound study of their principles; and then replied to the second question in the following manner :—'To have received a beautifully moulded soul appears to me to be undoubtedly the best of all dispositions. Next to this is elevation of mind and an unswerving consistency of thought. Then comes the deep knowledge of the Christian Religion, which, the more it is understood, the more it expands and strengthens the wings of the spirit, and enables it to reach the loftiest heights of metaphysical science. Then must be added perfect freedom from all those fetters by which the littleness of man impedes the flight of genius. The mind must be accustomed to gaze on the ideas themselves, stripped of all the trappings of words, schemata, and methods. It must be made to recognise truth under all forms and colours, to love it under all, to abhor every school or system that would impose limits to these forms of truth, and to study profoundly the meanings of words. It is clear from the observations of both Vico and Bonald, that in words are contained the knowledge and sciences possessed by the nations of the earth. We must, then, beware of altering the meanings affixed to words by mankind, or rather, I would say, by Providence, by God Himself. A strict adherence to propriety in the use of words, is the only means for maintaining clearness of ideas, for preserving and harmonising them. Of this propriety, St. Thomas was at once a most patient investigator and a most firm maintainer. Many ancient and modern sophists, and many profane philosophers, sought artfully to alter the true value and force of words. The world could scarcely be deceived except by such alteration. Abuse has been made of almost all philosophical and political terms, as has been frequently shown by various writers. Whoever takes note of the errors that have arisen from the abuse of the word *Nature*, in the sciences of Right and Politics—of the words *Sensation*, *Pleasure*, *Pain*, in Metaphysics; of the words *Equality* and *Liberty* in Politics ; of the word *Wealth* in Political Economy—and of the many others to which, generally, there has been added only a more extensive signification than that given them by common usage, will discover the sources of incredible deceptions to the mind, and of incredible evils to humanity.'[1]

7. When Rosmini first turned his attention to the history of the physical sciences, he was struck with the stupendous progress they have made in modern times. He asked himself to what this could be owing, and he soon found that it flowed directly from the method which such sciences, since the days of Bacon and Galileo, had persistently pursued. He saw that physicists instead of beginning as formerly with mere theory, and afterwards attempting to compel facts to adjust themselves to it, followed the very opposite course. They commenced with facts, carefully observing, analysing and classifying them, so as to enlarge gradually their knowledge of the laws that regulated them. After a close and long study of external nature under the guidance of the safe rules of inductive reasoning, they deduced cautiously their theories, and, by the help of these, proceeded, more enlightened, to further considerations of phenomena. Thus theory and fact were no longer enemies, but the fastest friends, and each gave the other a helping hand. 'Why,' demanded Rosmini, 'should not this method be applied to philosophy, to the internal and spiritual facts of the soul and of consciousness?' He already knew that the philosophers who preceded him had failed most whenever they had forgotten to follow the guidance of observation. He therefore resolved to commence his philo-

[1] *Introduzione alla Filosofia*, p. 387.

sophical researches, not by a criticism of reason, or of the forms
of thought, or of the faculties of the soul—not by inquiring
into the validity of human knowledge; not by attempting to
demonstrate that man possesses truth and certitude—but by
calmly and keenly observing the nature of our cognitions. The
result more than justified this course. Like Kant, he discovered
that whatever is *material* in our knowledge of things, is supplied by the senses and experience; and that all in it which
is purely *formal* is furnished by the mind. But, unlike Kant,
he discovered moreover that all the forms of the mind are
reducible to one, and that this is not subjective, not a creation or emanation of the human spirit, but objective, and
presented to the spirit from without, by God Himself.
Armed with this discovery, he at first thought he might
plunge at once into ontological speculation. But here a
serious reflection made him pause. His study of German
philosophers had convinced him that those powerful reasoners had fallen into grievous errors, because, before having
thoroughly understood the formal and material conditions
of thought, they had rashly endeavoured to carry, as it were
by storm, the almost impregnable fortress of the highest
metaphysics. Thus put on his guard, he determined to move
cautiously step by step; to observe, analyse, compare, so as
to be sure of his ground before making the slightest advance.
He therefore carefully examined the various forms in which
thought presents itself, and the various materials of knowledge furnished to the mind through the external and internal
senses. In this way, he was led gradually to the discovery
of the true nature, origin, and certainty of Ideas, and to the
composition of the *Nuovo Saggio* and the *Logica.* He
was thus enabled to arrive at a clear understanding as to the
nature of sensation, of intelligence, of the materials of cognition, and to write his profound treatises on Anthropology
and Psychology.

8. Having finished these preliminary labours, he felt himself sufficiently equipped to attempt a complete theory of *being.*
This he calls Theosophy, and he divides it into three parts.
In the first part he treats of being taken universally, or
being in general; in the second, of the Infinite or Absolute
Being, or God, in as far as He can be known by mere reason ;
and in the third, of finite being, or the created universe.
This is the pure metaphysical theory of Rosmini, which alone,
he says, deserves the name of theory, because it alone can
solve all the difficulties and antinomies of thought. It must
not, however, be imagined that Rosmini's philosophical system is mere theory, fit only for highly speculative minds and
without any practical importance. On the contrary, he
found in the origin of speculative thought the origin of all
human science, and applied his discovery in such works as
the *Principles of Ethical Science* and the *Philosophy of Right*
and the *Philosophy of Politics.* As in his preceding treatises
he had laid down the principles of all knowledge and science,
and pointed out their applicability to the arts of life, so in
his *Theosophy* he demonstrates where and how all those
principles have their full justification, how man can arrive at
the contemplation of the last reasons of all things, and what
gives dignity and worth to his every thought and act.

Rosmini does not begin with criticism like Kant; nor
with inquiry or methodical doubt, like Des Cartes. He does
not begin with theory, but with fact ; nor with reasoning, but
with observation. At his point of departure he is in a state
of methodical ignorance, thereby showing that he wishes to
find out the data which man must possess as the necessary
conditions for thinking, judging, and acquiring knowledge.
He does not therefore start with the avowed object of demonstrating the validity of cognitions. He simply wants to
discover first of all what these are. Demonstration may
follow, but it will be only a consequence of the method, not
what inspired the method itself. In a word, Rosmini's

method is eminently moderate, because, starting with, and ever accompanied by, an accurate and penetrating observation of external and internal facts, he is able to verify every conclusion at which he arrives. A careful study of the *Nuovo Saggio* will fully justify this last assertion, and will moreover show the superiority of his method over others with which, towards the end of the *Saggio*, he compares it.

9. As a specimen of Rosmini's method of observation let us quote, from his *Restoration of Philosophy in Italy*, a passage in which he tells us how he arrived at the persuasion, that what he terms the *idea of being in general*, is the light of Reason and the principle of Cognition. 'Behold,' he says, 'the principal points of view from which I examined human knowledge.

'I. First of all I took the greatest care to distinguish in it the *material* from the *formal* element. Although this distinction is more or less alluded to by all, I am nevertheless profoundly convinced that no philosopher as yet (I speak of those I have read) has seized it with that full and steady grasp of mind which is necessary for comprehending its nature and feeling its importance. I perceived that all that could be designated as *matter* of our cognitions lay in the subsistent individuals of a species—that *subsistence*, and nothing else, constituted such matter. I saw that the *species* alone (*idea*) was the object of the intellect; and that subsistence as such could not enter into the sphere of this faculty, was not through itself cognisable.

'But if subsistence is not cognisable through itself, shall we not, nevertheless, be able to perceive it?—Yes, but by an act essentially different from that by which our intellect contemplates the species or idea; an act which is not, of its own self, *cognition.* This act belongs, not to the world of ideas, but to that of realities. The world of realities is made up entirely of *sentiments*, of *actions* and *passions* ; whereas in the world of ideas there are neither passions nor actions, but purely *notions* and cognitions. The perception of real things is, then, a passion of our own—that is to say, a passion produced by an action exercised by those things on the substantial sentiment we have of ourselves, and which is called EGO. Thus far, however, there is nothing in the nature of cognition, we are perfectly in the dark. How then shall we pass on to the light ? I answer :—

'The perception of real things, *i.e.* of subsistences, takes place in ourselves ; and owing to this fact it has in us a relation with ideas, with the ideal world, which is also in ourselves. What is the foundation of this relation?—The absolute unity of the EGO. We who, on the one hand, feel struck by the action of the real thing, in other words, have the perception (not cognisable through its own self) of the *subsistence*, are the very same who, on the other hand, have also the intuition of the *idea*. In the unity, therefore, of our intimate selves, we confront the perception, the passion experienced by us, with the idea shining before us ; and through this comparison we are able to say to ourselves : " That of which I have the perception is a realisation of that which I see in my idea."

'It is thus that light is thrown on our perceptions—that the *subsistence* of things, although in itself dark, becomes (to use a scholastic term) *illumined*, in which state it takes the name of *intellectual perception*. What, then, is intellectual perception ? It is not simply the intuition of an idea ; it is an *affirmation*, a judgment. The idea remains what it was before. There is not, truly and properly speaking, any addition made of a new intellectual object. There is only a function of a principle different from the intuitive, the principle that applies the cognition (the idea)—an active principle belonging, as I have said, not to the ideal but to the real world—a principle which, taken in general as an activity displaying itself in a variety of special functions, I denominate by the name of *Reason.*

'The *subsistence* therefore of things is excluded from knowledge properly so called; it has nothing to do with the intellect, considered as the faculty receptive of intelligible entities, because the intellect, as intellect, is essentially incapable of taking in the *real,* and is purely the seat of that which is *ideal.* But if the *subsistence* of things is not by itself an intelligible entity, if it is excluded from the intellectual sphere, it is nevertheless the only thing upon which this exclusion falls. All the qualities of things, whether accidental or substantial, have alike an intelligible essence, and all belong therefore to pure and formal knowledge. This is what has not, so far as I know, been felt or affirmed as yet by anyone.

'I concluded, then, that the subsistence or reality of things, and this alone, constitutes the *matter* of knowledge, whilst the *form*—that in virtue of which knowledge has actually the nature of knowledge—is constituted by the ideal or notional element.

'Having thus cleared *knowledge* of its material part, and reduced it to *pure ideas* (the possibles, the essences; or, as the Schoolmen said, the *quiddities*), I proceeded to compare together the various ideas, and I found that there existed among them such an order that some were contained in others—the more determinate in the less determinate—and this in such a manner that between the contained and the containers there was a most perfect equation. I mean to say, that by putting any idea of the more indeterminate kind on the one side, and on the other that same idea determinate in all possible modes, and therefore multiplied into a countless number of ideas, I discovered that the latter all pre-existed in the former, and had no greater value than it, although they were not in it in a distinct form.

'Here one must not turn round and say: "How can this

be ? Why, the thing seems to me impossible ; for it seems
to involve a sort of absurdity ; I cannot believe it." This
manner of speaking would be quite unworthy of a philosopher. For, as I have so often remarked, there is no question
here of the *why* or the *how*, but simply of a matter of fact.
All we have to do, therefore, is to ascertain whether the
thing be so or not, and this can only be done by calm, close
observation. If we thus find that such is the fact, we are
bound to acknowledge it ; and if this seems a hard trial for
our reason, we must not lack the courage of humility, even
though it be at the cost of feeling all the immensity of our
ignorance.

'I observed, then, and saw that the less general ideas were
contained, though indistinctly, in the more general. Hence
I became aware, that if ideas were distributed in the form of
a pyramid—first the more particular and multiplied, and then
over these, in due order of succession, the less and less particular and consequently fewer and fewer in number—one
would necessarily come up at last to a first idea forming the
point of the pyramid : and it would be found that this one
idea was worth as much as all the rest taken together, that
it embraced them all within its one self, in fact that through
numberless distinctions and determinations it transformed
itself into every one of them. Thus did I arrive at a reflex
vision of the idea of *possible* or *indeterminate being*, and at the
discovery of the true and pure source of all the knowable.' [1]

10. The work from which we have quoted the above
passages may be described as a continuation, or development,
as well as a defence of the *Nuovo Saggio*. Some of the expressions used in the parts cited call for a few words of
explanation, because they have been made the occasion of
absurd charges and because they show how easy it often is,
even for men of high intelligence to confound a mere relation

---

[1] *Rinnovamento della Filosofia in Italia*, etc. pp. 499-501 (Milan, 1836).

of an object with the object itself, and then to impute to an author the result of their own comparison of thought. We allude, in the first place, to the expression 'possible being,' or 'possible essence,' as applied to the Idea. Rosmini gives in the *Nuovo Saggio* a long explanation of Logical Possibility and defines precisely in what sense an idea can be called a 'possible.' He shows that possibility taken logically, as it is in the *Nuovo Saggio*, is simply a relation between the idea and the real being it makes known; between the ideal essence and its realisation. For instance, suppose I fix my mind on the idea of man. By this idea alone, I do not know any particular subsisting man; but in it I see that there is implied no absurdity, no logical repugnance, no contradiction, no impossibility, in short, that a real man corresponding to my idea could subsist. Now, where do I see this possibility? In the idea itself and nowhere else. It is not, then, strictly speaking, the idea that is possible, but the real being to which the idea refers—the possibly subsisting man. Is it not, then, very extraordinary that, after Rosmini, in the *Nuovo Saggio* and elsewhere, had thoroughly analysed the term *possible*, and shown the several senses in which it may be and is often used, and how he himself understands and uses it, writers should be found who, whilst priding themselves on their logical acumen and power of analysis, accuse him of confusing the *idea* with the *possible*, and of laying down as the principle of his whole system a mere possibility?

But exception has been taken to the expression, *Idea of Possible or Indeterminate Being*. Let us therefore endeavour to explain the exact meaning attached to it by Rosmini, who bases his whole system on the intuition of *Indeterminate Being*. We must remember that Rosmini wrote the *Nuovo Saggio* in order to describe the nature of the *Light of Reason* and to point out how by means of it and combined with sensation and reflection man acquires all his ideas. When entering on this subject his attention was naturally drawn to the expression *Light of Reason.* He as naturally asked himself what analogy men had seen between the eye of the body with its medium of natural light, and the mind with its medium of intellectual light. The very universality of the expressions 'Light of Reason,' 'light of nature,' 'light of the intellect,' 'light of God's countenance,' 'light of truth,' &c., which had been used from time immemorial both by sacred and profane writers, by the unlearned no less than by the most learned and deep thinkers, showed that such analogy was no ordinary one. He therefore resolved to examine the whole subject exhaustively. The results of his observations may be thus briefly stated. To begin with the physical world, men have ever distinguished the light from the eye that sees it, from the object seen, and from the different acts of sight. The light then is not the eye, nor a modification of it, nor dependent on it. On the contrary, it informs the eye, enables it to see, shows the colour and shape and size of all the objects seen.

This light appears simple, indivisible, uniform, illimitable, universal, embracing within its sphere all objects of sight. If it had always been, and always were, present alone, with its unvarying brilliancy, men would have never consciously reflected on its existence. They would probably have remained persuaded that all the objects they saw were themselves so many separate lights, or that the eye saw without light. But as the light went and came, men's attention was attracted to it and they gradually arrived at the conclusion that all they saw in the several objects was but a modification of it, and that whilst those objects could be seen only in and through the light, *it* was seen in and through itself.

If we turn our gaze on the intellectual world, we shall see there, too, that the Light of Reason is distinct from the mind that sees it, from the object it illuminates and makes known, and from the different acts of mental vision.

This Intellectual Light is one and the same not only for a

single mind but for all minds. No one dreams of saying *lights* of reason. Wherever man is, there is reason, and there likewise is the one identical light of reason. In fact, were not the light the same for each human being, it would be quite impossible for men to interchange ideas, or, in fact, to understand one another.

11. If we apply our reflection to this light, far more marvellous and mysterious qualities and characteristics will disclose themselves to us than we can discover in the physical light. The mind not only contemplates it, but is *informed* by it in such a manner that it would not be *mind, i.e.* an intellectual faculty, except for this *informing*. It is in and through it, therefore, that we are able to understand things— their nature or mode of being, their worth ; to compare them together, to distinguish the like from the unlike, to discover their infinitely various relations, and expatiate freely over the boundless regions of speculative reasoning. The minds are many, but the light which informs them is identically one and the same. This light, then, is not *ourselves*, nor a part, nor a modification of ourselves. It is immeasurably above us, and yet, as has just been said, so united to us as to constitute us in the nature of *intelligent beings*.

Moreover, there is in this light something of the infinite ; for unless we saw in it what *infinity* is, how would it be possible for us to infer from the existence of this sensible world—in itself purely and simply finite—the existence of the *Infinite Being*, of God ? How could we see the difference between Him and finite things ? It is the mind, and the mind only, which, through its light, can and does, by looking at these things, perceive as a logical necessity that they could not exist unless an Infinite Power caused them to exist. Some might say that the *imagination* enables us to pass the bounds of the finite. But they would be mistaken. The imagination cannot of itself advance a single step beyond the images it

has received from the senses. It can indeed reproduce and
arrange them in a variety of ways, but it is necessarily enclosed
within the small circle of sensible forms.

A parity of reasoning will prove that the light of reason,
although manifested to man in *time*, is, in itself, eternal, therefore immutable, therefore necessary. We all know what
eternity, immutability, necessity is ; but this knowledge would
be impossible if our mind saw nothing beyond the *temporal*,
the *mutable*, the *contingent*, as all the objects falling under our
experience most undoubtedly are in themselves.

12. This should lead us to understand more clearly the
true nature of the Light of Reason. For, what does it tell us
regarding the things it makes known to us ? It can tell us only
of their existence or being, and of their modes of existence
or being. To these two heads all our knowledge of things
is ultimately and necessarily reduced. Now, if the Light of
Reason can show us being and the modes of being, we must
see all this in that light itself. But we cannot see the modes
of being except in being ; we may see and understand being
without its modes, but not conversely. In fact, if we look at
the Light of Reason as it is in itself, we shall discover nothing
but being or existence. This is why Rosmini says that the
Light of Reason is the simple essence, or, in scholastic phrase,
the quiddity of being. The other terms he applies to it
denote its relations. For instance, when he calls it *indeterminate
being*, he merely means that it has none of the determinate
forms, specific or generic, of the objects seen in it. If he terms
it *being taken universally*, or *being in general*, this signifies that
in its infinite extension and all-embracing universality, it
includes potentially all possible beings of whatever kind. If
again he calls it *objective* and *ideal*, he does so because this is
what a comparison of it with the mind assures us it truly is.
If he calls it *ideal*, it is because we can know things only
through ideas, and this is the parent idea of all. From this
comparison he saw that whilst the mind itself is a finite thing,

belonging to the world of reality, and subjective, the light of being is not only infinite, but presented and united to the mind in an essentially objective and ideal form. The term objective, like many others, has undergone considerable modifications of meaning. In the *Nuovo Saggio* Rosmini gives a long explanation of it; and therefore it will be enough to state here that for him, the being of the primitive intuition is essentially objective (placed opposite to us—*objectum*), because it enables us to see things as they are in themselves, in their true nature and essence; makes us see them without any relation to ourselves or to any other subject; and serves to measure the exact modes and grades of being they possess.

Rosmini maintains that there are three forms of being—the ideal, the real, and the moral. When speaking of ideal being, he always uses the verb *is* or *exists*; to the real form, he applies the verb *subsists*.

13. In his *Aristotle Examined and Explained*, Rosmini shows, that through not keeping the ideal and real modes of being quite distinct, great confusion of thought and ceaseless contentions have arisen amongst philosophers. He there proves that the controversies of the Realists, Nominalists, and Conceptualists, had their source and continuance in the same want of distinction. He is therefore ever on his guard to preserve the distinction perfect and to prevent his readers from losing sight of it.

Many other names are given by Rosmini to *being* according as we view it in itself or in its determinations; but they will present no difficulty when once we have mastered his leading idea; and several of them are explained in the *Nuovo Saggio*. If the reader remembers that for Rosmini the Light of Reason is simply pure *being*, infinite in extension and unchangeable in essence, he will easily understand the different names given to it in its relations with the objects of cognition. For instance, the expression *deter-*

minations of being, does not mean that being itself changes, or is limited, or really determined ; but only that when by its means we come to know any object, we restrict our gaze for the moment to this object, and thus seemingly limit being itself. In an analogous way the material light appears to contract itself to the size and shape and dimensions of the different things it enables us to see. In short, the indeterminate being of the first intuition always remains the same ; it is only our vision that changes as it passes from one known object to another, and we are said to contract or determine being, because we must use the whole of it, in order to form determinate ideas of finite things.

The expression, *Idea of indeterminate Being*, means, then, that we naturally and continually contemplate pure unlimited being, that in it we see the fount of the intelligible essences of the various particular beings we can know ; that it therefore constitutes their logical possibility ; that, knowing by means of it what is *being* in general, when any determinate being is presented to the mind, we recognise it as already contained virtually in the primitive intuition.

But we must call attention to Rosmini's phraseology as regards *being*. He uses two terms to express it. As he himself explains in the *Theosophy*, when he is speaking of simple *indeterminate being*, he uses the term, *essere*, which is equivalent to our word *being* taken nominatively and in its most general acceptation, to the Latin *esse*, the Greek εἶναι, the German *das Sein*. When he is treating of determinate being, he always makes use of the term *ente*, which corresponds to our word *being* used participially or with the articles. This *ente* is near in signification to the Latin *ens*, the Greek τὸ ὄν, the German *das Seiende*. The context will always tell which meaning to attach to our single term, *being*. Every determinate being, the *ente*, exists in each of the two forms, ideal and real. The ideal form contains the intelligible essence of

the real form, of the individual. In other words, the individual
or real being cannot be known except in and through the idea,
the universal. This is the teaching, not only of philosophy,
but of philology.

To know any real thing simply means to put it in the
class to which it belongs. Then alone can we give it a
name. All names originally signified general or universal
qualities. The words *know* and *name* are, in fact, traceable
to the same root. We can only name things as we know
them, and we can only know them when we throw upon
them the light of the idea that contains their intelligible
essence. Even now nearly all words have general significations, and to be able to restrict those significations we are
obliged to make use of individualising particles or proper
names. The term *man*, for instance, does not mean any
particular and real man, but the species, the reasonable being,
the essence seen in the idea. To make it refer to a real individual, we must use such expressions as *this* or *that* man, *the*
man *Peter*, *the* man *to whom I speak*, and so on. The more
language is studied philosophically, the more will it be seen
that the mind cannot apprehend the particular except through
the universal, that the idea, the intelligible essence makes
us know the real and the individual, and that every real
finite being is but a particular realisation of the essence
seen in the idea. Rosmini dwells on this subject at considerable length in the *Nuovo Saggio*, and we have only
said this much in order to prevent the reader from thinking
that the idea is a mere image, the modification of an impression or a sensation, or a *mere creation* of the mind, as seems
to be very generally assumed nowadays as self-evident.
Rosmini, on the contrary, maintains that an accurate observation of the nature of cognition will make manifest that
though we cannot obtain the positive idea of a real being
unless that being acts on our senses, yet that the idea once
formed has an existence in the mind quite independent of

the reality that gave occasion to its acquisition, and is essentially universal, necessary, and unchangeable.

We have thus tried to explain the meaning of some of the terms used in Rosmini's philosophy, because we believe that his system only requires to be understood in order to be embraced by all sincere lovers of truth. We are persuaded that it cuts up by the roots the chief errors of agnosticism, positivism, materialism, rationalism, sensism, subjectivism, and pantheism, in all the forms in which they can present themselves.

14. But we must caution the reader against fancying that Rosmini pretends to comprehend thoroughly the nature of the intellectual light. This he certainly does not do. Much less does he pretend to make his reader comprehend it. God alone can comprehend anything fully. Our knowledge of things is essentially limited. Every thinker worthy of the name recognises this at once. And yet a very clever writer composed a biographical history of philosophy to prove that philosophy was an impossibility because it assumes, as he asserts, that it can, not only discover and explain the true nature of things, but disclose the secrets of the universe. Had he confined his assertions to pure rationalists, he would have written the simple truth. They indeed began to philosophise on the assumption that they could with their finite intelligence reach the height and fathom the depth of the Divinity Itself. But even they, after repeated failures, felt obliged to say that man's mind is not only limited, but that it cannot know the nature of anything whatsoever, and that human knowledge is confined to phenomena. This last conclusion was, however, as baseless as the premises from which it was drawn—that the whole of our ideas must come through the senses. Rosmini proves incontestably how we cannot know phenomena without knowing something beyond them; how, though our most perfect notions of things are

only aspects of them, even when considered from all possible points of view and meditated on profoundly and frequently, they are nevertheless true, because we have within us the light of truth to guide us in acquiring them. Spiritual objects are certainly more difficult, at least for ordinary minds, to understand, than material ones, and the Light of Reason is the most spiritual of all objects naturally known to us. If, then, Rosmini can show us something of its true nature, if by means of it he can lift for us even but a little the veil that hides the face of truth—or if he can point out a solid foundation on which to build a system of philosophy and furnish us with genuine materials for the building, and does not assume to do more—we ought surely to accept with thankfulness what he has given us, and by aid of it, continue the work to which he devoted the best years of his life.

The better to do this, we should master his fundamental principle. We should follow him step by step in his path of observation. We should examine at each step whether his observations are correct. We should not inquire whether what he tells us *can* be ; that is, we ought not to begin by reasoning on the possibility of the results he places before us. To do this will cause the imagination and confirmed habits of thought to intrude where nothing but fixed and continued contemplation and accurate observation are of any avail. The only question we have a right to ask, is, whether he observes correctly and describes his object correctly, whether his results are true as far as they go. Now, as that object is the most simple and the most remote from sense of any we can positively know, and at the same time ever shines before us with unvarying light, it is difficult for us to keep it steadily in view, or to avoid confusing it with something quite extraneous to it.

The difficulty is certainly not lessened by the subjects and methods of study to which men have for a long while almost exclusively confined their attention. The outward world of sense, of matter and its various modifications, have so engrossed the thoughts of the learned for years, that they easily persuade themselves that not only is it impossible to acquire a strictly scientific and true knowledge of any other world, but that even if such a world exists, nothing can be known about it. At a time when all science is restricted to observing and classifying the various manifestations of physical phenomena ; when impressions, sensations, perceptions, images, memory, acts of thought, thought itself, consciousness and states of consciousness, are all jumbled together in an inextricable confusion, and are all regarded as only so many exhibitions of the potency of matter, a philosophy which starting from a wholly immaterial object, pretends that that matter is but the mere term of a sensitive principle, and holds the lowest place in the scale of existence, has apparently little chance of getting a hearing. When, further, this philosophy asks the learned to free themselves from the trammels of matter, from the circle of sensible images, from their special habits and forms of thinking, and to fix their gaze on something perfectly spiritual, ideal, universal, indeterminate—to take their flight to a world altogether metaphysical and eternal, where the laws of space and time have no sway—are not too many of them likely to deem it all the baseless fabric of an over-worked brain? Will they not stop when they come to its fundamental principle and be more than ever persuaded that nothing exists but matter and force ?

Possibly this may be the fate reserved for the *Nuovo Saggio* at the hands of many who cannot appreciate the high spirituality of its teachings. Still, we trust there are many more who, whilst attached, through education and habit, to physical methods of observation and research, will not refuse to read attentively and to meditate seriously upon a work like the one we here present to them. To these especially do we address ourselves ; and we would first of all ask them to consider that the very fact of our being able to think of what is immaterial, eternal, necessary, and infinite, proves to demonstration that there is something which neither matter nor imagination can teach. For, certainly, were men confined to what they see, handle, smell, touch, and picture to themselves in sensible images, they could not possibly ever conceive that anything else existed. Let them then persuade themselves that there is a world. which only the eye of the mind, illumined by the pure, spiritual, light of reason, can look upon. Let them, under the guidance of the *Nuovo Saggio*, begin to examine the phenomena of that world, and we are persuaded they will soon convince themselves that it is infinitely preferable to the world of sense. They will then be moved to observe it more closely, and though, as in the observation of physical objects, they may make mistakes, yet they have that within them which, if properly consulted, will lead them back to the truth, even to that Light of Reason which, being unalloyed truth itself, is the only guide to certainty.

15. Although the object of the *Nuovo Saggio* may be inferred sufficiently from what has been said already, it is important to explain more directly its purpose, and consider more attentively its method. Rosmini, as we have shown, added to an intense love of truth and most uncommon mental endowments, a comprehensive and appreciative acquaintance with the various systems of philosophy. He had more especially bestowed earnest and deep study on modern systems, had detected their principal errors, and had seen with grief the false and pernicious consequences, the speculative and practical errors, which had been logically deduced from them. He saw, too, how, by the sophistries of the self-styled philosophers of the eighteenth century, philosophy itself had been degraded in the eyes of many thinking and right-minded men ; how its very first principles were still

denied or perverted, to the grievous injury of all the sciences, of which it ought ever to be regarded as the queen and guide. The more he reflected, the more he felt, that to restore philosophy to its proper place, to make it the light and benefactress of mankind, it was necessary first of all to return to the study of its fundamental principle, nay, if possible, to one universal principle, which, accepted by philosophers, would give unity, strength, and harmony to the whole knowable. He thought that by means of such a principle, a system of philosophy could be constructed unassailable in itself, fit to combat and overcome every kind of error, and capable of giving a solid foundation to all the sciences. He found that men generally reason correctly, and that if they arrive at erroneous conclusions, it is only because they started from erroneous principles. 'Let philosophers then,' he said, 'but agree in the first principles of reason, and all will come right.'

16. The method Rosmini prescribed to himself, and which he rigorously followed, compelled him to examine the question of the origin of ideas from every possible point of view. He had discovered the principle of all cognition whilst yet a youth, and he dwelt upon it for at least eleven years, before he published the first volume of the *Nuovo Saggio*. During those years he studied the principal works of the greatest philosophers known to the world, in order to be able to compare his own conclusions with those of the great thinkers who had gone before him. The result of these long and arduous labours is given, for the most part, in the *Nuovo Saggio* itself.

When he sketched out this work, he foresaw that it would be useless to give his own theory on the nature and source of reason, till he had first criticised those already before the world, and shown with irresistible logic where they were defective. He undertook this task in the first volume.

As, at the time he wrote, the philosophy of Locke and his followers was in the main dominant in Italy, and as the many fatal conclusions which Hume and the French sophists had drawn from its principles had already penetrated so deeply into society and literature as to affect banefully both truth and morality, he felt the necessity of beginning with a criticism of the system of Locke. He pointed out how false was the method which Locke pursued; how, whilst claiming to adhere strictly to facts and observation, he started with theory, inadequate hypotheses, and groundless assumptions; how this carried him to deny some of the plainest and most universal dictates of common sense and consciousness, and how he unwittingly laid the foundation of the erroneous systems of Hume, Berkeley and Condillac, and, through an intellectual reaction, gave rise to those of Reid and Dugald Stuart, of Leibnitz, Kant and other German philosophers.

Having disposed of Locke, Rosmini proceeds to deal with all the offshoots of Locke's system, each in its own proper place, pointing out their weak points, and doing justice to all. It would take us too long to enter here into details, and we must therefore refer the reader to the book itself. This applies also to Plato, who, like Leibnitz and Kant, erred by assuming more than was necessary for explaining the origin of ideas, and to Aristotle, who, for obvious reasons, could not have been left out in a treatise of this description.[1]

17. The criticism on Kant terminates the first part of the *Nuovo Saggio.* Rosmini begins the second part by a brief recapitulation of what he had said in the first. This practice

---

[1] Some have found fault with Rosmini for not having made a distinct chapter on St. Thomas of Aquin. But they forget that his object was to *confute erroneous systems*, whereas he was most profoundly convinced of the substantial identity of his own system with the doctrines of St. Thomas, ' in whose footsteps, as well as in those of St. Augustine, it had always been his ambition to follow.' So he wrote in his preface to the *Theodicy.* A perusal, not only of the *Nuovo Saggio*, but of Rosmini's works generally, will show how very often he quotes St. Thomas in corroboration of his views, explains difficult and obscure passages in the Angelical Doctor, and brings them into harmony with other passages, their apparent contradiction notwithstanding.

of recapitulating is frequent with him and of the greatest service to the student of his works. In speaking of Plato, Leibnitz, and Kant, he directs the student's reflection to the fact, that from Plato to Kant the problem of the nature and source of thought approached gradually towards its true solution, and that had it not been for the labours of the great thinkers who preceded him, he himself would most probably have never been able to complete that solution.

He then proceeds to set forth the theory on which this solution is based, and begins by considering and analysing the fact of cognition. Having arrived at the reflex contemplation of the *idea of being* (after the manner explained in the extract we have quoted from his *Rinnovamento*), he dwells on its nature, and separates and distinguishes it from all that might be confounded with it,—from every sensible image, sensation, judgment, perception, and determinate idea. He next asks how the human mind could have become possessed of the idea of being, and whether it is possible to derive it from external and corporeal sensations; from the internal sentiment of our existence, or of the *Ego*; from reflection as conceived by Locke; or whether it is given at the moment of the intellectual perception, as seems to be supposed by the theory of Reid and others. He examines in turn each of the alleged sources of the idea of being, and demonstrates that even all combined are quite unequal to furnish it. He therefore concludes, by the principle of universal exclusion, that it must be innate. Lastly he shows that his own theory is only a development, an explanation, of what has all along been contained in Christian Tradition.

18. To this portion of the *Nuovo Saggio* we invite the reader's most serious attention; for it is the fundamental part of Rosmini's theory, on which the whole system is based, and by which, as a system, it must stand or fall. Rosmini might have claimed originality for his theory; might have affirmed

that he had reached the discovery of the origin of ideas by his own independent thinking. But instead of this, he is never tired of pointing out how he only states distinctly and in modern language, what most of his predecessors felt, and believed, and held at least implicitly; and how they failed to give that clear and unmistakable expression to their thoughts which prevents misconception in the minds of shallow or biassed readers, merely because, occupied in other questions, they did not give their full attention to that of the origin of ideas, and consequently did not consider sufficiently its supreme importance.

It must not however be inferred from this, that Rosmini brings the principle of authority into philosophy. No one knew better than he that philosophy is the science of pure reason, that it is wholly built on reason, and that no authority as such, can claim a place in it. But whilst fully aware of this, he had a truly humble opinion of himself as an individual thinker, and, therefore, though he felt the full logical force of his principles and reasonings, he felt too, and that deeply, the need of steadying and strengthening his steps by the aid of his brother philosophers. The student of Rosmini must, then, be careful not to confound the substance of his philosophy, which is derived from a supreme and self-evident principle by a pure chain of logical deduction, with the adventitious and merely accidental helps it receives from the opinions and authority of other philosophers.

19. Rosmini lays down four points, which serve as so many signs whereby one who has read the *Nuovo Saggio* may know whether he has understood the doctrine it contains. They are as follows :—

(1) The difference between *sensation* and *sensitive perception*.

(2) The difference between the *idea* of a thing and the *judgment* on the subsistence of that thing.

(3) The difference between *sensitive* and *intellectual perception.*

(4) The difference between an *act* of the soul and *advertence* to that act.

It is hardly necessary to show that these points are most closely connected with the difference between direct and reflex knowledge, or implicit and explicit thought, which is now so much insisted upon by metaphysicians generally, and of which the diligent student of Rosmini will learn from him the nature and great importance.

20. The third part of the *Nuovo Saggio* contains the corollaries of the author's theory,—on the criterion of certitude, on the force of *a priori* reasoning, and on the first division of the sciences. He begins with a description of what is meant by truth and certainty, by criterion of certitude, and by persuasion. He shows that man naturally possesses truth, that he is persuaded of having this possession, and that by reflection this persuasion becomes certitude. Certitude, then, he defines, 'a firm and reasonable persuasion in conformity with truth.' He next proceeds to examine the different forms under which truth presents itself, and shows that man has the power of attaining and recognising it, and of being persuaded and certain of it, under each form. He not only proves that the idea of being is the first and universal form of truth, but that it alone enables the mind to see and be sure of seeing truth under every shape it can take. He applies this light of truth to discover the value of the various kinds of human cognition pure and 'materiated,' and to demonstrate the validity of the principles of reasoning. He defends these principles against the attacks of sceptics. He makes these openly contradict themselves and acknowledge that they cannot by any possibility enunciate their fundamental assumptions, without asserting the existence of the truth they deny, without making use of the very principles they pretend to

reject. He reduces the various forms of scepticism to one, and shows its absurdity and its direct antagonism to the universal and invincible dictates of common sense. He inquires how it happens that man can be led by science to deny what by nature he knows to be true. He enters into an examination of the difference between thought and reflection on thought; between direct and reflex cognition, between popular and scientific knowledge, and between the declarations of common sense and the pronouncements of philosophy.

21. He is thus naturally conducted to the consideration of error: He asks; What is error? Whence does it proceed? How does man become its prey? A first observation of the subject shows him, that error could not exist in a pure intelligence, that if such a being were finite, its knowledge would be indeed limited, itself would be ignorant of much, but that what it did know must be true. But man besides intelligence, has feelings, sentiments, affections, passions, and will. If, then, error exists in man, it must come from these last. He then observes the nature of error, how it is negative; how, as truth is that which is, error, being its opposite, must be that which is not; how it is therefore a chimæra, a creation of the will under the influence of some blind sentiment or passion. He searches into the cause, the sources, the occasions of error. He distinguishes it into its kinds; he finds that whilst man may be necessarily led into material error, he cannot be compelled to fall into formal error. He discovers that it is only this latter which can really injure man, and he thence concludes that no one can truly harm him but himself, thereby demonstrating that man can, if he likes, become the author of his own intellectual and moral perfection.

Arrived thus far, he returns to the form of truth, the idea of being, and the starting-point of his philosophy. He com-

pares his point of departure with those of the German
philosophers and their followers, and dwells particularly on
Kant, Fichte, Schelling, Hegel, Bouterweck, and Cousin.
This comparison offers him opportunities for showing the
superiority of his system over those he criticises, and for
making many important remarks on the erroneous principles
and conclusions of the German school of thought.

22. Having vindicated the principle and starting-point of
his philosophy, he inquires how far this principle will, by
itself, enable the mind to proceed without the aid of knowledge derived *a posteriori,* or through the senses. This is
where he discusses the force and extent of *a priori* reasoning,
and where he shows how it can lead to a demonstration of
the logical principles of cognition, and of the existence of
God. Finally, always under the guidance of the *idea of
being,* he considers : What is the first division of the sciences ;
whether we should begin our scientific course from a universal
or a particular ; whether with observation or with reasoning ;
whether with a fact, and particularly with the fact of consciousness ; how man begins his first development ; how he
starts on the way of reflection ; and what is the difference
between doubt and methodical ignorance.

23. But we must close these preliminary remarks. We
have hitherto presented Rosmini to the reader merely as a
profound thinker, as the author of a philosophical system.
If, in consequence, it should be thought that he was nothing
better than a speculative philosopher or a metaphysician,
without human sympathies, without deep love for his fellow-
men, and without useful energy, we have been unknowingly
the occasion of a most erroneous view of his life and character. From his very boyhood he dedicated himself to the
service of his neighbour. For his fellow-men, or rather for
God seen in his fellow-men, he sacrificed ease, riches,

worldly ambition. The true good, the real happiness of his neighbour was the aim of his every thought and action. When he elaborated what he believed to be the system of truth, and laboured to bring it to perfection, he employed all the resources of a gigantic intellect, and a vast philosophical and theological erudition, it was simply because he was profoundly persuaded that the only way to make men better was through the truth. He held that truth understood, loved, embraced, followed unswervingly, must lead to goodness of heart, to moral perfection, and through this to rest and happiness. His spirit, then, was one of universal and most intense love of his kind. It breathed in all he wrote and did. It will be felt even in his driest scientific writings, and certainly in the *Nuovo Saggio.*

24. As to the present translation, we should be much grieved if its imperfections prevented the English reader from feeling the true spirit of its author in every line. We have, indeed, done our utmost to express Rosmini's meaning clearly and fully. We have sought to write as we imagined he would have written had he been now living to publish this work for the English-speaking world. But in spite of all our efforts, we know that we are far from having done full justice to the original. Sometimes we have been obliged to use inelegant if not harsh expressions, and occasionally words and phrases not in ordinary use. This is a necessity which our language imposes on all who try to accommodate it to philosophic phraseology. Nevertheless we trust that these and the many other blemishes, which may be discovered too easily, are not such as can mar the fidelity of the translation. We, therefore, send it forth in the fond hope that it will serve the cause for which the *Nuovo Saggio* was first written, and bring rest of mind and peace of soul to many a sincere lover of Truth.

THE TRANSLATORS.

*_** It may be necessary to explain that Rosmini's own Preface has not been used, because it was written with special reference to the Catholic public in Italy, and to the condition of philosophical controversies at the time the Nuovo Saggio was first published. However, in the Preface here substituted for the author's own, his arrangement has been carefully kept, and many of his remarks reproduced.

CONTENTS.

OF

THE FIRST VOLUME.

—◦◦◦—

═══════════

SECTION II.

*ON THE NATURE OF THE DIFFICULTY TO BE OVER-
COME IN EXPLAINING THE ORIGIN OF IDEAS:—
THE DIFFICULTY STATED.*

SECTION III.

THEORIES WHICH ERR BY DEFECT—THAT IS, BY NOT ASSIGNING TO IDEAS AN ADEQUATE CAUSE.

CHAPTER I.

LOCKE.

CHAPTER II.

CONDILLAC.

CHAPTER V.

xlviii   *CONTENTS OF THE FIRST VOLUME.*

SECTION IV.

THEORIES WHICH ERR BY EXCESS—THAT IS, BY ASSIGNING TO IDEAS A GREATER CAUSE THAN IS NECESSARY.

CHAPTER I.

PLATO AND ARISTOTLE.

CHAPTER II.

LEIBNITZ.

CHAPTER IV.

HOW PHILOSOPHY MAY BE SAID TO HAVE PROGRESSED BY MEANS OF PLATO, LEIBNITZ, AND KANT; AND WHAT IT STILL REQUIRES IN ORDER TO BE PERFECT.

SECTION I.

CHAPTER I.

ON THE TWO PRINCIPLES OF PHILOSOPHIC METHOD.

26. I beg to inform the reader that in the following disquisitions it is my intention to be guided by two principles.

The first is, that in explaining the facts of the human soul 'we must not assume less than is necessary for that explanation.'

The reason of this is evident : so long as we do not assume all that is necessary, we shall never be able to say with truth that the facts have been adequately explained. Thus, for example, if by way of accounting for the two different sensations of colour and of sound I were to say that both are produced by a single sense—*i.e.* either the sight or the hearing—my explanation would certainly be deemed insufficient ; for no one could ever be made to understand how it is possible for the eye to hear sounds, or for the ear to see colours.

27. The second principle is, that 'we must not assume more than is necessary.'[1]

Whatever is assumed over and above the requirements of the explanation is mere surplusage, an element introduced into the argument without any reason, and which can, therefore, be denied with as good a right as it can be asserted. For example, if some one were to tell us that two different

---

[1] It is easy to see that these two principles, taken together, are nothing but the principle of *sufficient reason*, divided into the two parts of which it is composed.

sensories are required for producing a single kind of sensation, we should only be astonished at his want of sense in assigning two causes to a fact for which one cause is evidently enough.

28. Wherefore those who apply themselves to investigate the nature of the human soul should always admit without hesitation what is really necessary, in order satisfactorily to account for all those characteristic facts which can be ascertained through an accurate and complete observation ; but *nothing beyond.*

Briefly : Of all complete explanations of the facts of the human soul, let that one be preferred which is simplest and requires fewest suppositions.

CHAPTER II.

TWO PHILOSOPHIES: THE ONE VULGAR, AND THE OTHER
LEARNED; THEIR TWO DEFECTS.

29. Now, as the correct and genuine method of philosophical investigation is governed by two principles, so whatever
errors there may be in the theories which have hitherto been
propounded on the human soul, they can only have arisen from
one or other of two causes—namely, from transgressing either
against the first principle or against the second : against the
first, by not assuming what is necessary for explaining all the
facts recognised by observation ; against the second, by too
easily introducing into the explanation things and suppositions
which, for the end in view, are wholly superfluous.

30. It is no easy matter to avoid both these extremes ;
and we may fairly say that if philosophy were once firmly
established on such a footing as to run perfectly clear of the
two, it would be as near perfection as possible. For this
would necessarily presuppose (1) that the observation of the
facts had already been carried to completion ; (2) that such
facts as are characteristic—*i.e.* forming *separate species*—had
been accurately distinguished from those which exhibit only
accidental varieties, or mere repetitions of cases belonging to
one and the same species : which, to say it *en passant*, is an
arduous task demanding no small degree of philosophical
acumen and discrimination ; and (3) that a just and thorough
perception had been formed, on the one hand, of the nature
of the difficulty to be overcome in order to explain the facts,
and, on the other, of the efficacy of the reasons with which it
was proposed to meet that difficulty ; for unless both these
sides of the question are balanced with great care one against
the other, the consequence will be that, unawares to ourselves,

either the reasons will be insufficient, or there will be in them something more than there ought to be.

31. The errors of that which I designate as *vulgar philosophy*[1] arise from the absence of some or all of these three things, and they are chiefly against the first of the two principles of method above laid down.

The vulgar philosophy never rests on a complete observation ; it does not know how to classify the facts which it has observed, or how to distinguish those that are characteristic of a species from those that are not so. On the contrary, when it has collected together a great number of facts, it already thinks itself very rich; forgetting that the value of observations does not depend on the number of facts similar in kind, but on the number of those features which are distinctive of a species. Lastly, it does not penetrate into the inner nature of the facts, nor understand where lies the real point of the difficulty of accounting for them ; nor, consequently, of what force must be the reason necessary for validly solving that difficulty. Such are the defects of vulgar philosophy.

32. The imperfection of the vulgar way of thinking may be easily noticed by anyone who is at all accustomed to reflection ; for we all of us come more or less in contact with

---

[1] By *vulgar philosophy* I mean that imperfect philosophy which is still found among the ordinary run of philosophers at a time when the world is already in possession of great and profound philosophical truths : such, for instance, as are deposited in so many books that have been transmitted to us from antiquity and in each succeeding age down to the present. In the eighteenth century the whole of the heritage left to us by our fathers was deliberately renounced, and philosophy made to start afresh in a state of infancy. It is in this state that I call it *vulgar*; for it is the custom of the common people to take questions in the first aspect in which they present themselves, even when they have already changed their state and nature, as is the case when a more mature and deeper philosophical reflection has been exercised on them. Des Cartes was the first to set the bad example of presuming to construct, by himself alone, as we may say, and with an exceedingly limited study of the writers who had preceded him, the philosophical edifice about which all former ages had laboured, and laboured with a high degree of success. His powerful mind, and the few ideas which he took from the schoolmen, and utilised without making an acknowledgment of the fact, perhaps even without being conscious of it, saved him from many errors ; and if his work was imperfect, it was nevertheless marvellous when considered as the work, I should almost say, of a single mind. Locke, who, with abilities far inferior to those of Des Cartes, ventured on the same bold course, inaugurated the real beginning of that vulgar and infantine philosophy to which I refer.

the common people, and have, therefore, opportunities of observing their intellectual habits.

We find in the illiterate class two things apparently opposed to each other, but which proceed from the same cause—*i.e.* from the absence of the three conditions which I have set down as necessary for sound philosophical thought (30). Observe how the illiterate, on the one hand, do not show the least surprise at things most wonderful in themselves, simply because they have them continually under their eyes. If you ask them to explain how these things come about, they have quite ready an answer which seems to them perfectly natural, and so obviously true, that they will be strongly tempted to smile at your simplicity in not knowing it already, or in pretending not to know it. As a matter of fact, the uneducated have very few queries to perplex them ; they see but very few difficulties—only such as are extraordinary—and these they have an off-hand way of solving .to themselves by reasons, or rather suppositions, not very intellectual, I confess, but yet entirely to their satisfaction. But just try and cause some doubt to arise in their minds as to the validity of the answer they have given ; talk to them so that they may come to clearly perceive a real knot in the question, and you will find that their first impulse is to rush into the opposite extreme. Whilst heretofore everything seemed perfectly smooth, now that they understand the objection, you will have the greatest difficulty in bringing them to appreciate that which is the only suitable answer to it : indeed, a difficulty fully as great as was the facility with which they had implicitly assented to the reason proposed by themselves.

33. My object in this allusion is to point out that the error of the theories which, in professing to explain the facts of the human soul, assume less than is necessary, coincides with the way of reasoning prevalent among the illiterate ; while, on the contrary, the error of those which assume more than is necessary usually proceeds from minds that are not altogether unused to philosophy, but have already made some progress in it and noted some of its difficult points, without at the

same time having discovered the simplest mode of explaining them—a discovery, be it remembered, which comes only after a long lapse of time. For the first explanations are always hypothetical and very complicated and involved, being accepted simply because the human mind, on the one hand, feels urgently the need of some explanation, and, on the other, cannot at the moment suggest anything better.

34. Hence philosophy may be, as it were, distinguished into three periods. To the first period belongs a vulgar philosophy, indulgent with itself, blind to difficulties, or perceiving them only obscurely, and therefore explaining them by hypotheses as gross, or at least as confused, as they are gratuitous. Then comes in that more intellectual or learned kind of philosophy, which, having become fully alive to the reasons that render its former hypotheses untenable, looks down contemptuously on the old and popular theories. This is the period during which systems are invented, clever and elaborate, but usually erring by excess, even as the former ones had erred by defect. In both these periods philosophy is imperfect. Its imperfection in the first period arises from not seeing the difficulties ; and, in the second, from not knowing the proper way of meeting them. When, having become more and more improved, philosophy corrects these faults, and renders its theories at once simple and complete, then it has entered on its third period—that of its perfection.

CHAPTER III.

ON THE DEFECT OF THE PHILOSOPHY OF LOCKE.

35. The revolution of ideas brought about by Locke and his followers does not, properly speaking, consist in any great restoration of philosophy, but in having drawn forth this science from the secluded enclosure of the schools, and thrown it open to the general public.

In this I recognise, not so much a personal merit of this author, as a need universally felt in the age in which he lived, and which, were it even for this alone, will be for ever memorable.

36. For my own part, nothing could delight me more than the prospect of seeing all men share in the knowledge of the highest truths—a knowledge which is so powerfully calculated to elevate the mind and ennoble the heart.

On the contrary, it fills me with pain and sadness to think that truths so excellent in themselves and so congenial to the human intelligence should be, as it were, monopolised by a small circle of individuals, as though none but themselves had a right to possess them. Is there not something odious and hurtful to human feeling in a science which, under the pretence of being scholastic, envelops itself in mystery; which seems to hate the light of day; which wears all the appearance of a sect, with a language, or rather jargon, of its own, and forbidden to the rest of men, and which assumes an ambitious, or at least a strange and exclusive, tone, as if it had some great secret to conceal, or some dark ends to accomplish? Why should this science, which boasts of being the mother of all the arts, keep itself aloof from, and sullenly refuse to hold friendly intercourse with, the human family? Has it, then, like some beast of a new species, impenetrable

lairs, where to abide in solitude, from fear lest its interests
should suffer by being mixed up with those of the world at
large? Or has heaven bestowed the gift of reason on a few
individuals only? And shall, therefore, the great bulk of
mankind for ever have to be led, like a flock of sheep, by the
command or the rod of those favoured ones? Must men
be for everlasting debarred from judging in a body or
pronouncing on matters on which their own dignity and
happiness depend?

These thoughts, which are so easily awakened in candid
minds, make one feel the liveliest gratitude for those who
labour with the intent of placing the very highest truths
within reach of the greatest number, and who on this account
seek to unfold and present these truths in language best
suited to the general comprehension. For if this were well
and successfully done, the masses would be able to enjoy in
some way the loveable aspect of those truths, and would rise
to that better condition which was heretofore attainable only
by the more subtle-minded, more inquisitive, or more fortunate few. Moreover (and this would be a great blessing), the
masses, by bringing their collective judgment to bear on the
interminable disputations of the learned, might perhaps speak
out with such an overwhelming weight of authority as would
effectually recall these disputants to more profitable occupations and sounder ways of thinking; and this especially when
they saw them—instead of working for the true benefit of the
individual and of society—wasting their time in catching at
that worthless sort of celebrity which consists merely in vain
and momentary triumphs over opinions adverse to their own.

37. But while a good instinct of our nature irresistibly
prompts us to applaud intentions so humane, and to wish
them God speed, when we ask ourselves the question whether
they will ever be fully realised, can our answer be in the
affirmative? I should be afraid to say so. But to expect
that the generality of men could in a short time be taught to
philosophise, and to philosophise on the most arduous subjects, on which the learned themselves—a very limited class
comparatively—have never as yet been able to agree, nay,

have frequently accused one another of not even understanding the question in debate, seems so great a stretch of philosophical credulity as to make the notion appear almost utopian. If it has been found so extremely difficult to generalise even so modest an institution as that of elementary schools, where little more is imparted than reading, writing, and cyphering (and the institution is not quite general as yet), how can we hope that philosophy can be not only presented to the masses in a language adapted to their capacity, but understood by them, and understood aright? And, what is very much more, can we believe that the masses will attain to so high a degree of philosophical proficiency as would qualify them to sit as a vast assembly of judges[1] on the respective merits of divergent philosophical views? In any case, if so flattering a notion as I am here referring to can be entertained at all, its fulfilment must certainly be remanded to a future so distant from our time, and so indefinite, that the most sagacious mind would be unable to fix it with anything like approximation. And even such a future as this—the thought of which will nevertheless be dear to all lovers of the human race—I would hesitate to hint at, were it not from fear lest I might thus be placing arbitrary limits to human perfectibility and to the workings of Divine Providence.

But let us return to Locke and his school.

38. It was but natural that, in suddenly offering the boon of philosophy to the masses, not yet prepared to receive it,

---

[1] There is a contradiction in terms as well in the opinion that subjects should be the judges of those lawfully placed over them as in that which says that those who have to be taught should be the judges of their duly appointed teachers. To claim for the lower classes the highest place would be manifest folly and the overthrowing of all order in human things. These absurdities, however, must not be confounded with the system which maintains that the *sensus communis* of men should be appealed to as the great judge in human affairs. Rationally understood, this system is simply a means for repressing individual rashness and presumption, and for asserting the superiority of collective mankind, without, however, taking away from society and humanity that *order* which is the bond of its union, and the form in which it has been constituted by Divine Providence. In noticing the difference between these two systems, and declaring the former self-contradictory and absurd, I have no intention of attributing the interpretation given by me of the latter to this or that particular writer. I speak of systems only, quite irrespectively of the personal opinions of anyone.

and in presenting it in the vernacular, one should give it a character somewhat in unison with the modes of reasoning proper to the masses themselves.

This is why the philosophy of Locke (1) exhibits everywhere evidences of an incomplete observation, and especially in regard to those facts which require for their detection a most vigilant attention to what passes within us, and sometimes an attention involving several orders of reflection—a task for which the great majority of men are utterly unfit ; (2) it exhibits a pitiable want of discernment in distinguishing those facts which are *characteristic* or constitutive of different species, from such as are only accidental varieties within the same species. As a general rule, the writers of this school are very industrious in collecting together facts similar in kind and in multiplying examples of them, but are extremely negligent in indicating their several species ; (3) it hardly ever sees where lies the real knot of the question, and hence is very prone to despise the labours of former philosophers ; thus giving up the precious legacy of truths bequeathed to us by past ages. When speaking of the great thinkers, who did their best to find a proper solution of the most thorny questions, it peremptorily sets them down as dreamers ; for it does not understand either the reason of their efforts or the necessity of the expedients to which they had recourse in order to overcome the difficulties seen by them. Accordingly, it dismisses their theories with a few words uttered with a show of dignity, perhaps even with a smile, congratulating itself on being exempt from such bad taste in philosophy.

Hence the defect of this school, especially in its earlier stage, consisted in over-confidence, or in pretending to explain the facts of the soul by means of insufficient reasons, much more than in the opposite extreme. But when, later on, its adherents were made aware of certain difficulties which had not been seen at the beginning, they put forth all their ingenuity in the attempt to solve them, and then they never seemed to be satisfied with any solution.

39. In consequence of this defect, the philosophy of Locke

was held in low esteem by some great men of his time[1]; but having obtained the popular favour, and the support of a sect which was just then gaining the ascendant by proclaiming itself the friend of the people, it succeeded in effecting a brief but almost universal triumph in public opinion.

At the period in which it appeared there were circumstances most favourable to it. Scholasticism had become, so to speak, rotten to the core; and Des Cartes had already given it its death-blow by substituting in its stead some profound thoughts, but too few for filling the place of that complete philosophical system of which the world stood in need. It was natural, therefore, that as the masses were growing more familiar with the cultivation of letters, and rising in social importance, their opinion should come to preponderate, not only in questions touching their material interests, but also in matters relating to philosophy.

40. Of the defects which I ascribe to the school of Locke, some little specimen will be seen in the question which I am about to treat. For, having to make good my contention that human reason has only one *Form*, which I call the *Form of Truth*, it will be my duty to demonstrate that on this principle alone can we avoid the two great stumbling-blocks which have so far proved fatal to the diverse theories broached in modern times. And, first of all, I shall have to speak of those systems which do not assume what is necessary for explaining the origin of ideas; then of those which assume a great deal more than is necessary; and, lastly, I shall have to prove that the theory which assigns one only form to human reason, by steering a middle course between those two extremes, keeps equally clear of both, and that of all complete explanations of the fact of which I speak, it is the simplest, and that which makes fewest suppositions.

---

[1] Leibnitz had a very mean opinion of the philosophy of Locke; but in writing against it, he perceived that it had the advantage of being popular, and to this he called attention in the preface to his *Nouveaux Essais sur l'Entendement Humain.* He says: ' Il est plus populaire que moi ; et moi je suis forcé quelquefois d'être un peu plus acromatique et plus abstrait ; ce que n'est pas un avantage pour moi, surtout écrivant dans une langue vivante ' (p. 2). It was, however, with the view of making these essays as popular as possible that he wrote them in French ; but the popularising of philosophical truths of the highest order was too difficult an undertaking.

As, however, what I am here pledging myself to do is, not to give a theory on everything which takes place in the human soul, but only to explain the origin of ideas, I must, before proceeding further, describe as concisely and as clearly as I can the intimate nature of this fact, that so the reader may see the true state of the question, as well as the knot which renders its solution a matter of no ordinary difficulty.

SECTION II.

ON THE NATURE OF THE DIFFICULTY TO BE OVERCOME
IN EXPLAINING THE ORIGIN OF IDEAS.

THE DIFFICULTY STATED.

41. The fact, then, which I propose to explain is that of
the existence in us of ideas or cognitions.[1]

We all know many things, we think of many things: in a
word, we have ideas. I do not now inquire what ideas are,
contenting myself with the notion which is commonly attached
to this word. But, whatever these ideas be, I want to know
how or whence it is that they are found in our mind.

This is a question which everyone can ask of himself, but
to which not all are equally able to reply. It is the celebrated
question of the *origin of ideas*, whereon the schools and
philosophers of all ages have been divided.

42. To indicate as briefly as possible, where its difficulty
lies, I reason as follows :—

In order that we may make a judgment, our mind must
be already in possession of some universal.

For instance, when I say, 'this sheet of paper is white,' or,
'this is a wise man,' my affirmation supposes in me the knowledge of the universals called whiteness and wisdom ; for
otherwise I could not attribute the predicates to these
particular subjects rather than to others.

It would take a long time to demonstrate by induction

---

[1] Every idea gives some knowledge. '*Pure* ideas,' *i.e.* those which
do not by themselves cause us to
know any real things, might perhaps
be thought an exception to this rule.
Some assertion to this effect is to
be met with in Aristotle. Nevertheless, all ideas without exception may,
in a broad sense, be called cognitions.
At all events, of whatever sort our
cognitions may be, ideas are always
the *formal part* of them, as will be
shown later.

that this applies invariably to all judgments; but it could always be done with strict logical accuracy. We may therefore lay it down as an incontrovertible truth, that a judgment is nothing but an intellectual operation by which we join a given predicate with a given subject; and hence that in this operation—

(1) We take the subject and the predicate as two things mentally distinct; that is, such that we can fix our attention upon one of them exclusively and thus distinguish it from the other.

(2) We recognise that these two things are united in fact; that is, we fix our attention on them, not as separated, but as joined together in the relation of predicate and subject.

Such being the operation called judgment, we can see that it implies, first of all, the knowledge of a predicate distinct from the subject, and that without this knowledge the judgment would be impossible. Now, a predicate distinct from the subject is always a universal; for so long as it is not actually united with this or that particular subject, it is capable of being united with many, indeed with an infinite number of possible subjects; which is precisely what we mean by the term *universal* as applied to ideas.

But if no judgment can be made without our being already cognisant of some universal, the question arises: How do we come by the knowledge of universals?

43. A very little reflection will suffice to show that there are only two ways in which this knowledge could be acquired— that is, either through *abstraction* exercised on a particular idea,[1] or through a *judgment.*

Abstraction may draw the universal from a particular idea by doing three things :—

[1] Here I must say a word about the expression 'particular idea.' An idea is particular only in so far as it is attached in our mind to an individual reality. No sooner is it separated therefrom than it acquires, or rather manifests, its character of *universality*; for by being thus set free, it becomes applicable at pleasure to an infinite number of individuals of the same class. Therefore, the only thing truly proper or particular in an idea is the individual reality with which it is joined, and which does not form part of the idea itself, but is an element heterogeneous to the *idea*, and united with it, not by nature, but by an act of the intelligent spirit. Hence, to me, a pure idea and a *universal idea* are equivalent phrases. All this will be fully explained in the progress of this work.

(1) Dividing that idea into the two elements of which it is composed—*i.e.* (*a*) the *common*, and (*b*) the *proper;*

(2) Leaving aside the proper; and

(3) Fixing the attention on the *common* alone, which is precisely the universal about which we are here inquiring.

Now, we must recollect that the particular idea is in us antecedently to these three intellectual operations, else they could not be performed on it, and that their object, therefore, is, not to cause the *common* to exist in our mind, but simply to *observe* it in such a manner that it may be seen by its pure self alone.

But it could not be thus observed unless it were already contained in that particular idea.

Therefore *abstraction* cannot account for the formation of universals, as certain philosophical schools have erroneously supposed. It can only serve for the purpose of disengaging them from heterogeneous elements, and placing them before our attention in a perfectly isolated state.

44. It only remains to say, therefore, that universals are formed by means of a *judgment*.

But we have already seen, that every judgment pre-supposes in us the knowledge of some universal (42). In fact, a judgment is nothing but an act by which we apply a universal to a given subject, or, in other words, assign this subject to a class of things determined by that universal. For example, by judging that a certain individual is virtuous, I place that individual in the class of things known to me under the general name of *virtue* : and the same must be said of all other judgments.

If, then, we cannot begin to judge except by making use of a universal, it is manifestly impossible to explain the *formation* of all universals by means of *judgments*. We must needs assume that antecedently to all our judgments we know some universal which renders possible to us the making of judgments, and, through them, the formation of other universals.

45. Such, in a few words, is the difficulty which presents itself to those who wish to explain the origin of ideas without

prejudices of school or without vulgar assumptions. This difficulty will show itself more and more clearly as we proceed ; and those philosophers who think that they can derive from the senses alone all the ideas which observation and consciousness certify that we are possessed of will see what a hard task they have undertaken.

SECTION III.

THEORIES WHICH ERR BY DEFECT—THAT IS, BY NOT ASSIGNING TO IDEAS AN ADEQUATE CAUSE.

46. The difficulty which I have now stated has presented itself under different aspects to the minds of all the principal philosophers, and they have devised various and ingenious hypotheses to solve it. Let us, then, begin by examining the systems which they invented, that we may see whether any of these systems can be considered satisfactory. The first which offers itself to our attention is the system of Locke.

CHAPTER I.

LOCKE.

ARTICLE I.

The system of Locke.

47. It must be confessed that the celebrated Locke perceived the difficulty of which we are speaking more imperfectly than any other philosopher, or at all events he did not seriously consider it. We shall nevertheless find that he also fell in with it in the course of his investigations.

This philosopher with the greatest *bonhomie* imaginable assures you at the outset that all our ideas are derived from *sensation* and *reflection*, in the same way, one might think, that the waters of a reservoir are supplied from two large fountains.

•ARTICLE II.

Locke, when coming to account for the origin of the idea of substance, stumbles upon the difficulty, but does not perceive it.

48. Having thus taken the principle of his system for granted at the very commencement,[1] Locke proceeds to apply it, passing in review the various species of ideas, and showing how their formation can easily be explained by sensation and reflection alone.

[1] Such is the method of Locke. We must not suppose that he starts from facts in order to deduce his principles from them : on the contrary, he begins by gratuitously assuming the truth of his principles, and on that assumption he proceeds to explain the facts. And such also, more or less, is the method of the adherents of his school down to Cabanis, Destutt-Tracy, Gioja, &c. In what, then, does the merit of these writers consist in connection with philosophical method? It consists in continually crying out to others, ‘ Don't do as we do : observe facts carefully, and lay down no principles except in so far as warranted by your observations.’ Well, it is no small merit to inculcate what is right. Let us take the good, from whomsoever it comes, and pass by the rest.

To test the principle of a system by its application is, undoubtedly, a thing much to be commended; for it is the only proper way of ascertaining if the principle be sound, or, if not, of discovering where its weak points lie.

49. In fact, it was during this process of application that Locke stumbled upon the difficulty. Among the various species of ideas which came in his way there was also the idea of substance; and by no amount of ingenuity could he, on the ' sensation and reflection' principle alone, account for the production of this idea.

Placed in this dilemma, what did he do? Rather than admit that his fundamental principle was defective, because insufficient to account for the formation of all our ideas, he boldly took it upon himself to assert that the idea of substance was a mere dream!

' I confess,' he says, ' there is another idea [1] which would be of general use for mankind to have, as it is of general talk,[2] as if they had it;[3] and that is the Idea of *Substance,* which we neither have nor can have by sensation or reflection.' [4]

50. The reasoning of Locke, put in the form of a dialogue, would come to the following :—

Locke: The origin of ideas, like everything else, must be discussed on the basis of facts.

Opponent: Nothing could be better; but pray what are the facts you would start from?

Locke: Sensation and reflection.

Opponent: Well, but how do you, from these two faculties, derive the idea of substance?

Locke: It cannot be derived from them; therefore it does not exist.

---

[1] Strange contradiction! There is an idea which is not an idea.

[2] How can that which is not an idea form the subject of common talk? That a *thing* which does not actually exist may form the subject of conversation, I can well understand; but that what is not even *thought* of, is not even an *idea*, can be talked about, is to me utterly unintelligible; it is a metaphysical mystery of Lockism.

[3] Again, men make use of an idea, and constantly introduce it into their discourses, without possessing it! Will these philosophers, who pique themselves so much on the clearness and accuracy of their reasonings, be good enough to explain how this can be?

[4] *Essay on the Human Understanding,* Bk. I. ch. iv. § 18.

Opponent: Pardon me, but I am unable to see the force of your deduction. Sensation and reflection are certainly two facts ; but it is also a fact that we have the idea of substance. Now, by what right do you exclude [1] this third fact, simply because it happens to be out of harmony with the two which you have selected as the basis of your philosophy? Questions of *fact* are not to be settled by *reasoning*, but by *observation*. You, on the contrary, start from reasoning in order to deny a fact. You say the idea of substance does not exist because it *cannot exist*, and it cannot exist because it is not derived from sensation and reflection. Is not this going counter to the method which you have, and very properly, laid down for us all ? According to this method, you ought to have examined, first, if the idea of substance exists ; and if you found that it *does* exist, you ought to have said, Therefore it *can* exist. Any one fact is as much a fact, and therefore as much entitled to recognition, as any other fact. This rule of justice you have clearly violated. From a desire to hold fast by your favourite theory, you have unduly extolled some facts at the expense of others, and I must therefore, on these grounds, be permitted to call your argument a blunder.

I do not see how this reply could be validly gainsaid by a follower of the school of Locke.

ARTICLE III.

Without the idea of substance the development of our intellectual life would be impossible.

51. Now, if Locke, instead of examining whether the idea of substance does exist, had directed his attention to the question whether it *can* exist, he would very soon have become convinced that its necessity is such that it *cannot but* exist.

---

[1] This systematic exclusion is not a fact, but a principle. Therefore have I said that Locke begins by an assumption of principles and thence proceeds to explain facts. To say, 'In accounting for the origin of ideas we must start from sensation and reflection only,' is to lay down an arbitrary law by which certain facts shall be admitted, while others are repudiated.

Without this idea it is impossible for us to make any reasonings either in thought or speech. Locke himself acknowledges that it forms the general subject of human discourse. Apart from it we should not be able to conceive the existence of anything, corporeal or spiritual. But we *do* conceive it ; therefore we possess the idea of substance.

Concerning this, a distinguished Italian philosopher writes as follows :—' The idea of substance must have greatly embarrassed Ideologists had they reflected on it in good faith. They taught that we perceive nothing but our own modifications. The consequence of this would be either that we have not any idea of substance, or that this idea must be in us independently of our sensations. The first of these suppositions is belied by our intimate consciousness, and by the very language of Locke and Condillac. These philosophers confess that we are obliged to imagine an unknown something as sustaining the sensible qualities, which is the same as to admit that we have, somehow or other, a notion of substance, independently of the sensations. Say what you will about this being a vague and obscure notion, you must needs allow that it is the centre to which all the sensible qualities are referred by us, and that, without it, we could never form the idea of any sensible object.' [1]

ARTICLE IV.

Why the idea of substance cannot come from sensations alone.

52. But whence the impossibility, acknowledged by Locke himself, of accounting for the idea of substance by means of sensations alone?

I am sorry to be obliged, at so early a stage of these inquiries, to enter upon the difficult task of submitting to analysis the idea of substance; for I would very much rather have reserved it till near the end, when my way would have been considerably smoothed by the previous treatment of easier topics. But, as I have no alternative, I shall endeavour to do it as clearly as I can.

[1] Galuppi, *Lettere filosofiche*, &c., Messina, 1827.

The difficulty, then, lies in this: every sensation we experience, whether external or internal, is purely an affection of our own—a modification of the feeling or sentiment which we naturally have of ourselves—a passivity; and in the receiving of it our understanding has no part whatever. A *substance*, on the contrary, cannot be conceived by us except as a thing which subsists in itself; which is in no way a modification, but is itself a subject of modifications; and which therefore cannot fall under the perception of our senses. Hence the idea of substance is entirely different from the idea of sensation. The properties of the one have nothing to do with the properties of the other. Consequently, this idea cannot be contained, nor therefore found, in sensations. But I will point out more distinctly some essential differences between the idea of sensation and that of substance.

53. *First difference*: A sensation is an accident subsisting, not in itself, but in us; a substance subsists in itself.

Second difference: A sensation is a modification of the sentient subject; while a substance may be the sentient subject itself.

Third difference: A sensation is the result produced by that which affects our sensitive organs. The substance of bodies, on the contrary, remains in our thoughts after being divested of all sensible qualities; which shows that it is something beyond the mere sensible.[1]

54. In short, the substance (*i.e.* of bodies) is conceived by us through the following reasoning:—' The sensible qualities could not exist without a support. But the sensible qualities exist; our sensations advertise us of the fact. Therefore, that which supports them—the subject to which they belong, and which is called *substance*—exists also.'

The sensations simply advertise us of the presence of the sensible qualities; they do not go any further.

To deduce from these qualities the necessity of a substance

---

[1] It may also be said that the *mere sensible* (whatever it may be) is not a substance, because without the addition to it of the perception of the understanding it is not yet a *being*, as will be said later: whereas the term *substance* includes the idea of a *being*.

is the work of the understanding ; and this faculty deduces it on the following principle :—' The sensible qualities cannot exist without a support.'

But whence does our understanding draw this principle? Certainly not from the experience of the sensible qualities, since the support of which we speak never falls within that experience (52).

How come we, then, to affirm with such absolute assurance, not only that the support exists, but also that it *must* exist? We could not do so, unless (1) we knew *what* a support (a *substance*) is, or, which is the same thing, had the idea of it ; (2) unless we possessed within us a rule whereby to discriminate between that which cannot exist without a support and that which can ; (3) unless we applied this rule to the sensible qualities, and found them to be of that class of things which cannot exist without a support, a subject to which they belong.

Hence the whole difficulty which is met with in explaining the origin of the idea of substance, consists in finding a satisfactory answer (which Locke felt unable to give) to the question, How is it possible for us to make the abovementioned judgment, 'the sensible qualities cannot exist without a support'?

Now, if we examine the three things which we have said to be necessary for making this judgment, we shall find that there is only one of them which is not supplied by the senses.

In fact, the third of those things is the act by which, applying the rule to the sensible qualities, we judge that they necessarily demand a support. Now, this judgment can be made as soon as our mind is in possession (1) of the said rule, and (2) of the idea of support.

But the idea of support is already included in the rule.

To make this plain, let us suppose that our mind is possessed of some principle in virtue of which it understands that the sensible qualities cannot exist by themselves alone. From this principle it is easy for the mind to draw at once the idea of support—*i.e.* of something (whatever that may be) which is found united with the sensible qualities, and renders it possible for them to subsist.

All that remains to be discovered, therefore, is, ' How our mind can be possessed of, or form to itself, a rule or principle authorising it to judge that "the sensible qualities cannot exist by themselves alone."'

Now, this rule is the major of a syllogism, and might be worded thus : ' Accidents cannot exist by themselves alone ;' the meaning of which formula is that the mind sees an intrinsic contradiction between the idea of a certain species of things called *accidents*, considered by themselves alone, and the idea of *existence*.

The analysis, therefore, of this rule gives us two elements —(1) the accidents, and (2) the idea of existence.

The accidents themselves are furnished to us by the sensations, since they are only the sensible qualities.

What the sensations do not and cannot furnish to us is the universal and pure idea of *existence*; that idea which mixes itself up with all our reasonings ; and this is where the point of the difficulty lies.

To recapitulate :—

The idea of the substance of external bodies cannot be formed otherwise than by a judgment.

This judgment is made by means of a rule.

This rule, when analysed, is found to be the compound result of two elements—that is to say, (1) the accidents, and (2) the idea of existence.

The *accidents* are supplied to us by the sensations.

The idea of *existence*, on the contrary, is a universal which cannot possibly come from the senses.   Consequently, on the supposition that all our ideas are derived from the sensations alone, the idea of substance remains inexplicable.

ARTICLE V.

The difficulty found in explaining the origin of the idea of substance is the same as that which I have stated in another form.

55. The impossibility of deriving the idea of substance from the senses arises, as we have just seen, from the fact that

such derivation is possible only through a judgment, for making which we must necessarily be in possession of a universal, which the senses cannot give : I mean the idea of existence.

Now, anyone who reflects well on the matter will perceive that this is the same difficulty which I have propounded in connection with the origin of ideas generally ; for the whole of that difficulty was reduced by me to this one question, ' How is our first judgment possible, supposing that we have not the knowledge of some universal, have not some idea, innate in us ? '

Indeed, how could that judgment be possible when it is in the very nature of a judgment to make use of a universal, and therefore to presuppose it in our mind ?

Antecedently to our knowledge of the universal, therefore, the making of any judgment about our sensations, or the causes which produce them, is utterly out of the question.

But if so, our understanding will never be able to advance ever so little beyond the sensations ; for to deprive this faculty of the power of making judgments, is to take away from it all its activity, and to doom it to a state of absolute inertness ; and therefore to disqualify it entirely from forming to itself any universal, because every such formation is only the effect of a judgment.

To illustrate this by an example, we will suppose that my senses are acted upon by some sensible agent—a tree, a stone, an animal, &c. I shall forthwith experience the sensations which that agent produces in me—the sensation of colour, of size, of form, of motion, &c. Now, so long as I am only a passive recipient of these sensations, so long as they remain pure modifications of my sensitivity, unaccompanied by any action of my understanding, I have not conceived any being in an intellectual way. To conceive it intellectually, I must make a judgment by which I say to myself, ' Here is something endowed with such and such qualities ' (the qualities perceived by my senses). Now, by pronouncing this judgment I simply attribute existence to a real thing of which my senses have perceived only the sensible qualities, or the accidents ; and I thus perceive intellectually the being itself. The universal applied here to the sensations is that of *existence* ; but if I had not the knowledge of this universal previously, I could not apply it, and therefore could not perceive anything intellectually ; since to perceive a thing intellectually is nothing but to judge that thing existent.

But this universal idea of existence, or being, cannot be supplied by sensations ; and why ? because they do not contain it ; for the existence of the sensible qualities which produce the sensations is not in *them*, but in the being (the substance) of which they are accidents, and which is entirely different from them. Hence they cannot be intellectually perceived by themselves alone, but must be perceived in that being (that substance). Here is the whole of the difficulty to which Locke himself bore witness by his inability to derive the idea of substance from sensations.

56. But the difficulty, in the form in which I have proposed it, extends a great deal further than this.

It is a fact, certified by observation, that we have no intellectual perception of any sensible thing except through an interior judgment by which we say to ourselves, ' This thing exists ; ' and it is equally a fact that, in order to pronounce this judgment, we must be possessed of the idea of *existence*, which we add to the qualities perceived by the senses.

This alone, in the first place, is an insoluble knot for those who imagine that all ideas can be drawn from the senses ; and the same knot is found in the formation of every idea—the idea of tree, of stone, of an animal, howsoever determinate it may be, &c. For in the formation of these ideas, as also of intellectual perceptions, a judgment in which we make use of the universal idea of *existence* is always necessary, because by them we affirm something as existent. But, for the reason already given, this idea cannot be had from the sensible qualities, and consequently cannot be had through sensations.

Therefore the formation also of particular ideas, or, to speak more accurately, of intellectual perceptions, is inexplicable unless cn the admission that we have, antecedently to them, the universal idea of existence.

57. We are therefore well justified in saying that the philosophers of the school of Locke have not carried their analysis of ideas far enough for them to see the truth which I have pointed out—namely, that there is not a single idea, even though relating to a particular, which has not in it a *universal*, at least the idea of *existence*. For to have, say, the idea of *tree*, referring it to a particular tree, is the same thing as intellectually to perceive a tree ; and intellectually to perceive a tree is the same thing as to judge a tree existent ; and to judge this is the same thing as to assign the tree to the class of things that have existence. Wherefore a sense-perception is not an *idea* until that which the sense perceives is classed, so to speak, among the things existing, either actually or potentially ; which cannot be done without the idea of existence—that is, of the class in which that thing is placed. But the philosophers of whom I speak were entirely unconscious of this truth. They supposed that there really were particular ideas without any universal or common element in them.

58. In arguing, therefore, with these philosophers, I would tell them that, on this their supposition, the forming of universals by means of abstraction is a sheer impossibility.

In fact, how shall I extract universals from particular ideas which, by the hypothesis, do not contain any universal at all? Is not this a manifest self-contradiction ?

However, in the opinion of our philosophers, nothing is easier than the making of this abstraction. All you have to do (say they) is this : When you have the idea of a tree, of a stone, of an animal, or of any other particular thing, observe what each of these things has in it of 'common' and what of 'proper.' Fix your attention on the common, totally apart from the proper, and that is the universal you were seeking for. Do you wish to form the idea of existence ? Forget all the other qualities ; think only of that quality which, in the objects known to you, is the most common of all, and the thing is done.

I shall not stop to enumerate the numberless inaccuracies contained in these sentences, but shall confine myself to what is sufficient for bringing out into full view the difficulty of which we are speaking.

I answer, then : You want me, in reflecting upon the particular ideas which I have of a tree, of a stone, &c., to fix my attention upon such of their qualities as are common, and to separate them from those that are proper. You assume, then, that each of these ideas is composed of two elements— the 'common' and the 'proper;' for otherwise you could not expect me to find these elements in them, nor, consequently, to fix my attention on one in preference to the other. You are, then, in contradiction with yourselves; for your supposition was, that the *particular* ideas contained nothing universal, and that I, having as yet no universal, could obtain it by means of those ideas.

The truth is, that these philosophers are taking unwarrantable liberties with the rules of logic, now asserting one thing, and the next moment implying the contrary ; first maintaining that we begin with particular ideas received only from the sensations, and then assuring us that we shall find in these ideas the universals which they have just told us are not in them !

And if they had supposed (as they should have done) that in the particular ideas some universal is contained, it would have been their duty to assign to the universal an origin different from the sensations which contain nothing but what is particular.

59. But what could have been the origin of this illusion of the followers of Locke ? I believe it to have been this, that they never properly realised to themselves this simple truth, that the sensations as well as the 'sensibles,' considered by themselves and independently of our understanding, are *particular* in such a manner that they contained positively nothing but particular qualities ; and that a common and universal quality exists in our understanding only. Of this truth I shall have occasion to say more in future. Having failed to notice it, our philosophers fell into the blunder of attributing

to the things perceived that which was only in the understanding; and from this first blunder the others came of
themselves, because the error was carried from the beginning
of the calculation down to the very end of it, to the ultimate
result.

60. Let us trace out the way in which the first error, unconsciously admitted, went on communicating itself, as if by a
natural reproduction, from one proposition to another down
to the last.

First error, then : ' The things perceived by the bodily
senses have really in them *something common* independently of
the manner in which they are perceived by the understanding.'

Now, if the ' common' be really in the things themselves,
and not in the understanding, it is clearly superfluous to seek
in the understanding for the origin of the 'common.'

Second error : ' The two elements of which the things are
composed—*i.e.* the "common" and the "proper"—pass into
the sensations so soon as the things are perceived by the
senses.'

This is a necessary sequel of the above. Assume that the
sensible qualities, as perceived by the senses, contain the
' common ' as well as the ' proper,' and you are bound to say
that the sensation perceives both of them.

Third error: ' If the sense receives into itself and perceives that which is " common " in the things, as well as that
which is " proper," the origin of *particular* ideas is very easy
to explain :' very easy, indeed, when the sense is supposed to
supply us so well with both of the elements which compose
those ideas.[1]

Fourth and last error : ' From the particular ideas one
can readily abstract universals.'

Just so. We only require for that purpose to divide the
two elements contained in these ideas, and to bestow our
attention on the 'common,' exclusively of the ' proper.'

All these consequences are unimpeachably correct if the

---

[1] The self-contradiction with which I have charged the Lockists would always remain, even though all this reasoning which they raise on a shaky basis were strictly accurate.

first of the above propositions be true—namely, that the 'common' and the 'proper' really exist in the things per-ceived by the bodily senses.   In fact,

1st. It is indubitable that universals can be drawn by analysis from *particular* ideas, if it be true that the universals are contained in them.

2nd. It is indubitable that *particular ideas*, composed of 'common' and of 'proper,' can be obtained from sensations alone, if it be true that the sensations themselves are the compound result of these two elements.

3rd. Lastly, it is indubitable that the sense perceives the 'common' as well as the 'proper,' if it be true that these are real elements entering into the composition of external things and their sensible qualities.

The capital sin of all this reasoning is in the proposition last named.

The *common* has no existence outside the understanding. It is an element of our ideas, not a real element of external things.   The existence of these things is purely individual and proper, and so are all their other qualities ; for the word *common* implies a *relation* seen by the understanding between several objects, and a relation is not even a species of quality, so that it may exist in a real thing.   It belongs to the order, not of things, but of thought.

61. If, then, the universal (the *common*) is found only in ideas, and if in external things there is an existence purely *particular* and *proper*, the question is, 'Whence do we get our knowledge of universals ?'

Not certainly from external things, which have it not to give.   And yet none of us is without the knowledge of uni-versals.   Therefore, the origin of that knowledge must be in the understanding itself independently of sensations.   This argument seems to me unanswerable.

Now, the difficulty proposed by me reduced itself to this very question, ' How is it possible for the understanding to have the knowledge of universals ?'

It is a fact, I said, that a person whose intellectual facul-ties are at all developed makes judgments.

Therefore, he must at some time or other have begun making them.

There is no middle term here, no gradation ; to pretend that there is would be a mere dream of the imagination. I must either say to myself, 'This which acts upon my senses exists,' or not say it.

Let us, then, go back in thought to the very first of our judgments. For making it we already stood essentially in need of a universal. But we could only have drawn the universal through reflection (1) on our sensations, (2) on our particular ideas. Not, however, on our sensations, because the universal was not in them ; therefore, on our particular ideas. It will then have to be supposed that we began to judge after having acquired some particular ideas. But either these ideas contained the universal, or they did not contain it : if they did, it remains to be explained whence it came into them. If they did not contain it, the difficulty returns. Take it, therefore, as you will ; this difficulty cannot be got over except on the assumption that the *common* or *universal* is supplied by the understanding itself, and that this faculty carries with it something not received from the senses.

62. Thus would be solved the first part of the question which I have proposed in this work—namely, 'Whether the human understanding has something innate in it?' There would remain the second part—*i.e.* : 'Assuming that the human mind has in it something innate, in what does that something consist?'

But the answer to this may be already surmised from the things which I have said, and which clearly point to the *idea of being* as that universal whence all other universals originate. Nevertheless, before treating professedly of this matter, I must fulfil the promise I have made (40), of passing in review the principal philosophical systems concerning the first part of the present inquiries.

ARTICLE VI.

Conclusion on the imperfection of the system of Locke.

63. Let us now briefly recapitulate all we have said thus far :—

I. Every particular idea contains, at the least, one universal—*i.e.* the idea of *existence*; for we cannot have the idea of any one thing until we have made a judgment in which we say to ourselves, ' This thing exists.'

II. We form particular ideas in the first instance by uniting the ' sensible' with the idea of *existence*, and thus placing that ' sensible,' as it were, in the class of existent things.

A particular idea, therefore, may be defined ' the perception which the understanding forms of a " sensible " by seeing it in the class of existent things ;' or also, ' a " sensible " to which is attributed the common quality of existence, which quality in virtue of this attribution becomes proper.' [1]

III. Hence it is impossible to form a particular idea without contributing thereto the idea of *existence*; and, since this operation may be called a *synthesis*, a particular idea implies a *synthesis* made by the understanding.

IV. The *common* or *universal* cannot be drawn from sensations, because it is not contained in them. The understanding must therefore carry it with itself.

V. From the particular idea the *universal* can be drawn through abstraction, because the universal is already contained in that idea. This operation is called *analysis*.

VI. Locke, not having the least suspicion that there was any difficulty in explaining the formation of *particular ideas*, supposed them to be furnished immediately by our sensations in the manner I have described. Hence he thought that *universals* could be easily obtained from these ideas through analysis ; because, in fact, the *universals* are contained in them.

---

[1] I consider, however, as will be seen later, that between the *intellectual perception* and the *particular idea* there is some difference, inasmuch as the particular idea is the *object* seen by us, tied to the affirmation which we make of its subsistence ; while the intellectual perception is the *affirmation* itself.

64. The imperfection of the system of Locke, therefore, consists in his having erroneously assumed that the *universal* really exists in the sensible things themselves, and, as a consequence, in not having perceived the difficulty which stands in the way of explaining the origin of the universal.

Owing to this error, he did not see the necessity of a *synthesis* preceding the *analysis*—that is, of an operation by which the understanding joins. that which falls under the senses with the universal idea of existence previously possessed by it, and thus makes that judgment whereby particular ideas are formed.

Supposing the *synthesis* to be already made in the external things themselves, he began his theory by the *analysis* of particular ideas, and derived from it, by a simple separation, the universals in their *abstract* form. He did not explain the formation of these ideas, but assumed it.

I shall conclude this article by quoting a passage from an Italian philosopher who, in language as accurate as it is clear, thus exposes the imperfection of the theory of Locke : ' In man's knowledge we must distinguish two epochs. The first consists in *synthesis*, which forms the objects of experience and composes the great book of sensible nature. In this epoch the first operation of the understanding must be *synthesis*. The second epoch begins by the reading of the book of nature : in it man reviews his own work, and his first operation is *analysis*. Locke occupies himself with the second of these epochs. He supposes the great book of nature as already formed, and introduces the intelligent spirit to read and understand it. He starts by the assumption that the senses give us complete ideas of the individuals which are the objects of experience. He supposes as given the externality of sensations, and their union in an object (*and I shall add, he supposes as given the universal idea of existence*) ; and, as a consequence, he derives all simple ideas (all *universals* [1]) from

---

[1] By saying *simple idea* we do not bring out the difficulty so well as we should do by the word *universal* ; for, to make the difficulty of drawing simple ideas from the phenomena of sensations properly understood, one would first have to prove the impossibility of the simple being found by analysing the composite. But when I say *universals*, I at once make it quite clear that they

experience by means of analysis.'   And further on he says :
'In truth, what does the English philosopher do?   In presenting to man's meditation the great book of nature, he
expects him to draw thence all simple ideas by means of
analysis.   Now, it cannot be concluded from this that all
simple ideas thus derived are data of sense, or that they are'
feelings distinct from and evolved out of other feelings.   If
in these simple ideas there should be found some subjective
elements,[1] these elements may, indeed, be derived from
experience by means of analysis. But why ?   Only because
the understanding has placed them there through that synthesis by which it has formed the objects of experience.
The fundamental question consists in determining whether
the first operation of the activity of thought be analysis or
synthesis.'[2]

cannot be found in the particular, because the particular excludes the universal as its contrary.

[1] *Subjective, i.e.* posited by the
intelligent subject himself, and therefore innate. This term, *subjective,* however, is not exact, and, as we shall see,
by its inexactness it has caused the
fundamental error of the system of
Kant. In fact, the human spirit may
have in it some universal innate without at the same time drawing it from
its very self, but, on the contrary,
receiving it from without ; in this case
the universal, though not subjective,
would be still *innate.* This remark is
of great importance for understanding
well the theory which I shall expound
in due course.

[2] Galluppi, *Lettere filosofiche,* &c.,
Lett. 7. It is not enough, however,
to know that the first operation of the
activity of thought is synthesis ; it is
necessary furthermore to know of *what
kind* of synthesis one speaks. *This* is
the vital question.

CHAPTER II.

CONDILLAC.

ARTICLE I.

Objections raised by D'Alembert against the system of Locke.

65. The first ideas which offer themselves to our analysis are those of corporeal beings; and it was these that engrossed the attention of Locke and his followers.

No sooner did this philosopher see the impossibility of harmonising the *idea of substance* with his system than, to save the system, he denied the idea (49).

He did not reflect that, without it, we should have no means of forming the ideas of external bodies, and that therefore the idea of *substance—i.e.* of an existence exclusively proper: of a subject, in short, of the sensible qualities— enters of necessity into them all.

Meanwhile, however, his declaration about the impossibility of deriving the idea of substance from the senses was a valuable admission; but, as it stood there isolated from everything else, it remained a long time without bearing fruit.

He had viewed this idea in an abstract way, and hence he could not see the connection it had with so many other ideas less extensive than itself. This explains why he spoke of it as of a mere creature of the imagination, which might be dispensed with in philosophy.

Nor did the philosophers who came after Locke feel at first the full import of his admission; nor did they give it that serious attention which it really deserved.

Instead of this, they occupied themselves with examining in particular the manner in which Locke had derived the

ideas of bodies ; and here it was that they discovered how
his proceeding had been arbitrary, and how difficulties which
should have been seriously grappled with had been simply
passed over.

The thought that it was necessary to enter upon a care-
fully-reasoned explanation of how it is possible for us to
form the ideas of things external to us had not occurred to
Locke, any more than it would occur to any illiterate man.
He had started from the proposition that 'the sensations
give us immediately the ideas of external bodies.' To his
mind this proposition expressed a primitive fact equivalent to
a principle—a fact so obvious that to delay over its explanation would be a mere waste of time.

66. D'Alembert observed that this could not be admitted
as a primitive fact,[1] and that there were in it certain difficulties which called for explanation. The difficulties seen by
D'Alembert were these :—

(1) The sensations are only modifications of our own soul ;
they exist only in us. How is it possible, then, for us to go
outside of ourselves, and to gain the conception of things
external to us, if our sensations are the only sources whence
we can draw ideas ?

(2) Each sensation stands detached from and independent
of the others. For instance, the sensation of smell has
nothing to do with the sensation of colour ; nor has the sensation of colour any resemblance with that of flavour or of
sound ; nor, again, is there anything in common between
these sensations and that of touch. Now, our idea of a body
is the assemblage of all these sensible qualities so utterly
different in their nature. It shows them to us joined together
in one only subject, which is precisely what we call *body*.
How, then, can this be, if the ideas of bodies are produced in
us by the senses alone ?

67. These objections made by D'Alembert against the

[1] And yet D'Alembert speaks of
Locke's *Essay on the Human Understanding* as of a complete treatise on
metaphysics ! That book was then the
rage of the day. The exaggerated
praises lavished at that time on Locke
have now become intolerable—a clear
indication of the progress since made in
the world of thought.

theory of Locke came in reality to the same difficulty which Locke had seen in connection with the origin of the idea of substance; only that Locke had, as I have said, proposed the difficulty in relation to the idea of substance in general, whereas D'Alembert was presenting it under a partial form—that is, by considering that idea in reference to bodies.

In fact, to think of an external body as the sole subject to which all the qualities perceived by our senses are referred is nothing but to think of a support, a centre necessary to those qualities—in a word, the corporeal substance.

But so far was the French philosopher from being conscious of the radical identity of his difficulties with that noticed by Locke,[1] that he, with all apparent good faith, proposed the question, 'Whence is the substantial idea we have of bodies derived?' and this (still more strange to say) while he was fully concurring with Locke in a total denial of the idea of substance.[2] So torpid is human thought! So true is it that even most perspicacious intellects are apt to grope their way slowly searching after truth in the dim twilight of uncertainty!

[1] One of the ways of simplifying philosophical questions is to clear our ideas, and to reduce the difficulties as well as the questions themselves to as few as possible. For the same question may be presented under a great many forms, and each new form appears as a new question, although it is not. This arises principally from the nature of language, which affords innumerable ways and forms of expressing one and the same thought. Those who wish to make a vain and useless parade of learning seek, on the contrary, to multiply questions, arguments, and objections. This is poverty assuming the garb of wealth; and it can impose only on the unwary. It is more than the folly of that madman who broke up into fragments all the household furniture he could lay his hands on, alleging as his reason that he was thus increasing the number of articles in his possession.

[2] In my opinion, the idea of substance was denied through a pure misconception—viz. through imagining that, to have it, more is required than is really the case. In fact, to have this idea, it is enough to know that there can be *no modification without a subject modified*. Now, the idea of this subject is the idea of substance. But you may tell me, 'I do not know what this subject is.' Perhaps not; nay, I will even go further, and grant you that you cannot know it—that for you it is essentially an x. Still, you know that it is the subject of such or such modifications, the cause of such or such effects. Now, what do you want more? It is true that if you strip this subject of its modifications, of its properties, of its effects, you have but an x remaining; but even then you still have the idea of it, because you know the relations which this x has with what you know. Such is the knowledge we have of substance considered in the abstract; nor have we a right to require more, since there is enough in that knowledge to give us the idea in question.

ARTICLE II.

Locke censured by Condillac.

68. D'Alembert proposed the two difficulties above mentioned, but did not solve them. Condillac followed and made the attempt.

The mere proposing a question in any way is already a right step made in philosophy, and to have done this is the merit of D'Alembert. He had, however, no thought of abandoning Locke's principle, that 'all ideas come from the senses.' This principle was then held as a foregone conclusion, and a surrender of it was therefore not to be dreamed of.

To ask how we can, from sensations which exist only *in us*, transport ourselves into the outer world, and form ideas of bodies, was tantamount to asking 'How we can form a judgment before possessing ideas.' In fact, to have the idea of anything external to me I must make the three following judgments: (1) something exists; (2) this something is outside of me; and (3) this something is the subject of the qualities perceived by my senses. But how can I make all these judgments without having some universal already in my mind? (55). The formation, therefore, of our ideas of bodies (the first ideas we acquire) is inexplicable unless on the supposition that there is some universal idea originally given us by nature.

69. Such is the real question when stated in its full extent. But Condillac saw only the first part of it. He perceived that judgments were necessary for forming the ideas of bodies, but he did not perceive that these judgments presupposed universal ideas. It was a short and easy step to make, but he did not make it. Tardy indeed and sluggish is the progress of the human mind.

Having, therefore, risen with his reflection to a more elevated point than had been reached by Locke, Condillac could censure the latter for not having taken into consideration the judgments which are mixed up with our sensations. Speaking of Locke in the beginning of his 'Treatise on Sensations,' he says: 'Nous verrons que la plupart des jugements qui se mêlent à toutes nos sensations lui ont échappé ;' and a little further on : 'Il était si loin d'embrasser dans toute son étendue le système de l'homme, que, sans Molineux, peut-être n'eût-il jamais eu occasion de remarquer qu'il se mêle des jugements aux sensations de la vue. Il nie expressément qu'il en soit de même des autres sens. Il croyait donc que nous nous en servons naturellement par une espèce d'instinct sans que la réflexion ait contribué à nous en donner l'usage.' (*Extrait raisonné du Traité des Sensations*, p. 6; Paris, 1821.)

ARTICLE III.

The system of Condillac.

70. From the above passage would it not seem that Condillac had clearly caught sight of the difference (unperceived by Locke) between our external sensations and the *judgments* that are found intermixed with them ? And that he would therefore have admitted two faculties essentially distinct—the faculty by which we feel the sensations, and the faculty by which we make judgments thereon ?

It would certainly seem so ; but the love of a preconceived system led him to do the very opposite—that is, to reduce everything to one only faculty, that of *sensation*. Thus, instead of adding anything by way of improvement to the two principles of Locke, *sensation* and *reflection*, he strove to make Locke's system more meagre and inadequate than ever.

His error is similar to that which I have mentioned above —namely, of a person who should pretend to account for different species of sensations by means of a single sense. The proposition, that the faculty by which we see colours is the same as that by which we hear sounds or taste the flavour of viands, is not less difficult to prove, nor less absurd, than the proposition which contains the whole pith and substance of Condillac's theory—*i.e.* 'The identical sense which has the sensation of touch judges of that sensation.' [1]

71. But the better to see the errors of this philosopher, let us follow him step by step, and observe the whole course of his reasoning.

He states the subject-matter of the second part of his ' Treatise on Sensations,' thus : ' La seconde partie traite du toucher ou du seul sense qui juge par lui-même des objets extérieurs.' (*Extrait raisonné du Traité des Sensations*, p. 9 ; Paris, 1821.)

One sole faculty, then, one sole sense, performs two operations, acknowledged by Condillac himself as so different from each other that he calls them by two different names : (1) to have the feeling of external things ; (2) to judge of them. [2]

These two kinds of operation he attributes also to the other senses ; but with this difference, that while the touch judges by a virtue inherent in itself, the judicative power of the other senses is *communicated* to them by the touch : and to explain how this truly mysterious communication takes place, is the object which he proposes to himself in the third part of the same treatise. The third part (he says) undertakes to show ' comment le toucher apprend aux autres senses à juger des objets extérieurs.' (*Ibid.*) [3]

---

[1] St. Augustine in many parts of his works notes very accurately the difference between feeling and judging, and finds an immense distance between these two operations of the soul. He says also that, to speak properly, the mind (*mens*) consists in the faculty of judging : ' Servat [mens] aliquid quo libere de specie talium imaginum judicet, et hoc est magis mens, id est rationalis intelligentia, quae servatur ut judicet' (*De Trinitate*, lib. ix. c. 5). ' The mind has in it something in virtue of which it can freely judge of these images [*corporeal things*]; and it has the name of mind, viz. of *rational intelligence*, for this reason, that its characteristic office is to produce judgments.'
[2] That the sense judges has been said also by Aristotle and the school-men. It seems, however, that they took the word *judgment* in a translated sense, owing to a certain resemblance which may be noticed between the effects of sense and those of judgment. I am induced to think so by some passages where Aristotle explains the judgments attributed by him to the sense, in a manner very different from that in which he understands the judgments made by the understanding. In any case, it seems to me difficult to absolve this philosopher from the error which I find in Condillac without charging him with inaccuracy and impropriety of expression.
[3] When I am told that one man *communicates* knowledge to another by teaching, I understand very well what the term *communication* means ; but when I hear it said that one sense com-

ARTICLE IV.

Defectiveness of Condillac's analysis.

72. In reading attentively this author, we see a man who evidently means to explain the successive development of the human faculties by that strict analytical process which does not allow of a single arbitrary admission, and who is, moreover, persuaded of his ability to succeed better than any of his predecessors in the same field of investigation. But we see, at the same time, that in his hands the art of conducting a reasoning with rigorous consecutiveness is as yet in its infancy. By following up his steps with the same intention of being exact, and with the art, improved nowadays, of closely observing everything, and admitting nothing without good proof being shown for it, we discover that his analysis of the operations of the soul is done very imperfectly, and that he sometimes introduces and sometimes supposes the most relevant facts without giving any explanation of them, without having distinctly observed them, or at least without perceiving that they require explanation.

As a proof of this, and to make it clear that Condillac did not so much as see the difficulty there is in accounting for the *act of judgment* without presupposing something innate in our minds, I will let the reader judge for himself how loose and how little ingenious is the way in which he reduces all the faculties of the soul to sensation alone.[1]

ARTICLE V.

Intellectual attention is not the same thing as sensitivity.

73. Condillac, in the first place, endeavours to reduce attention to sensation as follows : ' Si une multitude de

municates to another the faculty of judging which it has not by nature, I own that this is simply beyond my powers of comprehension. I can make nothing of it.

[1] Several other observations on the system of *transformed sensation* may be found in the little treatise which I have entitled *Breve Esposizione della Filosofia di M. Gioja*, inserted in the second volume of my *Opuscoli Filosofici*, and especially in the notes of pp. 358–365, where I have endeavoured to present a summary view of the absurdities of such a philosophy.

sensations se font à la fois avec le même degré de vivacité, ou à peu près, l'homme n'est encore qu'un animal qui sent. . . . Mais ne laissons subsister qu'une seule sensation, ou même, sans retrancher entièrement les autres, diminuons-en seulement la force ; aussitôt l'esprit est occupé plus particulièrement de la sensation qui conserve toute sa vivacité, et cette sensation devient attention, sans qu'il soit nécessaire de supposer rien de plus dans l' âme.' (*Extrait raisonné du Traité des Sensations*, p. 12 ; Paris, 1821.)

But surely it was not difficult to see that the action of external things on our sensitive organs, as well as the sensation which accompanies it, is different from that activity which the intelligent spirit puts forth in thinking of that sensation.[1]

74. A sensation may be received by us quite independently of any action of our will. All that is required for it is that we be passively in a fit condition to receive it. On the contrary, the attention given to a sensation is, not a mere passivity, but an activity subject to our will.

Suppose we were to receive simultaneously four sensations, and that owing to our remaining in a passive or, to speak more accurately, inert attitude, all these sensations had for us much the same degree of vividness. Now, suppose that, instead of continuing in that state of indifference, we concentrated our attention as much as possible on one out of the four : it is certain that the sensation thus specially ad-

[1] Condillac himself distinguishes in the soul a *passivity* and an *activity*. If these two terms convey, as they most certainly do, totally opposite ideas, must not the things which they express be different also ? How, then, can even the most active powers of the soul be reduced to sensation, which is purely a passivity ? No one has exposed this error of Condillac better than Baron Galluppi, in his *Elementi di Filosofia* (Messina, 1820, vol. ii. p. 192, &c.). In France, the birth-place of Condillachism, they now write as follows : 'Soit que, durant trente années, Condillac ait été dans l'illusion, soit que jamais il n'ait exprimé sa pensée avec une clarté suffisante, soit que moi-même j'aie

manqué de pénétration, il m'a toujours été impossible de concevoir, non pas que la sensation précède l'attention, mais que la sensation se change en attention ; non pas que dans l'âme un état actif succède immédiatement à un état passif, mais qu'il y ait identité de nature entre ces deux états, en sorte que l'activité soit une transformation de la passivité ; et je suis si loin de donner mon assentiment à cette proposition, qu'à peine sais-je ce qu'il est possible d'entendre par le rapprochement des termes dont elle se compose. (Laromiguière, *Leçons de Philosophie*, Partie 1ère, Leçon 5ème. Paris, 1844, page 102.)

verted to would be more vividly perceived by us, although perhaps not so vividly as to cause the others to pass totally unnoticed.

There is in us, therefore, besides the passivity of sense, a voluntary activity—a force through which we can, among several sensations of equal strength, select one for special attention, and thus increase the strength of its impression on us. Does not this observation show that the force by which we voluntarily reflect on our sensations, and on one in preference to another, is quite a different thing from the sensations themselves, which exist even without that force being set in motion at all?

A good case in point may be had in a musical quartette. If you listen in a quiet, passive way, you will take in the harmony and have all the sensations which are produced in you by the four instruments together. But experience will very soon convince you that you have also an activity quite different from this passive way of listening, and of which you can dispose at pleasure, either for attending more intensely to the whole harmony, or for taking special delight in the modulations of one particular instrument, or perhaps for admiring the skill of the performer. The *sensation*, therefore, belongs to a passive faculty, for the exercise of which the soul needs not to have any particular and, as it were, self-moving activity; whereas attention belongs to an active faculty, whose use is often determined by our free-will. In this sense it is true that, with sensation alone, man ' is as yet no better than an animal that feels.' But man is never with sensation alone. Besides the power of feeling he has always (whether he actually uses it or not) the power of turning his intellectual activity upon one rather than another of the things he feels; and this latter power from the very first moments of his existence divides him from and places him essentially above the brute.[1]

¹ By what I have said in this article respecting *attention*, or the power of directing one's intellectual activity, I do not by any means intend to deny that there is a *sensitive activity* necessary to sensation. On the contrary, I admit that in every human being who has the feeling of his body, this *sensitive activity* is always in act, and is modified by external impressions, and is some-

ARTICLE VI.

Memory is not sensitivity.

75. Nor is Condillac more fortunate when he attempts to
identify *memory* with *sensation.* He says: 'Notre capacité
de sentir se partage donc entre la sensation que nous avons
eue et celle que nous avons; nous les percevons à la fois
toutes deux; mais nous les apercevons différemment; l'une
nous paraît passée, l'autre nous paraît actuelle.

'Apercevoir ou sentir ces deux sensations, c'est la même
chose;[1] or ce sentiment prend le nom de *sensation* lorsque
l'impression se fait actuellement sur les sens, et il prend celui
de mémoire lorsque cette sensation, qui ne se fait pas actuellement, s'offre à nous comme une sensation qui s'est faite.'
(*Extrait,* &c. p. 13.)

It seems impossible for one to be so deceived as to affirm
that the perceiving of a sensation which is taking place at
this moment, and the perceiving of one which has passed
away, are acts of the same nature. Nay, can a sensation
which is gone by be perceived? Can that be felt which has
ceased to exist?

76. A former sensation may, indeed, exist in our memory;
but it cannot then be said to exist as a real sensation. Its
reality is past and gone, as we express by the phrase: 'I
remember having experienced such or such a sensation.'
For a sensation really to exist it is necessary that our sensitive organs be actually impressed in that way which causes
us to feel; and no sooner does the impression cease, than
there is an end to the sensation. The *memory,* on the con-

---

times equably diffused, and sometimes
more particularly concentrated on one
sensation, according to certain laws of
instinct.
  [1] Could there be a more gratuitous
assertion than this? Condillac does
not support it by the least proof. The
only proof which the philosophers of
this school offer us of the truth of their
opinions is their own bold assertion.
Bold assertions impose on unwary
readers, who take them for scientific
pronouncements. In this way it is
very easy for any writer to draw conclusions perfectly in harmony with a
preconceived system.

trary, continues ; or, to speak more correctly, begins when the sensation has disappeared. Therefore memory is not sensation.

77. What seems to have misled our philosopher is the common expression, ' Past sensations are preserved in the memory.' He ought to have known that the expression is, strictly speaking, inexact ; for in it the word *sensation* has not the same meaning as when one speaks of a real sensation. We preserve in our memory, not the *real sensations*, but only the *recollection* of them. Who does not see that to recollect an acute pain or an intense pleasure is a different thing from actually feeling with our senses that pain or that pleasure ?

The error arising from the double meaning of the term *sensation*, as applied to the senses and as applied to the memory, is in part similar to the error of a person who, on looking at a portrait and hearing some one say, ' This is Manzoni,' were to take that portrait for Manzoni's real self. Most assuredly the Manzoni painted on the canvas differs essentially from the great man who bears that name. The former is a mere likeness in oil or watercolour ; the latter is a real living personage who, I am sure, would emphatically deny ever having transformed himself into that likeness and those colours.

The sensation, therefore, which is said to be in us by recollection is not the real sensation which has caused us, for example, such agonies of pain when a sharp splinter of wood happened to be thrust into our arm or foot. This was felt in the arm or foot itself, whereas the other is a pure reminiscence of it, aided, if you will, by some image,[1] preserved or revived in the soul, but always different and entirely separate from the sensation itself.

---

[1] It cannot properly be said that an idea is an *image*. The word *image* is applicable, not to ideas, but to the phantasms of corporeal things, when we depict them to ourselves in that form in which they fell under our senses. To understand well what an idea is, it is necessary to accustom ourselves to consider it as it is in its own true self, without mixing up with it any comparisons or metaphors drawn from material things. An idea has a being exclusively its own, spiritual and transcending all corporeal sensations.

Therefore whatever dependence or relation may exist be
tween the actual sensation *and the sensation as preserved in
our memory*, and, though they may be even designated by
the same name of *sensation*, they can neither be confounded
together, nor the one be called a transformation of the
other.

In conclusion, then, sensitivity and memory are two
separate faculties, nor can the love of systematic simplicity
be a justification for blending them in one ; that is, for going
directly counter to the fact of nature.[1]

ARTICLE VII.

Attention is different from memory.

78. Having (as he imagined) shown that *memory* does not
differ essentially from *sensitivity*, Condillac boldly continues
as follows :—

‘Par là nous sommes capables de deux attentions ; l’une
s’exerce par la mémoire, et l’autre par les sens.

‘Dès qu’il y a double attention, il y a comparaison; car
être attentif à deux idées, ou les comparer, c’est la même
chose. Or on ne peut les comparer sans apercevoir entre elles
quelque différence ou quelque ressemblance : apercevoir de
pareils rapports, c’est juger.’ (*Extrait*, &c. p. 14.)

This is indeed going at full gallop. Before this man
obstacles seem to vanish as by enchantment.

79. First of all, very little reflection is required to perceive
that the act by which we concentrate our attention either on
the objects of memory or on the terms of sense, is neither
memory nor sense.

Attention is a force directed by the activity of our will, or
rather it is that activity itself. We give attention by an act
of our will, and that attention has a greater or less intensity
according as we will (73, 74).

[1] Condillac himself distinguishes
the *attention of the memory* from the
attention of the sense, characterising the
first as *active* and the second as *passive*—
in other words, making them contrary
to each other. Can there be a difference more essential than this ?

How sensation differs from attention by its passivity, and from memory by the difference of its term, we have already seen (n. 75–77).

That attention also differs from memory is likewise easy to see. Memory consists in the recollection of things past; but attention may be bestowed on things present as well as past. Therefore attention is different from memory.

80. There are, therefore, in us three faculties totally distinct: (1) the faculty of feeling present impressions; (2) that of remembering those impressions when they are past; (3) that of bringing at discretion our *intellectual activity* to bear in a degree more or less intense on some sensations rather than on others, whether present or past. *

ARTICLE VIII.

Judgment must not be confounded with simple attention.

81. Let us proceed:—

‘ Dès qu'il y a double attention il y a comparaison;[1] car être attentif à deux idées, ou les comparer, c'est la même chose.' (*Extrait raisonné*, &c. p. 14.)

This reasoning is altogether incorrect. The proposition that giving attention to two ideas is the same as comparing them together, will not bear examination. May I not, if I like, think first of one idea by itself, and then of another, without instituting a comparison between them and noting their differences?

82. But even if the attention given to two ideas necessarily implied their comparison and the knowledge of their points of difference, it would nevertheless be necessary to admit in this fact three distinct, although contemporaneous, intellectual operations—namely, (1) the attention given to one idea, (2) the attention given to the other idea, and (3) the attention given to the difference between the two; and it would still remain to be seen whether these three acts are of the same nature;

---

[1] Comparison is the result, not of two acts of attention, but of two objects brought simultaneously together by one sole act of attention.

for, if they are not of the same nature, they cannot, their contemporaneousness notwithstanding, be attributed to one and the same faculty.

83. Moreover, these three acts are not necessarily contemporaneous. Surely I can bestow my attention on one idea and then on another, without caring to think of their difference !

To see all this more clearly, it will be enough to glance at what takes place in regard to our ideas of numbers.

Suppose, then, that I have the ideas of number 35 and of number 49, am I obliged to institute a comparison between them and mark their difference? Certainly not. The knowledge of them is not the knowledge of that difference. They are respectively 35 and 49, but the difference is 14—a third number which I produce to myself by performing on them an intellectual operation of a nature peculiar to itself.

Nay, I have the power not only to fix my attention on both those numbers, successively or contemporaneously, but furthermore to exercise my mind on them in sundry other ways, without being at all bound to make that intellectual operation which reveals to me their difference.

84. Condillac's belief that our attention could not be fixed on two things without at the same time perceiving their difference, seems to have arisen from this, that he observed only what mostly takes place in those cases in which we think of things easy to compare together, and whose difference can be very readily seen.

85. Is it not surprising, however, that so obvious a distinction as that between the act of simple attention first to one idea and then to another, and the act of comparing them together and perceiving their difference, should have been overlooked by a philosopher? Even admitting that we were always necessitated by a law of our nature to do these two acts simultaneously, we should still be obliged to say that they are essentially different from each other ; and that the second is more than the first, and therefore deserving to be carefully analysed apart, instead of being so lightly passed over.

When I simply fix my attention on two ideas, I do not produce a new object for it, but occupy it with two objects which are already in my mind. When, on the contrary, I compare two ideas together and separate in them that which is proper to each from that which they have in common, I form to myself a new object of attention—*i.e.* their difference, of which, in so far as it is thus divided and distinguished from those ideas, I had no manner of thought before (95).

ARTICLE IX.

Condillac stumbles upon the difficulty without perceiving it: that is, he accounts for the formation of ideas by unconsciously begging the question.

86. If, instead of so heedlessly passing over the act by which we compare ideas together and find out their differences, Condillac had taken pains to analyse it, as is the duty of a philosopher professing to give a satisfactory explanation of the facts of the human soul, perhaps the difficulty which I have stated above, and which, as I believe, cannot be overcome except by admitting something innate in our mind, would have attracted his notice. Let us follow him :—

' Or, on ne peut comparer deux idées sans apercevoir entre elles quelque différence ou quelque ressemblance : apercevoir de pareils rapports, c'est juger. (*Extrait raisonné*, &c. p. 14.)

From hearing our author thus speak of the comparison of ideas, one would suppose that he had already explained what he meant by the word *idea*.

But his definition of *idea* comes much later. It was therefore natural that in this passage, where he attempts to show that a judgment is simply the result of a comparison of ideas, he should meet with no obstruction. For, the nature of an idea not being as yet defined, one cannot say what the passage really means ; and it is precisely when a reasoning appears to be correct in form, while the words of which it is

composed have no fixed meaning, that readers are apt to be
more indulgent with error.

87. That we may not fall into the same mistake, let us
first examine the value which Condillac assigns to the word
idea ; this will enable us to see whether his reasoning is proof
against all criticism.

He distinguishes sensations from ideas in the following
way :—‘ Une sensation n'est point encore une idée, tant qu'on
ne la considère que comme un sentiment qui se borne à
modifier l'âme.   Si j'éprouve actuellement de la douleur, je
ne dirai pas que j'ai l'idée de la douleur, je dirai que je la sens.

‘ Mais si je me rappelle une douleur que j'ai eue, le souvenir et l'idée sont alors une même chose.’   (*Extrait raisonné*,
&c. p. 31.)

It appears from this passage that, according to Condillac,
an idea is a sensation, not in so far as actually experienced
by us, but only in so far as preserved in our memory.

I have already pointed out that sensation, considered
only in so far as preserved in our memory, is quite a different
thing from the real sensation, or that passive modification
which we experience when our sensitive organs are being
impressed by external things (75-77).   Since, then, an *idea* is
here taken as identical with the *remembrance of sensations*—
which is not a sensation, and begins only when the sensation
has passed away—it is obvious that the word *idea* has a sense
essentially different from that of the word *sensation*.

But it will be well for us to see what it was that prompted
our philosopher to lay down the distinction between sensation
properly so called and the remembrance of a sensation.

The sequel proves that he did it for the reason that
the sensation, as such, does not represent anything outside
itself, whereas the remembrance represents, or rather recalls
to our mind, something different from itself—*i.e.* the sensation
whereof it is the remembrance.   Consequently, what in the
opinion of our philosopher causes an apprehension of our
mind to be an *idea*, is its property of *representing* an external
thing.   This is why he attributes to the sense of touch the
power of changing sensations into ideas—namely, because he

supposes that the touch, alone of all the senses, has the virtue of imparting a representative character to our sensations. But let him speak for himself :—

'Les sensations actuelles de l'ouïe, du goût, de la vue et de l'odorat ne sont que des sentiments, lorsque ces sens n'ont point encore été instruits par le toucher, parce que l'âme ne peut alors les prendre que pour des modifications d'elle-même.[1] Mais si ces sentiments n'existent que dans la mémoire qui les rappelle, ils deviennent des idées. On ne dit pas alors, "j'ai le sentiment de ce que j'ai été ;" on dit, "j'en ai le souvenir ou l'idée."

'La sensation actuelle, comme passée, de solidité, est seule par elle-même tout à la fois sentiment et idée. Elle est sentiment par le rapport qu'elle a à l'âme qu'elle modifie ; elle est idée par le rapport qu'elle a à quelque chose d'extérieur.

'Cette sensation nous force bientôt à juger hors de nous toutes les modifications que l'âme reçoit par le toucher ; c'est pourquoi chaque sensation du tact se trouve représentative des objets que la main saisit.

'Le toucher, accoutumé à rapporter ses sensations au dehors, fait contracter la même habitude aux autres sens. Toutes nos sensations nous paraissent les qualités des objets qui nous environnent ; elles les représentent donc, elles sont des idées.' (*Extrait*, &c. pp. 31-32.)

Now, I beg the reader to observe that the sense to which Condillac here attributes the power of changing sensations into ideas—*i.e.* of rendering the sensations representative of something external—is the very same which he had before credited with the faculty of judging of external objects (70, 71).

Indeed, his whole theory on sensations may be said to centre in the proposition that 'the touch is the only sense

[1] This is a gratuitous proposition resting on the mere *ipse dixit* of Condillac. We need not discuss here whether the thing be as he says, or not ; but I cannot refrain from observing that it is exactly by propositions like these, uttered in a tone of assurance, that errors are covertly introduced into philosophical systems.

which judges of external objects by itself, and communicates the power of judging of those objects to the other senses.' We are given to understand that the touch is likewise that sense whose sensations are, *ipso facto*, *ideas*, and which transforms into ideas the sensations of the other senses also.

Therefore according to Condillac, sensations are transformed into ideas through a judgment. Again, in the passage we have just quoted, he says that the only reason why the touch can transform sensations into ideas is because it has in itself the power of judging of external objects. Therefore the transformation of sensations into ideas is effected through that judgment by which this sense, on being modified by sensations, judges that external objects exist.

88. As against this I might refer the reader to the demonstration I have previously given of the absurdity of attributing to the touch the faculty of judgment—an absurdity as great as, if not greater than, it would be to claim for the sense of *sight* the power of *hearing* (70). Again, I might call attention to the great and very obvious difference which exists between the act of judgment and the sensation of touch—the former being wholly internal and done by the spirit alone,[1] while the latter is solely the result of an external impression actually made on our sensitive organs.

But for the present I will not oppose Condillac on either of these grounds. I will only take him on his own principles, and argue thus :—

89. You say that the act of judgment consists in comparing two ideas together, and making out their differences.

Then in another place, when explaining what you mean by an *idea*, you say that no idea can be formed except by means of a judgment ; and from this you conclude that the touch is the only sense which can transform sensations into ideas, because it is the only sense which has in itself the ability to judge of sensations.

---

[1] The senses furnish us only with the *matter* of the judgment. The act itself of judgment is formed within our spirit alone, quite independently of any particular part of our body or of external space.

Now, here lies precisely my difficulty. Will you be good enough to say how these two propositions can be reconciled ? (1) The judgment is formed through a comparison of ideas ; (2) ideas are formed through a judgment. Which of the two is formed first, the judgment or the idea ?

If every idea must be formed through a judgment, it seems that the judgment precedes the formation of ideas ; but if a judgment is only the result of a comparison of ideas, it seems that we must have ideas before we can form any judgment.[1]

ARTICLE X.

In every representative apprehension we contemplate a universal : hence the difficulty is seen still more clearly in the theory of Condillac, and remains in it unsolved.

90. The above is precisely the difficulty which I stated at the beginning, and of which we are seeking the solution : here it shows itself in all its generality.

It no longer applies to one particular class of ideas only — *i.e.* the universal ideas—but to all ideas without any distinction. It does not say, ' To make a judgment we must be in possession of some universal, and to form a universal we must make a judgment : query, then, which of the two is first—the universal or the judgment ? ' But it says, ' To make

---

[1] Fortunatus of Brescia made but a poor attempt to escape from the difficulty when he bethought himself of bringing in, as supplementary to Heineccius's definition of an *idea* (' objecti alicujus genuina imago quam mens immediate contemplatur,' &c.), the words 'quin tamen de re ipsâ quidquam a nobis affirmetur vel negetur.' Nevertheless, the mere fact of his considering such an addition necessary shows that he had some inkling of the difficulty. Can I, through a *particular idea*, become aware of the existence of external realities, unless I have affirmed that existence in my own mind ? And what is an affirmation but a judgment ? I deem it useful to notice these stumbling-blocks encountered by almost all the authors who have undertaken to explain the origin of ideas, as well as the various shifts to which they had recourse in order to get rid of the same ; for we see from them that the existence of a difficulty in that explanation is attested by a universal authority. Even those who did their utmost to dissemble it did not fail subsequently to reveal it by the embarrassment which they betrayed, by the uncertainty and incoherence of their expressions, and the paltriness of the expedients which they invented in order to hide it from themselves and their readers.

Of the elaborate although unsuccessful attempts made by Wolff to smooth away the difficulty, I shall speak under Section V.

a judgment we require some ideas to compare together, and to form ideas we require to make a judgment: query, then, which of the two is first—the judgment or the idea ?'

This interrogation, put in the form of a philosophical problem, may be expressed thus : ' To assign to ideas and to judgments such an origin that they will not reciprocally presuppose each other, and that we may thus avoid the absurdity of having to consider the effect as the cause of its cause.' Such, in fact, would be the case if all ideas were the result of judgments, and all judgments the result of ideas compared together.

91. Before proceeding to examine whether any other philosopher has succeeded in solving this problem, it will not be amiss to dwell a little longer on the theory of Condillac.

In this theory an idea is a perception representing something different from itself; and it seems evident that, in order to recognise that a perception is related to something different from itself in such a way as to be fit to represent it, a judgment is necessary.[1]

Certainly a simple modification of our soul, such as a pain or a pleasure, is felt by us without any need of a judgment ; but to be able to say that a modification represents something different from itself, we must make a judgment on it. Condillac implies as much by saying that the reason why ideas are representative of external objects is because they are produced by the touch—*i.e.* the sense which (as he asserts) has in it the power of judging and of teaching the other senses to do the same.

I need not repeat that I entirely disagree with his view of the nature of the sense of touch. To me this sense is one thing, and the faculty of judging is essentially another (88).

---

[1] The distinction between the faculty of feeling and that of judging was noted with great precision by St. Augustine (*v.* note to n. 70). The same Father observes in many parts of his writings, that if we had only the senses, the use of *signs* would be impossible to us, because we should have no means of distinguishing the *sign* from the *thing signified.* This observation is of great importance, and, if philosophers had turned it to account, it might have helped them very much to understand the manner in which the human spirit operates. See, among other places, the book on the *Eighty-three Questions,* q. 9.

The touch does not make judgments ; it only furnishes the occasion and the matter for them.

92. Nevertheless, this divergence between Condillac and myself does not in any way affect the nature of my objection against his system. Whether the faculty of judgment identifies itself with the sense of touch, as he will have it, or, as I contend, is a separate power of the soul, we are both agreed in this, that to form ideas a judgment is necessary.

Now, here will be seen in a clearer light the truth which I hinted when first stating the difficulty (43) : namely, that there is not a single idea, how particular soever it may be, which does not contain a universal. For we can always, even in ideas applied to particular things, find the 'common,' and separate it in our mind from the 'proper;' which we could not do if the 'common' was not contained in those ideas. Let us see this truth from Condillac's own theory.

For Condillac, to have an idea or a representative conception,[1] is the same thing as to have an exemplar to which to refer the objects represented and expressed by it.[2]

A portrait is representative of the person who has sat for it ; but this does not cause the person to be of the same nature or substance as the portrait : it only places him in the relation of similarity with it (77). Hence others besides himself might answer to the same portrait, because his relation with it is not so exclusive, so all-absorbing, that other individuals may not share in it through their personal appearance being more or less like his own. So with a perception. Once become representative of something different from itself, it is *universal* in this sense, that it can also represent other things besides the one from which it was taken. The applicability of the relation of similarity to

---

[1] I say *conception* ; Condillac would say *sensation* ; but we must remember that this author, misled by the want of precision in the popular way of speaking, extends, with a mischievous ambiguity, the word 'sensation' to signify 'the remembrance of a sensation.' Now, I need not repeat that a sensation properly so-called—that is, an actual sensation—does not *represent* anything. But the remembrance which we have of a sensation does certainly represent something—namely, the sensation itself—and a remembrance may also be called a conception.

[2] I have already shown in how limited a sense the words *exemplar*, *type*, *image*, must be taken when applied to ideas (*v.* note to n. 77).

things of the same kind, whether existing actually, or only potentially, is inexhaustible. By being similar to each other, two things are not inter-penetrated, made one in nature, wedded together, so to speak, in an indissoluble bond. Each of them remains perfectly free to resemble any number of other things. The one resemblance does not prevent or disturb the other : on the contrary, it implies and supposes it.

Therefore from the moment that Condillac affirms that all ideas are representative perceptions, he is bound to admit that there is a universal and common element in every one of them : *universal,* because this quality alone can make them representative ; *common,* because the only reason why many things resemble one another is that they have something in common : and this *common essence,* taken by itself, is what may be considered as the exemplar or type of all those things, inasmuch as all are referable to it. An exemplar, therefore, a type, is always a universal ; and if one chooses to particularise it by applying it to one thing only—for example, to that whence it was drawn—the particularisation is purely arbitrary and positive, and not natural and necessary.

Had Condillac observed this, he would not have spoken of *ideas* in one place, and then, in another place much further down, of *universal ideas.* He would at once have recognised *universality* as characteristic of all ideas generally ; and having done this, he could have proceeded to treat of the different ways of universality.

But that there may not remain any doubt as to this universality, intrinsic to all representative perceptions (I lay stress on the fact because it is of great importance), let us once more hear how Condillac explains the manner in which a particular idea becomes universal. ' Nous n'avons point d'idée générale, qui n'ait été particulière. Un premier objet que nous avons occasion de remarquer, est un modèle auquel nous rapportons tout ce qui lui ressemble ; et cette idée, qui n'a d'abord été que singulière, devient d'autant plus générale que notre discernement est moins formé.' [1] (*Extrait,* &c., p. 35.)

---

[1] What Condillac says in the last words of this extract is a fact certified by experience. 'Man generalises his ideas in exactly the inverse ratio of his

93. For an idea to be general or universal, then, is the same thing as for it to˙ be the exemplar of many objects (properly of many real individuals). Now, to be the exemplar of many objects is the same thing as to be representative of those objects. But every idea is a perception endowed with a representative property. Therefore, every idea has in it a universal element.

The reason why Condillac did not perceive this truth seems to me to have been this, that he confounded the *aptitude* which an idea has of representing an infinity of real individuals, with the *use* which we make of that aptitude—*i.e.* with the act whereby we explicitly recognise such aptitude in the idea.

If we have in our house the portrait of a venerated ancestor, probably the members of the family, who in those well-delineated features have so vivid a reminder of his former presence in their midst, will never think of that likeness except in connection with him. In this case, therefore, the relation of similarity will be determined to one object alone.

But it remains to be seen whether this determination arises from the nature of the likeness and an intrinsic inaptitude to represent more than one individual, or whether it depends on the accidental disposition of those who look at it, not simply in its natural relations, but in that conventional relation which is suggested by their knowing and remembering for *whom* the likeness was intended. Now, it is evident that the second of these alternatives is the true one ; and it is also evident that the accident of the likeness being viewed by the family in that particular light does not change its nature nor do away with the fitness it essentially has to represent all

intellectual development.' But this fact completely overthrows our author's theory. If the *universality* of ideas is the result of an operation of our mind, how does it happen that the less educated a man is, the fitter is he for the operation? If to *universalise* ideas is to rise from the *particular* to the *universal*, why should those least practised in the use of their intellectual faculties be the quickest in measuring the distance? Is it easier to do much than to do little? Or how does it happen that in the first stage of human development, this is the only thing in which the intermediate steps are jumped over? It is impossible to account for all this in the systems of Locke and Condillac ; but the explanation will appear very easy when we shall have proved that the most universal of all ideas (the idea of *being*) is innate in man.

persons who may exist with features resembling those of our ancestor.

In like manner, from the instant that a perception is *representative*, it has a necessary relation with all that can fall under its representativeness ; and this is independent of the use we make of it and of the attention we give to the several individuals which it expresses and represents. We may, if we please, take it as representative of one individual only, or of two, or three ; but this does not in any way detract from its natural fitness to represent any number of other individuals of the same class, although we may not think of them all, which, indeed, we could not do, because that number would go on *ad infinitum*. Hence a representative conception being once formed in our mind, the task of applying it to individual cases is left to ourselves ; and this becomes as it were an art which we learn in proportion as we advance in the knowledge of the use to which that conception may be applied. But, be our proficiency in this art great or small, the nature of the conception as representative of an infinity of individuals remains ever the same, even though we do not advert to the fact. The case is parallel to that of the portrait we were just speaking of.

Therefore, when Condillac pretends that his statue, in order to transform the idea which it has already acquired of a particular orange into the exemplar of all oranges generally, must see, not one orange only, or many oranges in succession, but two or more oranges simultaneously, and refer them together to the particular idea ; [1] he does not, as he imagines, explain how the particular idea passes into being an exemplar (*i.e.* a universal), but he only shows how we begin to make use of it as an exemplar. It is already an exemplar, and our beginning to make use of it clearly supposes it such. By referring to it the several oranges simultaneously seen by us we do not alter its nature ; we take it as we find it in our mind, and we make use of it for our purpose.

On the other hand, the universal representativeness of that idea is not at all increased by our applying it to

[1] *Traité des Sensations*, Pt. IV. ch. vi.

many oranges; even as the universal representativeness of the portrait above alluded to would receive no additions from being applied to all persons resembling the ancestor who sat for it. In both cases the representative property always continues to be precisely as it was from the first, whether one makes use of it or not, and whether one expressly adverts to it or not.

Therefore, given that such ideas as Condillac allows to be *representative* have been formed in our mind, there is no possibility of their being other than universal. The hidden and secret way in which they are formed has entirely escaped his attention. Instead of watchfully observing how they came into his statue, he found them there; and having thus unconsciously jumped clear over the real hard point of the difficulty, having gratuitously assumed that main point as explained, he found the further course of his investigations quite smooth and easy.

94. It is, therefore, one thing to have an idea, and another to know the use to which it may be put. Our mind, which always advances gradually, does not certainly come to know all the uses of which ideas are susceptible except through many successive reflections and a searching analysis of them. It is thus only that ideas reveal themselves to us under new aspects, both in relation to one another and in relation to external things; and as a consequence of this we find out new uses for these ideas. This, however, does not mean that the ideas on which our mind performs these diverse operations are not in it entire from the first. If the mind were not fully in possession of them, how could it make them the subject of these operations, or discover the relations and uses of which we speak? But such is the constitution of the human mind, that the act by which it receives the ideas of things must precede the acts by which it acquires the knowledge of the uses to be made of them. Now, the principal use which the human mind makes of ideas is, as Condillac truly says, that they serve as the exemplars of things. Thus the idea of *orange* is the exemplar by which all oranges are judged to be oranges. Hence when, seeing before us many oranges to-

gether, we judge of them by using the same idea as their
common exemplar, we do not, as Condillac seems to think,
gain a new kind of idea—*i.e.* a universal idea. The idea was
already universal by its nature, and the simultaneous sight of
many oranges was only the occasion for our bringing that
universality into requisition.

ARTICLE XI.

Continuation.

95. So true is the above doctrine that Condillac himself,
his preoccupation to the contrary notwithstanding, gives
evident signs of having caught occasional glimpses of it : as,
for instance, where he treats of judgments.

According to him, a judgment is simply an operation
whereby we refer the object—*i.e.* the actual sensation of
which we judge—to its exemplar already existing in our
memory.

He distinguishes, as we have seen, two kinds of attention :
the one proper to the memory, the other proper to the senses ;
the one active, the other passive. The first consists in the
reminiscence of things which we have formerly seen ; the
second consists in the actual perception of an individual
thing by the senses. These two attentions are, he thinks,
sufficient to account for the act of judgment.

We compare that which actually impresses our senses with
that which has impressed them heretofore, and the image of
which is preserved in our memory ; and a judgment is the
result. Now to make this comparison is nothing but to refer
the thing now acting on our senses to the exemplar antecedently formed in our mind. Here are Condillac's own
words :—

' Si après avoir senti à plusieurs reprises une rose et un
œillet, elle sent encore une fois une rose, l'attention passive
qui se fait par l'odorat sera toute à l'odeur présente de rose,
et l'attention active, qui se fait par la mémoire, sera partagée
entre le souvenir qui reste des odeurs de rose et d'œillet. Or
les manières d'être ne peuvent se partager la capacité de

sentir, qu'elles ne se comparent : [1] car comparer n'est autre chose que donner en même temps son attention à deux idées. Dès qu'il y a comparaison il y a jugement. . . . Un jugement n'est donc que la perception d'un rapport entre deux idées, que l'on compare.' (*Traité des Sensations*, Pt. I. ch. ii. §§ 14, 15.)

When in order to judge of a given thing we compare it with another, the latter is taken as the exemplar of the former, and the sole aim of the comparison is to discover whether the thing to be judged of corresponds with that exemplar or not. Such, indeed, is the nature of all judgments. Now, Condillac tells us that, while the exemplar is the idea which we have in our memory, the thing to be judged of is that which actually falls under our senses.

96. But if this is the case, that idea must be universal in the very sense which Condillac attributes to this word ; for he has already said that the universality of an idea consists in its being the exemplar of a great many individuals.

I would therefore ask how it is that he treats of judgments long before introducing us to the subject of universal ideas? for he speaks of universal ideas in the fourth part of the ' Treatise on Sensations,' while he treats of judgments in the second.[2] If, as his theory would clearly imply, no judgment

---

[1] I have already demonstrated that to have two sensations contemporaneously, and to compare them together, are two different things (nn. 81, 85). Each of these sensations attracts to itself a portion of our attention, and seeks to take the attention altogether away from the other, in order to occupy us exclusively with itself. Our spirit, on the contrary, when making a judgment, follows an opposite tendency—*i.e.* it gives its attention to both objects contemporaneously, without consenting that either should absorb it exclusively, which, if it did, a judgment would be impossible. Hence we can see how very absurd it is to attribute to sensations the act of judgment—an act which is directly contrary to that sort of action which the sensations exercise on our soul. Sensation seeks to draw our attention wholly to itself ; the faculty of judgment seeks to distribute it, as it

were, equitably among the various things which it must compare together in order to form a judgment. On the other hand, the expression ' *the sensations judge*' has in it something so inexact that it seems incredible that a philosopher should ever have used it. If the sensations judge, or if the senses judge, or if judgment is sensation, it follows that one sensation feels another sensation (for there is no judgment without a comparison) ; or that the act by which we feel one sensation is the same as that by which we feel another ; or that the apprehension of the relation between two ideas (which apprehension leads to the judgment) is the judgment itself. I need not say how absurd all these things are.

[2] It is true that he touches upon universal ideas in the First Part also, on occasion of explaining how his statue, supposed to be possessed of the olfac-

can be formed without our possessing universal ideas, it is impossible to explain the nature of judgments before having explained that of universal ideas.

Why, then, did he treat of universal ideas after speaking of judgments, except because he saw that, in his system, universal ideas could only be formed through judgments? Here are again his words : ‘ L'idée particulière d'un cheval et celle d'un oiseau deviendront également générales, lorsque les circonstances feront comparer plusieurs chevaux et plusieurs oiseaux ; et ainsi de tous les objets sensibles.’ (*Traité des Sensations*, Pt. IV. ch. vi. § 4.)

Now, let it be remembered that in the system of Condillac there is no comparison without a judgment. If, then, to transform a particular into a universal idea a comparison is necessary, evidently a judgment is necessary.

But, on the other hand, all judgments require some antecedent idea for their formation.

Thus, according to our author, judgments presuppose universal ideas (or simply *ideas*, because all ideas have a universal element in them) ; and, contrariwise, universal ideas presuppose judgments. His theory, therefore, does not solve the difficulty ; indeed, it ignores it altogether. He speaks of ideas, of judgments, and of universal ideas in three separate places, as if they were subjects independent of one another and had not that intimate connection which renders it impossible to speak of one without being well acquainted with the others. And then, after having explained universal ideas at his leisure, he ends by congratulating himself on the ease with which he has succeeded in accomplishing his task : ‘ On voit par là combien il est facile de se faire des idées générales.’ (*Traité des Sensations*, Pt. IV. ch. vi. § 6.)

tory sense alone, begins to form abstract ideas ; but he does this only in the fourth chapter, whereas he had already spoken of judgments in the second.

ARTICLE XII.

Conclusion on the intrinsic defect of the system of Condillac.

97. In addressing myself thus far to Condillac, I have made use of what is known as the *argumentum ad hominem*. Lest, however, I should present him in a worse light than he deserves, I feel bound in justice to add here a few explanatory words on what I alleged against him in the last article. Indeed, I myself have already said something which may fairly be quoted in extenuation of his error ; and I will state how.

Condillac, when giving his account of the formation of universal ideas, distinguishes ideas into two classes—the *particular* and the *general* (*i.e. universal*), and says that the particular are transformed into general through our using them as exemplars in that comparison through which we judge of individual things.

Now, I have shown, and this by Condillac's own definitions, that the comparison in question has nothing whatever to do with making our ideas universal, but that universality is intrinsic to their very nature. For Condillac says that an idea is 'a sensation representative of something,' as is the case with those sensations which are preserved in our memory ; and he says also that general ideas are those which serve us as exemplars. Now, to be representative and to be an exemplar is precisely the same. Therefore, according to Condillac himself, the character of universality is intrinsic to the nature of an idea.

The construction which we may equitably put on this seems to be that our author's error on the formation of universal ideas consists, more than in anything else, in a wrong application of the words 'how universal ideas are formed ;' instead of which he should have said, ' how we recognise and make use of the universality inherent in all ideas.'

If, then, the followers of Condillac were to own to this inaccuracy of expression, I should no longer have the right of insisting on the objection I was urging against them, and which was to this effect: 'You cannot form universal ideas without making a judgment, and you cannot make a judgment without having universal ideas: this is a vicious circle, from which your system affords us no possible means of escape.' They could answer me: 'We admit that it is inaccurate to say that our ideas are universal only from the moment of their being recognised and used as exemplars: they are universal from the very first, and the judgments which we make by means of them do not create their universality, but simply cause us to recognise its presence Being, therefore, independent of these judgments, the universal ideas do not require to be preceded by them.'

98. But if the followers of Condillac may, by correcting the above inaccuracy of language, evade the cogency of my last argument, which is wholly relative to the man whom I was addressing, and based on that inaccuracy, the difficulty which I have pointed out as being contained in the inmost nature of their system still remains entire and unanswered ; since it is impossible, on the one hand, to form an idea without a judgment intervening in the operation, and, on the other, to form a judgment without some idea pre-existing in our mind ; and this leaves the question in as great a perplexity as ever, or rather proves to evidence either that the system of Condillac is false, or else that the formation of ideas as well as judgments is inexplicable.[1]

---

[1] Those who wish to be still more convinced of this have only to read in full the passage of which only a few lines were quoted above : 'Si je me rappelle une douleur que j'aie eue, le souvenir et l'idée sont alors une même chose ; et si je dis que je me fais l'idée d'une douleur dont on me parle, et que je n'ai jamais ressentie, c'est que j'en juge d'après une douleur que j'ai éprou- vée, ou d'après une douleur que je souffre actuellement. Dans le premier cas, l'idée et le souvenir ne diffèrent encore point. Dans le second, l'idée est le sentiment d'une douleur actuelle modifié par les jugements que je porte, pour me représenter la douleur d'un autre.'—*Extrait raisonné du Traité des Sensations*, p. 31 ; Paris, 1821.

CHAPTER III.

REID.

ARTICLE I.

Origin of the Scottish School.

99. I have deemed it advisable to dwell somewhat at length on the system of Condillac, because this system still enjoys some favour in Italy. Not that it can be said to be the most conformable to the way of thinking of this nation, which, on the whole, has kept itself more free from the systematic and exaggerated spirit of modern times than has been the case with other nations.[1]

100. The system of Condillac is, in reality, nothing but that of Locke transplanted into French soil. The slight modifications which the latter system may have undergone in France since the time of Condillac—those additions of heterogeneous matter which only confuse and disguise the inquiries on the operations of the soul : such as things pertaining to medicine,

---

[1] In Southern Italy there is still (A.D. 1829) some leaning towards the systems of Des Cartes and of Malebranche, especially in the Roman States. This, I think, is to be attributed to the writings of Cardinal Gerdil and of other philosophers who have modified and improved those systems. The kingdom of Naples can still boast of intellectual celebrities not unworthy to be associated with the name of Vico—such as Galluppi on this side of the Sicilian Straits, and Miceli on the other. The more prevailing tendency of the Italian mind seems, however, to be in favour of a kind of eclecticism. In the Lombardo-Venetian provinces Padre Soave, doubtless with the best intentions, has done a great deal of harm by diffusing everywhere the doctrines of Condillac, and reducing philosophy to a pitiable meagreness which, while enticing the vulgar by its apparent facility, generates presumption. People who were never made for philosophy are thus deluded into believing themselves to be good adepts in this science, and, as a consequence, looking contemptuously on the great questions which are far above their own loquacious and sententious mediocrity. Nevertheless, even in this part of Italy, powerful thinkers have not been wanting, who, as if in manly protest against the common lassitude, have fearlessly grappled with the highest philosophical problems. Suffice it to mention one for all—the Barnabite Father, Ermenegildo Pini, author of *La Protologia.*

anatomy, and chemistry—need not be noticed here, since they do not offer any new explanation of the origin of ideas.

101. In England the philosophy of Locke was dealt with by much more acute minds than in France: I mean, by such thinkers as Berkeley and Hume, who with dauntless courage pushed it to its last consequences—namely, to Idealism and to Scepticism ; took away the foundations of all the sciences, and, in effect, asked that human nature should consent to doubt its own existence.

102. Consequences so startling, and the dismal project of an abyss where, first the material, and then the spiritual world, together with man himself, would be swallowed up and anni-hilated, could not fail to arouse a strong intellectual reaction. Earnest men began, therefore, to ask themselves whether the great facility with which the sensation-system had been accepted, and the popular favour so freely lavished on it, might not, after all, have been due to inconsiderate haste in assuming its principles as self-evident, when in reality they were pregnant with grave error. Accordingly, a searching scrutiny was instituted into all its premises, and clear posi-tive proof demanded for each of those which, without being necessarily self-evident, seemed nevertheless true at first sight, that it might thus be discovered where lay the fatal error—if such there were—that inevitably issued in such terrible conclusions. In short, it was human nature which entered its protest against the dominant philosophy, and which, seeing itself brought by a false guide to the very brink of the abyss, shrank back with horror, for no other reason than that it could not possibly proceed further.

When, therefore, the irresistible force of nature, combined with the promptings of common sense, had made men feel that that philosophy could not be true, because irreconcilable with human nature,[1] then there arose in Scotland a new school, which, taking the *common sense of mankind* for its

[1] It was natural that the need of a philosophical reform should be felt in Scotland more than elsewhere ; be-cause, as Dugald Stewart assures us, the idealism of Berkeley and of Hume had made its way into all the schools of that country.—*Dissertation exhibit-ing the Progress of Metaphysical, Ethi-cal, and Political Philosophy*, part iii.

guide, proposed never to deviate from it, and not to make use of the individual reason except for explaining its pronouncements.

103. These new philosophers saw the impossibility of attacking the conclusions which Berkeley and Hume had drawn from the principles of Locke, those conclusions being deduced with a force of logic which admitted of no reply. Nothing remained but to re-examine the principles themselves, in order to find the real source of the latent error. Having to deal with subtle adversaries, and being obliged to proceed with strict logical accuracy in their reasonings, it is no wonder that the Scottish philosophical reformers made so little account of the teachings, although then still popular, of Condillac.

If I am not mistaken, Reid never quotes this author. Dugald Stewart speaks of him generally with contempt, calling him a mere commentator of Locke, and one who has not so much as understood his master.[1] Of his philosophical style he writes as follows: 'The clearness and simplicity of Condillac's style add to the force of this illusion, and flatter the reader with an agreeable idea of the powers of his own understanding when he finds himself so easily conducted through the darkest labyrinths of metaphysical science. It is to this cause I would chiefly ascribe the great popularity of his works. They may be read with as little exertion of

[1] Dugald Stewart shows great partiality for Locke, and speaks of him with that sympathy which is inspired by the feeling of a common nationality. Nevertheless, he admits in many places that the system of Locke is deficient and chargeable with many errors. He says that he 'considers it a loss of time to argue with those who adhere to passages of this author as to an infallible guide in metaphysics.' What is still more remarkable, knowing as we do the favourable opinion which this author so often expresses of Locke, and, on the other hand, his contempt for Condillac, is, that he in one place explicitly allows that 'the difference between the theory of Locke and that which derives all our ideas from sensa- tion' (*i.e.* the theory of Condillac) 'is rather apparent than real' (*Elements of the Philosophy of the Human Mind,* vol. i. part ii. chap. i. sec. 4). It was for this last reason principally that— thinking it would be well to speak at some length on Condillac, because of his more immediate influence on ourselves here in Italy—I said less on Locke than I would otherwise have done; for I wished to avoid useless repetitions. Besides, whatever there might remain for me to say on that which relates to my purpose in the theory of Locke, will be supplied in the course of the remarks I shall make on Reid, who confutes some fundamental propositions of Locke, as well as of Berkeley and of Hume.

thought as a history or a novel ; and it is only when we shut the book, and attempt to express in our own words the substance of what we have gained, that we have the mortification to see our supposed acquisitions vanish into air.'[1]

ARTICLE II.

System of Reid on the distinction of the human faculties.

104. The difficulty to be overcome in explaining the origin of ideas did not present itself to Dr. Reid in that generality in which I have endeavoured to propose it. He never had occasion to consider it under so wide an aspect, and this is perhaps the reason why we have not on this subject as much as we might have expected from a philosopher of so solid a mind.

Nevertheless, he saw it partially, and did his best to solve it in the part which he saw ; for it is impossible to answer, as Reid professes to do, the arguments of the Idealists and Sceptics, without entering into that difficulty at least to some extent.

105. To see in what form the difficulty was viewed by him, we must know what were the opinions he undertook to impugn.

As I have before observed, Condillac, misled by the double meaning attributed by him to the word *sensation,* maintained that between the object of sense[2] and the object of memory there is no essential difference, the first being a present sensation, and the second a sensation also, but past. He thus believed that these two faculties could be reduced to one ; and not only these, but likewise all the other faculties of the human soul ; for, according to him, the objects of

---

[1] *Dissertation exhibiting the Progress,* &c , part ii. (Sec. vi. Collected Works, Edinburgh, 1854, vol. i. p. 360.)

[2] The expression *objects of sense* is an inaccuracy which has given rise to many errors. It must be obvious to everyone that a large class at least of our sensations namely, all those which consist in mere pleasure or pain --have no *object*; they are simple; they are (if I may say so) a self-object. They have, indeed, a cause outside of them, but not an *object*. Nevertheless, until the proper time arrives for me to clear up this matter, I am obliged, in order to make myself understood, to ad pt sometimes the common phraseology, especially when commenting upon systems whose authors have freely made use of such phraseology.

them all do not differ essentially, being, as he expresses it, nothing but *sensation transformed.*

Locke had known that the object of the memory was not the same as that of sense; and he had therefore made a specific distinction between these two faculties. For instance, when we remember a rose which we smelt yesterday, the object of our memory is not the actual smelling of the rose, but an idea, an exemplar, a phantasm, something, in short, which that sensation had left behind it in our soul.

Berkeley and Hume, who perfected the erroneous system of Locke in England, as Condillac had done in France, strove likewise to bring the objects of sense and memory to one only; and this by supposing that those objects differed merely in the degree of their vividness.

106. Singular as it may appear, Dr. Reid, while directing his fine talents to combat the idealism and scepticism of these two philosophers, thought it necessary to abolish the distinction which Locke had made between the objects of sense and ideas.[1] He writes: ‘In the mean time I beg leave to think with the vulgar that when I remember the

---

[1] In his *Inquiry into the Human Mind on the Principles of Common Sense*, chap. ii. sec. 3 and 5, Dr. Reid seems to attribute indiscriminately to Locke, Berkeley, and Hume, two opinions that are contradictory—namely, first, that the immediate object of memory is only an idea, an image, an exemplar of, and therefore something specifically different from, the actual sensation, and this specific distinction between the objects of sense and of memory would point to a corresponding distinction between those two faculties. Second, that the sensation and the object of memory differ only in the degree of force and vividness with which our soul perceives; in which case there would be nothing to forbid the objects of these two faculties, and therefore the faculties themselves, from being specifically one and the same. It may be, and in fact is, the case, that these authors are not consistent in their expressions, and that while saying in one place that sensation does not differ from the object of memory except in the degree of force with which the

soul perceives, in other places they speak as if they considered the object of memory not to be a sensation at all, but only an idea of a sensation. Hume does certainly lay himself open to this charge. For example, in his *Essay on the Origin of Ideas*, he tells us sometimes that an idea is only a sensation in an attenuated form, and at other times he describes it as a perception whereby the soul reflects on its sensations. But surely to *reflect* on a sensation is not simply to have a faint sort of sensation. In no sensation is there such a high kind of activity displayed as in this reflection.

Nevertheless, I have thought it fair to attribute the first of these two conflicting opinions to Locke, and the second to Berkeley and Hume, because such is the sense which appears to predominate in the writings of these authors, and to be directly intended by them; whereas when they express themselves in an opposite sense, they seem to do so almost against their will, and from not having better modes of expression at hand.

smell of the tuberose, that very sensation which I had
yesterday, and which has now no more any existence, is the
immediate object of my memory; and when I imagine it
present, the sensation itself, and not any idea of it, is the
object of my imagination.' (*Inquiry into the Human Mind*,
&c., chap. ii. sec. 3.)

107. The mind, then, can actually think of a thing which
is in no way present to it—*i.e.* neither through an idea,
because Dr. Reid repudiates all ideas, exemplars, or signs
whatever of the same; nor through the thing itself, because
its presence is excluded by the hypothesis! How this can
be, I am wholly at a loss to comprehend. Neither do I
believe that on this point the vulgar are at one with Dr. Reid.
It seems to me, on the contrary, that when an illiterate man
remembers a thing which he has seen or felt, he believes, not,
indeed, that he has before him the actual thing itself, but that
he recognises it as that thing, because he has the idea of it,
and the trace left in his soul.[1]

---

[1] Dr. Reid would fain eliminate
ideas from philosophy, because he
finds them somewhat embarrassing.
In that case it would be necessary to
erase the word *idea* from all vocabu-
laries, to expel it from every language,
and to forbid mankind at large to pronounce it, to think of it. In fact, this
is a word used by the vulgar not less
than by philosophers, in scientific not
less than in social discourses. Now,
what does Dr. Reid propose to himself?
The title-page of his work, from which
I have quoted, assures me that his
object is no other than to defend the
principles of common sense against
that philosophy which leads to their
destruction. Would he, then, be one of
those who stand up as the apologists of
those principles, so, however, as to begin by opposing them? To declare that
one's philosophy is in unison with the
general sense of mankind may be a
true statement, so long as nothing is
meant by it save the intimation of an
intention; but it is, to say the least, a
daring assumption if it be further meant
as an assurance that one's philosophy is
really in accordance with that sense.
No amount of assertion can make a
philosopher to be any other than he is
—a poor fallible being, a mere individual unit. A philosopher may tell
you seriously, 'Mine is the philosophy of the common sense of mankind.'
Nothing of the sort; it is only your
philosophy. Another will cry out,
'All who do not follow my system are
the victims of prejudice; all must follow reason alone, even as I do.' Vain
and rash words! Man will, at best,
follow what he believes to be conformable to reason; but he cannot set himself up in the place of reason; he is
not reason in person. Even if the
entire human race (I mean taken
abstractedly from revealed truth) were
to proclaim with one voice, 'This is
the truth,' one would always have the
right of refusing assent to that declaration, emphatic as it is, and could
frankly reply, 'Corrupt humanity!
Thy very first utterance is a falsehood.
Thou art not infallible. Say, "This
is my opinion," but presume not to say,
"What I think is absolutely the truth."
Deity alone can speak thus.' But man,
both individually and collectively,
always aspires to exaggerate his own
importance. Thus the political de-

108. Nevertheless, although Dr. Reid reduces all the cbjects of the human faculties to one only, he does not do

signer will address a gullible audience in the name of the nation; every journalist will assure you that he is simply the interpreter of public opinion; and every demagogue is only the mouth-piece of the people standing up for their rights, unjustly invaded by in-human oppressors. How long will these miserable pretensions continue? How long will credulity allow itself to be victimised? Or when will the world cease to go in leading-strings?

I make these remarks all the more willingly now that I have occasion to speak of the philosophy of Dr. Reid, because as he is one of the most modest and circumspect writers of our times, what I say acquires increased force, and shows how easy it is for a philosopher to promise more than he can accomplish, and how common this defect is among those who in their philosophical *dicta* rely on human reason alone. Let us be just; the Fathers and a multitude of writers of the Catholic Church are the only ones whose sin-cere, profound, and unvarying modesty is of that kind which man requires in order to arrive at the truth.

Nevertheless the question of the existence of ideas, as raised by Dr. Reid, is of the highest importance, as well as of the greatest difficulty; and the mere fact of having brought it into prominence is an incalculable merit of this great man.

It had, however, been already seen by the Schoolmen of old. They clearly perceived that when we think of a real thing, the object of our thought is not a mere idea, but the real thing itself. But how could this be, seeing that the thing was outside of us? They answered that the thing, although not present through itself, became present through its idea (or image). I confess that this explanation, if taken in its most obvious sense, cannot be con-sidered satisfactory. For one may always rejoin, ' By saying that the idea is only the means by which we think of the thing external to us, you admit that the object of our thought is, ultimately, something outside of our-selves; and, by consequence, that there is nothing absurd or impossible in our

mind going outside itself to lay hold of objects at a distance from it. But if so, what need have we of the idea? The reason for introducing the idea lay simply in the supposed necessity of keeping our mind, so to speak, within itself. But now it turns out that the idea is only the means for enabling the mind to do the very opposite of this. The question was, not as to what means the mind requires in order to get at external things, but purely as to whether it is possible for the mind to get at them. If this is possible, we can dispense with the idea. It is enough that on occasion of the sensations we turn our mind straight to the external objects, and thus gain the perception of them.' Such is the rejoinder which might be made to the scholastic or Aristotelian solution when taken in its *prima facie* aspect.

In my opinion, however, that solu-tion admits of a more satisfactory in-terpretation which I shall submit later on, when I shall have cleared up certain points which are necessary for properly understanding it.

I shall also, in due course, offer that solution of the difficulty raised by Dr. Reid concerning ideas which it seems to me to admit. I shall show that this difficulty arises in part from want of clearness in the language used by philosophers, or at all events from a wrong way of understanding certain philosophical expressions. For ex-ample, when I say that the idea ex-presses the thing—is, as it were, an image, a likeness, an exemplar, a sign or indication of it— the words must be understood with great circumspection, else very serious misconceptions may be the result. Let us see this briefly.

If the reader remembers the propo-sition which I have proved above, viz. that 'for an idea to be representa-tive is the same as for it to be common or universal '.—he will understand in what sense I say that an idea is some-thing representative. We will consider this proposition from both its sides.

(1) *That which is representative is common or universal.* Why so? Be-cause that which is representative of one thing is equally representative of

the same with the faculties themselves ; and herein his system differs altogether from that of Condillac. Let us hear how he continues after the words we have quoted above : 'But though the object of my sensation, memory, and imagination, be in this case the same, yet these acts or operations of the mind are as different and as easily distinguishable as smell, taste, and sound. I am conscious of a difference in kind between sensation and memory, and between both and

all things that are like to that one ; according to the axiom that 'any two things similar to a third are similar to each other.' There can be but one exception to this rule—namely, when the thing represented is the only one possible of its kind.

(2) *That which is common or universal is representative.* Indeed, one thing is representative of another only in so far as it has some quality in common therewith. Thus a portrait is representative of all the persons who resemble it, not in so far as it is an individual painting, for, considered thus, it is nothing more than a piece of canvas, with a mixture of oil and colours laid on it in a certain way. In these things, which make up its own proper, individual and real entity, it can have no relation with any other thing, since all *relations* are excluded by the hypothesis, and therefore it represents nothing.

The only reason, then, why the portrait is representative of persons is because it possesses something in common with them – that is to say, because the sight of it produces in us an impression similar to that which we receive by looking at those persons. The similarity, therefore, between the portrait and the persons is discovered by ourselves through comparing together the two impressions. In virtue of this comparison we find that certain qualities—the fair complexion, the lineaments of the countenance, the curve of the lips, the expression of the eyes, &c.—exist in the portrait as well as in the person, and make the two similar to each other. Such qualities we term *common qualities.* In itself, therefore, a *common quality* is but one thing, but the one thing is seen by us as existing in two or more subjects, determined by the qualities proper to

each and individuated by the real existence of each, and it is seen by us through different acts of our intelligent spirit. It is also called *species—i.e.* 'the medium through which we intellectually see many things on occasion of these things striking individually our senses. To recognise, therefore, that many things are similar to one another is the same as to see them *through one sole species.* This species shows them in that part in which they are similar. It also shows us, through the particular and proper impression which each of them produces in us, that part which consists in their own individual existence, and in which, therefore, they have not any relation of similarity. I say '*in which they have not any relation of similarity,*' because each thing, in so far as individually existing, is wholly and exclusively limited to its own proper self. If, then, we see them to be similar, or (what comes to the same) see them by means of one sole species, we must perforce say that what enables us thus to see them is not that which exists in their own proper and individual selves, but it is the *species* which is in our mind ; and this species is precisely what goes under the name of *idea* ; and it is representative in this sense, that it is a quality exemplified in many subjects.

I cannot here enter more fully into this matter, which belongs to the treatise on the *nature of ideas* rather than to that on their *origin.* It was my duty, however, to demonstrate the existence of ideas, so strongly impugned by the Scottish philosopher ; for, to explain the origin of ideas, it is necessary, in the first place, to demonstrate that they exist, lest we build a theory in the air, as I am sorry to say is often the case with merely human systems.

imagination.'[1] And elsewhere he says :—' If a man should maintain that a circle, a square, and a triangle, differ only in magnitude and not in figure, I believe he would find nobody disposed either to believe him or to argue against him ; and yet I do not think it less shocking to common sense to maintain that sensation, memory, and imagination, differ only in degree and not in kind.'[2]

ARTICLE III.

The difficulty as seen by Dr. Reid.

109. But to come to our difficulty, we must see what Dr. Reid understands by the three words, *sensation, memory,* and *imagination.* He says :—

' A sensation—a smell, for instance—may be presented to the mind in three different ways.[3] It may be smelled ; it may be remembered ; it may be imagined or thought of.[4] In the first case it is necessarily accompanied with a belief of its present existence ; in the second, it is necessarily accompanied with a belief of its past existence ; and in the last, it is not accompanied with belief at all, but is what the logicians call *a simple apprehension.*'[5]

110. It being immaterial to the correctness of a reasoning in what sense words are used, provided that one takes care to define them beforehand, and then never to use them in any other meaning, I shall not stop to examine whether the sense given by Dr. Reid to the three words *sensation, memory, imagination,* be the same as is attributed to them

[1] *An Inquiry,* &c. chap. ii. sec. 3.

[2] *Ibid.* sec. 5.

[3] I beg to note how nearly akin this manner of speaking seems to Condillac's theory of *transformed sensation.* Nevertheless, Reid admits, as we have said, an intrinsic distinction between the above faculties. In any case, the exception which I took to the phrase *transformed sensation*—namely, that it has the serious defect of involving in a metaphor the principal idea, and thereby confusing and misleading the minds of the readers—is applicable here also.

[4] Here Dr. Reid confounds two things which are widely different. The *image* or phantasm belongs to our soul in so far as animal, whereas the *idea* belongs to it in so far as intelligent. The latter is the *simple apprehension* of the Schoolmen. Nevertheless, the image constitutes the positive and material part of our perceptions of corporeal things, as I shall show more clearly in another place.

[5] *An Inquiry,* &c. chap. ii. sec. 3.

in common discourse. Instead of doing this, I shall ask the reader to note well the concepts which Dr. Reid wishes respectively to convey by those terms

First of all, I would call attention to the difference he makes between the first two and the third. By the first two (*sensation* and *memory*) he wants us to understand, not the bare perception of a being, but a perception united with the persuasion of the real existence of that being ; with this sole distinction, that, in the case of the sensation, we are persuaded that the being really exists now, and in the case of the memory, the being really existed heretofore. On the contrary, by *imagination* he means the faculty of perceiving the being, but without any persuasion of its existence, either present or past, accompanying the perception ; which kind of perception the Schoolmen designated—and, I think, with greater propriety—by the name of *simple apprehension.*

111. The question now arises as to whether *the simple apprehension of a being*, or the act of imagination taken in the sense of Dr. Reid, precedes in our soul the sensation and the memory, as Locke and Hume appear to maintain, or whether it is preceded by them, as Dr. Reid contends.

Now, it is precisely by following up the controversy between these philosophical antagonists, that we see the difficulty which I proposed at the beginning, brought out to full view. That difficulty is, in substance, ever the same; but it assumes a great variety of forms according to the aspects in which it has happened to fall in the way of philosophical inquirers. Let us see, then, whether either party has succeeded in untying the knot, or in showing us the way out of the labyrinth.

112. The system of the adversaries of Dr. Reid, or, as he calls it, the *ideal system*, is described by him as follows : ' The ideal system teaches us that the first operation of the mind about its ideas is simple apprehension : that is, the bare conception of a thing, without any belief about it ; and that after we have got simple apprehensions, by comparing them together, we perceive agreements or disagreements between them ; and that this perception of the agreement or disagree-

ment of ideas is all that we call belief, judgment, or knowledge.'[1]

Such is what we may call the last expression of the
system of Locke and of his followers both in England and
France.

In analysing the system of Condillac I pointed out how
its whole essence consists in this, that it places the formation
of ideas first, and then, through a comparison between these
ideas, the formation of judgments. But here at once the
difficulty of which I speak showed itself, and in such a way
that, according to that system, it could not possibly be
solved. For Condillac himself supplied me with arguments
which necessarily led to the conclusion that no idea could be
formed except through a judgment ; and that therefore the
question of ideas could not be treated separately from that of
judgments.

But as on the other hand no judgment can be formed
except through some idea, there remained to explain how a
judgment was possible antecedently to all ideas, in Locke's
and Condillac's hypothesis that all ideas are acquired (nn.
86–98).

Now, this was the difficulty seen and noted by Dr. Reid,
though in a more partial form : on which account he could,
indeed, confute the systems of his adversaries, but not, as it
seems to me, propose a system capable of affording a satisfactory solution of the difficulty itself.

ARTICLE IV.

*The difficulty found by Dr. Reid in the system of Locke had in some
way been perceived by Locke himself.*

113. If writers would only listen attentively to the voice
of their own conscience, they would probably avoid much of
the adverse criticism which is heaped on them by the public.
For it seldom happens that anything deservedly reprehensible
is found by the public in their productions, of which the
authors themselves had not beforehand some secret fear, some

---

[1] *An Inquiry into the Human Mind*, &c., chap. ii. sec. 4.

suspicion, but which they unfortunately had not the courage to look straight in the face and thoroughly sift to the bottom.

114. I should think that some such feeling as this must have been experienced by Locke as regards the opposition which his system would be likely to encounter, and of which Dr. Reid became afterwards the exponent. I have already noticed the uncertain tone of Locke in speaking of the idea of substance. A similar embarrassment may be observed in him where, in defining *knowledge*, he refuses this name to whatever in our mind is not accompanied by a judgment.[1] This, in reality, is the same as to say, that without making a judgment it would be impossible for us to know anything.

I have no desire to dispute about words ; but I believe I may safely say, that either Locke is not consistent, or else he attributes to the word *idea* a sense different from that in which it is generally used. For the generality of men, *to have the idea of a thing* and *to have knowledge of a thing*, are equivalent expressions. Nor could anyone understand how it would be possible to have the *idea* of a thing without having some *knowledge* of that thing. If, then, it is a contradiction to say, in the ordinary sense of the words, ' I have an idea of a thing, but I have no knowledge of it whatever,' it must be conceded that, according to the common belief of men, the idea of a thing always includes a knowledge of some sort. From which it seems legitimate to infer, that since Locke perceived that every cognition necessarily supposes a judgment, he had also some suspicion that the same must be said of ideas. But as, on the other hand, he was unable to explain to himself how our first ideas are formed—since before them there could be no judgment, because every judgment supposes some antecedent idea—so, to escape from the troublesome dilemma, and to supply the need he had of

---

[1] Book II., chap. 2. Professor Laromiguière, in his *Leçons de Philosophie*, P. II. Leç. i., enumerating the different synonyms that have been used for the word *idea*, mentions also the word *cognition*, which, he observes, is a barbarism in the French language. In point of fact, the sense which this philosopher attributes to the word *idea* exactly corresponds with what Locke calls *knowledge*, as may be seen by comparing the two authors in the passages quoted above.

making it appear that some ideas could be acquired independently of any judgment, he betook himself to the imaginary distinction between *knowledge* and *idea*, and to the absurd supposition that there are ideas wholly devoid of knowledge.

It seems to me, therefore, that it was the love of system which led him to adopt an expedient as repugnant to the general belief of men as it was a deviation from the practical good sense, free from frivolities, which he usually exhibits. Such was the consequence of his pledging himself to the principle, that ' There is nothing innate in the human mind, but all knowledge is acquired through sensation and reflection.'

ARTICLE V.

Objection urged by Reid against Locke.

115. Reid, then, perceived that the system of Locke was defective, and although he did not clearly see in what the defect consisted, he was nevertheless in a position to urge some weighty objections against it.

He presented the whole problem of the origin of ideas in the following form : ' Does the simple apprehension of things precede the judgment which affirms their existence, as Locke and his followers maintain, or, is the simple apprehension preceded by this judgment ? '

Of these two alternatives, he declared for the second.

' It is acknowledged by all,' he says, ' that sensation must go before memory and imagination;' and hence it necessarily

---

' Let the reader again take note of the meaning here attached by Dr. Reid to the word *imagination*. He understands by it the faculty of *simple apprehension*—in other words, the faculty by which, in contradistinction to what he says of sensation and memory, we conceive a thing in the state of pure *possibility*, quite abstractedly from the question of its real existence. The impropriety of this manner of speaking has already been po nted out. It gave Dugald Stewart the occasion to enter upon a long discussion on the question as to whether it can be said that the *imagination* is not accompanied by the persuasion of the things imagined (see the third chapter of his *Elements of Philosophy*). So true is it that the want of precision in the use of words gives rise to many useless questions. Mr. Dugald Stewart rightly observes, that if the imagination of a thing is very vivid, we conceive the thing as present, although we are speculatively convinced that it has no real existence. Now, it is precisely on this speculative knowledge of the non-existence of the thing that we should fix our attention ; for this is the very knowledge of which

follows that apprehension, accompanied with belief and knowledge, must go before simple apprehension, at least in the matter we are speaking of. So that here, instead of saying that the belief or knowledge is got by putting together and comparing the simple apprehensions, we ought rather to say that the simple apprehension is performed by resolving and analysing a NATURAL AND ORIGINAL JUDGMENT.' [1]

ARTICLE VI.

Reid places judgment before ideas.

116. Certainly in the words just quoted there is a flash of light.

Dr. Reid sees quite clearly that the supposition of his adversaries, that man acquires in the first place the *simple apprehension* of things, and then, through comparisons and judgments, the *persuasion* of their real existence, is inadmissible.

His adversaries, on the other hand, saw not less clearly that it is impossible for a man to be intimately persuaded that a certain thing exists, without affirming its existence by a judgment. But they saw, at the same time, that no man can make a judgment if he is supposed to be wholly devoid of ideas. They imagined, therefore, that the persuasion of the existence of the things perceived was not contemporaneous with the perception itself, but followed afterwards, when man, having already perceived the things, is in possession of their ideas, and can compare these together, and through this comparison make the judgment affirmatory of the real existence of the things, and thus have the persuasion in question.

we are here speaking. By it we contemplate, coolly as it were, the thing in itself, for the sole purpose of examining its nature, and without at all caring to know whether it really exists or not. It is what I have termed the *simple apprehension* of a thing, to the faculty of forming which the name of *imagination* is improperly given. To speak accurately, it could not even be said that by it the thing is known not to exist. We think neither of its existence nor of its non-existence. We consider it simply *in se*, in a state of pure possibility, or as involving no contradiction. The faculty which forms this *simple apprehension* is, properly speaking, called the *Intellect.*

[1] *An Inquiry*, &c., chap. ii. sec. 4.

But to Dr. Reid this 'appears to be all fiction,' prompted by the love of system, and 'without any foundation in nature.'

In his opinion, an unprejudiced observation of the fact as it really takes place, will show that we perceive external things by means of our senses, and that thereupon we instantly make 'A NATURAL AND ORIGINAL JUDGMENT' which persuades us of the real existence of those things. The perception having thus been formed, we, by an act of abstraction, separate the things from their real existence, present as well as past, and contemplate them purely in that manner which is called *simple apprehension*, or the concept of a thing divested of the persuasion and thought of its real existence.

ARTICLE VII.

Dr. Reid maintains, against Locke, that the first operation of the human mind is, not analytic, but synthetic.

117. Dr. Reid considers that the above is the only satisfactory account of the formation of our first cognitions ; and hence he maintains that the operations of our mind begin by synthesis, and not by analysis. Accordingly he proceeds as follows :—

'It is with the operations of the mind, in this case, as with natural bodies, which are indeed compounded of simple principles or elements. Nature does not exhibit these elements separate, to be compounded by us ; she exhibits them mixed and compounded in concrete bodies, and it is only by art and chemical analysis that they can be separated.' [1]

ARTICLE VIII.

The system proposed by Dr. Reid cannot be considered satisfactory.

118. It must be admitted that the adversaries of Dr. Reid can have nothing to say against his description of the facts. Most undoubtedly, the simple apprehension of an

[1] *An Inquiry*, &c. chap. ii. sec. 4.

object,[1] or the concept of it divested of the persuasion of its existence, cannot be had by us until we have perceived that object as existent, and then by an intellectual operation divided it from the persuasion of its existence, and considered it only in that abstract state.

119. But if Dr. Reid's appeal to the fact as presented to observation is decisive against his adversaries, they may in their turn take the offensive, and show him that the system which he would substitute for theirs is not by any means free from objection.

Their rejoinder might be expressed in some such form as the following :—

'We will for the sake of argument suppose that the intimate persuasion of the existence of the things perceived by man is, as you have said, antecedent to the simple apprehension of them, and that this apprehension is the result of an abstraction which man exercises on the judgment whereby he has affirmed their existence. Yet we fail to see in this a proof that you have gone up to the first and highest of the facts of the human spirit in connection with the origin of ideas. You suppose that the first product of the action of the human spirit is composite; for such is that persuasion which you place before simple apprehension. In short, you make the development of man's intellectual life start, not from ideas, but from judgments. Now this is precisely what we cannot understand. To say that the composite goes before the simple, judgment before ideas, seems to us a contradiction in terms. We will explain ourselves more fully.

'If, as you assert, the first operation of the human spirit is a judgment, you must concede that it contains all the essentials of a judgment, and, therefore, that it is, not a simple, but a composite operation—*i.e.* resulting from several elements.

'It is true that you qualify this judgment by the epithets of *natural* and *original*; which is tantamount to saying that man makes it by necessity, by an intrinsic force or, as you express it, a certain "*inspiration*" (*Essay* ii. chap. 6). But this does not

---

[1] What is said here relates particularly to corporeal beings, which are the first realities different from ourselves, which we externally perceive.

make it any the less a veritable judgment, and you yourself
call it so. Indeed, how can a man be persuaded of the
existence of a being until he has said within himself, "This
being exists"? and what is this interior pronouncement
but a judgment by which existence is attributed to the
being?

'We beg to repeat it; it is quite immaterial whether this
judgment which is immediately conjoined with the sensations
be made from an internal and natural movement which man
cannot resist, or whether it be made freely: in either case its
nature as a judgment remains unchanged. So far it seems that
we are agreed.

'You may, if you like, change the formula, and instead of
saying, "I judge that this being exists," say, "I feel that
this being exists," or, "My consciousness tells me that what I
now perceive by my senses has existence;" or you may use
some other still more accurate expression.[1] But the self-same
concept of a true and complete judgment will remain. It
will always be true that you inwardly feel that there is a
relation of identity between what affects your senses and
existence; and that to feel this is the same as to make a
judgment. There is, therefore, no gainsaying the fact, that
the natural and original judgment which you have laid down
as the basis of your theory is a *judgment* in the strict sense of
the word, and must precede our persuasion of the existence of
external things.

'But if so, you certainly begin the development of man's
intellectual life, not by a simple but by a composite operation,
by the conjunction of a predicate with a subject; for this, and
nothing else, is what all philosophers, your ownself included,
understand by a *judgment.* Thus, in the judgment we are
discussing ("such or such a thing really exists"), *existence* is

---

[1] A more accurate way of expressing
this original judgment would be: 'The
sensation which I experience demands
a something existent (other than myself).' Be it also observed, that to
say, 'This object exists,' would be to
repeat the idea of existence twice over;
for when I say *this object,* I already
signify something which is perceived by
me as existent; and, therefore, the proposition *this object exists* does not
simply express an original judgment,
since the first two words of it, *this
object,* suppose a judgment formed
before the third word, *exists,* is uttered.

the predicate, and the "*sensible*," or the thing in so far as felt, is the subject.

'We ask, therefore, how can man thus join the predicate of existence with the thing which affects his senses, unless he be already in possession of these two elements? And how can you, therefore, call this judgment *original* in the sense that it is not preceded in man by any knowledge? If to make such a judgment it is necessary, on the one hand, to experience the sensation, and, on the other, to have the idea of existence, surely you must acknowledge that this operation is not *original*, but preceded by the two simpler operations, of feeling the *sensation*, and intueing the idea of *existence*. The fact of the judgment taking place immediately upon our experiencing the sensations in no way invalidates the force of our argument. The two elementary operations must exist before they can be conjoined.

120. 'Now, think, if you please, of the idea of existence. The object seen in this idea is a *universal*, and you assume it without giving any account whatever of its origin in our mind. It is a necessary element in the formation of the judgment; it is simpler than the judgment, and must precede it, logically at least. With what consistency, then, can you charge us with error for maintaining that man's intellectual development begins with ideas, when you do the very same by representing it as starting with a judgment which is necessarily conditional upon an antecedent idea?'[1]

[1] The efforts made by philosophers in order to extricate themselves from a difficulty which harasses them on every side, are a subject well worthy of attention. In their eagerness to find an escape, they will not hesitate even to falsify the notions of things, to deny the most approved definitions, to call evidence itself in question. For this end they will be lynx-eyed in scrutinising every word which is used in connection with their argument; and if there should be in it any inaccuracy, which it may serve their purpose to detect, they will most probably detect it through that same activity by which they distort the meaning of so many other words, and misrepresent the nature of so many ideas.

Among the attempts made by philosophers to evade the force of the objection which I here urge against Dr. Reid, there is that of denying the definition of judgment. Degerando says that judgment cannot consist in a comparison of ideas, because if it did, one would have to admit that ideas are antecedent to judgment—an admission, he adds, no longer to be thought of after what has been written by Reid.

Although Degerando's remark is very far from answering my objection, it nevertheless brings to light a real inaccuracy in the common definition of

ARTICLE IX.

Defect common to Reid and his adversaries.

121. The adversaries of Reid have certainly the best of the argument so long as there is only question of demon-

judgment. Let us see where his remark holds good, and where it is at fault.

Degerando argues thus :—' When we affirm to ourselves the existence of an external object, we make a judgment. Now this judgment on the existence of external things cannot be the result of the comparison of two ideas ; for by comparing two ideas together, I do indeed discover the relations which exist between these ideas ; but this operation takes place wholly within my own mind, and cannot, therefore, enable me to affirm that things external to me really exist. Therefore the judgment by which I affirm to myself the real existence of an external object cannot be simply the result of a comparison of my ideas.'

This argument (supposing it to refer to the real existence of corporeal beings) is, in my opinion, unanswerable. So far, then, Degerando's remark is correct, and deserves to be turned to account.

But what consequence can we draw from it ? Simply this, that the definition which makes judgment consist solely in a comparison of ideas is defective. Further than this the argument has no force.

It does not, therefore, affect in any way the definition which I am wont to give of judgment, namely, 'an operation by which we attribute a predicate to a subject.' This latter definition has a wider scope than that which simply places judgment in 'a comparison of ideas.' It does not speak of ideas, nor limit itself to their comparison ; but it speaks of the application of a *predicate* to a *subject.* To bring it within the definition censured by Degerando, it would be necessary to prove first that the *predicate* and the *subject* are neces-
- sarily two ideas. Now this is precisely what I demonstrate not to be the case. I maintain, on the contrary, that only the *predicate* must always be

an idea ; but not so the *subject.* I say that the subject may be a feeling, an assemblage of sensible qualities, a something sensitively perceived. By this doctrine I am enabled to explain our first judgments, those by which we affirm for the first time the real existence of things outside of us. I show that these judgments are the result of the union, not of two ideas, but of that which is felt by our senses (in which state it is not as yet for us a *being*, but only an assemblage of sense-perceptions) with the idea of existence. Through this union we at one and the same time affirm the real existence of external things, and form to ourselves a concept of them.

Accordingly, between the two propositions, ' A judgment is always the result of a comparison of two ideas,' and ' To make a judgment no ideas are requisite,' there is a middle one, namely, ' A judgment is sometimes made by uniting an idea with a sense-perception.' But Degerando did not see this intermediate link. Having, therefore, proved conclusively that the first of these propositions was erroneous, he thought himself justified in concluding also that judgments were made quite independently of ideas ; that is, by an act not resulting from the union of two elements (predicate and subject), but perfectly simple.

He therefore endeavours to make it out that ' there are elementary judgments which consist in the simple perception of objects,' and that with these our cognitions begin.

' Our first cognitions,' he writes, ' are at once perceptions and judgments—perceptions, because their objects are seen by the mind ; judgments, because those objects are seen as real.' (*Histoire comparée*, &c. t. ii. chap. x.)

This is a strange sentence, and I shall reply to it in the words of the Baron Galluppi, a writer whose views on this matter are radically the same as

strating that to make a first judgment without some idea
pre-existing in the mind is an impossibility ; but they are not

those of the French philosopher. ' If,'
says Galluppi with his usual good sense,
'the simple perception of objects is
nothing but perception, why give two
names to one and the same thing?
This serves only to perplex the reader.
On the other hand, it would be merely
raising a question of words. . . .

' Degerando tells us that our first
cognitions are judgments, because in
them the objects are seen as real.
Therefore, I say, by these cognitions
we unite the idea of the object with
the idea of reality or existence ; for
how could we say to ourselves, "The
object which I see is real," unless we
had both these ideas in our mind ? Consequently, this operation is subsequent
to the perceptions or ideas, a conclusion evidently fatal to the hypothesis of
our author. Here there is no middle
term. Either our spirit stops at the
simple vision of the object, and then it
has a perception ; or it turns its attention to the reality of the object, and in
that case it instantly unites together two
ideas, and makes a judgment—an operation, therefore, which comes after
perception and presupposes it.' (*Saggio
Filosofico sulla Critica della Conoscenza*,
by Pasquale Galluppi, Naples, 1819,
vol. i. chap. i.)

Galluppi therefore falls back on the
opinion that simple perception is our
first intellectual operation, and hence
that the *simple apprehension* (the idea)
of objects precedes the judgment by
which we affirm their real existence.
But this theory, after what has been
said on it by Reid, can no longer be
defended.

Reid, having shown that our first
intellectual operation could not consist
in a simple apprehension (idea), concluded that it must be a judgment.
This conclusion, however, was too
hastily drawn, and wholly unjustifiable ;
since a judgment without some antecedent idea is an absurdity.

Degerando, noticing this difficulty,
said :—' Well, let us change the definition of judgment ; let us invent a definition which may embrace both theories
at once. Some maintain that our first
intellectual operation is a *simple apprehension* ; but the observation of the
fact seems evidently to tell against this

hypothesis. Others will have it that
this operation is a *judgment* ; but a judgment without some simple apprehension
is impossible. Let us say, then, that
it is an operation which has the singular
property of being at once a judgment
and an apprehension—a judgment as
simple as the apprehension is simple.'

Galluppi, examining this proposal
of Degerando, finds it self-contradictory, and he is right ; for, on the one
hand, a simple apprehension can never
be a judgment, because there are not
in it the two terms necessary for forming a judgment ; and, on the other,
a judgment can never be a simple apprehension, because if the two terms
could be reduced to one, the judgment
would be destroyed, or rather rendered
impossible. Therefore the middle
course suggested by Degerando is as
absurd as it would be to say that two
are one, or that one is two.

We shall find our way out of the
labyrinth if we admit (1) That the simple
intuition of existence (the idea of being
in general) is innate in us ; and (2) That
(leaving aside that natural act which
constitutes us intelligent beings) our
first intellectual operation is a *judgment* whereby we unite the sense-perceptions with the idea of being, and
thus form the ideas of bodies.

In this system the judgment of
which I speak is the union, not of two
ideas, but of a predicate and a subject,
the subject consisting in what is felt by
the senses. Prior to this judgment we
have not the simple apprehension or *idea*
of the several corporeal things : we
have sensation only. We affirm the
real existence of these things, and then
from this judgment and the persuasion
consequent thereon, we draw the simple
apprehension (or idea) of them by
means of abstraction ; that is, by contemplating them wholly apart from the
persuasion of their real existence.

In conclusion, either we must confess that the problem of the origin of
ideas is unsolvable, or else we must
acknowledge the truth, so unpopular
nowadays, that there is something
which we know from our origin and
by nature. I trust that this truth will
be made perfectly clear in the progress
of this work.

equally fortunate when they have to defend the proposition
that ' The simple apprehension or pure idea of a thing precedes the judgment which affirms its real existence.'

On the one hand, this proposition seems quite true ; for
how can I judge that a being exists of which I have no idea ?
Looking, therefore, at the matter under this aspect, it would
appear that the idea or simple apprehension of that being
must precede the judgment on its subsistence.

But, on the other hand, this is altogether contradicted by
experience. To anyone who looks at this matter in the light
of experience, it must be obvious that, as regards external
things, we, in the first place, form a concrete idea of them —
i.e. an idea coupled with the actual perception and persuasion
of their real existence, and that only later on do we draw
from it (by abstracting from this perception and persuasion)
that pure idea which is called simple apprehension. For
instance, who thinks of a purely ideal or possible horse
without ever having seen some particular horse in actual
existence ?

122. This knot of the question was not clearly seen either
by Reid or by his opponents. Hence it came to pass that
each side could successfully attack the position of the other,
while it was unable to defend its own.

Reid confounded together two questions which are very
different. For it is one thing to ask 'whether a judgment on
the real existence of external things can be made by us without some universal idea pre-existing in our mind ; ' and
another thing to ask 'whether, before we can make that
judgment, we must have the simple apprehension or abstract
idea of the things themselves.'

The adversaries of Reid answered the latter question in
the affirmative, and in this they were wrong.

Now, Reid did not restrict himself to opposing them on
this particular ground, which would have been enough to
overthrow their system. He further undertook to prove that
we affirm the existence of external things by an original
judgment, not only without possessing the simple apprehension of the things themselves, but also without possessing

any universal ideas at all ; that is, by a judgment wholly involved in darkness and mystery.

By thus unnecessarily widening the controversy, Reid
damaged his cause in such a manner that his adversaries,
although silenced by his argument as against themselves,
could nevertheless turn round upon him, and convict him of
grievous error.

In fact, it does not require much effort to see that no one
can make a judgment who does not possess some universal
idea ; and, therefore, the thesis which Reid, in his zeal for the
truth, undertook to maintain, was exaggerated and altogether
untenable.

Moreover, the task of showing to his adversaries, by an
appeal to experience, that our first judgments on the real
existence of external things must precede the simple ideas of
them, was an easy one ; but it was far from easy to find a satisfactory answer to the formidable question :—' How can I judge
that a thing exists of which I have no idea ? '

The answer to this question would have led the Scottish
philosopher very far in his investigations ; but whether it was
that he despaired of finding it, or that he considered it of no
importance, he did not even seek for it. He contented himself with enveloping his ' original judgment ' in a cloud of
mystery, thus, possibly, to screen it from all further question-
ings on the part of inquisitive minds.

123. There could be only one way of finally settling the
point.   This was by devising a system where the object
judged to exist, was the effect of the judgment itself, or, which
comes to the same, ' where the specific ideas of things were
produced by the self-same act which affirmed the real existence of those things.' The whole difficulty, therefore, lay
in finding a judgment of this description.

124. Now, by passing in review the various species of
judgments which we make on things, we find that, so long as
the judgment is merely about some *quality* belonging to a
thing, the idea of that thing necessarily exists in our mind
before the judgment, as well as before the idea of the quality
which the judgment attributes to it.   On the contrary, when

the judgment is such as to fall on the existence itself of the thing, then the idea of the thing judged of is not in our mind prior to, but in virtue of, this judgment. For until a thing is thought of by us as existent, either really or potentially, it is nothing so far as we are concerned ; it is not an object of our thought, an idea. Therefore the judgment by which we affirm the *existence* of things, different in this from all other judgments, is itself the producer of its object. This fact shows that such a judgment is possessed of a peculiar and almost creative energy which eminently deserves the attention of the philosopher.[1] For us, then, the object begins to exist, at the very most, simultaneously with the judgment of which I am speaking.

There is therefore, in us, a special intellectual power, the power of thinking of things as existent.

125. About this power three questions may be asked :—

(1) How is it moved to think of a thing as existent ?

(2) Whence does it draw the universal idea of existence which is indispensable for forming that thought ?

(3) How does it come to limit that universal idea to a determinate thing, in such a way that this thing, and not any other, is the object it thinks of as existent ?

126. The first and third of these questions are easily answered by the aid of experience.

For our understanding is moved both to think of an object as existent, and to determine it as such or such, by the sensations. These produce in us a certain modification, and in response to that modification we say to ourselves, ' That which causes in me these sensations exists.'

The only difficulty, then, is as to how we come by the idea of *existence*, without which it would be impossible for us to make that judgment whereby we know for the first time that a certain external thing exists. Here is the great problem of Ideology.

---

[1] ' That there is in every man a first intellectual operation which produces to itself its own object,' was also held by St. Thomas. His words are : *Prima actio ejus* (intellectûs) *per spe-* *ciem, est formatio sui objecti, quo formato intelligit: simul tamen tempore ipse format et formatum est, et simul intelligit.* (De Natura Verbi Intellectûs, Opusc. xiii. *Opera*, ed. Parm. vol. xvi. p. 179.)

127. To recapitulate in other words. To the question, 'How can I judge that a thing exists of which I have as yet no idea?' the answer is as follows: This judgment includes two parts; first, the thought of existence (or being) in general, and secondly, the thought of the particular thing which I have now before me, with all its determining properties.

So long as I think only of existence in general, or not determined in any way, I make no judgment. I begin to judge when I apply that thought, or determine it to this or that particular thing.

Now, suppose that I were already in possession of the idea of existence (or being) in general; all that I should then require in order to make the judgment 'Such or such a thing exists,' would be the sensations, for they would give me the determination of the existence (being) which by the hypothesis is present to my mind. The whole difficulty therefore reduces itself to explaining the origin of the idea of *being*, the great *sine qua non* in all first judgments.

128. But, whatever be the origin of this idea, let us for the present continue to speak on the supposition that we have it prior to all our judgments on the actual existence of this or that determinate and sensible thing.

In this case the judgments may be very easily explained and analysed in the following manner:—

We are by nature at once sentient and intelligent; that is to say, we are endowed with both sense and understanding.

The sense is the faculty of perceiving things in so far as *sensible*; the understanding is the faculty of perceiving things as *existent in themselves.*

Now, the reason why all that is perceived by our sense becomes the *object* of our understanding is, because WE who experience the sensations are the identical human subjects who are also possessed of understanding.

Given, therefore, that our sense has perceived the sensible qualities, what will be the intellectual operation which we exercise on them?

The understanding, as I have said, is the faculty of perceiving things as existent in themselves. It will therefore

perceive the 'sensibles'—not as the sense perceives them—
i.e. not in the intimate relation they have with ourselves in
so far as they are sensations [1]—but as existing in themselves
independently of us. Now, to perceive in this manner is
nothing but to judge that there is a being outside of us wherein
are the sensible qualities; although as to how those qualities
are in it (and certainly there must be a way in which they
can be there), this first judgment does not make any pronouncement.

Let us, then, seize well on the difference between the two
species of judgments which are made by us on external
objects.

One species consists of those judgments by which we
simply think of a *quality* as existent in a *being* of which we
have already the idea. Thus when I say, 'This man is
blind,' I attribute the quality of blindness to a person whom
I already know, and to whom my judgment refers.

By the judgments of the other species, on the contrary,
we think of a *being* as adhering to certain sensible qualities.
Such is the judgment we make when we say to ourselves,
'Here is a being determined by these and these qualities
which fall under my senses.'

In the first species, the object exists to us antecedently
to the judgment we make on it; in the second, the object
does not exist prior to the judgment, but only the elements

---

[1] I use the word *sensation* to express the modification which we experience when perceiving the *sensible
qualities*; and I use the phrase *sensible qualities* when I consider these
qualities in the relation they have
with the bodies to which they are referred.
This distinction is grounded on the
analysis of sensation. In fact, when
our sensitive organs suffer a modification, and as a consequence we have a
sensation, we are conscious of two
things : (1) of the pleasure, pain, &c.,
which we experience ; (2) of our being,
not the agents, but the patients. Now,
the consciousness of our passivity
necessarily involves the idea of an
action done, indeed, in us, yet not by us,
but by something different from ourselves.
    If, therefore, this action which takes
place in us is neither ourselves, nor the
effect of our activity, and if the conceiving of a determinate action supposes
all that is necessary for the concept of
an action, it must perforce be admitted that with the action we also
conceive an agent different from our
own selves; for an action necessarily
implies an agent. This agent, thus
conceived by us, is not by any means
left indeterminate, but is determined by
the effects or action which it produces
in us; and this effect, this action,
considered in so far as it affects and
modifies us, we call by the name of
sensation.

of it—that is, (1) the sensations, not yet become cognitions ; (2) the idea of existence, which illumines the sensations by adding *being* to them, and causes them to be known in and through being.

To conclude : judgment does not always refer to an object previously thought of, but it sometimes refers to 'sensibles' which become objects of our thought in virtue of the act of judgment itself.

129. From all this we can easily see what is the right solution of the two questions on which Dr. Reid and his adversaries are divided.

First Question : 'Is it necessary that the simple apprehension, or pure idea, of the external objects should be in our mind antecedently to the judgment by which we affirm their actual existence ?'

Answer : No ; it is only necessary that we should have the sense-perception of the sensible qualities.

The mistake of the adversaries of Dr. Reid in thinking that we have first the idea of a thing, and then form the judgment on its existence, arose from their not having well mastered the distinction between a *sensation* and an *idea*. By confounding these two things together, and at the same time seeing that it is only by the sensations that we are led to judge of the existence of a body, they concluded that before making this judgment we must have the *idea* of that body. Had they reflected that the sensations give us the *particular sensible qualities* only, whereas by an *idea* we think of a *being* endowed with those qualities, they would easily have seen, that our idea of a body presupposes a judgment—I mean, that judgment which to the particular sensible qualities supplied to us by the sensations joins the thought of *existence* and thus forms the idea of the body determined by the qualities which actually fall under our senses. This idea is the *object* understood by us, and it is formed, as I have said, by the judgment itself. Then reflection comes in and by considering the object apart from the persuasion of its actual existence— that is to say, leaving it before the mind in a state of pure possibility—forms that species of abstraction which the Schoolmen called *simple apprehension.*

Second Question : ' Is it necessary that before making that judgment by which we affirm for the first time the existence of a body, we should be in possession of some universal idea ? '

Answer : Undoubtedly it is ; because a judgment not preceded by some universal idea is an impossibility ; and to have overlooked this truth was the great blunder of Reid. He admitted an original judgment, qualifying it as mysterious and incapable of any explanation. Now, it is certainly in some cases lawful for a philosopher to admit a principle which he declares to be mysterious, and, if you will, utterly inexplicable ; but it is none of the attributes of a philosopher to admit an absurdity : and a judgment made independently of all universal ideas is an absurdity. Nor is it less unbecoming in a philosopher to lay down a principle and at the same time not to examine the conditions which are necessary to make it possible : for in that case, even if the principle were not shown to be manifestly absurd, the fact of its not having been examined would at least leave a doubt as to its truth. Now, an antecedent universal idea is a condition absolutely necessary for that judgment by which we affirm for the first time the existence of a body. Therefore, Dr. Reid should not have abruptly suspended the process of analysing the ' original and natural judgment' on which he based his theory, but should have prosecuted it until he found whether or not it had all the essentials requisite for its formation.

ARTICLE X.

The part in which the system of Reid holds good as against that of his adversaries.

130. Nevertheless, from all that has been argued thus far we may see that the system of Reid has in it a very strong point as compared with that of his adversaries.

We will suppose that Reid, having by some means or other discovered the error he had committed through giving

an undue extension to his thesis, had wisely corrected
himself. This would have entitled him to speak with force
to his adversaries in the following way : 'I am willing to
acknowledge that the interior judgment by which we affirm
the real existence of the things which strike our senses, is
composed of two elements—the idea of existence and of sensation. Still you must on your part admit, that at the very
moment in which we receive the sensations, our intellectual
nature obliges us to affirm the presence of a being, to make
that judgment which I call *original,* and *natural* : not, indeed,
because it precedes all ideas, for, as I now find, to say this
would be a contradiction, but because it precedes all other
judgments.'

In truth, the real merit of the system of Reid consists in
his having fully grasped the fact that no sooner does our
sense happen to be affected by the action of external agents
than we necessarily affirm their existence, by 'a simple act,'
as he says, though he is wrong when he adds, 'by an act
which cannot be defined.' [1]

What I have said in the preceding article proves that
there is no need in this case of admitting a principle wholly
sui generis, incapable of explanation, a sort of occult quality,
a philosophical *arcanum.*

131. If Reid had clearly seen in what consisted the
deficiency of the system of his predecessors in the philosophical arena, he, instead of insisting upon the necessity of
placing judgments before ideas, would have ascended higher,
and, to use his own phrase, brought a 'more refined chemical
analysis' to bear on those simple apprehensions which are
supposed by his adversaries to precede the persuasion and
judgment of the existence of external objects.

Even from this side he could have driven them to close
quarters by arguing as follows : 'You suppose that the
simple apprehensions or ideas of things precede the judgment we make on their real existence, and you therefore
describe the development of the human mind as proceeding
in accordance with this principle.'

[1] *Inquiry,* &c., chap. ii. sec. 5 (London, 1821, p. 31).

Now, I find a great difficulty here ; for it seems to me that you cannot have the idea or simple apprehension of a thing except by means of a judgment.

To see whether I am right or not, let us come to particulars. Let us take, for example, the idea or simple apprehension of a horse. I ask, 'On what condition is it possible for me to have this idea or simple apprehension ? If, as your books positively state, I get it by *abstracting* from the perception which I now have, or formerly had, of some particular horse, it is evident that this perception, of the horse in the concrete, together with the affirmation and persuasion of its existence, which this perception implies, has preceded the idea or simple apprehension. Indeed, how could I make an abstraction if there was nothing for me to abstract ? Therefore, your two assertions—*first*, that the simple ideas of things precede all the judgments which we make on them ; and, *second*, that these ideas originate in abstraction--are in palpable contradiction with each other.'

132. Nay, he could have pushed his argument still further, thus : You say 'that the simple ideas of things are anterior to all our judgments ;' but if you will take pains to analyse any one of these ideas, you will find that it necessarily includes a judgment. Let us keep to the idea of a horse. When you conceive a *horse*, even though apart from its subsistence, present or past, what are you really thinking of ? Is the object of your thought so simple that it cannot be decomposed into several distinct ideas, or is it not rather the contrary ? Assuredly, if I think of a horse in the abstract, I think (1) of a *being*, and (2) of all those constitutives of it by which the idea of a being in general becomes determined to that particular kind of being which is called *horse.*

Therefore, this idea is composed of two kinds of ideas ; (1) the idea of a being in general, and (2) the ideas of those constitutives whose aggregate gives the idea of the *nature* of a horse—an idea much less extended than the first.

Let us now see how these two ideas come to be so bound up together as to make but one idea.

A very little reflection will suffice to show that the narrower is conceived by us as existing in the wider idea; which is the same thing as to say that we conceive the horse as belonging to the class of *beings*; or, again, that to have the idea of a horse is to have the idea of a being possessed of those determinations which constitute the animal known by the name of *horse*.

Now, from this analysis it is easy to see that the idea of *horse* has in it all the requisites of a complete judgment.

To make a judgment (1) there must be two terms, the one less extended than the other; and (2) the less extended term must be conceived as existing in the more extended. And both these conditions we have found in the idea of *horse* as just explained.

Therefore, the simple apprehension of a finite thing is itself a complex idea, and such as to include a judgment. It is one of those ideas which cannot be formed except by comparing or joining together other ideas or apprehensions.

Therefore, the proposition that 'the simple apprehension of things is anterior to all the judgments which we make on them,' must be considered as altogether untenable.

ARTICLE XI.

Conclusion.

133. Such, then, is the nature of the controversy between Locke and Reid. Both sides find themselves in such a position that, although very well able to destroy, they are utterly incapacitated by their principles from building up a theory that will bear examination.

Reduced to its simplest form, the question upon which they differ may be stated as follows :—

Locke says to Reid, 'Ideas must be anterior to judgments, because it is absurd to suppose that a comparison can be made between two things which do not as yet exist;' and his reason seems to be evident.. Reid replies, 'Judgments must be anterior to ideas because it is impossible for us to form the idea of a thing before we have judged that the thing exists:' and his reason seems also to be evident. How are these two propositions, each apparently true, and yet mutually contradictory, to be reconciled?

As we have already seen, the difficulty involved in these propositions ultimately reduces itself to the origin of the idea of *existence*. I trust that the theory I shall set forth at length in the second volume will offer a satisfactory solution of this important question, which forms the whole theme of the present work.

CHAPTER IV.

DUGALD STEWART.

ARTICLE I.

Various aspects of the difficulty.

134. As I have already observed, all the principal
philosophers have fallen on the difficulty so often mentioned,
as upon a rock standing in the way, so to speak, of their
philosophical course.

It has always been so in the solution of great problems.
A great problem is nothing but a great difficulty to be overcome. Now, we must not imagine that in the proposing of
difficulties a philosopher has his own free choice, as though
he knew or surmised them all beforehand, and could take up
for consideration whichever of them he pleased. If difficult
problems have been solved only after the lapse of many
ages, this arose not so much from the greatness of the difficulty involved in them, as from the circumstance that they
were not known. It may be said with truth, that a difficulty
once brought under the notice of men is already half solved,
and that it is sometimes brought under the notice of the
learned by a mere accident. This we see, for instance, in the
case of the oscillations of Galileo's lamp, to which mathematical science owes its theory on isochronous arcs ; and in
that of the falling of the apple, which resulted in Newton's
system of universal gravitation.

But it is not sufficient that the difficulties be seen in any
sort of way. To be solved aright, they must be seen aright.
The tardiness of their solution is in great part to be attributed
to the length of time which must elapse before the state of
the question can be presented to the student with simplicity

and fulness, so that he may look at it, not merely sideways, on occasion of his thinking of some other thing, but straight in the face.

This is precisely what has happened in reference to our difficulty. Thrown in the path of nearly all philosophers, it was nevertheless lightly passed over by them, because they had not made it the direct object of their inquiries ; while the greater number of them saw it only in a confused way and under an accidental form.

I take note of this in order that I may deal fairly by those authors ; for it seems nothing but equitable to believe, that, had they only been able to put the difficulty to themselves as clearly as we now can, thanks to the labours which they accomplished, and of which we reap the benefit, they would have solved it quite as well as we.

135. To recapitulate, then, the various accidents which have placed our difficulty in the way of modern philosophers :—

Locke stumbled upon it when obliged to speak of the idea of substance, and also when coming to define the term *knowledge*—he perceived that he could not define it without having recourse to *judgments.* Condillac came very close to it when he had to distinguish *ideas* from *sensations,* and to treat of *general ideas.* Reid did the same thing while seeking to account for the persuasion we have of the existence of external bodies ; for he then discovered that Locke had erred in making the development of the human mind begin with acquired ideas, and that the acquisition of ideas presupposed an original and natural judgment. And how was the difficulty seen by the late Dugald Stewart, who had been in his time the mainstay of the meritorious Scottish school? He also went very near it, though not near enough to see it clearly. This was on occasion of his trying to explain how general ideas can be formed through the imposition of names to things. Let us examine carefully how it fared with him.

ARTICLE II.

Dugald Stewart grounds his theory on a passage of Adam Smith.

136 In that chapter of his 'Elements of the Philosophy of the Human Mind' where he undertakes to treat of the faculty of abstraction, Dugald Stewart quotes a passage from the 'Dissertation on the Origin of Language,' by Adam Smith, which, as it contains the principal idea of his theory on abstraction, I shall insert here.

'The assignation of particular names to denote particular objects—that is, the institution of nouns substantive—would probably be one of the first steps towards the formation of language. The particular cave whose covering sheltered the savage from the weather; the particular tree whose fruit relieved his hunger; the particular fountain whose water allayed his thirst, would first be denominated by the words cave, tree, fountain, or by whatever other appellations he might think proper, in that primitive jargon, to mark them. Afterwards, when the more enlarged experience of this savage had led him to observe, and his necessary occasions obliged him to make mention of, other caves, and other trees, and other fountains, he would naturally [1] bestow upon each one of those new

---

[1] The reasoning drawn out in the above extract, whether logically correct or not, is certainly no narrative of facts. It is purely the work of an *imagination* which seeks to describe what seems to it likely to have taken place on the supposition of a man found in a savage state. Hence it would be a mistake to suppose that all the philosophy of Adam Smith, of Dugald Stewart, and of other such modern thinkers, rests solely on *observation* and on *facts*. Even in these authors imagination plays a part, aye, and a very large one, as may be seen from the sample here produced. The question of which it treats is of capital importance to philosophy; indeed, the whole of philosophy depends on it. Now, what is the method pursued by Adam Smith and Dugald Stewart for solving so vital a question? They begin by laying down the bases for the reasoning which is to follow, and those bases

are taken from the imagination! That is to say, they begin by inquiring how, according to their fancy, a savage, on the *assumption* that he was at first wholly without ideas and without speech, would be most likely to proceed in the formation of both words and ideas. Having treated the reader to a pretty little romance about this savage, they draw from it their conclusions. Such is the method of the philosophers of whom I speak! But how will you refuse to believe them when you see their narrative interspersed with such assuring declarations as *the thing is certain, it must naturally be so,* &c.? You have their word for it, *i.e.* the authority of their imagination, and is not that enough?

In spite of all this, however, I make bold to think that it is permissible to examine (1) whether that which their imagination sets down as a *certainty,* as

objects the same name by which he had been accustomed to express the similar object he was first acquainted with. And thus those words, which were originally the proper names of individuals, would each of them insensibly become the common name of a multitude.

' It is this application,' continues Smith, ' of the name of an individual to a great number of objects whose resemblance naturally recalls the idea of that individual and of the name which expresses it, that seems originally to have given occasion to the formation of those classes and assortments, which in the schools are called *genera* and *species*, and of which the ingenious and eloquent Rousseau finds himself so much at a loss to account for the origin. What constitutes a species is merely a number of objects bearing a certain degree of resemblance to one another, and on that account denominated by a single appellation, which may be applied to express one of them.' [1]

137. This mode of explaining how the ideas of genera and species are formed, seems at first sight very easy and natural. But if we diligently search into it we shall find that the explanation, its plausibility notwithstanding, is no better than an illusion. I look upon it as one of those explanations which, owing to the seductively elegant form in which they are presented, divert the minds of unwary readers from the things contained in it. Being charmed with the pleasing smoothness with which the argument seems to proceed, these readers do not think it necessary to verify for themselves

the thing *naturally* to be expected, be in accordance with the real facts, I mean with what has actually been known to take place in similar cases, and consequently, (2) if the supposition which they make, and on which their entire system is grounded—*i.e.* if the supposition of a savage absolutely without either speech or ideas—be allowable. This is what I shall endeavour to do by the following remarks on the passage of Adam Smith and on the theory of Dugald Stewart.

[1] Chap. iv. sec. 1. Dugald Stewart confesses that ' the same account of the progress of the mind in the forma-

tion of *genera*, is given by the Abbé de Condillac.' The merit of Condillac in having called the attention of philosophers to the mutual relation of speech and thought is well known. Hence in speaking of the system of Condillac, I might have anticipated some of my observations on the system of Dugald Stewart concerning the formation of *genera* and *species*; but to avoid unnecessary length I have thought it proper to reserve them for this chapter. The reader may by himself apply to the theory of Condillac much of what is said here on the views of Smith and of Stewart.

what is said, but confidingly take its truth for granted. As regards myself, however, having been taught by a painful experience that under reasonings of the most plausible kind there often lie errors pregnant with numerous evil consequences, I must be forgiven if, before accepting the reasoning above quoted, I consider it my right as well as my duty to scan it carefully.

ARTICLE III.

Defects in the above passage.—First defect: It does not distinguish the several species of names indicating multitudes of individuals.

138. The first thing I have to observe on the above passage is that it speaks of common names as though they were all of one and the same kind. Now, it being well known that there are several kinds of common names, I must examine whether it be correct to treat of these names without indicating their diverse species, and whether the reasoning of Adam Smith be applicable to every species or to one only.

The only notion which he gives us of a common name is, that it signifies a 'multitude' of individuals. Let us see, then, in the first place, if this applies to all the species of common names—in other words, if all names expressing a 'multitude' of individuals are *common* in the true sense of the term.

The first species consists of the numerals—two, three, four, five, &c. Leaving aside the abstraction belonging to these names, and owing to which we cannot apply them to a species of individuals without naming the particular species which we mean—*e.g.* two, three, four, five men, &c.—we will consider them only in so far as they are capable of representing to us a multitude of individuals.

Now, when I say *ten men, ten cities,* &c., I certainly denote a 'multitude' of individuals ; but it cannot on that account be said that the numeral *ten* is *common, i.e.* applicable to each of those individuals—to each city, to each man, &c. It is not true, then, that all the names indicative of a multitude of individuals can, with propriety of language, be called 'common.'[1]

The *numerals* have therefore this peculiarity, that, together with the multitude, they state its numerousness, they fix precisely the number of the individuals contained in that multitude.

139. The second species is formed of those words which in naming a multitude of individuals do not define its numerousness with precision, but only in a general way. Such are the words *few, some, many, a great many,* &c. These also, not being applicable to each of the individuals of the respective multitudes, are not entitled to the appellation of 'common.'

The third species comprises those names which do not express the numerousness of the multitude indicated by them, either precisely or in a general way, but only relatively to some idea which is connected therewith : for instance, the words *nation, tribe, family, assembly,* &c. Now, although the word *family* does not by itself give us any clue for knowing how many persons there are in the family, or whether it be large or small, yet from the nature of the thing we can at once understand that a family is a far smaller collection than would be suggested by the word *nation.* But inasmuch as these names also, indicative though they be of a multitude, are not applicable to the single individuals belonging to it, they must be excluded from the category of *common names.*

140. Lastly, all the plurals, such as *men, animals, houses,* &c., indicate multitudes of individuals, but in such a manner as to determine nothing whatever about their numerousness. Hence they constitute a fourth species of collective names to which, for the reason already stated, the qualification of 'common' cannot be attributed.

[1] The word *ten* is common to every aggregate of things amounting to a decade; but this in no way invalidates the truth of what I have said as to its not being a word applicable to each individual of the multitude indicated by it. If it is common to all such aggregates, the reason is because it then contains another abstraction, and is used in another sense. It expresses not merely the multitudes as such, but also a *qualification* of them—*i.e.* their equality as regards numerousness.

Regarding this indeterminateness proper to plurals some other observations ought to be made ; but, not to interrupt the thread of our discussion, I will, for the present, go on with the enumeration of the various kinds of names, that we may see which among them are of such a nature as easily to be mistaken for those to which the designation of *common names* properly belongs.

ARTICLE IV.

Second defect : Smith does not distinguish the names indicating multitudes of individuals from those which indicate abstract qualities.

141. There are names which do not indicate individuals but only their qualities, whether essential or accidental, and considered apart from the rest that goes to make up an individual. It were useless either to deny or blink this fact. For example, when I say *human nature, animality,* &c., I express essential qualities ; and when I say *whiteness, hardness, fluidity,* &c., I express accidental qualities.

Now, these names may, indeed, be called *general,* but not common ; *general,* because they do not signify individuals, but *qualities* common to many individuals ; not *common,* because the quality to which they severally apply, although found in many individuals, is but one.

That these names cannot rightly be styled 'common' is also seen by the fact that, in contradistinction to all common names, they can never be used in the plural number. Each of them expresses a single thing, abstract and entirely simple, one and indivisible, and therefore [1] impossible to be confused with any other.

Thus while we all speak of *human nature, animality, vegetativeness, whiteness,* &c., no one with any regard for propriety of language would ever dream of saying *human natures, animalities, vegetativenesses, whitenesses,* &c.

[1] By this I do not mean to affirm that these *abstract ideas* may not be analysed and resolved into simpler ideas. Nay, all those which represent the species of things—*e.g.* the species *tree,* &c.—are nothing but the compound result of simple qualities reduced to unity. But what I mean to say is that the joining together of these qualities, and their being seen by us as a thing one and indivisible, is our own work (how we do it I need not explain here). This operation, by which we unite several qualities into one concept, is necessary for the invention of common nouns.

Here, then, is a distinct class of names, which neither designate individuals nor fall under the denomination of ' common ; ' but can only be called *general* or *abstract*.

ARTICLE V.

Third defect : Smith confounds with common names the names indicating multitudes of individuals and those indicating abstract qualities.

142. From these general or abstract names, or rather from the *idea* represented by them,[1] spring those names which are with all propriety called *common*, because they are applicable to each of many individuals ; for instance, the words *man, vegetable, animal, cavern, tree, fountain*, &c., as also the adjectives *white, hard*, &c., whether they be used simply as adjectives, or whether, by an elliptical mode of speech, they be taken as substantives.

Now, unless, in analysing the meaning of these names, we proceed with great caution, we shall easily be deceived by the artificial character of modern languages. We are generally inclined to believe that to each word there corre-

---

[1] I wish to observe that, for the existence of a common name indicative of the *being* which possesses the abstract property, it is not necessary that there should also be the name representing the abstract idea itself. There are many *common* names which have not the abstract words corresponding to them. Thus the English language has the terms *tree, cavern, fountain*, but not *treeishness, cavernousness, fountainousness*, which would be the corresponding abstract terms. The existence of the latter sort of names, as also of names generally, depends on the need which men have of them ; for it is only to supply a need that men invent a word. But if the whole process of ideas is not always indicated in languages, because this is not always necessary for men who only make use of language to express their thoughts, it does not follow that such process is not continuous and complete in the mind itself. Were it interrupted, the human mind would proceed *per saltum*—that is to say, would advance in knowledge without discoursing, which is absurd. And still more absurd would it be to suppose that men's minds become possessed of composite ideas without having first thought of the elements of which those ideas are the result. We must therefore admit that whenever a common noun has been invented, as for instance, *cavern*, there must have been in the mind the idea which responds to it, and which, if it were separately expressed, would be termed *cavernousness*. The fact of this idea not being expressed by a distinct word does not render it (the idea) any the less necessary for the invention which has taken place of the word *cavern* ; for the idea conveyed by this word, resolved into its elements, simply indicates a something endowed with those properties which (did such a word exist) would be called *cavernousness*. And, nevertheless, this does not prove that those properties have been, in the first instance, conceived separately from the subjects to which they belong, but it rather proves the contrary.

sponds but one idea, whereas that is not so. On the contrary, instances of this kind are extremely rare. The nature of language, and especially of modern languages, is such that in by far the greatest number of cases a single word expresses an idea of the most complex description ; that is to say, composed of many other ideas. Not only this, but that very same word indicates also the link which binds all those ideas together and gives them unity. Hence it comes to pass that on submitting the meaning of a single term to analysis, we can often translate it into a proposition, and even several propositions.

This is true of the names of which I speak. The word *man*, for example, is equivalent to the proposition, ' A being possessed of humanity ; ' the word *tree* is convertible into the formula, ' A being possessed of those properties which constitute a tree, and which, if they were to be summed up in a single word, which is wanting in the English language, would be called *treeishness.*' And so with these names generally. In all of them we attribute to beings a certain quality they are found to possess. Hence, under each of these names there lurks a judgment by which, as often as we pronounce or think of them, we attribute a predicate to a subject, while for the sake of brevity we express this operation by a single word which gives us its result, by representing in a single *coup d'œil* the relation which we have discovered between that predicate and that subject. Now, it is only these names which can with propriety be designated as *common*, since they are applicable to each individual of a certain class. Thus the word *man* applies severally to every member of the human race ; the word *tree* to every tree, no matter which ; the word *cavern* to all caverns without exception ; and so of all the rest.

143. Such being the case, I must entirely disagree with the opinion of Adam Smith, that a common noun indicates a ' multitude' of individuals. On the contrary, it invariably indicates one ' individual' only ; but it does so through a quality common to many, and this is why, after being applied to one individual, it can, *ad libitum*, be applied to another, and

then to another, and so on in succession to all the individuals characterised by that same quality. If it were true that the word *tree*, for example, signified a 'multitude' of trees, the consequence would be that, when we said *trees*, we should express many such 'multitudes,' But no one has ever thought that, when using this plural, he was expressing anything more than a number of individual trees.

ARTICLE VI.

Fourth defect : Smith does not understand the true distinction between common and proper nouns.

144. I think that by this time the reader must already have begun to feel serious misgivings about a reasoning which, although it seemed at first sight very plausible, and based on the apparently truthful description of a perfectly natural fact, has been found, upon examination, to contain, in a few phrases, so many inaccuracies.[1]

Adam Smith gave us to understand that common nouns simply signified 'multitudes' of individuals; but on enumerating the four kinds of names expressive of such 'multitudes,' we discovered that not one of them was common to many individuals.

We next examined the general or abstract names, which denote single qualities, essential or accidental, and we found that they also are not common to many individuals, but proper to a common quality.

Lastly, in these general or abstract names, or rather in the ideas which they represent to us, we have seen the origin of common nouns ; and we have found that their nature consists simply in expressing a judgment whereby a quality is attributed to a subject, or in designating an object through a quality which indicates or makes it known to us, and which

[1] My motive for analysing somewhat closely this passage of Adam Smith, which Dugald Stewart has adduced as one of singular merit, is that I may undeceive, if possible, those many superficial persons, young and old, in our country, who imagine that the capacity for deep and philosophical thought is a prerogative/ exclusively reserved for students living beyond 'the Alps and the sea by which,' as Dante says, 'beautiful Italy is encircled.'

being common to many subjects, causes the same name to be applicable to each of them.   But we must proceed.

145. The nature of *common* nouns being now ascertained, let us see what is the nature of *proper* nouns.

Both common and proper nouns express individuals and not collections of individuals, but with this difference : that while the common noun designates and distinguishes an individual through a quality belonging to it, the proper noun makes known the individual, not through a quality of it, but directly ; it expresses, so to speak, its individuality.   Now, *individuality* as such is essentially incommunicable, essentially exclusive of everything but its own proper self.   One individual cannot be another.   Hence a proper noun can apply to one individual only.   On the contrary, a common noun, by indicating a being through a quality which may be found equally in other beings, does not single it out with such precision as absolutely to contradistinguish and isolate it from all others.   Whatever being has the same quality is entitled to the same name.   Thus the word *man*, unless when used in the abstract sense of *humanity*, signifies not many but only one man ; yet as the one man is named from humanity, a quality common to all other men, the same word can be applied to them as well as to him.   But the case would be different if, instead of calling him *man*, I were to call him *Peter* ; for this second name would not be derived from a quality common to other men, but would be used by me expressly to signify that individuality which belongs exclusively to Peter, and which in consequence cannot be communicated to any other person.

ARTICLE VII.

Fifth defect : Smith does not understand the reason why common nouns and proper nouns are severally so called.

146. Having thus cleared up the ideas attached severally to the words *proper noun* and *common noun*, let us continue our analysis of the reasoning of Smith.

The proper name, then, is imposed on a being to express its individuality alone.   But as this name has no necessary relation with that individuality, one is free to apply it to the individuality of any other being one pleases.

Thus, for example, a father who has twelve sons may, if so inclined, call each of them in succession by the proper name of *Peter*. I will, moreover, suppose that all persons now living who answer to the name of *Peter* are assembled together before us. Does it follow that this name of *Peter*, · because applied to so many people, is a *common* noun? Certainly not; and the reason is clear. The fact of a name being common or proper does not depend upon its being used for naming one individual or many, but on the *manner* in which it names them. If it names them, in consideration of a quality common to them all—as, for instance, in the case of the term *man*, which distinguishes human beings through *humanity*—then it is common. But if it names them purely and simply with reference to their individuality, it is proper. Hence even if every man in this world were called *Peter*, all that we could say of it would be that every man had two names, one common—i.e. *man*; and one proper—i.e. *Peter*. As a matter of fact, each of us has the two names, and it is a mere accident that our proper name is, or is not, the same as that of our neighbours. Indeed, the number of proper names is very small in comparison with the whole human race; nay, there might even be but one proper name for all men alike.

147. Now, this reveals a new fallacy in the reasoning of Smith—I mean, in that part where he says, though without any proof, that the savage changes proper names into common, simply by applying them to many individuals; as if nothing else were wanted for effecting such a change. So far is this from being true, that even if the name of *Peter* were, as I have said, given to all the men of a province, of a kingdom, of the world, it would still remain *proper*, since it would indicate men, not through their common humanity, but through the individuality of each.

Suppose, then, that the savage had given a proper name to the first cave which sheltered him from the inclemency of the weather, another to the first tree with the fruit of which he relieved his hunger, a third to the first fountain at which

he quenched his thirst; and suppose, further, that on seeing
afterwards one, two, or three similar caves, one, two, or three
similar trees or fountains, he had also given each of them the
same name as he used in the first instance, we should thus
have four caves, four trees, four fountains, called respectively
by the same name; but it would still remain to be seen
whether this savage, in applying one and the same name to
four similar things, used it as a proper or as a common noun.

Now, it is clear that in no case did he, as Smith asserts,
denote a ' multitude' of individuals; since each time he said
cave, tree, fountain, he meant only one cave, one tree, one
fountain.   But even if he had made these names collective by
saying in the plural *caves, trees, fountains,* that would not have
sufficed by itself to prove that the names were ' common '
(146).   The only criterion for judging whether they were
common or proper consists in knowing whether in them he
contradistinguished the individuals by means of qualities
which they held in common, or designated those individuals
through their own individualities alone.

ARTICLE VIII.

*Sixth defect: Smith does not see that the first names given to things
were common nouns.*

148. For my own part, I think it more probable that the
names given by the supposed savage to his *tree,* to his *cave*
and to his *fountain,* would be *common nouns* from the very
first.

Be it observed that, generally speaking, proper names are
not imposed on objects of the description here spoken of—
i.e. caves, trees, fountains, &c.—but rather on persons, places,
rivers, &c.; because this is found necessary for not confounding such things together.   Usually there is not any necessity
for individuating by a proper name a tree, a cave, a fountain;
and if there is, men are accustomed to secure such individu-
ation by referring to circumstances connected with the thing.

Thus, for example, a cave would be called the cave of
Polyphemus, from the man who was dwelling in it; or the

cave of Hebron, from the district in which it stood; and so with the expressions the cedar of Lebanon, the rose of Jericho, the palm of Cades, from the places where these trees flourished; the well of Jacob, from him who dug, or discovered, or made use of it; the healing fountain, from the medicinal properties of its waters, and so on. For things of this kind there never is an imperative need of inventing proper names.

149. Hence we can see why proper names, denoting as they do the individual substance of a thing, far from being the most frequent, are, even in the richest and most copious languages, wanting to numberless objects; whereas there is not a single thing in the world without a common name of some sort. The common name is more necessary than the proper, and it is probable that men did not invent proper names until they perceived that without them a confusion of similar things would ensue. When a case of this kind occurred, they would fix for the one particular thing a name significative of that proper and individual substance, whereby alone that thing became unmistakably segregated from all others of the same species.

150. In this connection it is important to observe that the imposing of a name on that exclusive property which individualises a being, and unmistakably singles it out from among all others of the same species, demands a much more difficult exercise of abstraction than is required for naming that being from a quality it possesses in common with other beings. Speaking in particular of bodies, their common qualities are the first to strike our senses, and to be cognised by us. Consequently, it is much more likely that we should name a corporeal being from these qualities than from its own proper and individual substance, which, as separate from its accidents, does not fall under our senses, and can only be separated from the accidents by means of an abstraction, or rather a series of abstractions. I therefore believe the real truth to be, that it is only after a very long lapse of time, and after many comparisons have been made between things of the same species, that men's intellectual powers grow

so far developed as distinctly and expressly to notice that, besides the common qualities which fall under the senses, there is in each being a something so exclusively proper as to divide it completely from all other beings ; and that something is its own self.

Accordingly, my firm persuasion is, that our supposed savage would not at first have felt the need of giving to his tree, cave, or fountain a proper name, but only at a much later period, when having already seen many caves, trees, and fountains, he would have learnt to separate in his mind the individuality of each, and, what is still more, to see the necessity of singling out that individuality by a special name, so that he might in speaking, for instance, to his wife and children point out to them that particular cave, tree, or fountain with such precision that they would not be able to mistake them for other caves, trees, or fountains. I do not, however, believe that a necessity like this would arise while he continued in a savage state, nor yet for a good while after, even though he should have considerably advanced in civilisation. Even were the necessity to occur he would doubtless supply it by a much readier process than the most difficult one of inventing proper names : for example, by the context of his discourse, or by means of those accidental adjuncts which I have mentioned, or by some other expedient.

151. Moreover, as we cannot know that a name is common simply from the fact of its being applied to many individuals, because, as we have seen, many might be called by the same proper name, so on the other hand we cannot say that a name is proper simply from finding it applied to one individual only. For even a single individual may be designated by a common name. Thus, in the supposition that only one man were left in this world, there would be no necessity whatever of a proper name for him, since the common name of *man* would then be quite sufficient to identify him beyond the possibility of his being mistaken for another. And yet this would still be a common name, because derived from *humanity*—a quality which would equally belong to other human individuals if there were any in existence.

Nor is all this mere conjecture, based on imagination, like the narrative of Smith. It is the fact as described in the inspired book of Genesis. There we read of a time when there was only one man on the earth. No proper name was given to this man, for none was required ; but he was called *Adam*, which in the Hebrew language conveys the same meaning as our word *man*. And that we may better see how this was truly a common name, let us look at its origin. It was derived from *earth*, the material of which the same sacred record declares man to have been formed, and it was intended to signify a 'being composed of earth.' Therefore, the first person ever named in this world was not designated through his individuality, but through a quality common to all men who should come after him, and hence by a common noun.

152. Instead, then, of having recourse to an imaginary savage, and of losing themselves in an arbitrary supposition— a method which is, by universal consent, the reverse of philo- sophical—would not our philosophers have acted much more wisely by consulting the monuments of antiquity, which give us the real facts ?

A sober investigation of these facts would have made them see the impropriety of assenting without careful exami- nation to the opinion, certain as it might seem at first sight, that 'proper nouns were invented before the common.'

It is just in propositions like these, which make an apparent show of evidence, that the most pernicious errors lie concealed, and in such a way as to render their detection a matter of no small difficulty. The false evidence causes these propositions to be gratuitously accepted even by men otherwise circumspect, as Mr. Dugald Stewart is generally reputed to be, and makes them believe themselves dispensed from a diligent and painstaking study of the facts.

Had these respectable philosophers examined, as I have said, the manner in which the first men really imposed names on things, they would most certainly have found that those primitive names were never chosen arbitrarily, as is the case with proper names. The first men did not express individual objects through their individuality, but always through a quality they held in common with other objects. Thus Cain meant 'a thing acquired or newly gotten;' hence in giving this name Adam said, 'I have gotten a new thing through God.' Applicable as this word is to everything acquired or 'newly gotten,' it is clearly a common noun. Abel meant 'vanity;' Eve, 'life-giver;' Seth, 'a being substituted;' Enoch, 'dedicated;' Lamech, 'poor,' 'humbled;' all of which are, again, common nouns. And the same may be said of the other Hebrew names of persons or things. All of them designate the individual through common qualities, and are therefore common nouns.[1]

[1] The earliest historical record we have of the imposition of names is found in the second chapter of Genesis, where we are told that 'Adam called all the beasts by their names' (v. 20) ; and the sacred historian says that 'whatsoever Adam called any living creature, the same is its name'—'Omne enim quod vocavit Adam animæ viventis, ipsum est nomen ejus' (v. 19). Commenting on this passage, Eusebius says that Moses intended by this remark to intimate that the names imposed by Adam on the animals expressed their nature. 'Quum ait *ipsum est nomen ejus,* quid aliud quam appellationes, uti natura postulabat, inditas esse significat?' (*Præp. Evang.* l. xi. c. 6.) Now, these names, given to the different species of animals created by God, so as to signify their nature, are nothing but common nouns. Thus the most ancient and authoritative of all documents extant concerning the formation of language unmistakably proves that the first names imposed on things were, not proper, but common nouns. With the opinion of Eusebius accord all the Hebrew traditions and the Rabbinical teachings, as anyone may see by reading John Buxtorff, jun. (*Dissert. Philologico-Theologicæ,* i. § xxi.), or Julius Bartolocci (*Biblioth. magna Rabbin.* tom. i.), or other authors of that class.

But the Hebrew antiquities are not the only source from which we learn that the first and most ancient names were 'common,' and signified the *nature* or the *qualities* of the things named, and not their individuality.

This is the opinion of antiquity in general, as well as a fact embedded in all ancient languages. I have not here the time to dwell on the countless proofs that I might easily produce in support of my statement. Suffice it to observe that the *Cratilus* of Plato aims in substance at establishing three points : (1) that names were originally imposed on things, not arbitrarily, but for a reason ; (2) that when the necessity arises for imposing new names, we should in like manner endeavour to adopt such as may express the qualities—that is, the nature—of the things we wish to name ; (3) that as regards the names already imposed, they should always be used with strict propriety, so that the meaning they had at first may be unchangeably preserved.

It is in great part for the reason that the oldest names were *common,* or significative of *common qualities,* the *species,* the *essences* of things—that the ancients generally were deeply impressed with the conviction that all wisdom consisted in the science of names, and that these should therefore be jealously guarded against all change, and transmitted to the children in that same state in which they had been received by their fathers. For they regarded them as a precious and sacred heritage containing the deposit of religion and of knowledge, as well as the secret of human happiness.

To the same source may also be traced the superstitions observable in the use of certain names. For the reverence with which those names were

A similar observation may be made as regards Greek names, and, indeed, the names of all antiquity, in which it may safely be affirmed that men never knew how to impose truly proper names, indicating the individuality itself of a thing, such as have come to be, in modern languages, Peter, Paul, Italy, France, England, the Adige, the Tiber, the Po. Nay, even these names only became proper from the time that their etymologies were lost or forgotten.

That these proper nouns which modern languages have inherited from antiquity were originally common nouns, is proved by all that remains to us of their etymologies ; for from these we can see that the men of those early times designated the said persons, countries, rivers, &c., not by the individuality exclusively proper to each,[1] but by qualities which were or might be possessed by other beings of the same species.

regarded, and the importance which heads of families attached to the duty of preserving and transmitting them intact to their descendants, degenerated in course of time into a blind and unreasoning veneration, thus exhibiting an instance of that excess into which all human affections are ever prone to fall when the imagination has full sway and is allowed to produce the most capricious effects.

[1] Hence the ancients were in a much better position than we now are for noticing the chronological priority of *common* over *proper* nouns.

Aristotle took note of it in the first chapter of his first book ' On Physics.' He there says plainly that the common nouns are invented first, and afterwards the proper.

And it is most remarkable that Aristotle grounds his opinion on a fact most similar to the one adduced by Smith in order to prove precisely the contrary. So true is it that facts, when not accompanied by a sound and proper discernment in him who makes use of them, are not of themselves sufficient to lead to the truth, but become the occasion of abuse and error.

Smith says : ' The savage calls by the name which he gave to his own cave all the caves he sees ; therefore, he invented the proper name first, and then made it common.'

Aristotle says : 'A child calls by the name of *father* every man it sees, until it has learned to distinguish its own father from other men ; therefore, the name which the child gives to its father is for it a common noun, and the child does not restrict the meaning of this common noun to designate its own father alone, until it has perceived the differences which exist between him and others, and consequently the error it was committing by taking him for any other man. Therefore, the understanding of the child proceeds from the general to the particular, from the genus to those differences which mark out the species.' (Arist. *Nat. Ausc.*, lib. i. cap. 1.)

ARTICLE IX.

Seventh defect: Smith does not see that to know in things that which is
' common' is easier than to know that which is ' proper.'

153. The study of antiquity, then, reveals to us the fact
that the invention of common nouns is of a very much earlier
date than that of proper nouns ; that in ancient languages
common nouns were employed even when necessity compelled
the naming of individual objects ; and hence that for truly
proper nouns we must look to modern languages only.

This mode of progression in the formation of languages
may at first sight appear strange ; but if we examine it attentively we shall find that it is perfectly natural—nay, the only
one possible to the human mind.

In the first place, a much more difficult abstraction is required, as we have said, for noting and naming the individuality itself of beings, than for giving attention to their common
qualities and naming them accordingly (150).   Now, the
development of man's faculties is gradual, and therefore must
commence with the easier, and not with the more difficult,
operations.

In the second place, words are only invented to supply a
need (see note to n. 142).   Now, the first need which men
experience is that of designating things through their more
general qualities.   Then comes a time when things must be
named by means of more special qualities, both to prevent a
confusion and the damage or annoyance that result from it.
Then, again, as experience and the use of things proceeds
further and further, men feel called upon to make smaller and
smaller subdivisions, and to indicate them by names less and
less common ; and so on until the social development reaches
a stage so advanced as to necessitate the marking by proper
names of the individuals themselves.   Proper names are,
therefore, the very last to be invented.   They give to language its ultimate completion and perfection.

Accordingly, we find that there is not a single thing
which has not a common name : not all have the name of the

genus ; still fewer have also that of the species ; while those distinguished by a proper name form but a very insignificant fraction, and this in modern languages only.

It is therefore manifest that the philosophers of whom I speak, in describing the progress of the human mind in the formation of languages, began precisely at the point where they ought to have ended ; and they did this because, instead of taking the real facts for their guide, they hastily abandoned themselves to hypothetical speculations. They imagined the invention of proper nouns to be the first step in human speech, whereas in very truth it is the last. It, in fact, supposes the very highest degree of social culture ; so much so, that even in the modern European languages, brought though they are to so great a perfection—thanks to the civilising influence which Christianity has happily been exercising for nearly two thousand years—proper nouns can still be traced to their origin, and there recognised as having, at first, been nothing but common nouns.

ARTICLE X.

Eighth defect : Smith does not know in what way common nouns pass into being used as proper.

154. When Smith, therefore, pronounced so confidently that the first cave, tree, and fountain with which his savage became acquainted were *naturally* the first objects he would designate by proper names ; that these names would become common simply through the savage applying them to other caves, other trees, and other fountains ; and that all the common nouns we have at this day were originally proper, he expressed the direct contrary of the real facts.

He owed this error to his incorrect notion of what constitutes respectively a proper and a common noun. He thought—and at first sight it would seem truly—that a proper noun is a name given to a single individual, and a common noun a name applied to many. Herein, however, he mistook that which accidentally happens in connection with these nouns for what properly constitutes their nature. It is, indeed, customary for a common noun to be applied to many individuals, and for a proper noun to be applied to one only ; but, as I have just said, this is merely accidental. The contrary would not only be possible, but is actually seen in practice. Sometimes a common noun is applied to a single individual without ceasing on that account to be common, and *vice versa* a proper noun is applied to many individuals without ceasing to be proper (146, 151). In point of fact, the proper as well as the common noun is never applied except to one individual at a time ; their only difference being, as I have so often pointed out, that the common noun is taken from a certain quality in which many other individuals do or may participate ; whereas the proper noun aims direct at the *individuality itself, which is essentially proper and incommunicable.

The truth, therefore, is, not that proper nouns have gradually passed into common, but that those which were once common nouns have been made to serve as proper, by transferring them to signify that individuality which originally was not expressed but only understood.[1]

The better to see how this could have been done, we must bear in mind that a common noun does not of its own nature determine (as a proper noun does) an individual in such a way as totally to divide it from all the others which do or may share in the common quality whence it has been derived (145). It only acquires this determinative force[2] from

[1] On the cause of the error of Smith, as well as on what there is of truth in his reasoning, see the next note. The same subject has also been treated under another aspect by the author in his *Psychology*, vol. ii. n. 1460, p. 366, and n. 1462, p. 370, of the Milan edition. Note of P. Perez in his *Rosminian Anthology*, p. 172.—[TRANSLATORS.]

[2] Sometimes a common noun is used to designate individuals even before it passes by general consent into being taken as a proper noun. When this takes place, the usual practice is to supply for the indeterminateness of the noun by the external adjuncts accompanying our employment of it. Thus

when I wish to speak to a stranger who happens to be the only person before me on the road, I call out, '*Good man!* I want to speak to you.' Hereupon he stops and turns towards me, in the belief that *he* is the individual addressed. Nor can he be mistaken in this ; for there is no one else there. But if others should happen to be there, several would perhaps turn round at the same time, precisely because the word *man* which I have used is common to them all. In that case I should immediately determine the one man I mean, by pointing my hand at him, by emphatically throwing my voice in his direction, or by some other sign calcu-

a tacit understanding, or, to speak more correctly, an understanding expressed by the fact that men mutually agree that

lated to single him out from among the rest.

Now, this must exactly have been the case with the first names given to things. They must have been *common* in themselves, but employed and regarded by the speakers as *proper.* In other words, although each name expressed nothing but a *common quality,* the speakers always understood it as conjoined with the individual, and tacitly referred it to the same in their thoughts. In fact, the human mind, while in that early stage in which it is not yet accustomed to dwell on abstract ideas, always looks at objects in the concrete.

The order in which the human mind forms reflex ideas is as follows : (1) First of all, the mind has the idea of *being in general* ; but we may safely say that it does not reflect on this idea, nor is distinctly aware of its presence, till after it has reflexly gone over all the other ideas. The series of *reflex ideas* does not, therefore, begin here. (2) In the next place the mind, aided by the senses, acquires the perceptions of individual beings ; and these perceptions are composed, (*a*) of a common element (ideas), and (*b*) of a proper element (the sensible realities). This twofold term of the perception is that which first arrests and occupies the attention.

(3) Only after this, begin those *abstractions,* whereby man's attention dwells solely on the most common notions.

Now, man does not give a name except to such ideas as he reflexly knows. Consequently, the ideas first named by him are ideas applied to individuals. Now, I think it is this fact that led Smith into error. From it he concluded that the first words were proper nouns ; which is directly at variance with history and therefore with reason. He did not observe the nature of ideas as applied to individuals ; he supposed that individuals were thought of by means of abstract ideas alone ; whereas those ideas by which individuals are thought of consist of a common element united with the proper and real. Now, I maintain that

although the ideas first named are not abstract, but applied to individuals— that is to say, are perceptions or recollections of perceptions—nevertheless the names are given in consideration of the common element which those ideas contain. Hence, although the intention of those who use them and the peculiar external circumstances in which they are used, may give them the aptitude for serving as proper nouns, they are in themselves common nouns.

If the first ideas named by man are individuated, those which he names next are not so, but separated by abstraction from the individuals with which they are at first united. To make this separation, to fix the attention on those ideas in an isolated state, and lastly to name them, is a subsequent intellectual operation.

I have said that individuated ideas are named from the common element contained in them ; and that the aptitude which these common nouns have for serving as proper—*i.e.* designating exclusively a particular individual— proceeds solely from an implied conventional understanding on the part of those who use them. To see ideas in an individuated state, is to see the common in the individual. But now the question arises as to how the common can be seen apart from the individual, and in this state be expressed by a name.

This question divides itself into two, namely : (1) How is it possible for the human mind to acquire the first abstract ideas (universalisations) ; and (2) How is it possible for man to give these ideas a name ?

Now, it is evident that if we suppose these abstract ideas as already conceived, there will be no difficulty in understanding how man can name them. He can do so, either by common nouns such as *man, animal,* &c. ; or by substantives indicating abstract ideas, such as *humanity, animality,* &c.

With regard to common nouns, he is, by the hypothesis, already in possession of them ; all that remains to be ascertained about these is, how man begins to use them purely and simply

the name, although 'common' by its nature, shall be taken to signify exclusively a certain particular being.

Thus the aptitude which the common noun has for being applied to a single individual is not expressed in the noun itself, but implied by those who make use of it with that intent. And the reason why the individuality is not directly expressed but only implied, lies precisely in the difficulty which the human mind encounters in concentrating its gaze on the pure individuality of a being apart from all its qualities—a most arduous mental operation, and one of the very last to be performed.

155. But let us proceed : be it well understood, then, that the first step which the human mind makes towards knowing the individuality of things is to perceive that individuality as united and bound up together with all the common qualities, and to fix the attention on it less distinctly than on them.

According to this, man at first designates with names the common qualities, and afterwards makes use of these names for indicating the individuality ; so, however, as to show that the idea of that individuality is not as yet distinctly noticed by him, and therefore not capable of being expressed by itself alone with a strictly proper noun. Indeed, the invention of a strictly proper noun is so difficult a task that hardly any instances of it can be found even in modern languages.

Returning, therefore, to our savage, and supposing for sake of argument that the names of his cave, tree, and fountain

---

as *common*, and without referring them to any one individual. To know how he can do this, is to know how he is moved to his first abstractions. This, therefore, depends entirely on the first of our two questions.

As to the names expressive of abstract ideas, there can be again no difficulty in explaining the invention of them, if we suppose that man has already reached that intellectual stage in which he descries the abstract qualities of things apart from those which are proper ; since he can give a name to any idea of whose presence to his mind he is distinctly aware. The whole of the difficulty, therefore, centres on the first question : ' How the human mind is moved to its first abstractions.'

Now, to be so moved, it requires some *external sign*, such as language, marking exclusively the quality which is being abstracted, and capable of fixing his attention on that alone. Hence to invent a language suitable for this purpose would be quite impossible to man in a state of perfect isolation.

were to be invented by himself, we should have to describe the probable process of his mind during that operation in the following way :—

At the outset, he would notice in his cave, in his tree, in his fountain, some one of the more prominent qualities, which more readily and vividly struck his senses, as for instance in the cave, hollowness ; in the tree, gnarledness, or height ; in the fountain, depth or the rising of the water, or some other such quality. Then by means of these qualities he would invent truly common nouns, which in his mind would be equivalent to the propositions : ' That which is hollow ; that which is gnarled ; that which is deep or rising.'

Then feeling, as he must do, that the constant supplying of his own wants was intimately connected with the particular objects in which he had noticed the qualities I have referred to, he would very soon make use of those same common nouns for designating them—*i.e.* his particular cave, tree, and fountain—pursuant to the law we have stated, that common nouns can be made to answer the purpose of proper nouns, not, indeed, in virtue of their own nature, but by the intention of him who uses them, and the circumstances in which he uses them.

As, however, the supposition is that our savage at this stage would know only one cave, one tree, and one fountain, he could not apply the names he had invented except to these alone. But when he afterwards came to discover other caves, other trees, other fountains, he would instantly perceive that they possessed qualities similar to those of the objects with which he had first become acquainted, and that, therefore, the same names would equally do for them.

Consequently, he would now apply his names to many trees, many caves, and many fountains ; and thus that which had been a common noun from the beginning would undergo no other change than that of being actually used to indicate several individuals at once, each, however, distinct from the other, while at first it had been used to designate one only. This, then, would be a second step.

But when circumstances arose of a nature to make our

savage feel that it was needful for him to distinguish his own
cave, &c., from all the others, he would make a third step;
but it would not be as yet that of the invention of strictly
proper names. He would probably distinguish several caves
of his forest through some addition made to the common noun
itself in the form, for instance, of the possessive pronoun
mine, thine, his: saying, *my* cavern, *thy* cavern, *his* cavern,
&c.;[1] or in any other form he might think fit for indicating
the cavern belonging to himself, or to the person he was
addressing, or to a third person.

Before arriving at the invention of proper nouns he would
have still a long way to go. He would have to pass from the
state of a savage into that of an orderly social being. It
would be necessary that the society which began in his woods
and was at first limited to a single family should expand into
much larger proportions, should attain a very high degree of
culture and civilisation, and at last the state of perfection—a
state in which men are not only fully equal to the most subtle
and most sustained abstractions, but able to keep their minds
fixed on them—a state in which artificial wants are multiplied, and moral wants developed, diversified, and refined. I
say artificial and moral wants; for it is by them that men are
impelled to draw ever closer and closer distinctions between
things,[2] to divide the greater into lesser classes; to designate

[1] Here also I can appeal to facts.
The ancient languages supply us with
many examples of words consisting of a
common noun with the possessive pronoun affixed to it. For instance, *Sarai*
in Hebrew signifies ' My lady '; and
many other Hebrew names ending in
the letter *i* are equivalent to the English
my.

[2] The fact mentioned by Captain
Cook in his account of a small island
called Wateeoo, which he visited in
sailing from New Zealand to the
Friendly Islands, so far from witness-
ing, as Mr. Dugald Stewart thinks, to
the truth of Smith's theory, seems
rather to tell very decisively against
it; and while confirming, on the one
hand, the view which I maintain, it
affords, on the other, an instance of
the great difference there is between

quoting facts and quoting them to the
purpose.

Smith and Dugald Stewart will
have it that the savage first invented
proper names, and then rendered them
common through applying them to many
similar things; and that these names
thus applied stood as substitutes for
species and *genera.* Such is the account
which these philosophers give of species
and genera.

Here is Captain Cook's description
of the fact to which I refer : ' The in-
habitants of this island,' he says, ' were
afraid to come near our cows and horses,
nor did they form the least conception
of their nature. But the sheep and
goats did not surpass the limits of their
ideas, for they gave us to understand
that they knew them to be birds.'
And then he adds : ' It will appear

the species which are narrowest and approach nearest to the individual; to arrange these species in all possible ways, necessary as well as arbitrary; and, lastly, to fasten on the individuals themselves by means of names exclusively significative of their individuality—which is the last and most refined operation of all.

ARTICLE XI.

Ninth defect: Smith, while professing to explain abstract ideas, gives no such explanation at all.

156. Thus far our consideration has been restricted to the progress of language, on the supposition that man was its author. We have therefore examined only the external product of the interior operation of the mind, and said nothing as yet of how and by means of what faculties this operation must

rather incredible that human ignorance could ever make so strange a mistake, there not being the most distant similitude between a sheep or a goat and any winged animal. But these people seem to know nothing of the existence of any other land animals besides hogs, dogs, and birds. Our sheep and goats they could see were very different creatures from the two first, and therefore they inferred that they must belong to the latter class, in which they knew that there was a considerable variety of species.' (Dugald Stewart, *Elements*, &c., p. 154; London, 1811.)

For my own part, I should be more disposed to think that the distinguished English sailor, not being sufficiently acquainted with the language of those islanders, misunderstood what they were saying, than to believe that those islanders, who had the same senses as other men, did not see that sheep and goats bore a nearer resemblance to swine and dogs than to birds.

But since Mr. Dugald Stewart finds no difficulty in accepting this narrative, I shall content myself with the remark that so far from its being an illustration of the way in which proper nouns pass into common, there is no mention made in it except of common nouns. Those islanders possessed the names of the species, and not of the individuals, and they applied those names to such in-

dividuals as came under the species signified by them, or could in some way be reduced to it. By applying a common noun to several individuals one does not enlarge its meaning. But even if we were to suppose that the islanders in question widened the meaning of the word *birds*, the extension would be from a narrower species of things to a wider, and, therefore, from species to species, and not from individual to species; which is precisely the knot of the present difficulty, and the solution of which is in no way helped by the above narrative.

Besides, when there is a word received by common usage as signifying a given species of things, if anyone should happen to employ that word for indicating an object not included in the said species, it would be more just to say that this person errs in the meaning of the word or in the judgment whereby he assigns a certain object to a species to which it does not belong, than to say that the word itself has received a wider signification. Thus, if on seeing a camel I were to call it a horse, the only legitimate inference would be that I had mistaken either the species of the animal or else the meaning of the word 'horse.' That meaning would still remain as it was; nor could it be altered except with the general sanction of society.

proceed so that it may end in that external result. If we can succeed in correctly describing all this, the progressive steps which we have detailed as taking place in the formation of language will have received an adequate and satisfactory explanation.

Most men are satisfied with seeing the process of the mind described in its outward manifestation ; because their attention is absorbed by the external forms of the discourse. This is so much the case that even such a thinker as Dugald Stewart, when wishing to account for the formation of genera and species, unhesitatingly endorses the views expressed on the subject in the passage he has quoted from Smith, and declares that ' Smith's account appears to him to be equally simple and satisfactory.'

Now, I will admit, for the moment, that the whole of what Smith says in that passage is true, and that man did really pass from proper to common or appellative names. But I am still at a loss to see that our author has in any way explained the manner in which man forms those assortments of individuals which he afterwards calls genera and species. To tell us that man passes from proper to common names is not as yet to inform us what takes place in his mind. It is not to examine the interior operation corresponding to that transformation of names, nor to seek what faculties must necessarily be supposed for such an operation—in a word, it is not to give us any clue to the solution of those difficulties which, as Dugald Stewart himself says, have caused some philosophers to look upon the formation of genera and species as one of the most perplexing problems in metaphysics.

ARTICLE XII.

Tenth defect: The language of Smith throws a veil over the true point of the difficulty to be overcome in explaining the origin of abstract ideas.

157. Observe, moreover, how the language of Smith tends to mystify the reader respecting the nature of the difficulties which are to be met in explaining the formation of

the ideas of genera and species, or more generally of abstract ideas.

This it does by conveying incorrect notions and, as a consequence, misleading the mind and preventing it from seeing the real knot of the question.

Smith began by assuming that common names signified merely a multitude of individuals; but we have found that they apply only to single individuals of a given species.

Then in this use of the word 'multitude' for that of *species* there lurks another fallacy. A multitude of individuals always consists of a determinate or at least a finite number. The word 'species,' on the contrary, does not indicate a determinate number, but all possible individuals endowed with that character or quality which has been assumed for determining the species. This difference is of the greatest relevance to our question. Let us see how.

If there be question of explaining how man, after having given a name to an individual, may apply the same name to five others—and if it be assumed that by that name he means to indicate only one individual at a time, without any regard to the similarity which this individual has with others—it will only be necessary to suppose two faculties in him, namely, (1) the faculty of perceiving individuals (singulars), and (2) the faculty of indicating each of them by an arbitrary sign. He has had in this case five individuals and five signs; but as the signs, as well as the individuals, were independent of one another, instead of taking five different signs, he was free to repeat the same sign five times over, only attaching a different meaning to it each time.

But if, on the contrary, there is question of explaining how a proper has passed into a common name—or, in general, of how it was possible for man to invent common names—then the problem is changed into this other: 'How was it possible for man to name individual objects through a quality common to all?' And to answer this it will be necessary to suppose in man, not two, but four faculties—namely, (1) the faculty of conceiving individuals; (2) that of fixing his attention on their common qualities, or of forming abstract ideas ; (3) that of considering individuals in so far as endowed with these common qualities ; and (4) that of expressing by words all these things which he knows—that is to say, the individuals as such, the common qualities also as such, and the individuals in so far as endowed with these qualities. This last manner of naming individuals is what corresponds to the invention of common names.

To invent a common name, therefore, is, not to apply a proper name to a determinate number of individuals, but to designate by a name all the individuals characterised by one and the same quality. The inventor does not seek to know the number of those individuals. Whether they be few or many, it is no concern of his ; for his name stands equally good for all, even for those which have only a potential existence, and whose number is infinite.

On the contrary, when the same proper name is repeated and applied to several individuals, the repeater is obliged to know each of those individuals one after the other. In this case none of the individuals which is not present to his mind can be said to be called by that name ; whereas a common name embraces within its meaning those objects which are not individually known by the inventor—nay, which are pure possibilities and will never be realised.

Thus, assuming that a father has given the name of Peter to each of nine sons who now compose his family, it does not follow that if he were to have a tenth son, Peter must necessarily be his name. It would simply rest with the father to decide whether the same name should be repeated, or another introduced. So in the event of other sons following : each of them might be called Paul, or Anthony, or Andrew, or by any other name the father pleased. With common names the case is different. The word *man*, for instance is not applicable to one man only, or to those whom the inventor happens to know, and specially intends to indicate at the moment. Its applicability extends *per se* to all the individuals endowed with those common qualities which, taken in their assemblage, constitute what is known as *human nature.* No new act of the will is ever required to make valid the particular applications of this name ; for they were all virtually decreed through that act by which the inventor first imposed it and which in his mind was equivalent to this proposition : ' Every being which has or will have these qualities, I term a *man.*'

It is therefore manifest that a decree of this nature necessarily presupposes in the mind a universal and abstract idea, and is therefore not limited to a particular number, like that which is used in the imposition of proper names.

Let us conclude : to the assertion that a proper name has become common merely by being successively applied to many individuals, I would reply by the following distinction : Either that name has been applied to those individuals so as to be proper to each, and then it has not become a common name ; therefore the formation of common names has yet to be explained. Or else the proper name, being applied to many individuals, has acquired a new meaning, so that it now signifies, not the individual itself, but its *species*—that is to say, indicates individuals through a quality common to them all ; and in this case it remains to be explained how the change has been effected. In other words, how has it come to pass that the thought of a pure individuality has been replaced in the speaker's mind by the thought of a quality common to many individuals ; whence did the speaker draw this common quality ; and what is this quality which he has conceived and which he can separate from everything else and express by a distinct name ? In short, we are once more confronted by all those ideological problems of the Schoolmen of old, over which the elegant little narrative of Smith and Dugald Stewart may, indeed, throw a veil concealing them from the notice of incautious readers, but the solution of which is thereby rendered none the less necessary or difficult if we are to account for the existence of ideas.

On the supposition, then, that man has no other faculty but that of perceiving individual objects, it is quite impossible to explain the invention of common names, or the ideas of genera and species. Smith and Dugald Stewart, in their eagerness to make us believe that a proper name becomes common simply by being applied to a certain number of individuals, and that therefore a common name represents merely a ' multitude,' forgot to inform us of how many individuals that multitude ought to consist ; whether of two, or three, or four, &c. ; and it was well that they did so, since, as we have said, a common name is applicable of its own nature to all the individuals possible of a given species ; and their number is infinite.

158. As a further proof of the erroneousness of the opinion that a proper name becomes common simply by being applied to a certain number of individuals,[1] I may point out an absurdity which would follow from it. If what changes a proper name into common is its application to a certain number of individuals, clearly for every additional application the name will be ' more common,' or, which comes to the same, it will denote a wider species of things ; which is evidently false. Thus if a father has given the name of Peter to two of his sons, this name, according to Smith, has already become ' common ;' but if he should go on applying it to three or four, it will be more common ; and still more so, if to five, or six, or seven.

Certainly, if one wishes to abuse the meaning of the phrase *common name*, the thing may pass. One may very well, in a certain sense, call *common* that proper name which is applied to a number of distinct individuals—*e.g.* to those three, four, five, whose name happens to be Peter. But this is not the sense in which that phrase is used either by grammarians or by philosophers. It does not bring to our mind either a species or a genus of things ; and our business

---

[1] Our philosophers do not think it worth their while to support this opinion by proofs. They suppose it taken for granted by the reader. Their mode of reasoning is as follows : ' A name is common when it is applied to many individuals. Therefore, to invent a common name, man has only to apply a proper name to many individuals.' The argument would be perfect, provided the major proposition were certain ; but there lies the weak point. By a method like this you may demonstrate anything you please. Do you wish to establish some strange but favourite theory ? Have the precaution to frame from the first a proposition which implicitly contains that theory. Then declare positively that the proposition is certain ; or suppose it generally admitted ; or, if it suit you better, imply it throughout your discourse. Then analyse it and draw from it explicitly the theory which was already there ; and the thing is done, or rather it was done from the moment that your gratuitous premiss was unsuspectingly swallowed by your readers. The method is a most convenient one.

here is to explain how the ideas of *genera* and *species* are formed. Speaking in the first sense, the name becomes more common in proportion to the number of the individuals to whom it is successively applied. But in the sense understood in this our present discussion, a common name is common from the very first; nor does its commonness increase by adding ever so much to the number of its applications; for, as we have so often seen, it belongs of its own nature to all the individuals, not only actual but potential, of a given species. Take, for instance, the word *man*, apply it successively to one, to two, to three, to ten, to a hundred, or to a thousand human beings; will it mean anything more than an individual possessed of human nature quite irrespective of number, time, or place? Will its commonness ever be enlarged beyond that which it originally had? No.

159. From the systems of philosophers I appeal to the good sense of anyone. For a philosopher who stands formally pledged to a certain opinion, dreading the consequence which a frank and complete avowal of error would involve, is sometimes apt to deny that which is quite plain to everyone else; whereas any ordinary person with an average amount of good sense, is very well able to pronounce on matters that fall within his competence, as is, for instance, the signification of words, which is not by any means the exclusive property of philosophers, and, fortunately, cannot be so readily altered by their cavils. I take, then, the word *man*, though any other name would do as well, and I ask, Does this word denote only a certain number of individuals? Or is not its meaning equally applicable to an indeterminate and indefinite number of individuals, to every being which exists, actually or potentially, with human nature in it?

Now, if a common name, taken in the ordinary sense, includes the idea of the possibility of other individuals besides those in actual existence, it remains to be explained what this *possibility* linked with common names is; and how we come to have an idea which makes the meaning of a word fully as extensive as that possibility.

That everyone who uses a common name includes in its

meaning the idea of the possibility of all the individuals of the species which the name expresses, is an undeniable fact. And this idea is not merely universal but universal in the highest degree; for it has nothing to do with the individuals themselves: it only enables us to conceive an indefinitely greater and greater number of them.

Let us imagine a class of intellectual beings of such a nature as to be devoid of the power of conceiving this possibility, and therefore incapable of perceiving any but a given number of individuals. The perceptive power of these singular beings might be very unevenly distributed. In some it might be restricted to only five individuals; in others it might extend to ten; while again in others it might reach up to as many as a hundred, or a thousand, or a million, and so on; but never beyond an appointed limit, which it would be impossible for them to transcend. Now, with an intelligence like this let us compare that of man. He has, indeed, the power of perceiving a certain number of individuals actually existent —five, ten, a hundred, a thousand, &c.; but he can also in each case add, by a capacity natural to him, the concept of all the individuals existing only potentially, which is a very great deal more.

Now, the beings of the class we have imagined could invent no other than proper names; man, on the contrary, is able to invent common names, because his mind can conceive individuals in the state of pure possibility. And even if those beings were supposed to apply the same proper name to each of the individuals perceived by them (although this also would be impossible), the name would never be any other than proper (146); no common name would have been invented. Man, on the contrary, has power to invent common names; because, as I have said, he is able (1) to name an individual object in so far as endowed with a quality which can be held in common with it by other individual objects, irrespective of number, time, and place; and (2) to conceive the possibility of the indefinite repetition of such quality in any number whatsoever of like individuals.

160. In the signification of every common name, therefore, the following ideas are included: (1) the idea of a *quality*;

(2) the idea of the *aptitude* of that quality to belong to an individual ; (3) the idea of the *possibility* of the same quality being shared in by an indefinite number of individuals. And these same ideas are all included in every *specific* as well as *generic* idea. For a common name expresses a quality conceived as possible to be shared in by an indefinite number of individuals ; and that quality is what constitutes either a species or a genus, as the case may be.

What are we, then, to conclude ? That Smith's way of accounting for the formation of the ideas of genera and species is a failure. Reduced to few and clear expressions, his reasoning comes to the following : ' Proper names become common by being successively applied to many individuals. These names so applied hold in man's mind the place of the ideas of species and genera.'

My reply, stated also in a few words, is this : The mere application of a proper name to many individuals does not make it common. To become common that name must change its meaning. It must, instead of designating individuals by what constitutes their individuality, denote them by means of some quality which they hold in common. For this purpose an internal operation of the mind is required ; because it is only by the mind that the meaning of a word can be changed. But the mind cannot change the meaning of that name except (1) by directing it to signify a common quality, whereas previously it signified the individuality alone ; (2) by conceiving that quality as possible to be possessed by an indefinite number of individuals.

It is not, therefore, the common name that holds in our mind the place of these ideas ; but it is these ideas that give the name its signification. In other words, it is through ideas that the mind transforms proper into common names.

Therefore, even if it were true (which it is not) that man invents proper names first, and then renders them common, we are still left in the dark as to how he comes to form the ideas of genera and species ; for these ideas must be in his mind antecedently to, or at least simultaneously with, his invention of common names.

ARTICLE XIII.

What form the ideological problem takes in the reasonings of Smith and Dugald Stewart.

161. If what I have said thus far is correct, the theory of Smith and Dugald Stewart contributes nothing to the solution of the difficulty which I proposed at the beginning of this work.

Viewed in reference to the special question which we have now been discussing—namely, of the origin of the ideas of genera and species—that difficulty takes the following shape : ' We cannot form a generic or a specific idea without having the idea of a common quality ; and we cannot form the idea of a common quality without making a judgment. But a judgment presupposes the idea of a common quality, or of one of those very classes of things which go by the name of genera and species. How, then, is it possible for us to begin making judgments if all our ideas of common qualities, all our universal ideas, are acquired, and there is none innate in our minds ? '

ARTICLE XIV.

The system of the Nominalists does not solve the ideological problem.

162. Smith and Dugald Stewart, and Nominalists generally, have taken to denying the existence of universals and pronouncing them to be mere *words*, as the only means which they knew of disposing of the terrible questions : ' Whence are these mysterious universals ? How is it possible for the human mind to come by them ? '

Indeed, the difficulty which forms the main theme of the present work, and which may be called the *Syrtis* of philosophy, always confronts us when we seek to explain the formation of universals. Many of the modern philosophers, not knowing how to get out of this difficulty, have sought to persuade themselves that it is only a chimera, and that therefore, as Dugald Stewart says, what the ancients (poor creatures!) considered as one of the most difficult problems in metaphysics 'has a very simple solution,' such as that given by Smith.

But thus to evade the force of a difficulty is not to solve it ; for words can never fill the place of things, nor common names be a substitute for universal ideas. On the contrary, no common name can be formed without there being in the mind the corresponding universal idea.

This seems self-evident. But what truth is there which philosophers will not deny if they do not like it ?

And since the number of Nominalists, who imagine that they have discovered a very easy way of overcoming so grave a difficulty, is nowadays on the increase (A.D. 1830), I think it will not be useless to demonstrate still more clearly that the arguments by which Dugald Stewart seeks to corroborate his opinion are mere fallacies, and vitiated, every one of them, by a *petitio principii.*

ARTICLE XV.

How Dugald Stewart's error originated.

163. Words which have no meaning are but worthless sounds ; nor can they be of any use to us as a means of interchanging our thoughts. This proposition would seem to be as clear as noonday.

Now, general terms, as common names are, do not signify particular individuals. Therefore, they must either have no meaning at all, or signify universal ideas.

This argument could alone have sufficed to convince Mr. Dugald Stewart that to suppose that universal ideas have no existence, and that what we call a universal idea is in reality nothing but a word, was an absurdity. It is an argument so simple and so conclusive that one may well wonder how it could have escaped the attention of the Scottish philosopher.

164. If I were to offer a conjecture as to what may have been the cause of such an oversight, I would say that it was this : he found that he could describe the use which we make of general terms or common names without once introducing the words *genera, species, universal ideas* ; and having suc- ceeded in eliminating these words from the discourse, he

thought he had also succeeded in proving that we could dispense with the ideas attached to them.

Let us hear how he accounts for the use of general terms :
' When we speak of conceiving or understanding a general proposition, we mean nothing more than that we have a conviction (founded on our previous use of the words in which it is expressed), that we have it in our power, at pleasure, to substitute instead of the general terms some one of the individuals comprehended under them.'[1] By this passage it seems to me that he wished to say : In using general terms (common names) we have no need of connecting universal ideas with them. All that we require is, to have contracted the habit of substituting for them in our minds, *ad libitum*, one or another of the individuals which they designate. Given, then, that we have the power to conceive individual objects, and that we have formed the habit of using words in the manner aforesaid, the formation of reasonings of general signification can be readily explained.   Thus it is, according to him, that words take the place of universal ideas.

ARTICLE XVI.

The theory of Dugald Stewart sins by a petitio principii.

165. But in the argument of our philosopher there is a *petitio principii.*

To show this I argue as follows : How do you account for the habit which you say we contract, of substituting for a given general term, not individuals taken at random, but only certain individuals designated and determined by that term ? For example, you never take the term *man* to signify a beast or a stone, but always an individual of the human species.   What is the reason of this ?   Is there, perhaps, in the term taken materially an intrinsic virtue which prevents your taking it in any sense but one ? This you can by no means say ; for between the word materially taken and the individuals signified by it there is no necessary connection.

[1] *Elements of the Philosophy of the Human Mind*, chap. iv. sec. 3, p. 196 ; London ed. 1811.

The word itself is a mere sound, although it often reminds us of things which are neither sound nor anything like it. I should wish to know what connection the sound which you utter when you say *man* has with the individual designated by it. Between that sound and this individual there can be no other connection than such as is established by our mind.

166. You will say that this connection is arbitrary; and I agree with you so far as this, that in case it were proposed by the word *man* to signify what we now call *animal,* and the proposal were unanimously agreed to by a society, the members of that society would understand one another when using that word to signify *animal,* just as we now understand one another in using it in the more restricted sense of *human being.*

Well, then, let it be granted that the power of substituting for a given common name certain individuals, and not any others, is simply the result of a free conventional understanding. But here comes the difficulty. I ask: How can such a result be brought about? Perhaps by connecting with that name a fixed number of individuals. Doubtless this may be, if we suppose, for example, a compact to the effect that three different men shall be called by one and the same name, for which no individual may be substituted save one or another of these men. But either this would be only a proper name— that is, a word chosen arbitrarily for signifying each of the three men (146)—or, if it were a common name (as, for example, the word *friend*), the determination of its meaning to one or other of the said three men would be due to the compact in question; and in this case two things instead of one would have to be accounted for—*i.e.* (1) how is it that the name is 'common'? (2) how can a name which is common be used as 'proper'? In short, the difficulty to be solved is: Whence comes it that we connect certain individuals with one of those names which are called 'common'? And this difficulty, make what suppositions you will, can never be avoided.

As I have already said, the question is not as to how we can substitute for common names certain individuals which we have numbered and determined for that purpose beforehand. If this were the only question there would be no difficulty in it. We should only require an association of ideas or a simple reminiscence, which, on our hearing that word, would awaken in us the thought of one of those two, three, five, ten, determinate individuals, to designate which exclusively we have appointed it. The case stands far otherwise with common names. What must be explained in regard to a common name is, how we are able to substitute for it, not an individual purposely determined upon beforehand from among a fixed number of individuals experimentally known by us, but an individual taken from an indefinite number, including, not only those which have subsisted or subsist now without falling under our experience, but also that inexhaustible number whose existence is and shall ever be merely potential.

Thus, for example, when we use the common name *horse*, it is not by any means necessary that we should substitute in its stead one of the subsistent horses which we have seen, nor yet one of those which subsist without our having seen them. Indeed, that word, taken by itself, does not mean a subsistent horse at all. And even were we obliged to substitute for it one of the subsistent horses, would it not be indifferent which of them we substituted? But why indifferent? Is it perhaps because we have seen one by one every member of the equine family in this world, and made as many distinct compacts to call each of them *horse*? This certainly cannot be the reason. The thought of our imposing a name on so many animals one by one, and of our neighbours entering into so many compacts with us, is too ludicrous to be entertained. Especially when we consider that horses are only one of the multitudinous species of things for each of which we require a separate name so as to render possible our daily intercourse with one another. If, then, to have a common name for which we may be able to substitute this or that individual, we must follow the process traced out by our philosopher, we may as well give up the hope of ever possessing one. And what would put a climax to our misfortune would be this, that as often as a new individual thing happened to appear, we could not know its name without resuming the task which we had so laboriously gone through before ; and thus our whole life would have to be consumed in the drudgery of imposing names. What a prospect !

167. No ; it is not in this way that common names are formed. We connect with them, not a determinate number of individuals cognised one after the other, but a *species* of individuals—that is to say, all possible individuals characterised by a common quality. When using a common name we, indeed, substitute individuals for it, but individuals taken (1) not at random ; for if this were the case there would no longer be any distinction of species or of genera ; and (2) not in consequence of conventional understandings made in reference to particular individuals; for this would be an infinite process. On the contrary, the substitution (1) proceeds in accordance with a universal rule, that makes us see whether the individuals are possessed of the *common quality* on account of which the common name has been imposed ; and (2) it is not limited to individuals known to us, nor yet to such as exist around us or anywhere, but is open alike to all individuals that are *possible*, or mentally conceivable as possessed of that common quality.

Hence it is that so soon as one of the individuals possessed of that quality comes under our notice, even though for the first time, we at once know what to call it, being already acquainted with the *species* to which it belongs, and with the name by which that species is denoted.

168. Therefore, the substitution-theory, as unfolded by Dugald Stewart, is of no avail for explaining the difficulty in hand ; since the substitution of which he speaks could not extend either to things merely possible, or to those which are not individually known to us; both of which classes fall, nevertheless, within the scope of our thought.

Consequently, by denying on the one hand the necessity of universal ideas, and by maintaining on the other that it is enough if, when speaking, we substitute certain determinate individuals in the place of common names, our philosopher simply contradicts himself, inasmuch as the power to make this substitution essentially implies the possession of universal ideas. Without these ideas we could not know which among all the individuals ought to be substituted for a given common name rather than for another. In other words, before one can call anything by its right name, one must needs know to what species or genus the thing belongs. Thus, so long as a flower remains hidden from me under the grass, I cannot apply to it the name of *flower*; but the instant it is uncovered and I see it, I know that it belongs to the class of things called flowers.

ARTICLE XVII.

Another error of Dugald Stewart.

169. Similar to the above is the error committed by Dugald Stewart where he expresses his views on the formation of common names in this other way : 'According to this view of the process of the mind, in carrying on general speculations, that IDEA which the ancient philosophers considered as the essence of an individual is nothing more than the particular quality or qualities in which it resembles other individuals of the same class, and in consequence of which a generic name is applied to it. It is the possession of this quality that entitles the individual to the generic appellation, and which therefore may be said to be essential to its classification with that particular genus. But as all classifications are to a certain degree arbitrary, it does not necessarily follow that it is more essential to its existence as an individual than various other qualities, which we are accustomed to regard as accidental ; in other words (if I may borrow the language of modern philosophy [1]), this quality forms its nominal, but not its real essence.' [2]

170. Whoever examines this passage can easily see in it the style of an author who, not feeling quite sure of his main point for want of clear proof, seeks to uphold it by a

---

[1] Poor modern philosophy if this s its language !

[2] *Elements of the Philosophy of the Human Mind*, chap. iv. sec. 2, p. 173 ; London ed. 1811.

reasoning filled with that sort of phrases which, without laying down anything fully definite, are yet, when taken together, sufficiently plausible to make one believe that there is a logical connection of ideas even when such is not the case.

To begin with the last part, I would remark that the proposition ' this quality forms the nominal but not the real essence' supposes that there are two essences instead of one ; and therefore admits more than the author wishes to deny.

171. But I will not be too exacting about the use of words ; I will only ask whether by *nominal essence* Dugald Stewart means a mere word, as would seem from his way of expressing himself in other places, as well as from the aim of his reasoning, which is to prove that universals are nothing.

If he takes a *nominal essence* as being more than a mere word, then all his reasoning is thrown away ; for in this case general terms (or common names) would express something beyond themselves, something objective.

172. Now, that this is his view of a *nominal essence* we know from his words in the passage just quoted, for he says that this essence is a quality truly possessed by the individual, and also that ' it is the possession of this quality that entitles the individual to the generic appellation.'[1] If this quality were nothing, the individual could not possess it, nor receive from it the name of the genus. Moreover, he admits in the human mind the faculty of thinking of one of the qualities of an individual without thinking of the others which equally enter into its composition : as for instance when he writes, ' The classification of different objects supposes a power of attending to some of their qualities or attributes without attending to the rest.'[2]

We have, then, three admissions from him—namely, (1) that the several qualities of individuals are something real ; (2) that we have the faculty of thinking of each of these qualities by itself alone, and apart from the individuals in

[1] *Elements*, &c., chap. iv. sec. 2, p. 173 ; London ed. 1811.
[2] *Ibid.* p. 155.

which it exists; (3) that when we think of these qualities alone and isolated, we have before our mind a veritable object, because they are true.

Let us apply this to the qualities of bodies, such as colour, flavour, smell, sonorousness, size, hardness, fluidity, &c. Now, as we are not at present treating of the question of the existence of bodies, but assuming with Dugald Stewart this existence to be real, it will be enough for us to bear in mind that, according to his own principles, we have as many distinct objects of our thought as are the corporeal qualities. But if so, the names of these qualities—*i.e.* the words *colour*, *flavour*, &c. (all of them abstract words)—must likewise have an objective meaning. They are not, therefore, mere sounds; there is something truly corresponding to them, that is to say, the qualities themselves—whatever these may be in the things in which they are found. But if abstract words really signify something, it follows that the same must be said of common or appellative names, such as *coloured*, *flavoured*, &c., *body*, *man*, &c.; because these names merely signify in general *that which has colour, that which has flavour*, &c., *that which has corporeity, that which has humanity*, &c. Therefore, on Dugald Stewart's own showing, common names are not meaningless words, but truly significative of an object distinct from them.

ARTICLE XVIII.

Other errors of Dugald Stewart: the inadequacy of his theory to solve the ideological problem is further demonstrated.

173. Here Dugald Stewart might reply: I accept your proof that abstract as well as common names indicate something truly objective, and I am therefore ready to cancel whatever I may have in any way intimated to the contrary. But what I still maintain is, that that objective something is merely 'the particular quality, or aggregate of qualities, on account of which one individual resembles others.' As, then, this quality or aggregate of qualities is only in the individuals, it cannot itself be any other than individual or particular. There is, therefore, no universal here.

I shall certainly not reopen the question proposed by Plato, as to whether abstract qualities have an existence outside of a mind, and distinct from the individual beings in which we see them realised. This would in no way serve my present purpose. Very willingly do I concede to Mr. Dugald Stewart that the qualities of which we are speaking do not exist outside of a mind, except in the individuals themselves. But he, on his part, has conceded that our mind has the power of considering these qualities, and does actually consider them separately from the individuals, just as if they existed by themselves alone. Indeed, this is a fact about which there can be no doubt.

Now, such being the fact, the conclusion which I draw from it is, that our mind has a universal for the immediate object of its attention ; because a quality considered separately from the individual is a universal wholly independent of the word which expresses it.

174. If I can succeed in making this last assertion good, I believe the following consequences will flow from it : (1) that our mind can have a universal for its object ; (2) that to this object we can give a name; (3) that, therefore, there are names which express universals, and hence are not words devoid of objective meaning, for which we through mere habit substitute certain individuals.

When we say that a quality considered by our mind separately from the individual is a universal, we mean neither more nor less than that we can conceive it as existing in an indefinite number of individuals : and in the ordinary acceptation of language, ' to be conceivable as existing in an indefinite number of individuals,' or ' to be a universal,' or ' to be common,' is all one and the same.

To the existence of a quality as universal corresponds its existence as particular : by which is meant an existence that cannot be conceived as common to many individuals, but only as determined and proper to one individual.

What renders a universal or common quality particular is the individuality of the being to which it is applied. Hence, so long as qualities are not conceived by us as existing in determinate individuals, they remain common for us ; so that we are at liberty to associate them with any individual we please.   But no sooner are they conjoined with an individual than they are also individualised through it, and therefore are called particular : hence the whiteness, size, &c., of one body is not the whiteness, size, &c., of another body.

Since, then, on the one hand a quality is particular only in so far as it really exists in an individual, and on the other, as Mr. Dugald Stewart himself allows, we can think of a quality without thinking of the individual to which it belongs, I conclude that we have the power of conceiving it simply as possible to be realised, and this quite irrespectively of any of its actual realisations—which is what Dr. Reid calls *simple apprehension*, and Dugald Stewart seems to call *conception*. And if we have this power, then I maintain that the object before our mind in this case is a universal in the sense which Ideologists attribute to this word.   The quality of whiteness, for example, is not conjoined with any one body so exclusively that we may not conceive it as communicable to an indefinite number of bodies ; so much so that if we had creative power we could, through the idea which we have of this quality, produce any number of white bodies we thought fit.

175. Hence it follows that the whiteness so conceived by our mind is not a meaningless word, as Dugald Stewart seems to hold ; neither is it any of those whitenesses which we have seen really existing in white bodies.   I say it is not any of these whitenesses, because every one of them was particular ; and, as we have said, a particular whiteness is in the particular body in such a manner that it cannot be transferred from it to any other body, nor yet be common to many bodies even in thought.

For how could I conceive the whiteness of one body transferred to another body, without the first being deprived of its whiteness?   Either the body of which I speak is white only at the surface, while its bulk is of another colour, or else it is white all through—like chalk, for example, which, owing also to its friableness, leaves its own colour on the bodies over which it is rubbed. Now, let the reader consider the differences between bodies being made white by means of the whiteness really existing in a particular body, and being made white by means of the idea of whiteness in general, which, as I contend, is in our mind.

First difference. However white a body may be, it cannot communicate its whiteness to other bodies, unless it be friable, and this to a degree sufficient to allow the removal from it of those white particles which are to cover the surface of the body to be coloured. On the contrary, he who being, as we suppose, possessed of creative power, brings into existence a number of white bodies, simply copies in each case from the idea of whiteness he has in his mind, and which has certainly no need of friableness or any such quality in order to be communicated to bodies.

Second difference. If the body which is used for giving whiteness to another has but a very thin coat of this colour, the process will cause its own whiteness to fade, or even to vanish altogether. On the contrary, the creation of white bodies by the intelligent being of whom we speak, would neither destroy nor cause the least diminution in his idea of whiteness in general.

Third difference. Supposing even that the colouring body is friable and white all through—as, for instance, chalk—it cannot whiten another body without suffering a loss proportionate to the amount of whiteness which it imparts. It will, no doubt, still present a white appearance, but not the same white surface it exhibited before. This surface has gone from it, and passed to the other body.

Hence we may draw the conclusion that, speaking accurately, it cannot be said that by the whitening process the whiteness really existent in one body is communicated to another. All that takes place in that process is, that a multitude of white particles are removed, as I have just said, from the first body, and given to the second instead. But a removal, a change of place, is not a *communication.*

It is thus manifest that the whiteness really inherent in a particular body is so strictly particular as to be wholly incommunicable. It cannot, then, be, with its identical self, in more than one body at the same time.

On the contrary, a being capable of creating could never be imagined as taking off their real whiteness from existing bodies in order to give it to such others as he chose to create. He could only be conceived to give existence to the new particular whitenesses, by taking for his exemplar the general whiteness which his mind contemplates.

Fourth difference. Even if a white body were supposed to share its whiteness with others, it could not go on doing this *ad infinitum*, since by each fresh communication of itself it must necessarily suffer a diminution in its mass, and at last disappear altogether.

Not so with the idea of whiteness in general. By means of this idea a being possessed of creative power could go on producing white bodies to any extent, without the idea itself ever growing less, or being less capable of other and other realisations *ad infinitum*.

Therefore, the ideal whiteness which would enable the said being to create an indefinite number of bodies, is not that particular and essentially incommunicable whiteness which is received in an individual body.

176. Nor would it do to say, that a being possessed of creative power would produce white bodies by virtue of this power alone, without having any need of the idea of whiteness. For we must bear in mind that creative force, taken by itself alone, does not determine its possessor to create bodies of one colour rather than another ; nay, it cannot even be conceived as determined to the act of creation at all, unless the mind present to it the objects to be created.

In the same manner it would be unreasonable to object that because creation is a thing which transcends our way of understanding, and cannot, therefore, be brought within our rules of reasoning, the supposition I have made of a creating being is no solid basis for an argument. For I have not introduced this supposition as the basis on which to raise my argument, but simply as a means of better elucidating the point in discussion. For the validity of my argument it would be sufficient to suppose a man who imagines to himself any number of possible white bodies he pleases, and then ask whether the whiteness thus imagined by him is identically the same whiteness which he has actually seen in individual bodies; and it seems to me evident that it is not, even as it seems evident that it is not the whiteness which a creating being would impart to the bodies produced by him. The whiteness actually seen in individual bodies is inseparable from them, individual in its nature, and not communicable; whereas the whiteness which one imagines in possible bodies can be communicated indefinitely.

To be convinced beyond the possibility of doubt, that one of these two whitenesses is not the other, we have only to consider that while, on the one hand, we are all conscious of perceiving the whiteness of white bodies, whenever we see them, and understand very well that the particular whiteness of those bodies is inseparable from them, we are, on the other hand, equally conscious of having it in our power to imagine other and other bodies similar in whiteness to those we have seen.

Let us suppose that at a given moment a man brings up simultaneously before his imagination all the white bodies he has seen in his life. Could he not then still picture to himself as many more bodies, also white, but only possible to exist? Now, I ask, is the whiteness of this additional array of bodies imagined and conceived by this man the same as that which he had really seen in existing bodies, or is it another? It cannot certainly be the same; for the whiteness of the bodies seen is strictly individual; and we have supposed that all the white bodies ever seen by him are present to his interior sight. It is clear, then, that no matter how many cases of whiteness may have fallen under our experience, there is still in us the power of conceiving other similar cases without end —I mean, cases of a whiteness which is not real, but only pictured by the imagination, nay, only conceived in thought. I say, only conceived in thought, for it must be remembered that here we are speaking purely of the objects of thought.

177. If our capabilities extended no further than to recalling

the whiteness which we had actually seen in individual bodies, it might then well be said that the only faculty which we possessed, in addition to the faculty of sense, would be that of the reminiscence of phantasms. But besides the faculties of sense and reminiscence, we have also, as all admit, the faculty of simple conception, as well as the imaginative faculty, by means of which we may, if we wish, go on indefinitely multiplying to ourselves individual objects similar to those which we have seen. Now, it is of the existence in us of these last two faculties that an account must be given ; and given it cannot be so long as we suppose with Dugald Stewart that our mind is devoid of universal ideas —*i.e.* ideas representing qualities detached from the individuals—and of the power of attributing these qualities to an indefinite number of merely possible or thinkable individuals.[1]

[1] Galluppi and Degerando, in consequence of what had been said by Dr. Reid, declared themselves against ideas as defined by the ancients— *i.e.* as *representations of external objects* – and this on the ground that, if that definition were admitted, the truth of ideas, or their conformity with the objects represented, would be impossible to prove, and that thus scepticism would be inevitable. ' Ideas,' says Galluppi, ' are true, not because they accord with the objects, but because they act immediately on the objects and take hold of them.' Degerando writes : ' In the primitive truths, ideas invest and-take an immediate hold of the objects ; I grant him this doctrine.' (*Critique de la Connaissance*, vol. i. pp. 38, 41.)

As I have already observed (n. 106), the Schoolmen had seen this difficulty, and, in order to meet it, had said that ideas are not the *objects* of our thoughts, but simply the means through which our mind perceives the objects. But this solution, taken in its *primâ facie* sense, did not explain the difficulty, but merely removed it a step. The same remark may be applied to the theory of Galluppi and of the other authors I have named.

' Ideas take hold of and invest external objects :' this is a strange sentence, and savours much more of poetry than of philosophy. There is no necessity for it ; and moreover it is false and absurd.

But, leaving this aside, I have to observe that it is not enough to know whether—to use the language of our philosophers – ideas invest and take hold of the objects themselves. It is necessary to know furthermore whether this is only accidental to some ideas, or whether it constitutes their very nature. If it constitutes the very nature of ideas, it must be true of all of them ; for nothing can exist without that which constitutes its nature.

If it is only accidental to some ideas, then the original question returns ; and we must (1) define what is an idea ; and (2) explain how it happens that ideas invest and take hold of external objects ; for, this being only accidental to them, they could exist without it.

Now, I maintain that not all our ideas can be such as to invest and take hold of their external objects really existent, and that this union with those objects is not essential to their nature.

To prove this, I make use of all those arguments by which the difference between *ideas* and *real things*, as also their independence of each other, is established. For example, whiteness considered in general is different from and independent of the real whiteness which we see on a wall ; and not only whiteness considered in general, but also the

Now, if we have the power of which I speak, and if, therefore, the whiteness which we conceive only as possible is not the whiteness really existing in the particular individuals which we have seen (for by the definition it stands before our mind wholly apart from the individuals to which it really belongs), I contend that it is not, and cannot be, a mere name. Although what I have already said in reference to common names seems sufficient to demonstrate this, I will nevertheless prove it also in another way. The strong

particular whiteness of an individual wall conceived merely by way of *simple apprehension.*

This distinction between our ideas and the real things of which we think by means of them is established by St. Augustine in a similar way. He observes that if it were true that our ideas invested and took hold of real things it would necessarily follow that no change could take place in these things without a corresponding change in the ideas we have of them. For instance, I love Paul because I believe him to be virtuous. Now, Paul might alter for the worse without my knowing it, and I should still go on loving him as before. It is evident from this that I love Paul for what I think him to be, and not for what he really is; in other words, I love him as he is in my idea, and not as he is in himself. Therefore, my idea does not invest and take hold of his real self. If he were always in my idea exactly as he is in his own self, I should cease to love him for his virtue the very moment he became a bad man. Contrariwise, the good opinion I have of a man might be altered without any change taking place in him. He might be as good as ever, while I, deceived perhaps by some false appearance, thought very ill of him. In this case, says St. Augustine, ' in illo homine nihil mutatum est ; in mente autem mea mutata est utique ipsa æstimatio quæ de illo aliter se habebat et aliter habet ' (*De Trinitate*, lib. ix. c. 6). In short, if our ideas invested and took hold of the real object itself, they would always have a necessary conformity with it ; we should then be infallible ; and thus in order to avoid *scepticism* one would have to fall into the opposite extreme,

of upholding the doctrine of human *infallibility.*

What may be said, therefore, of our ideas is, not that they of their own nature invest and take hold of the object in real existence, but that we believe that, through them, we invest and take hold of it when, on occasion of its acting on our senses, we refer them to it. But to be certain that we are not deceived in this belief, we stand in need of a logical demonstration the nature of which I shall endeavour to set forth in another place.

For the present I shall only add one more remark in elucidation of this question. I ask : ' Does the belief of which I speak—namely, that when we refer an idea to a being in real existence, our idea or, to speak more accurately, our thought invests and takes hold of something really existing—belong to the idea itself ? Is it an element entering into its formation ? '

No. The *idea* and the *belief* that there really exists a being corresponding to the idea (nn. 60, 64, 90, 98) are two wholly different things; so much so that the idea is perfect and entire even without such belief; nor does this belief add anything thereto. In other words, the act by which we come to know that a certain object really exists differs essentially from the act by which we have the idea. Thus our intellectual operations are of two different kinds—*i.e.* (1) that by which we have the idea of a thing; (2) that by which we are persuaded that a thing corresponding to that idea exists really and in itself. This distinction of the two principal operations of our understanding is of the greatest importance.

tendency which modern philosophy exhibits in favour of Nominalism must be my apology for detaining the reader so long on this one point.

If the whiteness conceived in thought, but not really existing in any of the objects actually seen by us, were a mere name, the necessary inference would be that whenever we might happen to imagine a white body or a number of white bodies, without naming them, we should be doing nothing at all. But who will ever believe that when he imagines things which he has never individually seen or heard of or named, he does nothing? Is there anyone amongst us who has not at some time or other found a soothing relief in cheerful imaginings, although purely chimerical? Who does not occasionally feel pleasure in indulging in those sweet reveries which that wonderful power, the intellectual imagination, conjures up before him in his gayest moments, and while he is in a perfectly wakeful state? Who will be able to persuade the lover that the flattering visions by which he constantly nurtures his fondest hopes have nothing objective in them, do not exist even in his mind, in his soul? Who can persuade the poet that his melodious lays when not expressing things individually seen and handled by himself are but 'a tale full of sound, signifying nothing'? If they are this, how does it come to pass that, if he be a poet of the highest order, he, with an art almost divine, enchants his contemporaries and fills all succeeding ages with admiration, while no one else can produce a similar magic effect? Whence does he fetch such sounds as these? What deity inspires him with them? What spirit makes him break forth into them automaton-like? Has he, then, ere giving them utterance, no concept, no thought, no imagery to inspire his soul when, on the contrary, his whole song is one stupendous flight from the miserably narrow boundaries of these individual things called the sensible world, up to those interminable fields of the unseen, where an inexhaustible imagination can expatiate with the utmost freedom? Finally, what would a man who, being gifted with inventive genius, is eagerly striving after some new discoveries for the good of his fellow-men, say to a philosopher who were unceremoniously to address him thus : 'Pardon me, but you must be very simple. What is the use of wasting your time and energy in pursuits of this sort ? I say *wasting*, because, as you ought to know, for a man to try to think of anything except individual objects in actual existence is as good as the attempt to put wisdom into the head of an incurable idiot, or to make first-class music out of the rattlings of a lot of pebbles shaken together. This, in very truth, is what people are pleased to call the applying of oneself to new inventions, to the writing of original works, and such like novelties. Talk of ideas not yet realised in some concrete form ! I tell you that they are mere names—*vox et præterea nil.* I would advise you, therefore, to set aside these Utopian aspirations, and take to the more sensible plan of being content with what is practicable—the perceiving and recollecting of concrete objects.'

Those, then, who assert that man has no ideas of the several qualities of beings except when he regards these qualities in the individuals known to him—and that, therefore, qualities considered abstractedly from all individuals, or in a state of pure possibility, are mere names without any objective meaning—fall into a great mistake. However unconsciously or against their will, they stand committed to a principle which logically involves the abdication and denial of all the sciences and of all the arts. They leave themselves no means of accounting for the intellectual imagination. The man of these philosophers can have nothing but a meagre and inexplicable reminiscence of the things he has seen.[1] He is without power to

---

[1] From this we see that *Nominalism* is a system which sterilises humanity. According to it, the ethical and metaphysical sciences, and, indeed, all sciences generally, are nothing but a dream. For every branch of the human knowable is necessarily based on universal principles. Now, with the abolition of knowledge disappears, as a matter of course, all hope of any noble action, and of the true well-being of society. Such is *Nominalism*, so far-reaching are the consequences of certain doctrines which, considered in themselves, seem to be mere intellectual puzzles reserved for a few speculative thinkers, who would fain quit this real world of ours in order to live in one made up of abstractions. But they do not in fact quit the real world. No one can quit the real world as regards the effect of his thoughts. Let once an erroneous and apparently abstract principle be put into a theory, and that principle will be sure sooner or later to develop into practical results. It will introduce itself into the affairs of human life, into the order of society, and will, to your surprise, befoul the first and disturb the second, sowing evil broadcast everywhere. Everywhere it will pass from the aerial minds of the most abstruse

imagine possibilities. Thus the source whence flows all rational and human action is for him a sealed fountain. For human action springs from the power of working for and obtaining future and possible goods ; and possible things cannot be imagined unless the mind has conceived their qualities as possible— *i.e.* participable by an indefinite number of beings not yet subsistent.

ARTICLE XIX.

The Nominalism of Dugald Stewart flows from the principles of Reid.

178. The preceding observations have a special force against the system of Dugald Stewart owing to the circumstance that he follows the principles of Reid on the nature of ideas.

Locke, in common with the Schoolmen of old, distinguished

metaphysicians even into the manual occupations of the skilled artisan and the illiterate rustic, and everywhere leave its mark—*i.e.* degeneracy and corruption.

Modern *Nominalism* had its origin in *Materialism.* As a rule .*Nominalists* have always been *Materialists.* Hobbes was a staunch supporter of *Nominalism.* After him, those who sturdily denied the existence of universals were La Mettrie (*L'Homme Machine*), Helvetius (*L'Homme,* Vol. I. sect. ii. ch. 5), the author of the *Système de la Nature* (ch. x.), and others of that stamp.

Locke, on the other hand, placed the difference between man and the brute precisely in the faculty which the former has of forming abstract ideas (see *Essay on the Human Understanding,* Book I., ch. xi., § 10).

He admitted abstractions and universal ideas for the same reason for which the Materialists gainsaid them—namely, because in them consists the characteristic difference between man and animals. The Materialists wanted to do away with this difference ; Locke acknowledged its existence, and had at least the intention of establishing it.

,If man's capabilities do not reach any further than the perceiving of sensible and individual things, he can have no higher faculty than that of sense ; for to the sense belongs the perception of individual things. There-

fore, human reason, taken as distinct from sense, is nothing but an empty name. Now, whatever may be the principle of the corporeal sense, it is always such that at least its identity must cease with the dissolution of the corporeal organ. Hence the saying, ' Unus interitus hominis et jumentorum' (Eccl. iii. 19).

As to Mr. Dugald Stewart, I am full sure that the thought of this intimate connection between *Nominalism* — a system so abstract and theoretical—and *Materialism,* never crossed his mind ; else I sincerely believe he would never have been a Nominalist. In thus regretfully recording my impression that by not sufficiently calculating the consequences of his principles he was, for once, wanting in his usual caution, I think I do him an honour.

Speaking in general, it seems to me that it would be an excellent thing if certain philosophical writers of our day had by their side some friendly counsellor to dissuade them from trying conclusions with Scepticism, which is, in point of fact, the ultimate outcome of Materialism ; or at least to give them some wise hints on the way of discharging that duty better than they do. The best of all advisers would be a reverential and attentive study of the great masters whom the Church possesses on all these matters—I mean her Fathers and her Doctors.

the idea of a thing from the thing itself, and held that the first, and not the second, was the proximate term of the act of intellectual perception. According to him, therefore, the idea stood intermediate between the external realities and the mind which perceives them. Reid, on the contrary, maintained that these realities are perceived by us, not through any ideas (universals), but by a direct and immediate act; and such is also the opinion of Dugald Stewart.

Now, so far as individuals are concerned, the real object perceived by the mind truly exists, since the real individuals exist. But with ideas the case is different; since they have no existence outside the mind, there was no way of accounting for them in the system of Reid. Dugald Stewart, therefore, discarded them altogether, and set them down as mere empty names.[1]

[1] Dugald Stewart, speaking of the opinion of Dr. Reid respecting universals, passes the following judgment upon it : 'The long experience I have had of the candour of this excellent author encourages me to add that, in stating his opinion on the subject of universals, he has not expressed himself in a manner so completely satisfactory to my mind as on most other occasions' (*Elements of the Philosophy of the Human Mind*, ch. iv. sect. 3, p. 194; London ed. 1811).

To me it seems, moreover, that it would be difficult to reconcile in this matter Dr. Reid with himself. Certain it is that Dugald Stewart, when trying to conjecture what was on this point the opinion of that excellent philosopher, and to bring it into harmony with his principles on ideas, finds himself embarrassed. Here is the passage in which Dr. Reid expresses his opinion concerning universals : 'A universal,' he says, 'is not an object of any external sense, and therefore cannot be imagined ; but it may be distinctly conceived. When Mr Pope says "The proper study of mankind is man," I conceive his meaning distinctly ; although I neither imagine a black or a white, a crooked or a straight man. I can conceive a thing that is impossible; but I cannot distinctly imagine a thing that is impossible. I can conceive a proposition or a demonstration, but I cannot imagine

either. I can conceive understanding and will, virtue and vice, and other attributes of the mind ; but I cannot imagine them. In like manner I can distinctly conceive universals, but I cannot imagine them' (*Ib.* p. 195). The obvious and natural interpretation of this passage would seem to be that Dr. Reid looked upon universals as being true objects of thought, and not mere empty names. But then this would be in contradiction to his theory on ideas ; for in it he denied the existence of any such thing as an object of thought distinct from our mind as well as from external things. Hence Dugald Stewart endeavours to construe these words of Reid in a sense consistent with other passages of the same author ; but his interpretation—very ingenious, I must say—does not seem to me at all satisfactory. He writes : 'It appears from this passage that by *conceiving universals* Dr. Reid means nothing more than understanding the meaning of propositions involving general terms' (*Ibid.*). But to be convinced that this is not in accordance with the mind of Reid, it is enough to observe that in the passage quoted from him just before, he distinguishes 'conceiving a proposition' from 'conceiving universals,' and says that as we 'can conceive propositions', so we 'can distinctly conceive universals.' Moreover, I have already proved that general terms could not be of any

179. I shall not now inquire whether the system of Reid be, in this part, true or false, as the reader is already in possession of my views on the subject. Neither shall I examine whether Dugald Stewart formed a correct estimate of that system, or whether it follows as a necessary consequence of the same that one might deny the existence of universals, and suppose that mere names can take the place of them.

For my present purpose it is enough to note that Dugald Stewart believed himself bound to his conclusion by the logical necessity of the system ; nor, indeed, could he do otherwise from his own point of view. Having previously adopted the principle that there are no ideas intermediate between the external objects intellectually perceived by us and ourselves who perceive them, he had no alternative left but to throw universals completely overboard, since in them there is no external object really existent.

Now, as I have already proved (1) that mere empty names do not suffice to account for that act by which our spirit imagines beings which are only possible, and in an infinitely greater number than those which it has individually perceived by the aid of the senses; (2) that the same insufficiency applies to the ideas of the qualities perceived in the individual beings themselves, and considered in so far as adhering to these beings ; (3) but that, moreover, it is necessary that our mind should conceive these qualities in themselves, apart from the individuals, and therefore in a state of pure possibility— it is manifest that the system of Dugald Stewart is defective, because insufficient to account for this last mode of conceiving whereby universals are formed as well as contemplated by our mind.

use to us unless we attached to them true universal ideas (nn. 162-167). It is therefore necessary either to seek for some better way of reconciling the theory of Reid on universals with his theory on ideas, or to concede that one or the other of these theories is erroneous. On the other hand, it seems to me evident that we cannot establish a true theory on ideas before having solved the question about universals—a question which has so much exercised all the philosophers of antiquity ; and this observation ought, to say the least, to make us entertain very grave doubts concerning the soundness of the theory of Reid.

ARTICLE XX.

*In explaining how our mind conceives the similarity of obj.cts, the same
difficulty is met with under another aspect.*

180. There are many other reflections to be made upon
the passage I have quoted from Dugald Stewart.

In the first place, I beg the reader to consider how he
defines the essence of an individual: ' The essence of an
individual,' he says, ' is nothing more than the particular
quality or qualities in which it resembles other individuals of
the same class ; and in consequence of which a generic name
is applied to it' (*Elements of the Philosophy of the Human
Mind*, ch. iv. sec. 2, p. 173 ; London ed. 1811).

The singular thing in this definition is, that no one can
disagree with it, and I am full sure that Plato himself would
not have anything to add thereto. This simply means that
the question of which it professes to speak has been passed
over.

181. It is true that we do not see in it the words *universals,
general ideas*, and such like ; but what I maintain is, that the
sense which these words express is there all the same, and
that our philosopher, therefore, by formulating the definition
in this way has not by any means eliminated universals from
philosophy, but has only avoided indicating them by their
proper name, as though he were afraid of it.

182. To see how this is, I will take the liberty of asking the
reader to tell me what he conceives to be the real meaning
of that phrase used by Dugald Stewart, ' the quality in which
one individual resembles other individuals.'

Possibly I may be answered that this is an idle question,
inasmuch as everybody understands what it is for ' one thing
to resemble another.' Well, I also believe that everybody
understands it, and for this reason I think it must be easy to
define what similarity is.

When anyone says 'two or more things resemble one
another,' he means something less than if he said, 'two or more
things are equal.' For things cannot be called equal unless

they be exactly alike in their every part and quality; on the contrary, in order that they may be similar, it is enough that they mutually correspond to a certain extent. A similarity amongst several objects, then, necessarily imports that there is in each of them some quality common to all, which makes all equal in some respect. Now, I do not wish to stop here to examine what inference I might draw from this concerning the nature of the said common quality. I shall remark, instead, that it would be impossible for me ever to know either the similarity or the equality of different objects if I have only the individual idea of them, or the idea of their individual qualities. In fact, the qualities of two objects in so far as they are individualised— *i.e.* attached to an individual—can in no wise be compared together; because the qualities which exist in one individual are in a different place from those which exist in another; and so long as two things remain separated they cannot be compared together. To institute a comparison between several things or qualities and to discover how far they are equal or unequal, similar or dissimilar, there must be an intelligent spirit which has not only the faculty of perceiving them individually, but also that of mentally detaching them[1] from the individuals, and, when thus detached, of setting them one against the other, and by this means finding out what they possess of common and what of proper.

When a geometrician wants to ascertain if two triangles be equal, he, in his intellectual imagination, lays them one upon the other, and observes if they fit each other perfectly. In like manner, a carpenter, when requiring to know whether two boards be of the same size, places them the one upon the other. But the carpenter's operation is very different from that of the geometrician. It should be carefully noted that the mere fact of placing those boards closely together in that mechanical way, would be of no use towards making him see

---

[1] Were anyone to object that 'to detach mentally' is not 'to detach in reality,' and that therefore my argument rests on a false basis, he would clearly show thereby that he has not understood the question now under examination. We are now treating of the operations of the human mind—of that which takes place, not outside, but in it. As regards the mind, to detach or to unite means simply to fix its attention either on a part or on the whole of the object which is before it.

whether they are equal, unless he had also within him an intelligent spirit capable of conceiving them as compenetrated with each other- *i.e.* occupying an identical space. If we wish mutually to compare two lines, we must with our mind put the one of them in the place of the other ; and we must do the same if we wish to compare two superficies, or two solids. It is only by this kind of compenetration that we can see whether they are equal or unequal, or which of them is the larger or the smaller. However near to one another, however coherent, two solid bodies may be, they always remain each outside the other. The particular existence of each ends in itself, and has no relation whatever to the existence of the other ; and where there is no relation, there can be no comparison.

But it may be asked : Why, then, does the carpenter bring the two boards closely together, if this gives him no comparison outside his mind ? I answer : He does this, not because he expects that a comparison will thereby be effected outside his mind, but because that external act will assist his mind—and, I may also say, his imagination—to make the true comparison within himself. Anyone who has attentively considered the way in which we institute comparisons between different things, will be persuaded of the truth of what I say.

183. I shall only add that what I have now stated by way of example concerning bodies and space is equally applicable to all individual things, of whatever kind they may be.

No two individual things can ever be blent into one only, without losing their individuality. For each of them has its own existence, separate from and independent of the other. It may therefore be laid down as an incontrovertible truth, that if individuals were all that exists, there would be no possibility of comparing them together ; for they could not be together in the same place, or, to speak more generally, they could not be joined in one and the same existence.

184. What does, then, our mind require in order to be able to compare together two or more individuals, and discover

how far they are equal or unequal, similar or dissimilar?
According to Dugald Stewart, and to Dr. Reid before him,
our mind has none but individual ideas. But those individual
ideas do not suffice for the instituting of comparisons any
more than do the individuals, from which, so far as distinction
and mutual independence are concerned, they do not differ.
In fact, the idea of a quality would cease to be individual
if the quality which is seen in it could be conceived as transferred from one individual to another; because a quality is
particular or individual only on condition of its being conceivable as adhering to one individual and no more. As,
therefore, no comparison is possible between two individuals
apart from the mind which compares them together, so none
is possible between two ideas if we suppose them to be
purely individual. In order, therefore, that our mind may be
able to discover that two individuals are similar or dissimilar,
it is absolutely necessary that it should possess, besides
individual ideas, universal ideas also. Let me explain this by
an example.

185. Given two walls, both white, but not in the same
degree, how is their similarity to be ascertained?

As we have already said, neither the walls themselves nor
their individual whitenesses can be transferred one into the
other; and if they could, the result would be, not a comparison of two whitenesses, but simply a third whiteness as
individual as they. By parity of reasoning the idea of the
individual whiteness of the one wall cannot be compared
with the idea of the individual whiteness of the other, except
there be something common to both. For when we say
individual whiteness, we mean a whiteness with an existence
so strictly proper, that it cannot go out of itself, nor be
transferred to another, nor receive any other into itself—in
short, a whiteness which has not and cannot have anything
to do with others. That it may, therefore, be possible for
us to make the comparison here spoken of, we must, besides
seeing those two individual whitenesses in actual existence,
have in us a power by which we form to ourselves the notion
or idea of whiteness in general. Thus, and thus only, shall

we be enabled to make that comparison, and to judge how
far each of the individual whitenesses partakes of the nature
of the whiteness of which we have the idea.

Let us suppose, then, that this idea of whiteness in
general—*i.e.* a whiteness not actuated in this or that particular
individual, but possible to be actuated in any number of
individuals—has already (I do not now inquire in what way)
been formed by us.

An idea of this description, free from the prison-house, so
to speak, of the individual, is by its nature a type, an exemplar, a rule, by means of which we can at once judge of the
similarity or otherwise of any individual objects which fall
under our eyes. Let us examine how.

In the case now supposed, when we look at a white wall,
two whitenesses are present to our mind—(1) that which we
behold on the wall, or individual whiteness, and (2) that of
which we possess the abstract idea (abstract or universal
whiteness). We then compare the first with the second, and
thus judge of it. This comparison is possible, because the
abstract or universal whiteness which we contemplate in our
idea, not being restricted within any one individual, can be
conceived by us in all possible individuals, and therefore also
in the wall at which we are looking. In this way the individual whiteness perceived by means of the bodily eye, and
the abstract or universal whiteness apprehended by the mind
alone, are compenetrated or found together, without being
confused, since the universal cannot be confused with the
particular; but the particular is comprehended under the universal, and can be seen in it without at all losing that determination proper to itself which renders it particular.

Now, if we make a similar judgment concerning another
white wall, we shall have two individual walls, both adjudi-
cated white in a greater or less degree.

Hence, by the axiom that two things similar to a third
are similar to each other, we discover the similarity of the two
white walls.

In order, therefore, to ascertain whether two or more
individuals resemble one another, I say that it is necessary

to assume the existence in our mind of a common type or exemplar of that quality in virtue of which those individuals are similar; and this type or exemplar is nothing but the quality itself contemplated by our mind abstractedly from all individuals, or—which is the same thing—as a universal; in other words, it is nothing but that same quality, yet not in so far as really existent in any one individual, but in so far as possible to be received in an indefinite number of individuals.

186. If any of my readers does not feel satisfied with this explanation, I should be glad if he would suggest a better.

In any case, however, it will always appear to me strange that in a discussion which has for its object to inquire what a universal is, and how the mind forms it, a philosopher should content himself with saying that it is nothing but 'the particular quality in which one individual resembles other individuals of the same class;' thereby clearly implying that he deems it useless and superfluous to explain how the resemblances of individuals come to be known. If it be useless to ask how similarities and dissimilarities are known by us, it is equally useless to institute any inquiry about universals; for these are not two, but one and the same question expressed in different words. For my own part, as I said just now, I cannot conceive how a judgment respecting either the equality or the resemblance of two or more things is possible without a common measure to try them by—a measure which, precisely because it is common, cannot be individual, but must be universal.

187. If these measures, these common qualities, these universals—all which terms are used here as synonymous—present a difficulty to our mind; if there is perhaps in them something mysterious and recondite, will that be a reason for denying their existence? Such, alas! is the presumptuous tendency of human philosophy. Is there something which it cannot well comprehend—something which savours of mystery? This philosophy denies it straightway, rejects it as a chimera, as a dream of bygone dark ages, or, at best, pronounces it inexplicable, each philosopher gauging the calibre of the human mind by that of his own; and this is

the extreme of the modesty shown by this kind of philosophy.

But whatever may be said of writers of this or of that period, a true lover of wisdom will ever feel bound not to deny a thing whose existence has been well ascertained, simply because he does not comprehend it. He will candidly confess that he does not as yet understand its nature, rather than peremptorily declare that it transcends all human capacities, and ought not, therefore, to be made a subject of human investigation. To act in a contrary spirit should be left to such men as the compilers of the *Encyclopédie.*

ARTICLE XXI.

In explaining how individuals can be classified, the same difficulty presents itself again.

188. I beg leave to make one more observation on the passage quoted from Dugald Stewart. He says, 'It is the possession of this quality [by the individual]. . . . which may be said to be essential to its classification with that particular genus. But as all classifications are to a certain degree arbitrary, it does not necessarily follow that it is more essential to its existence as an individual than various other qualities which we are accustomed to regard as accidental' (*Elements,* &c. ch. iv. sect. 2, p. 173, London ed. 1811).

When a philosopher undertakes to give an account of some fact on which most serious differences of opinion exist, he ought, I think, to be strictly upon his guard against using any phrase which by its equivocal meaning may give rise to doubt or uncertainty. He ought especially to submit to a close and careful examination the ideas attached to every word. Now, the idea attached to the phrase employed by Dugald Stewart of '*classification with a genus*' does not certainly seem to have been examined by him. For had he examined it, he would easily have seen that a *classification* cannot be made except by means of a *universal idea*, or the idea of that quality which, being common to many individuals, causes them to resemble one another. Therefore, as in the former use of the word *resemblance*, so here in the use of the word *classification*, he has fallen into what is called by logicians a *vicious circle*.   In order to explain a fact, he has assumed its explanation.   He has supposed that the *classi-fying* of objects and the finding of their *resemblances* present no difficulty, whereas this is precisely the difficulty to be explained.   In short, he has defined a thing by the thing itself —*idem per idem*.

ARTICLE XXII.

Uncertainity observable in the expressions used by Dugald Stewart.

189 Again I have to note how singular is that expression of Dugald Stewart, 'as all classifications are to a certain degree arbitrary.'   Surely this is not speaking with philo-sophical accuracy.

By saying that classifications are *to a certain degree* arbitrary, you manifestly own that they are not arbitrary altogether.   Is it not therefore your duty to examine how far they are arbitrary and how far they are not so ?   The omission of this inquiry gives your reader a right to suspect that what in the classification is not arbitrary may be the very part containing the knot of the question which you so hurriedly pass over. He will tell you that, since the classifications of objects are, as you say, based only on certain qualities in virtue of which those objects are similar, or, as others would express it, on certain common qualities (these two expressions being the same in meaning), it follows of necessity that none of those classifications which we call *genera and species* are arbitrary, since the common qualities are not arbitrary, nor yet mere names, but are qualities existing in the individuals.   However fugitively, therefore, you may have admitted that in forming those classes of possible individuals denominated genera and species there is something not arbitrary but necessary, this admission is quite sufficient to make a prudent reader, first, entertain serious doubts about your whole system, and then, on further reflection, find that it is fatal thereto.

ARTICLE XXIII.

Dugald Stewart confounds together questions which are totally distinct.

190. Lastly, in the above short passage Dugald Stewart confounds together two totally distinct questions.

The first is this : Are there such things as universals known to the human mind? That is to say, does man think of common qualities, not as actuated in individual objects, but only as possible to be so actuated?

The second is : what are these universals or these common qualities, outside the human mind?

These two questions must not be confounded together ; and the second must be subdivided into several others, as I shall have occasion to say further on.

191. The question whether a common quality as such exists in itself independently of the mind, is irrelevant to our present argument.

Here we are all agreed. Outside the mind a common quality as such has not any isolated existence. The only way in which it exists really is by being individualised—that is, attached to real individuals.

But, this our agreement notwithstanding, the first question still remains to be solved—namely, whether the common quality exists in our mind, is truly an object of thought.

This last inquiry will certainly not present any difficulty except to those whose minds are mystified by the vain subtleties to which the world has been treated by the philosophical instructors of the day, who, through an exaggerated confidence in their own intellectual powers, have woven a variety of cobwebs for the taking in of men rather than of the truth.

192. Sober good sense is abundantly sufficient to convince us, that the qualities of things are true objects of our thought, not only in so far as they are individual, but also in so far as they are common. Whoever reflects a little on what passes within himself, will readily perceive that his mind is able (1) to know those qualities as existing in this or that particular individual; (2) to conceive them abstractedly from the

individual in which it has known them to exist ; and consequently (3) to understand that certain qualities are possessed
by several individuals contemporaneously, and might be
equally participated by an indefinite number which exist only
potentially. If this were not so, I could not think of it now, or
express it in words.

ARTICLE XXIV.

*Dugald Stewart does not understand the doctrines of the ancient
philosophers whom he censures, concerning the formation of genera
and species.*

193. Before proceeding further with the subject of universals, I wish to remark that Dugald Stewart has, without the
slightest necessity, introduced into his discussion the question
of common qualities considered as the essences of things. The
same is done by other philosophers also.[1] They confound
the Platonic question with the one we are treating here ; and,
what is worse, they state it in a very inaccurate and erroneous
way.

I should wish to know what authority Mr. Dugald Stewart
has for saying that the ancient philosophers placed the
essences of things in their common or universal qualities. I
find on the contrary that they, like ourselves, divided the
common qualities into two classes, the essential and the accidental ; and I also find that they formed genera and species
by means of the one as well as of the other of these two kinds
of qualities. And so they might ; for an essential, no less
than an accidental quality, can serve as the basis of a genus
or a species. Thus, if I say 'the man-species,' I characterise
this species by an essential quality—*humanity.* But if I say,
'the species of white men,' and 'the species of black men,' or
if, with Aristotle, I classify animals by the number of their
legs, I take for the basis of these species an accidental
quality—the white colour, the black colour, the number of

[1] This confusion of the two questions may be said to be a prevailing
sin among modern philosophers. Not
knowing how to solve the first, they introduce the second, and heap upon
the former whatever condemnation and
ridicule they may consider due to the
latter.

legs. Between these two ways of forming genera and species a clear distinction was always drawn, so far as I am aware; and the property of containing the true essence of individual things[1] was attributed to the genera and species of the former class only, while those of the latter were reputed to contain an essence simply relative to that accidental quality which was arbitrarily chosen for their foundation.

194. This second kind of essence might in a certain sense —although still not without some impropriety—be called nominal;[2] but to the essence of the first kind this appellation can never be properly given. In genera and species founded on accidental qualities, there is, as I have just said, something arbitrary; for when there is question of forming one such genus or species, we may be at liberty to take, among the accidental qualities, whichever we deem best for our purpose. But there is nothing arbitrary in genera or species based on essential qualities; because a determinate being has but one essence, and therefore we must either take that, or else the genus or species cannot be formed.

I have said, however, that even as regards essences consisting of accidental qualities the appellation of *nominal* would not be free from impropriety. The reason is, that by designating these essences as *nominal*, one might suppose that they are mere names. Now, this I have shown to be false, for the common qualities of things, be they accidental, or be they essential, truly exist, at least as objects of our mind.

[1] Thus it is by the essence of the thing that the genus or the species is formed, and not the essence by the genus or the species. The generic or specific idea presents to our mind a multitude (although indefinite as to numbers) of individuals existing at least potentially.

[2] An essence would be *nominal* in the proper sense of the word, if a name alone was that which formed the genus; for example, 'the genus of *Peters*, of *Pauls*,' &c., would be a genus having for its foundation a mere name. On comparing this kind of essence with the other essences, this genus with the other genera, the reader will see what a difference there is between it and them, and will conclude that it would be preposterous to confound all these things together, as Mr. Dugald Stewart attempts to do.

ARTICLE XXV.

Dugald Stewart does not understand the question debated between the Realists, the Conceptualists, and the Nominalists.

195. To Dugald Stewart it is inconceivable how there can be an object present to our mind without its existing externally. Hence, when—after setting forth the opinions of the Realists and the Nominalists, and declaring himself in favour of the latter—he comes to speak of the intermediate sect of the Conceptualists, he candidly confesses his inability to form a clear idea of their teaching, and seeks to conjecture or rather guess at it.

As a result he reduces it to two propositions. Let us hear himself :—

'From the indistinctness and inaccuracy of their [the Conceptualists'] language on the subject, it is not a very easy matter to ascertain precisely what was their opinion on the point in question ; but on the whole I am inclined to think that it amounted to the two following propositions : first, that we have no reason to believe the existence of any essences or universal ideas corresponding to general terms ; and, secondly, that the mind has the power of reasoning concerning genera or classes of individuals without the mediation of language.' [1]   Then he continues : 'Indeed, I cannot think of any other hypothesis which it is possible to form on the subject distinct from those of the two celebrated sects already mentioned (*the Realists and Nominalists*). In denying the existence of universals, we know that the Conceptualists agreed with the Nominalists. In what, then, can we suppose that they differed from them, but about the necessity of language as an instrument of thought in carrying on our general speculations ?' [2]

196. The Conceptualists agreed with the Nominalists in denying that *universal essences* subsisted in themselves ; but they did not agree with them in denying that *universal ideas* exist in the mind. [3]

---

[1] *Elements*, &c., ch. iv. sect. 3, (p. 192).

[2] *Ibid.*

[3] Whoever reads with attention

In other words, they admitted that our mind was, indeed, possessed of universal conceptions or ideas, but that these had no real existence outside of the mind—were, in short, fabricated by it on occasion of the particular perceptions of the things which act on our senses.

will easily perceive that, whilst regarding the system of the *Nominalists* as utterly erroneous, I do not by any means endorse that of the *Conceptualists.* Neither am I disposed to call myself a *Realist*; because this name does not, any more than the term *Nominalist* or *Conceptualist,* designate a clear and well-defined system of doctrines, but rather a congeries of diverse opinions. In fact, as John of Salisbury informs us, the Realists were divided into six different classes, and serious discrepancies of views prevailed as well among the Conceptualists as among the Nominalists. Therefore, to take a name so vague in its meaning would either be doing nothing, or else siding with a particular faction without clear knowledge of cause. This is why, as I have remarked elsewhere, the history of Philosophy will never attain perfection until the philosophical systems are classified by means of an exact description of the opinions severally propounded in them, and not by the names of their authors, or of the different sects. (See ' Fragment of a Letter on the Classification of Philosophical Systems,' &c. in my *Introduction to Philosophy,* vi. i.)

But to state briefly in what sense I have said that I do not adhere to the *Conceptualists,* I will observe that by this name one may not improperly designate those philosophers who hold that a *universal,* a common quality, is conceived by our mind in such a way that there exists nothing external corresponding to the conception. Now, than this sort of subjectivism nothing could be further from my opinion.

I take a universal idea, and, submitting it to analysis, I find that it consists of two elements: (1) the *quality* thought of in it, (2) the *universality* of that quality, noted also by St. Thomas, who calls it *intentio universalitatis.*

As regards the *quality thought of,* I say that there is a reality corresponding to it in the external individual thing

perceived by us. But as regards the *universality* of the quality thought of, I say that there is no external reality corresponding to it, and that it exists in the mind only.

To speak properly, the *universality* is not the quality thought of, but a mode which that quality takes in our mind. This distinction should be well grasped.

But how does the *quality thought of* take in our mind the mode of *universality?* I answer:—

It is a fact that after we have perceived a given quality actually existing in an individual, we can, and this not once, but as often as we please, imagine that same quality as existing, successively or contemporaneously, in any number of individuals. This power results (1) from the intuition of the possible with which our spirit is endowed, and (2) from the capacity we have of repeating our interior acts. This twofold power belongs exclusively to an intelligent spirit. It is, therefore, our spirit which, by means of such power, adds to the quality it thinks of, the character of *universality,* which, in ultimate analysis, is nothing but the possibility of a quality being conceived by us as existing in an indefinite number of individuals.

Here I cannot refrain from remarking, that if Degerando had duly observed the difference there is between saying that *universal ideas* are pure conceptions, and admitting that the *universality* of ideas exists only in the mind, while the *ideas* themselves, in so far as they are representative of qualities, have an external reality corresponding to them, he would not have asserted that S. Thomas is *un vrai conceptualiste* (*Histoire comparée,* &c. 2nd edit. t. iv. p. 498)—a title which he would also apply to Ockam (*Ibid.* p. 582), whose philosophical principles, however, differ very widely from those of the Doctor of Aquin.

197. In this system the mind had (1) particular perceptions and (2) the faculty of exercising itself upon these perceptions in such a manner as to add to them a new form—*universality.*

In truth, has not our spirit the power of performing some operations upon its ideas, and causing them to take new forms?[1] What are all the idols of phantasy but creations and forms of the activity of our spirit, which as such have no external reality? Do they not witness to the existence in us of a power to operate on our sensations and on the ideas we have of sensible things?

ARTICLE XXVI.

Dugald Stewart confounds the question of the necessity of language with that of the existence of universals.

198. On the other hand, Dugald Stewart regards the treatment of the question of the necessity of language as necessary for arriving at a correct estimate of the opinions of the three sects of which we are speaking—the Realists, the Conceptualists, and the Nominalists. He considers this question an essential part of that upon the solution of which these philosophers were divided, and supposes that the Realists are bound by their system to believe that words are not necessary to the formation of universals. After saying that the difference, as regards the use of language, between individuals and genera, consists in this, that we can, without it, reason upon the former, whilst we cannot upon the latter, he goes on thus: 'This observation deserves our attention the more that, if I am not mistaken, it has contributed to mislead some of the Realists; by giving rise to an idea that the use of language in thinking about universals, however convenient, is not more necessary than in thinking about individuals.'[2]

[1] To say that a *sensation* is transformed into an idea is an absurd expression ; because a sensation is, in the strictest sense of the word, *particular,* and hence, in order to be transformed into an idea, it would first have to be destroyed. With the *thought* of a thing the case is different. That thought embraces an object or idea containing universal as well as particular elements. In so far as the idea is universal, it can be variously determined and particularised, and this may legitimately be called a changing of form.

[2] *Elements,* ch. iv. sec. 2, p. 173.

199. The question of the necessity of language, however, is wholly independent of that upon which those three philosophical schools were divided, and the confounding the two questions together can only have the effect of rendering the main point in dispute more difficult and inextricable than ever.

I, who have never had any thought of becoming a *Nominalist*, am, nevertheless, firmly persuaded of the necessity of language for bringing man into that stage of intellectual life in which he begins to reflect on universals (*v. Teodicea*, nn. 100–102).

There is a wide difference between supposing that universals are mere names without either things or ideas corresponding to them, and supposing that they are things existing in themselves, or at least ideas existing in our mind, so, however, that we could not know the first, or have the second for the first time, without the aid of words.

The adherents of the first opinion, as well as those who follow either of the two last—I mean Nominalists not less than Realists or Conceptualists—can equally admit that, in order to make it possible for man distinctly to conceive universals, language is indispensable. On this point there is only one difference between them. Nominalists *must* believe language to be necessary ; Realists and Conceptualists *may* believe it, for they are not bound to this belief in virtue of the opinion they profess to hold on the nature of universals. Nominalists must believe it, because they maintain that universals are mere names. If, on the contrary, Conceptualists and Realists believe it, their reason is, not that they look upon names as a substitute for ideas, but that they regard them as means suitable and requisite for arousing and directing the attention of our mind, inert in the absence of a stimulus, to the common qualities,[1] or for causing it to exercise itself upon our perceptions in such a manner as to gain the possession of universals.

---

[1] If the question on the necessity of language be taken by itself, separately from that on the nature of universals, it will not be so difficult to know the opinions of Locke on it as Professor Dugald Stewart seems to imagine. He charges Locke with having in this matter made use of an 'inaccurate and paradoxical' manner of expressing himself, and so given occasion to his

ARTICLE XXVII.

Another Petitio Principii : *Dugald Stewart, whilst professing to explain how the mind forms the ideas of genera and species, begins by presupposing these ideas as already formed.*

200. I have waited advisedly till I had come to the end of my remarks upon the theory of Dugald Stewart on universals, to quote the strongest of all the passages written by him in support of his cause, in order that the reader might all the more easily understand its force as well as the force of the refutation which I am about to oppose to it.   The principles that have been expounded thus far in examining other passages of the same author, may here be found of service.

In the subjoined extract he does his best to explain how man can discourse on universal truths by means of words alone —that is, words without any ideas regularly affixed to them. Although somewhat lengthy, I will give it in full, lest anyone should doubt the accuracy of my statement of his views. The way, then, in which, according to Dugald Stewart, we arrive at universal truths is as follows :—

'There are two ways in which general truths may be obtained : either by fixing the attention on one individual in such a manner that our reasoning may involve no circumstances but those which are common to the whole genus, or (laying aside entirely the consideration of things) by means of the general terms with which language supplies us.'

being considered as holding conflicting opinions. I believe Dugald Stewart to be right; but the contradiction does not seem to me to be where he thinks it is. He finds Locke in contradiction with himself for having in some passages insinuated that language is not indispensable for the operations of our understanding, while at the same time he does not profess to be a Realist. Locke admits that universals are something in our mind ; but this opinion is wholly independent of that on the necessity of language. For one may very well hold that universals are objects of the mind (*entia rationis*), and yet be at liberty to think what he pleases as to the necessity or non-necessity of language for the forming of these objects, these universals which constitute a class of ideas by themselves.

What, I think, may justly be said of Locke is, that he did not penetrate into the real gist of either of these questions, and that the ridicule cast upon him by Doria, Martin Scribblerus, and other subsequent writers was not altogether undeserved.

He believes, then, that we can reason on universal truths by merely fixing our attention either on single individuals or on certain words. And he proceeds to elucidate his idea thus :—' In the first case, our attention being limited to those circumstances in which the subject of our reasoning resembles all other individuals of the same genus, whatever we demonstrate with respect to this subject must be true of every other to which the same attributes[1] belong. In the second case, the subject of our reasoning being expressed by a generic word which applies in common to a number of individuals, the conclusion we form must be as extensive in its application as the name of the subject is in its meaning.'[2]

201. Here I would interrupt him for a moment, to ask what he is aiming at by this mode of reasoning.

He replies that his object is to explain how universal truths may be obtained, and, in particular, how our ideas of genera and species are formed. If so, will he allow me to request his attention to the two expressions he has just used— ' *The circumstances which are common to the whole genus ;*' ' *The circumstances in which the subject of our reasoning resembles all other individuals of the same genus*' ? These two expressions (to limit myself to them) certainly suppose the genus as already formed, and they suppose likewise that we make use of the same. How can he, then, introduce the ideas of genera and species as already formed, into a discourse the object of which is precisely to explain how these ideas are formed by us ? Is not this an evident begging of the question ?

ARTICLE XXVIII.

Another Petitio Principii : *Dugald Stewart assumes that general ideas are something, in the very discussion in which he attempts to prove that they are mere names.*

202. He proceeds : ' The former process is analogous to the practice of geometers, who in their most general reasonings direct the attention to a particular diagram ; the latter,

---

[1] But what if these attributes or common qualities are only words?

[2] *Elements*, &c. chap. iv. sect. 2, pp. 171, 172.

to that of algebraists, who carry on their investigations by means of symbols.'

Quite so ; the fact is really as stated here. But what remains to be seen is whether, such being the fact, we ought to conclude from it that universals are nothing but empty words, or rather affirm the contrary. The exposition of our author's theory will suffice to give us a clue to the right decision.

The observation which he himself subjoins on the two ways by which, according to him, we 'obtain general truths,' appears to me not less beautiful and shrewd than calculated to throw light upon the argument.

'These two methods,' he says, ' of obtaining general truths proceed on the same principles, and are, in fact, much less different from each other than they appear to be at first view. When we carry on a process of general reasoning, by fixing our attention on a particular individual of a genus, this individual is to be considered merely as a sign or representative, and differs from any other sign only in this, that it bears a certain resemblance[1] to the thing it denotes. The straight lines employed in the Fifth Book of Euclid to represent magnitude in general differ from the algebraical expressions of these magnitudes in the same respects in which picture-writing differs from arbitrary characters.' (Note to p. 172 of *Elements*, &c.)

Nothing could be truer. By this beautiful observation the two ways of obtaining universal truths are reduced to one—namely, the use of signs. These, however, may be of two species ; for there are signs that have some resemblance to the thing signified, and there are signs that have no such resemblance. A painting, or the figures used in geometry, belong to the first species ; the letters of our alphabet, or those used in algebraic calculations, belong to the second.

203. Now, speaking particularly with reference to the latter species of signs, I maintain that, so far from their being sufficient of themselves to account for our reasonings

[1] Is this nothing ? You should explain in *what* this resemblance consists. That is the real knot of the question (180-187).

on general truths, as our author would have us believe, the mere fact of our making use of them supposes in our minds the existence of these truths.

He tells us that by these signs we *obtain general truths.* Now, if these truths were nothing, or if they did not differ from the signs themselves, what would be the sense of such an expression ? It would be as good as this other, ' By means of signs we get at signs, and precisely at the signs of which we are making use.' What a strange kind of philosophy this would be! What a statement to place before one's readers! In the name of common sense, let me ask Mr. Dugald Stewart whether the very word *sign* does not at once carry our mind to the thing signified ? Could anyone ever understand what is meant either by a *sign* or a *thing signified*, without at the same time conceiving the idea of both these things as of two correlatives, neither of which can be without the other ?

ARTICLE XXIX.

The use of signs does not suffice to account for our knowledge of universals.

204. Wherefore, signs are not sufficient to explain how we obtain universal truths, unless it be admitted that these truths also are something.

To say that signs cause us to think of individuals is not yet enough, as I have already shown (nn. 198–199).

In fact, when I am told that a sign must lead me to think of one individual alone and determinate, I can quite under-stand how two ideas may suffice me for this purpose—the idea of the sign, and that of the individual signified by it. But when I hear it said that a sign must lead me to think, not of one individual alone and determinate, but of any in-dividual among those contained in a given genus or a given species, to the exclusion of all those which are not of that genus or species, I am unable to conceive how this can be, unless I have, not two, but three ideas in my mind : (1) the idea of the sign, (2) that of the individual signified, and (3) that of something which may enable me to know of what genus or of what species is the individual of which I have to think; this something can only be the idea of the genus or of the species itself.

205. Nor is this all. The names or, more generally, the signs expressive of universals, serve us for two purposes.

The first is, that they arouse our attention, so that we can think of any individual of a given genus or a given species. For example, by means of the word *man*, which signifies an individual of the human species, we are enabled to think of some one of those particular men whom we happen to know, or of any man whatever, real or imaginary, just as we please.

As regards this first service rendered to us by universal names, it will be seen that it consists in causing us to descend from the species or the genus to the individual. Now, this is sufficient to prove that we could not make the first use of such names if we had only the idea of the individuals. We must necessarily have two ideas —namely, the idea of the individuals and that of the species or also of the genus to which they belong. Therefore, the ideas of genera and species cannot be mere names.

A similar conclusion will be arrived at by considering the second service which the words in question render us.

It consists in enabling us to form theories—that is to say, to reason in abstract and general ways without at all descending to individuals.

Here the individuals are entirely lost sight of, or else they are taken only as signs to help our mind to reason, without being themselves in any way the subject-matter of the reasoning. Dugald Stewart gives an example of this in the use which geometers make of signs. When the geometer draws upon his black-board a triangle in order to demonstrate a general proposition—for instance, that the three angles of the triangle taken together are equal to two right angles—he makes use of that particular triangle simply as a sign by which he seeks to facilitate his abstract reasoning; and the demonstration which he gives does not apply to that one triangle only, but to all triangles generally. It is not, therefore, the individual triangle that forms the object of his attention; that triangle is only a sign which helps him to carry his thoughts up to something higher, and this something is precisely that general truth which he proposes to arrive at, and which, although arrived at by the help of signs, is of a nature entirely different from theirs.

206. Dugald Stewart approaches so near to the truth without grasping it, that he seems like Horace's charioteer, who wheels round the goal without touching it; and certainly the touching of the goal by our philosopher would have been fatal to his system.   He says that in general reasonings individuals have no place, and that when they are introduced into them, they very often tend to disturb the train of our thoughts and to mislead us from the truth; and he says all this in the very part of his work in which he treats of universals, without seeming in the least aware that this fact alone is enough to overthrow his whole theory.

But let us hear his own words: 'In cases of this last sort'—*i.e.* when arbitrary signs are used for assisting us in our reasonings, as is done by the algebraist—'in cases of this last sort it may frequently happen from the association of ideas that a general word may recall some one individual to which it is applicable. But this is so far from being necessary to the accuracy of our reasoning that, excepting in some cases in which it may be useful to check us in the abuse of general terms, it always has a tendency, more or less, to mislead us from the truth.'[1] And he makes the same observation on occasion of repeating the statement of his opinion respecting universals thus: 'When we reason, therefore, concerning classes or genera, the objects of our attention are merely signs: or if, in any instance, the generic word should recall some individual, the circumstance is to be regarded only as the consequence of an accidental association, which has rather a tendency to disturb than to assist us in our reasoning.'[2]

When an author has committed himself to a false system, it is incredible in how many contradictions he is obliged to entangle himself, to how many inaccuracies he must submit

---

[1] *Elements*, chap, iv. sec. 2, p. 172.   [2] *Ibid.* sec. 3, p. 191.

so as to give some air of plausibility to his reasonings; and
the more ingenious he is, the farther will he push his error.
In such a case it is well worth while to follow him diligently
through his errors, and to watch the tortuous paths of the
maze in which he has lost himself. By thus seeing what has
befallen others, we can take a useful lesson for ourselves.
This is why I take the liberty of noticing yet another strange
fallacy of reasoning which I find in this writer.

ARTICLE XXX.

Another fallacy in the mode of reasoning adopted by Dugald Stewart.

207. He maintains that 'individuals alone can be objects
of our thought, and that those which we term general ideas
are nothing but words or signs.' But then, seeing that this
raises at once the difficulty, How, on such a principle, are
general reasonings possible? he, in order to get rid of it,
engages to prove the strange proposition that we can reason
by means of words alone, wholly regardless of the things
which those words express.

Indeed, in his case this was a necessity; for, as the words
which we use in making general reasonings do not express
individuals, he had no alternative but to say, either that
general terms are meaningless sounds, or else that there is
something universal which they signify and suggest to our
mind. The second proposition being excluded by his theory,
he was bound to maintain the first.

The proper way to establish the proposition would, in my
opinion, have been, to take as an example any *general* reasoning, and to see if by substituting for the general terms of which
it was composed other general terms taken at random, that
reasoning still preserved a meaning. For if the general terms
of which a reasoning is composed are, as he asserted, mere
signs devoid of all sense, it must be quite indifferent whether
we use those signs or others, since we do not pay any attention to the relations which signs may have with the things
signified.

208. But Dugald Stewart does nothing of the kind; nor,

indeed, could he. What method, then, does he follow instead?
We shall come to it presently; and I shall leave the reader
to say whether it be right. He takes a *particular* reasoning ;
eliminates from it the names of certain individuals, or puts in
their place the names or signs of other individuals; and then
turns to his reader and says: 'You see that the names are
changed, and yet the reasoning has the same meaning as
before.' Hence he deduces, that it is possible to reason by
means of mere signs without attaching any sense to them.
Now, I ask, is this deduction correct? The only legitimate
inference would be, that in cases of a particular reasoning the
names of the individuals may be changed at pleasure, and
common names be substituted in lieu of them. The
example of Dugald Stewart proves nothing more than this.

Here, then, is the example: ' As the decision of a judge
must necessarily be impartial when he is only acquainted
with the relations in which the parties stand to each other,
and when their names are supplied by letters of the alphabet
or by the fictitious names of Titius, Caius, and Sempronius ;
so in every process of reasoning, the conclusion we form is
most likely to be logically just when the attention is confined solely to signs, and when the imagination does not
present to it those individual objects which may sway the
judgment by casual associations.'

The first thing to which I must take exception in this
passage is the implied assumption that, in the case he speaks
of, our 'attention is confined solely to signs.'

It is quite true that parties suing before a judge may be
indicated to him either by their own proper names, or by
fictitious ones, or by letters of the alphabet; but this only
means, that when there is question of arbitrary signs, such as
proper names are, it is wholly immaterial which of them we
use. This indifference, however, regards the signs and not
the ideas ; which is a clear proof that what the judge's mind
really rests upon is the idea signified, and not the sign itself.
Nay, for the sign, taken irrespectively of what it signifies, the
judge does not care. Hence, provided the idea remains
unchanged, the means by which the parties are designated

may, so far as he is concerned, be altered at pleasure. And this is easier in the case of proper names, for the reason that as their connection with the thing signified is entirely arbitrary, that thing may be expressed by a letter, by a word of one syllable or of many syllables—in fact, by any sign which one thinks proper. But the same does not hold, or at least not to the same extent, with regard to common names or universal terms. Here it only holds when a synonym, a word or phrase conveying exactly the same universal idea can be found. And this is a confirmation of the truth of what I have said, that in reasonings the ideas alone are the essential element, while the signs have no value except in so far as they signify and suggest those ideas. So much, then, for Mr. Dugald Stewart's declaration that reasonings can be made through mere signs without any ideas attached to them. The example which he has adduced goes dead against himself.

209. This will appear all the more manifest the more that example is considered. If it is not necessary for the judge to know the true names of the litigants, this is simply because he has no need of knowing the *individuals* themselves, nor those private relations which have nothing to do with the case in dispute. All he requires is to know the individuals in relation to that case. The true names make them known to him as individuals ; but fictitious names, or the letters of the alphabet used for designating them, cause him to know them as belonging to a genus of things, or, 'as men standing to each other in those relations which result from the case he has to decide, and nothing more.' In order to know them in this second way, the judge must be in possession of universal and abstract ideas ; for the accidental relations of one individual to another are nothing but universal ideas taken abstractedly from the real individuality ; and the individuals between whom such relations exist belong to an accidental species constituted precisely by those relations. Therefore, the substitution of those fictitious names for the true ones has had no other effect than to substitute, in the judge's mind, a *generic* for an individual idea. Thus the example quoted by Dugald

Stewart proves the contrary of what he intended. His object was to show that a reasoning can be made without universal ideas, though not without individual ones ; and he has shown instead, and very conclusively, that we can reason both *without* individual ideas and *with* universal ideas alone. Such is the outcome of his argument.

Therefore, individuals are not the only objects of human thought, nor can mere signs supply the place of universal ideas. In order to reason, our mind has more need of universal than of individual ideas, since a reasoning is possible even abstracting entirely from individuals, as shown in the example referred to by Dugald Stewart ;[1] but we cannot conceive the possibility of making any reasoning without universal ideas ; for even when a reasoning turns upon mere individuals, it is absolutely necessary to consider these individuals as possessed of common qualities or of common relations.

---

[1] The error of Dugald Stewart concerning the existence of universals seems to have arisen also from his failing to observe that the *relations* of things resolve themselves into so many *universal ideas*, and are the foundation of *common* names. In fact, a common name designates a being through a *common quality* as well as through a relation which it has with something else. Thus when I pronounce the common name *man* I denote an individual of the *genus* constituted by the common quality '*humanity.*' When, on the contrary, I say *son*, I denote an individual of the *genus* constituted by the relation of sonship, also common to many individuals. To conceive a *relation*, then, is to have a *universal idea*—one of those ideas which form genera and give rise to common names. Had Dugald Stewart observed this, he would not have been deceived into the belief that he had demonstrated the non-existence of *universal ideas* by substituting for them the ideas of *relation* ; nor yet that he had demonstrated how a reasoning can be understood irrespectively of *general ideas*, and simply by means of the *ideas of relation*. Here are his words : ' From what has been said it follows that the assent we give to the conclusion of a syllogism does not result from any examination of the notions expressed by the different propositions of which it is composed, but is an immediate consequence of the relation in which the words stand to each other. The truth is that in every syllogism' (*in this I agree with him, and it proves precisely the necessity of universal ideas*) 'the inference is only a particular instance of the *general axiom*' (*therefore not of mere signs*) 'that whatever is true universally of any sign must also be true of every individual which that sign can be employed to express' (*in a syllogism nothing is predicated of the sign, but all of the thing signified*). Now, observe the strange consequence which Dugald Stewart draws : 'Admitting, therefore, that every process of reasoning may be resolved into a series of syllogisms, it follows that this operation of the mind furnishes no proof of the existence of anything corresponding to general terms distinct from the individuals to which these terms are applicable.' (*Elements of the Philosophy of the Human Mind*, ch. iv. sect. 2, p. 175.)

ARTICLE XXXI.

Conclusion: The Scottish school, conscious of its inability to overcome the difficulty in question, has tried in vain to eliminate it from Philosophy.

210. To conclude, then : the existence of universals is a fact. Indeed, if they did not exist, neither could we ourselves speak, nor could anyone else ever have spoken, of them. Therefore, neither the industry nor the high intellectual powers exhibited by the representatives of the modern Scottish school can destroy them. This philosophical school cannot, then, be complimented on the score of having, as it flatters itself, eliminated that which Professor Dugald Stewart declares to have always been considered one of the most difficult problems in metaphysics, I mean the problem of the origin of universals—that problem which, to present it once more under its most simple form, may be thus stated : ' To form universals we must necessarily make a judgment. But a judgment necessarily presupposes in us the knowledge of some universal. Therefore, either we must admit that there is some universal known to us by nature, and hence antecedently to all our judgments ; or, if we will not admit this, we must find some other explanation of the difficulty.'

In any case, it is the duty of philosophy to solve this problem ; and the examination which we have thus far made of those systems which pretend to account for the operations of the human mind while admitting in it nothing, or next to nothing,[1] innate, shows that they are unable to untie the knot of the question, and that their authors have not even sufficiently understood its nature.

---

[1] I say *next to nothing*, because the Scottish school, by holding that we perceive the existence of external bodies, not because of their images being presented by the sensations, but by a *quasi-inspiration*—a faculty wholly *sui generis* —which on occasion of the *sensations* causes those bodies to be perceived by us, admits more of the innate than does the school of Locke or of Condillac ; for it admits a *new faculty*, though obscure and altogether mysterious.

CHAPTER V.

WHAT STEPS HAS PHILOSOPHY MADE BY MEANS OF THE SYSTEMS WE HAVE EXAMINED THUS FAR?

211. I shall not here propose the question whether Locke and the philosophers who came after him, and whose systems we have been examining till now, have benefited the cause of philosophical science.

To see how superfluous this question would be, we have only to consider that even error itself is, in the grand order of Divine Providence, made to subserve the progress of the human spirit; to give occasion to the more important developments of truth, to place it in a clearer light, to excite towards it the love of man, and to persuade him to acknowledge, after having long and bitterly suffered from the agitations of error, that there is nothing so precious or so salutary as truth. Therefore, even admitting that the philosophers above spoken of had fallen into grave errrors, they would not on this account have been of any the less benefit to humanity. Witness, in proof of this, that yearning, so general nowadays, for the invaluable boon of a true and sound philosophy, a yearning which is due precisely to the uncertain utterances of those authors, and to the imperfect and unsatisfactory systems which they have propounded.

Wherefore, it may not be unprofitable at the end of this section, to pause awhile with a view to survey the ground we have traversed in commenting on the pronouncements of modern philosophy, and to observe in what state it was at the time of Locke, the period from which we started; as also what vicissitudes have been caused by this philosophy to the principal doctrines relative to the great question which forms the theme of the present work.

212. For this purpose, I think it will not be amiss to refer to a small elementary treatise by a contemporary of Locke's, which, as it records in simple language the principal philosophical ideas of the time when it was written, will afford us an easy means of ascertaining by comparison the modifications which those ideas subsequently underwent. I speak of the *Traité de la Connaissance de Dieu et de Soi-même,* composed by Bossuet[1] for the Dauphin of France—that is to say, for a young prince who, though he could not be supposed to have had much leisure for going deep into the mysteries of metaphysics, yet had to be made acquainted with the substance of the then known doctrines, presented in as plain and easy a way as possible.

Let us see, then, what truths were known at that period, and let us compare the principal ones with the opinions of the new school, set up and put in motion by Locke.

213. We have already seen how from the days of Locke down to our own, a numerous class of philosophers has made every attempt to confound or rather to identify the faculty of sense with that of understanding (nn. 70-85). And the works of these authors, now so widely diffused, and so much read, are so replete with materialistic sophisms, which fill their readers with prejudices and confusion of mind, that, very often indeed, it is no easy matter to make them see clearly the distinction of those two faculties.

The contemporaries of Locke knew this distinction fully, and held it as a thing past doubting. Bossuet's book establishes it at length. There the understanding is defined to be : 'The faculty of knowing the true and the false—a property entirely denied to sense.'[2]

---

[1] Bossuet was born in 1627, and Locke five years later. Both died in the same year, 1704.

[2] Ch. i. 7.—Let us suppose that at the time of Bossuet there had arisen some man of genius who, instead of diverting philosophy from the path upon which it had been set by Des Cartes, had simply preferred to help it on in that course ; who, with this object, had accepted and preserved such truths as had been established, and, having cleared them of all extraneous elements, had increased their number. Such a man might, for instance, have developed the principle contained in Bossuet's definition of the understanding, in such a way that, without materially departing from what was then known, but simply connecting its parts better, and elucidating it, he would have greatly advanced the cause of Philosophy.

The development I mean is this : —

214. Condillac confounded sensation with judgment even worse than Locke (nn. 81-89). In the days of Bossuet these two operations of our soul were accurately distinguished. It had been noticed, moreover, how important is the operation of judgment in connection with our knowledge.

'Les sens,' says Bossuet, 'ne nous apportent que leurs propres sensations, et laissent à l'entendement à juger des dispositions qu'ils marquent dans les objets. . . . La vraie perfection de l'entendement est de bien juger. Juger, c'est prononcer au dedans de soi, sur le vrai et sur le faux ; et bien juger c'est y prononcer avec raison et connaissance.'[1]

215. Reid and Dugald Stewart have sometimes confounded the imagination with the understanding (nn. 117-135). Before their day these faculties were kept so distinct as to make their confusion impossible. 'Comme il est beaucoup à craindre,' says Bossuet, 'qu'on ne confonde l'imagination

The understanding, as we have said, was defined to be 'the faculty of knowing the true and the false.'

Well, it only remained to inquire, 'What is truth and falsehood?' To give a full answer to this question was to confer a boon of priceless value on philosophical science; and this, as I have also said, could have been done without any great departure from the ideas already in possession at the time. In fact, how did Bossuet define truth and falsehood? 'Truth' (he says in the same book, ch. i. 16) 'is that which is; falsehood is that which is not.' Therefore, according to Bossuet, truth is *being*. Therefore, the understanding is nothing but the faculty of perceiving *being*. Once on this track, it was necessary to work out carefully the demonstration that sense can in no way perceive *being* (nn. 52-62), but merely the *accidents* of being; and hence that the *idea of being* must have been implanted in us by nature (n. 51); that it is by means of this idea that substances are perceived; that substances, therefore, are perceived only by the understanding (nn. 48-50); that the idea of being divested of all its determinations, which are received through the senses, is *the most extensive of all*

universals; that it is from this idea that all the others borrow the character of universality ; that all ideas are endowed with this character, and that their nature is constituted by it (nn. 90-98). After all this it would have been easy to pronounce that the understanding is not only 'the faculty of knowing truth and falsehood,' but also the 'faculty of ideas,' which cannot belong to the senses. In short, one could have gradually evolved all those truths 'which I have endeavoured to set before the reader of the present work.

[1] Chap. i. 7, 16. How easy would it have been from this doctrine of Bossuet to pass to the conclusion that no idea, unless innate, can be formed except through a judgment, and that therefore, the first operation of the understanding must be a judgment, while, on the other hand, this judgment must be preceded by a universal known to us by nature, since no judgment is possible without a universal! This development of truths which issued quite spontaneously from the ideas with which minds were familiar at that period will, perhaps, be difficult nowadays, when with a view to facilitate it I write this volume. (See in particular nn. 41-45, 117-135.)

avec l'intelligence, il faut encore marquer les charactères
propres de l'un et l'autre. . . .

'Il y a, par exemple, grande différence entre imaginer le
triangle, et entendre le triangle. Imaginer le triangle, c'est
s'en représenter un d'une mesure déterminée, et avec une
certaine grandeur de ses angles et de ses côtés ; au lieu que
l'entendre c'est en connaître la nature, et savoir en général
que c'est une figure à trois côtés, sans déterminer aucune
grandeur ni proportion particulière. Aussi, quand on entend
un triangle, l'idée qu'on en a convient à tous les triangles,
équilatéraux, isocèles, ou autres, de quelque grandeur et proportion qu'ils soient. Au lieu que le triangle qu'on imagine
est restreint à une certaine espèce de triangle, à une grandeur
déterminée. . . .

'Mais la différence essentielle entre imaginer et entendre,
est celle qui est exprimée par la définition. C'est qu'entendre
n'est autre chose que connaître et discerner le vrai et le
faux ; ce que l'imagination, qui suit simplement le sens, ne
peut avoir.'[1]

216. Some of the philosophers who have reduced the
understanding to sense and imagination have argued thus :
'Such or such a thing cannot be felt by our senses or pictured
by our imagination. Therefore, it is inconceivable or unintelligible.'[2] In this way, they excluded from the sphere of
human knowledge all spiritual beings.

The doctrine held at the time of Bossuet was, on the
contrary, as follows : 'Il y a encore une autre différence
entre imaginer et entendre. C'est qu'entendre s'étend beaucoup plus loin qu'imaginer. Car on ne peut imaginer que
les choses corporelles et sensibles, au lieu que l'on peut entendre les choses tant corporelles que spirituelles, celles qui

[1] Chap. i. 9. The development of which the doctrine here referred to by Bossuet was susceptible would have consisted in showing how the under-standing, the faculty of knowing the true and the false, was also the only faculty capable of forming universals ; while, on the other hand, the senses and the imagination could only perceive sensible individuals and consequently no universal relation between them, &c. (156-159).

[2] This is in substance the argu-ment used by modern Nominalists in order to gainsay the existence of uni-versals (177-179).

sont sensibles et celles qui ne le sont pas : par exemple, Dieu et l'âme.

'Ainsi ceux qui veulent imaginer Dieu et l'âme, tombent dans une grande erreur, parce qu'ils veulent imaginer ce qui n'est pas imaginable : c'est-à-dire ce qui n'a ni corps, ni figure, ni enfin rien de sensible.' [1]

The substance and the nature of external things cannot be felt, because they do not fall under the senses or the imagination. Hence the philosophers who reduced the understanding to sense maintained that we had no idea of these things ; whereas before their time it was known that we had the idea of them, though not the images or the sensations ; and this because a clear *distinction was drawn between sensation, imagination, and understanding.* Bossuet places the distinctive character of the understanding in ' knowing the nature of things.' [2]

217. We have seen how D'Alembert noted in the philosophy of Locke the omission of two important questions—viz. (1) ' How, on the principle of that philosophy, it was possible for us to think of what is outside of us, and (2) how, on the same principle, we could unite in a single subject the various sensible qualities perceived by us ' (nn. 65-67). By pointing out these omissions, D'Alembert was helping Locke's philosophy to make a step in advance ; and to have done this at a time when modern philosophical science was in its very infancy reflects much credit upon this author.

Nevertheless, before D'Alembert or even Locke was heard of in the philosophical world, those two questions had, well or ill, been treated by Des Cartes, and therefore were not unknown. Bossuet, who had been brought up in the philosophy of Des Cartes, knew them also, and he proposes the second of them in the following manner : ' Toutes différentes qu'elles sont [les sensations], il y a en l'âme une faculté de les réunir. Car l'expérience nous apprend qu'il ne se fait qu'un seul objet sensible de tout ce qui nous frappe ensemble, même par des sens différents, surtout quand le coup vient du même endroit. . Ainsi quand je vois le feu d'une certaine couleur, que je ressens le chaud qu'il me cause, et que j'entends le bruit qu'il fait, non seulement je vois cette couleur, je ressens cette chaleur, et j'entends ce bruit, mais je ressens ces sensations différentes comme venant du même feu.

'Cette faculté de l'âme qui réunit les sensations, soit qu'elle soit seulement une suite de ces sensations, qui s'unissent naturellement quand elles viennent ensemble, ou qu'elle fasse partie de l'imaginative, dont nous allons parler ; cette faculté, dis-je, quelle qu'elle soit, en tant qu'elle ne fait qu'un seul objet de tout ce qui frappe ensemble nos sens, est appelée le sens commun, terme qui se transporte aux opérations de l'esprit, mais dont la propre signification est celle que nous venons de remarquer.' [1]

218. Dugald Stewart did not perceive that the conceptions of the relations as well as of the resemblances of things were nothing but universal ideas, and therefore belonged, not to the senses, which do not go beyond corporeal and individual sensations, but to the understanding (nn. 180–188). At the time of Bossuet, on the contrary, it was perfectly understood that the knowledge of the relations and of the order of things could be obtained only through the intellectual faculty. Here is the proof :—

'Mais il y a des actes de l'entendement qui suivent de si près les sensations, que nous les confondons avec elles, à moins d'y prendre garde fort exactement.

'Le jugement que nous faisons naturellement des proportions, et de l'ordre qui en résulte, est de cette sorte.

'Connaître les proportions et l'ordre, est l'ouvrage de la raison qui compare une chose avec une autre et en découvre les rapports.' [2]

219. I ask, then : In all that we have seen and examined in this Section regarding the opinions of philosophers posterior to Locke, is there anything that can fairly be called an addi-

---

[1] Ch. i. 4. This could have received a most beautiful development, and it is but just to say that subsequent philosophers have, in this matter, made noble efforts, which I shall turn largely to account in the second volume of this work.
[2] Ch. i. 8.

tion to the philosophical lore of which the world was in possession when Locke stepped into the arena ?

All that, in reference to the main question of this work, I am able to find in any way worthy of that name, are the doubts raised by Dr. Reid against those who looked upon simple apprehension as the first operation of the human understanding. But Bossuet had no difficulty in adopting this view. Let us hear him :—

'Entendre les termes : par exemple, entendre que Dieu veut dire la première cause, qu'homme veut dire animal raisonable, qu'éternel veut dire "qui n'a ni commencement ni fin"; c'est ce qui s'appelle conception, simple appréhension, et c'est la première opération de l'esprit

'Elle ne se fait peut-être jamais toute seule, et c'est ce qui fait dire à quelques-uns qu'elle n'est pas.[1] Mais ils ne prennent pas garde, qu'entendre les termes est chose qui précède naturellement les assembler; autrement on ne sait ce qu'on assemble.'[2]

220. It is clear, then, that, at the time of Locke, truths were well known which the new school did not sufficiently appreciate, and therefore neglected. And in proportion as the new ways of thinking prevailed, those truths faded away more and more from men's memories, until at last they seemed to have fallen into utter oblivion. Hence it is now no easy matter to bring them once more to the surface, and to ensure their recognition; and this all the more as many mistake for new discoveries things which are very old indeed.

Whence, then, the spread of the new philosophy, and the consequent forgetfulness of those truths which were known at the time it started ?

In great part from the negligence of those who, being in possession of such truths, did not pay sufficient attention to the inroads of that philosophy, and at first treated it with contempt. These were the followers of Des Cartes, the only class of thinkers competent to judge of the same, but who

[1] We see from these words that even before Dr. Reid this difficulty had been mooted in no ambiguous language. [2] Ch. i. 13.

unfortunately professed and defended their own doctrine in a partisan spirit. Hence, while they stood heedlessly looking on, Lockism was daily gaining ground through the power of the many allurements it presented to human vanity by its superficiality, and to the passions by its sensuous tendency : to which must be added the circumstance of its having appeared just at the time when a taste for dabbling in philosophy was setting in amongst the general public. Naturally enough its influence was principally felt by the young— a new generation superseding the old, which was fast falling away, and with it the doctrines of the past.

Nor must the reader think I stand alone in thus accounting for the fall of Cartesianism, in spite of the many excellent truths it taught, and still more in spite of the most praiseworthy spirit which animated it. There are others who begin to see this matter in the same light. As a proof, I beg leave to quote an extract from a French publication, purporting to describe how the above transformation of philosophy was brought about, and how the Lockism that supervened was simply the continuation of an old sensual philosophy which, although vanquished in argument by Cartesianism, still had, as it always has in mankind, many more practical followers than it ought to have.

' Dans la lutte qui s'éleva' (thus writes the Paris *Globe*) ' entre le matérialisme et le spiritualisme, au temps de Des Cartes et de Gassendi, le spiritualisme triompha, en ce sens qu'après Des Cartes, sa doctrine continua à être représentée en France par une suite non interrompue de philosophes jusqu'au milieu du dix-huitième siècle, tandis que celle de Gassendi fut abandonnée par les métaphysiciens. Mais cette dernière[1] conserva des partisans parmi les hommes du monde et, depuis Bernier, Molière et Chapelle, on peut suivre sa trace jusqu'à Voltaire. Dans cette école d'hommes aimables et voluptueux, les traditions d'épicuréisme pratique, et d'incrédulité religieuse,

---

[1] The writer might have said the same of the philosophy of Hobbes, who was born before and died after Gassendi, and who had lived a long time in France.

se gardèrent mieux que les dogmes métaphysiques du matérialisme ; on ne songeait guère au principe de la sensation
chez Ninon de l'Enclos ; et depuis longtemps la philosophie
de Gassendi était morte en France, même chez ses disciples,
lorsque la traduction du livre de Locke vint la ramener. Il
n'y avait guère alors dans ce pays que les Cartésiens qui
fussent capables de comprendre "l'Essai sur l'Entendement ;"
mais, préoccupés de leurs vieilles idées, ils furent les seuls qui
ne consentirent point à l'examiner. Peu au fait des questions
métaphysiques, ceux qui embrassèrent la nouvelle doctrine
se méprirent sur son véritable esprit, et tandis que Berkeley
et Hume en déduisaient rigoureusement le spiritualisme en
Angleterre, Condillac en France y·trouva le matérialisme.'[1]
(3 Janvier 1829, page 5.)

As Locke treated the doctrines of Des Cartes with contempt, so did Des Cartes those of his predecessors.[2] This
contemptuous spirit exhibited by philosophical writers towards
one another is a source of great mischief. It induces man to
set aside some precious truths in his possession ; it drives him
back continually to intellectual infancy ; it forces on him the
necessity of recommencing studies which he had already
undertaken and carried to very good results ; it thus entails
on him an immense waste of time, and at last so wearies out
his patience that he grows sick of philosophy itself, of which
those authors are supposed to be the representatives. The

---

[1] I would not dare accuse Condillac
of *Materialism*. He stops at *Sensism*.
Berkeley and Hume, on the other hand,
do not abandon Sensism, but build upon
it. As regards, however, the philosophy
of Locke, it is true to say that it contains
the seeds both of Materialism and Idealism. The faculty of *Reflection*, which
might have saved his teaching from
absolute Sensism, is introduced by him
in too superficial a manner ; and, as I
have already shown, he does not even
seem to understand its nature.

[2] It must be acknowledged that, of
all countries, Italy is the one in which
the thread of traditional ideas was less
interrupted than in any other, thanks
to the great principles of Christianity,
which are, so to speak, inviscerated in
it. Hence we have seen that in Italy
the innovations of Locke were immediately met with a dignified opposition by
Paolo Doria, and those of Des Cartes
by Giovambattista Vico. These two
great men would have saved Italy from
many aberrations, had there not been
introduced into her midst a love, not so
much of what was new, as of what bore
on it a foreign impress. It was not a
philosophy but a party that prevailed.
Unfortunately it was an anti-social and
anti-religious party. But the eighteenth
century is now gone, and the nineteenth
has commenced a severe judgment upon
it.

true philosophical spirit can never be exclusive and individual. It is conservative, impartial, and large-hearted. It receives with respect the traditions of mankind, as well as of particular sages. In a word, it is not the vain spirit of the world, but rather the spirit of Christianity itself, applied to the study and meditation of natural truths.

SECTION IV.

THEORIES WHICH ERR BY EXCESS, I.E. BECAUSE THEY ASSIGN TO IDEAS A GREATER CAUSE THAN IS NE-CESSARY.

221. Hitherto I have spoken of those systems which have failed to assign a sufficient cause to the fact of the existence of ideas. I must now speak of those which, in explanation of the same most important fact, have assumed a cause greater than was necessary. The authors of the first systems, by being satisfied with an explanation which fell very far short of the mark, showed very clearly that they did not understand the true nature of that knot which renders the solution of the ideological problem so extremely difficult (41–45). The authors of the other systems, on the contrary, by their great efforts to invent expedients with a view to untie that knot, proved as plainly that, though they had understood it, they were not so fortunate as to hit upon the simplest and most natural mode of satisfactorily disposing of it. Both these classes of philosophers have transgressed against the method whose principles I laid down at the beginning of this volume— *i.e.* the former class against the first principle, or by defect; the latter against the second principle, or by excess (26–28). Among these, the first to offer himself to my attention is a man of rarest genius, Plato.

CHAPTER I.

PLATO AND ARISTOTLE.

ARTICLE I.

The difficulty of the problem of the origin of ideas as proposed by Plato.

222. Plato saw the difficulty which stands in the way of those who wish to give an exact account of the genesis of our ideas ; and moreover he thoroughly felt its force.

To be convinced of this it is enough to call to mind some one of the many passages which occur in his most beautiful dialogues, wherein the difficulty which I have proposed concerning the origin of ideas is set forth in a luminous manner and in substantially the same way as I have put it myself.

Here is one of the most celebrated of those passages :—

Menon of Thessaly, a friend of Aristippus of Larissa, and a follower of the presumptuous philosophy of the Thessalian sophist, engages in a discussion with Socrates, who professed not to know anything except perhaps this, that he could direct .the attention of others to the difficulties contained in even the simplest philosophical questions ; and here, in fact, comes very soon the difficulty of which we speak.   The dialogue between Menon and Socrates is of the following tenor : —

Socrates having said that he did not know the definition of virtue, but wished to investigate it, Menon makes to him the following objection : ‘ But how will you, O Socrates, seek after that of which you are entirely ignorant ?   How can you represent to yourself what you are in search of, if you do not know it at all ?   Or if you should happen to meet with this thing, how will you recognise it as that which you were looking for, when you have no idea of it whatever?’   In reply

Socrates brings out to view the whole force of the objection, which probably had not been perceived even by Menon himself. He says, ' I understand you, O Menon; but, pray, are you aware of what a very stubborn question you have raised? Methinks the import of your words is simply this, that a man can make no investigation of any kind, either about what he knows or about what he does not know. In fact, if he already knows it investigation will be needless, and if he does not know it investigation will be impossible, since he does not know what to investigate about.' [1]

The difficulty was indeed a most serious one, and whoever considers it attentively will not fail to perceive that in every investigation it is necessary that the thing inquired about should be in part known and in part unknown. I say *the thing should be in part known*, since if we had no knowledge of it whatever, it would not exist for us, and therefore could not form the subject of our investigation. And I say *it should be in part unknown*; for if we knew it fully there would be no sense in our seeking to know it.

The remark made by Menon, therefore, and whose point Socrates adroitly brought out into full relief, was solid, and, as I have just stated, led to this conclusion : ' Nothing can be inquired about unless it be partly unknown and partly known.'

223. In the first place, we must note the difference which passes between seeking some real thing in order to possess it, and seeking some truth in order to know it.

When we seek, for instance, a friend who has been lost in the crowd, or an article which we have mislaid somewhere in the house, the difficulty alluded to has no place. We may know

---

[1] St. Augustine treats this difficulty with great acuteness in the 10th book *On the Trinity*, and concludes thus :— 'Quilibet igitur studiosus, quilibet curiosus non amat incognita etiam cum ardentissimo appetitu instat scire quod nescit. Aut enim jam *genere* notum habet quod amat, idque nosse expedit etiam in aliqua re singula, vel in singulis rebus quæ illi nondum notæ forte laudantur, fingitque animo imaginariam formam qua excitetur in amorem.' This second way by which we sometimes desire to know that which is unknown supposes in us a certain degree of intellectual development, as well as a certain amount of acquired knowledge. But the first way by which we desire to know in particular that which we already know *in general*, may lead even to the discovery of the origin of all our cognitions ; but more of this later.

the friend or the article perfectly, and yet go in search of them. But Menon's discourse turned upon truths which are to be investigated—that is, sought after that they may be known. In this case possessing is the same as knowing, and we are therefore confronted with the difficulty of explaining how it is possible for anyone to seek after truths of which he knows nothing, or, if he knows them, why he seeks after them.

In short, that discourse pointed to the admission of something which is neither entire knowledge nor entire ignorance, but stands between the two ; and in determining the nature of this sort of middle-knowledge of the thing sought after, of this mixture of light and darkness—of as much light as suffices to enable us to recognise the thing as soon as found, and of as much darkness as makes us feel the need of inquiring after it in order that we may be able to say truly that *we know it*—was to consist the solution of the difficulty.

ARTICLE II.

Plato's solution of the difficulty.

224. It was precisely to a middle kind of knowledge that Socrates had recourse in order to extricate himself from the difficulty proposed to him ; and he placed it in a knowledge which we had forgotten on coming into this world.

To impart probability to his opinion he referred to a fact with which we are all familiar—namely, that there is in us at times a knowledge of which we have no present recollection, and which lies as it were dormant in the soul, but wakes up in vivid distinctness so soon as the objects of it are again brought to our notice. We then remember having known those things before—that is, we recognise in them what we knew already, but had slipped from our memory. Now, Socrates thought he could make use of this obvious fact as affording a satisfactory explanation of the difficulty in question. His reasoning came to the following : 'I observe that there are in us two kinds of knowledge—one which has been obliterated in us, and one which we distinctly remember. No inquiry is needed as regards the latter, because we have it already in our possession ; but we can very well investigate the former, because we retain a sort of general recollection of it—sufficient, if not to satisfy us, certainly to guide us in investigating more fully that which had been cancelled from our memory, and to cause its revival in it. If, then, we find this to be a matter of every-day occurrence, what is there to forbid the supposition that we carry with ourselves from birth, not an actual but a potential knowledge of things similar to that which we have of subjects once learnt but subsequently forgotten, though not to such a degree as that on their being again presented to us we may not remember having formerly known them ? Given this one supposition, we can easily explain how it is that a human being from his earliest infancy exhibits a most lively curiosity to know the truth of things, and that in proportion as he discovers it he feels satisfied as having thus attained the object of his desires.'

225. Doubtless this hypothesis suggested by Socrates was very ingenious, and fully met the requirements of the case. That great dialectician, however, did not stop here, but went on strengthening his position by further observations and by the allegation of other facts.

One was that of children who had never yet been trained in any scientific subject. Socrates called to him one of those children from the crowd, and plied him warily with questions so well connected together as to elicit from him quite naturally a number of geometrical truths, first of an easy and then of a difficult nature. As by this method Socrates went no further than to interrogate, he could truly say that he had never taught the child anything, for in point of fact he never said out and out, ‘The thing is so or so,’ but had left him to answer for himself. From this experiment he concluded that the boy could not have thus enunciated those truths unless he had had them within himself, and that they had lain in him, though in a dormant state, so to speak, or in a sort of oblivion, to make them emerge from which it was only necessary that some one should help him by properly directing his attention to them, and so recalling them to his memory.

The fact to which Socrates was appealing in support of his

view could not certainly be gainsaid by anyone. For it was quite certain (1) that the boy had not learnt from anyone the truths to which he gave utterance ; (2) and that on being questioned in a suitable manner he was able to discover them without anyone telling him distinctly what they were.

Now, whoever attentively considers this fact will find that its real drift may be expressed in the following manner :—

The youth, when interrogated as above, answered aright, even regarding what had never been communicated to him ; therefore he had in him the faculty of judgment. Such was the only inference which one could legitimately draw from the fact adduced by Socrates. Therefore, all that required to be explained in connection with that fact was how a human being can make judgments even on things which fall for the first time under his senses—on things he has never known before.

Now, this can only be explained in one of two ways. We must say either that the judgments formed by the child have been taught him by others, and this is excluded by the hypothesis ; or else that he has had in him from his birth something whence he can derive those judgments [1]—that he is, in fact, possessed of what St. Augustine terms *naturale judicatorium*,[2] or a rule which directs him to judge thus and not otherwise. Now, Socrates assumed that those judgments, or the truths to which they related, were themselves innate in the child, though obliterated ; and this, it must be confessed, was amply sufficient to explain the singular fact in question.

ARTICLE III.

The difficulty seen by Plato is in substance the same as that which has been proposed in these pages.

226. The reader will perceive that the difficulty of explaining the origin of ideas, as seen by Plato, is the very same which has been proposed by myself, and which, reduced to its last expression, comes simply to this, ' How is it possible for us to make judgments, seeing that no acquired idea can be had except through a judgment ? '

---

[1] A judgment is but an interior word, an affirmation.   [2] *De Libero Arbitrio*, ii. 10.

The only difference between Plato and myself as to the way of stating the difficulty is, that I have restricted it to the first of the judgments we make when beginning to use our intellectual faculties, whereas Plato gave it a much wider extension, from a belief that it applied to all our succeeding judgments as well.

That belief arose from his not having duly adverted to the connection which ideas, or truths, and consequently judgments, have one with the other. This connection is such that, given the explanation of the first of our judgments, the others do not present any difficulty, since on it they all entirely depend. Indeed, the whole knot of the difficulty lies in explaining how, on the hypothesis that we have no idea to start from, we can make that judgment by which we acquire the first idea, when, as I have said, every acquired idea is the effect of a judgment. But if we suppose even one antecedent idea, the possibility of the first judgment is accounted for, and, with it, the possibility of acquiring other ideas, which in their turn serve for other judgments; in short, we then see how it is that we have the faculty of judgment, which is the same as the faculty of reasoning.

227. Of this defect in the argument of Plato, I shall yet have to speak more at length. What I now wish to insist on is the fact that, Plato saw perfectly well that the whole difficulty of assigning to ideas their true origin consisted ultimately in explaining how there could be in us a faculty capable of producing them, since this faculty would be impossible if our reason were devoid of ideas.

To be all the more convinced that the Athenian philosopher was very deeply impressed by this difficulty, let us consider how thoroughly he understood the nature of human thought. He made thought to consist simply in interior judgments and reasonings. 'For me,' he says in *Theætetus*, 'thought is the discourse which the mind holds with itself.' Hence the reason, or the faculty of thought, was also called by him *discourse* or *word* (λόγος). Nor did Plato stand alone in this, for the same value of the term λόγος lay deep in the Greek tongue. Indeed, to look upon human thought in this light seems a prompting of common sense ; and, were it necessary, I could easily produce unmistakable evidence that it by no means began with the opening of the philosophical era of the Greeks, but sprang from a tradition dating from a most remote period, and common to all the Orientals. There is nothing truer or more natural than to conceive of a man who thinks as saying something to himself, pronouncing an interior word. Now, to say something to oneself, to pronounce an interior word, is nothing but to affirm or to deny something ; and every affirmation or negation can be resolved into a judgment. Thought, therefore, commences with a judgment ; a judgment is the first act of our thinking faculty ; it is by a judgment that our reason is set in motion ; and the fundamental error of the modern treatises on Logic and on Psychology is to place acquired ideas first, and to speak of the faculty by which they are formed as anterior to and independent of the faculty of judgment.[1]

[1] A symptom of the error lurking sometimes in a received philosophical opinion is the uncertain manner in which writers express themselves, and their excessive anxiety to justify it by means of elaborate subtleties. This proves that they do not feel well at ease on the matter, and that in their inmost conscience there is a voice murmuring against the hidden error which, did they but lend an attentive ear to that voice, they would discover. No philosophical doctrine, perhaps, is more in vogue at present than that which places the operations of the human understanding in the following order : (1) idea, (2) judgment, (3) reasoning ; and there is none, perhaps, in the exposition of which the symptom I speak of is more visibly betrayed in the books one reads on it.

I have already noted how, at the time of Bossuet, there were some who doubted the correctness of the above order (219); and how Fortunatus of Brescia (n. 89), to get rid of the difficulty by which he felt embarrassed, prudently added to the definition of *idea* the express clause 'that an idea, to be truly such, must contain no judgment'; as if the idea could cease to contain what it really contains, because a philosopher thinks fit to expel it from his definition. Now, since all these tokens which authors exhibit of their misgivings about the errors into which they were falling are valuable in this sense, that they turn wanderers from the truth into witnesses for it, and thereby show how extensive is truth's dominion over men, it will not be amiss to notice here the efforts made by such a writer as Wolff, in order to preserve for *notions* or *ideas* the place which is commonly assigned to them—I mean, that of being the first of the operations of the human understanding.

Wolff did not grasp the force of Plato's *dictum* that thought 'is simply an interior discourse.'

He distinguished, therefore, between an idea as merely apprehended by the understanding, and the same idea as expressed by words or signs. The first he called *intuitive cognition*, and the second *symbolical cognition*. And he said that ' in the *symbolical cognition*, the first operation of the understanding (*the idea as simply apprehended*) identified itself with the second ' (*Psychologia Rationalis*, § 398) ; but that such is not the case as regards purely *intuitive*

228. But if judgment is the first operation of our understanding, and if therefore this operation has not been pre-

cognition. Now, this distinction is only an evasion of the difficulty. For why should I, when expressing ideas by words, be bound to express them in the form of a judgment? Am I, then, obliged to say more than the ideas contain? If so, in so far as I insert what is not contained in the ideas, I make use of words without meaning, without anything corresponding to them in my mind; which would be an absurd *Nominalism.* For example, if I wish to express my idea of a triangle, I shall say : ' The triangle is a figure of three sides.' Now, the verb is, by which I express the triangle in its notional or ideal form, is not an empty sound, but has something corresponding to it in my mind—the idea itself, which I perceive as a thing different from me, the perceiver.

But says Wolff, ' The word is does not merely indicate that the triangle is regarded as a subject of some sort, but it also expresses the inexistence of the three sides in this subject.' (*Psychologia Rationalis,* p. 316.) ' Now, the purely intuitive cognition does not consider this *nexus*; by it, the qualities found in a given thing are represented as different both from one another and from the thing in which they exist.' (*Psychologia Empirica,* § 331.) ' In the *symbolical cognition,* on the contrary, we must necessarily express these qualities both as joined together, and as inexisting in the subject; this cognition, therefore, includes a judgment ; the other does not.' (*Psychologia Rationalis,* p. 315.)

On this reasoning of Wolff I beg leave to make the following observations.

1. I deny that in the proposition adduced the word is has the force which Wolff attaches to it. The proposition ' The triangle is a figure of three sides ' is perfectly equivalent to this other, ' That which I conceive and call a *triangle* is a figure of three sides.' The verb is, therefore, expresses nothing but the existence in my mind of the idea of triangle, without causing the least alteration in the same idea as expressed by the words 'a figure of three sides.' If, on the other hand, I were to say, 'This figure of which I

think *has* three sides,' then the verb *has* would express the inexistence of the three sides in the figure I think of ; but the verb is does not in any way refer to such inexistence.

2. Wolff says that in the intuitive cognition we perceive the qualities of the thing entirely apart from one another as well as from the thing itself. Now, is this possible? or is it thus that our first cognition of things really takes place? Does not the contrary rather seem to be the fact—viz. that our mind first perceives the thing in union with its qualities, and then, by means of abstraction, divides this composite object of its perception, and considers it part by part? It appears to me that experience tells decidedly in favour of this second view. Moreover, I have already demonstrated the impossibility of the contrary (nn. 55-61)—that is, of our mind perceiving in the first instance the accidents without the subject in which they exist. It is altogether different as regards the corporeal senses ; for these perceive only the accidents, while the idea lies entirely beyond their sphere ; and the error of Wolff must, perhaps, be ascribed to his not having sufficiently distinguished the characteristics of *sensation* from those of *idea.* It is true he claims for ideas — the object, according to him, of our first intellectual operation—the mark of universality, a mark which could very easily have enabled him to form a perfectly genuine concept of the nature of intellectual cognition. Now, with regard to this cognition, I say that it is impossible for us to conceive, first, the accidents separately from their subject, and afterwards to unite them with it, as Wolff maintains we do. In fact, when we perceive the accident of a subject, either we know at the very outset that it is an accident, and in this case we conceive it in relation with its subject ; or we do not know that it is an accident, and then we take the accident itself for a subject—that is, we conceive it as a thing standing by itself, and, therefore, as having *existence* and a *certain mode of existence* ; and to conceive in this way is still to conceive a *subject* (a being), and a *predicate* (the mode of that

ceded by another which could supply us with ideas, we must perforce admit that, antecedently to our first intellectual operation, and as a necessary condition of its possibility, there must be some idea innate in us.

ARTICLE IV.

The system of Plato solves the difficulty, but is at the same time vitiated by excess.

229. Plato, then, had proposed the difficulty of which we speak, in much too wide a form. He should have contented himself with demonstrating that the first act of our reasoning faculty was a judgment, because the acquisition of any idea whatsoever is not a simple passion of our senses, but an action of our understanding ; it is a word which we utter to ourselves—in short, it is a judgment which we pass on our sensations, pronouncing by it, at least implicitly, what that is of which we experience in ourselves the sensible action. This

being). Consequently, that which our author would lay down as the basis of his doctrine is an impossibility.

But the same can also be proved by examining Wolff's definition of the first operation of the understanding: 'Prima intellectus operatio (he says) est plurium *in re una* singillatim facta repræsentatio.' (*Psych. Empir.* § 330.) Mark the word *singillatim.* Wolff puts it in to indicate that all the qualities of the thing of which we have the idea are perceived by us one by one. Letting alone that this successive perception of the several qualities that are to be found in a thing, cannot be our first intellectual operation (for it is rather a series of intellectual operations), I would ask, where do we perceive these qualities? *In re una,* replies our philosopher ; all in the one thing of which we have the idea. Therefore, say I, we do not perceive them in themselves, apart from the thing, but we perceive them as qualities or parts belonging to the thing and existing in, and not out of it. Now, what is this but attributing them all to the thing itself, by at least an implicit judgment? Our perceiving those conditions, or parts, or qualities singly, as he asserts we do, would only add force

to my argument ; for it would mean that we make a distinct interior judgment on each of them, attributing each to the thing to which it belongs.

But I do not ask our philosopher for so much as this, nor do I accept all he so generously offers me, however materially it may favour my cause. I limit myself to saying that, whether the above-mentioned qualities be perceived as joined together, or as separate from one another, they are always perceived by our first intellectual operation, in a subject either real, or imaginary, or purely potential ; and hence that in this first intellectual operation, we always perceive two things—(1) *being* (a subject), (2) *a mode of being* (a predicate), and perceive them united together. Therefore, this first operation contains a judgment.

The outcome of all this is that the distinction invented by Wolff between *intuitive and symbolical cognition* with the object of justifying the commonly received order of our intellectual operations, has no solidity in it, but is only one of those subtleties whose hollowness bears witness to the weakness of the cause which is believed impossible to stand without their support.

would have put him on the way to demonstrate that, in order
to form that first judgment through which our first acquired
idea is obtained, it was necessary that there should be some
notion pre-existing in our mind, to serve us as a rule for the
said judgment; since to judge is simply to apply a certain
rule to the thing judged of.

230. But, instead of concentrating his thoughts on the
difficulty presented by the first of all the judgments made by
man at the commencement of his intellectual development,
and seeking in its explanation that of all the other judgments,
Plato imagined that the same difficulty existed in all judgments alike. His way of arguing was this: 'When in the
exercise of his reasoning powers, a human being judges of
anything, he discovers by himself a truth he did not know
before. Now, the question arises as to how he is able to say
that what he has discovered is the truth, and how he can
distinguish it from falsehood. The only way in which he can
do this is by having previously in his mind the exemplar of
the particular truth of which he is in search. Through comparing with this exemplar the truth which his investigation
has brought to view, he is able to recognise it as what he has
been looking for.' Thus was Plato led to suppose that we
have innate in us the exemplars of all truths—in other words,
that all ideas are in our mind *ab initio*, but, as I have said,
obscured until the senses, by perceiving external things as
copies or similitudes of the same, bring them out, and set
them clearly before us.

The defect of this mode of reasoning (to say in other
words precisely what I have expressed before) consisted in
not observing that although it is quite true that when we
make a judgment on anything, we thereby gain a new truth,
it by no means follows that we must have in ourselves, for
this purpose, the *particular exemplar* of that identical truth
itself. To guide us in discerning which among the various
judgments possible to be passed on the thing is the true one,
and which the false, a *general exemplar* is enough. We do
not seek for the new truth that we may recognise it as a particular truth which we had previously singled out in our own

mind, but that we may know what the truth is in the case in hand, whatever that truth may be. Such, and no other, is the aim of our every judgment.[1] We do not, therefore, require

[1] When, for instance, I seek to discover by experiments the properties of the electric or magnetic fluid, I do not know as yet what those properties will be; but in order that, when I shall have discovered them, I may know that they are precisely those I am in search of, it is enough that I can make sure that they are the *true* ones. Once certain of this, I know that they are what I seek, because I seek only the truth, whatever it may be. I must, therefore, have in me the faculty of discriminating the true from the false, or, in other words, I must know beforehand what is *truth in general,* so that I may recognise it whenever I happen to find it actualised in particular cases. Now, *to know beforehand what is truth in general,* is for me the same as to have in my mind the *exemplar of truth,* and consequently the means by which I can test the different opinions which may be formed upon the subject of my investigation. By applying the test, I shall be able to know which among all those opinions is in accordance with it, and therefore true, to the exclusion of all the others. In fact, were I not acquainted beforehand with the distinctive marks of truth I should never be able to recognise it as truth, and should thus be destitute of the faculty of discerning between truth and error. Now, to be acquainted with the distinctive marks of truth is nothing but to know how truth is constituted, to contemplate as it were its physiognomy, its exemplar, its notion, its form. In this sense, and in this only, is Plato's reasoning conclusive. It proves that to be able to make any judgments we must have the genuine *countenance* of truth present to our mind (*a*). But it does not prove that we must have as many exemplars as are our judgments, or the ideas which we acquire through them; for, given in us the possession of the *sign* by which truth can be known and distinguished from error, we can apply it to numberless things, to anything we please.

From that moment we have the faculty of judgment, the faculty of descrying and enjoying the truth, which has the same countenance everywhere; in a word, it is in our power to judge of things. One rule suffices us for all cases, because in all cases we seek *but one thing*—viz. that which is true, in contradistinction to that which is false; more briefly, we seek for that which is. By analysing still more closely the observation of the Athenian philosopher, we may divide the inquiries that may be instituted about it into three classes. (1) Sometimes we investigate and cognise truths taken, so to speak, at haphazard—that is, just as the occasion for making use of our reasoning powers is given us; (2) sometimes we seek after new truths connected with a thing which is already known to us under another aspect; and (3) sometimes we do the same in regard to truths already included in some idea, but on which we have not reflected, and consequently have not perceived them distinctly, and each by itself. This third kind of investigation takes place every time that we submit an idea to analysis. We then add nothing to the subject-matter of our cognitions (analytical judgments); we aim purely at seeing in a divided form that which we already know in a composite and united form. We acquire or augment only the *reflex* knowledge, whereas before we had intuitive and *spontaneous* knowledge. We examine what is known to us in one way, in order that we may know it in another; because the reflex or analytical knowledge serves us for diverse uses, in which we could not be assisted by the synthetical and undivided. To this class of inquiries, therefore, the reasoning of Plato is not applicable; since in them there is no question of discovering an entirely new truth, but only of finding, so to speak, the parts of that which is already known as a whole. Should anyone, however, wish to

(*a*) I shall demonstrate in due course that this countenance or primitive exemplar of truth is nothing but the innate idea of being, the *only constitutive form of human reason.*

to have innate in us as many exemplars as are the ideas which we obtain by judging.   All we require is the *exemplar*

consider the parts of this whole as constituting each a new truth by itself, then this third kind of inquiries could be reduced to and classified under the second.

The second class of inquiries is when we seek after a truth not known to us in itself, but linked with one which we know. For example, if I experimentalise with a view to ascertain the specific gravity of diverse bodies, what I inquire about is as yet unknown to me ; but at the same time I know the bodies to which it belongs, and I know, too, what is gravity in general. When, therefore, I come to discover the specific gravity in question, it is clear that, although I did not know it before, I have fully the means of knowing that it is precisely the thing I was in quest of, because I knew the bodies to which it was to belong. This relation which the gravity has with the bodies determines that gravity for me in so unmistakable a manner that no sooner do I find it than (my previous ignorance of it notwithstanding) I instantly identify it as the object of my search. The same principle is of very wide application in the concerns of our daily life. Thus, for example, if some one were to say to me, ' The man whom I shall salute on the way is he whom you must put under arrest,' it would be immaterial for the purpose in view whether I personally knew the man or not ; the sign given me by my informant would be quite sufficient to make me know the individual. In this class of inquiries, therefore, the truth we discover is recognised as being the one we were seeking after, not because we knew it beforehand, but because we were cognisant of a relation (I speak of a well-defined relation) which it had with something we knew. All the algebraical problems called *determinate* fall under this head. By means of them we obtain results which are entirely new to us, and this simply because such conditions are given in them as must lead infallibly to those results. The reasoning of Plato, therefore, has no bearing even on this species of inquiries, because they do not suppose in us the knowledge of the truths themselves about which we investigate, but only the knowledge of some relation which connects them with some other truths of which we are previously cognisant.

With the first of the three classes of inquiries I have named, the case is different. As I have said, we do not in them seek after a particular truth which we deliberately set to ourselves as an object of research. We are left as it were to chance. We seek, or rather find, truths according to the occasions which happen to offer themselves to us in the course of our intellectual development. No sooner, for example, has an infant entered into this world than he receives a great number of sensations from the things that surround him. Being at once susceptible of these sensations, and endowed with the faculty of reason, he, on feeling thus variously affected in his sensories, says, or, to put it more correctly, cannot help saying, to himself ' Here is something outside of me : this thing, that thing,' &c. He does not, indeed, as yet formulate all this in so many distinct words ; but his interior assents concerning the external realities which present themselves to his attention are there, and each of those assents is a judgment. Through such assents or judgments he knows the existence of those realities ; or, which is the same thing, attributes existence to them, even as he attributes existence to himself. Thus is formed in him that special class of judgments by which he produces to himself his own objects (synthetical judgments).

Now, it is for these primitive judgments that the human being necessarily requires to possess some antecedent notion, and precisely the notion of existence, which is the *sign* or indication whereby alone he can know that existence of bodies is a truth. Here, therefore, lies the solid part of Plato's reasoning. This first kind of inquiries, or rather these primitive findings of the truth, would be impossible to man unless there were an innate principle in his mind to enable him to discern the truth, and to discern it intuitively, and, as it were, by its own physiognomy ;

of truth. By referring to this one exemplar, we shall be able in all things which come before us to distinguish error from truth, since truth has the same countenance everywhere. Plato did not consider this, and, as a consequence, his solution of the difficulty overshot the mark by assuming more than was necessary to account for the origin of our ideas, against the second of the canons of method which I have laid down (n. 27).[1]

for it cannot be known through its relation with other truths, none of which, by the hypothesis, have as yet been acquired.

In fact, with the one supposition that the distinctive and common *mark* of truth (which, as we shall see, consists in notional existence or the idea of being) is imprinted on the soul of man from his origin, all the difficulties of which we speak disappear at once. By means of this *mark* he apprehends whichever truths happen to come before him first ; not as though he was purposely seeking for those in particular, but because by a natural prompting of his reason he feels a general hankering for truths, and is therefore always in wakeful expectation to receive them from whencesoever they may show themselves, that he may welcome them as congenial with his intellectual constitution. Now, to apprehend determinate truths is, as I said above, nothing but to judge that something is true. Consequently, for our reason to perceive bodies is nothing else than to judge that bodies truly exist, or, which is the same, to assent interiorly to the fact of their existence.

When the human being has made this step, and is therefore in possession of diverse truths, there is no difficulty in explaining how he can pass on to inquiries of the second class ; for the truths now known by him have relations whereby he can determine other truths as yet unknown, which may therefore be made a particular object of his inquisitiveness.

It is here, properly speaking, that those which we usually term *inquiries* after truth begin ; for those of the first species ought to be termed perceptions or findings rather than inquiries. In the same way there is no longer any difficulty in explaining the inquiries of

the third species, inasmuch as the existence of the ideas which are therein submitted to analysis has already been duly accounted for.

It was, then, from not having drawn a clear distinction between the above three ways in which we seek after truth, or at least find it, that Plato fell into the mistake of extending the difficulty of which we speak beyond its proper limits ; hence the solution which he offered could not be perfectly satisfactory.

[1] It could hardly be expected that a man who was the first to penetrate so deeply into the question regarding the origin of ideas should express what he saw with a faultless precision of language. Original men, when some great truth happens to be noticed by them for the first time, feel so enraptured by it, so satisfied and overjoyed on account of their new acquisition, that they do not trouble themselves much with sifting it from every particular flaw by which it may be, and usually is, surrounded. Unable any longer to doubt the certainty of their discovery, and carried away almost in spite of themselves by its unexpected beauty, they seem powerless to attend to it in minute detail, or to call its excellence in question. They take it as it is in the main, and idolise it. Thus are systems born ; and something of this kind seems to have happened to Plato in the matter of the origin of ideas.

Nevertheless, there are moments in which calm reason brings these men, unawares to themselves, nearer to the exact truth. In certain passages Plato approaches it so closely, that were these the only declarations we have of him, one would say that he had fully attained it.

Thus in *Theatetus*, to explain how it is that we carry within us the know-

ARTICLE V.

Aristotle points out the inaccuracy of Plato's reasoning.

231. The inaccuracy contained in Plato's reasoning seems to have been the cause of the defection of Aristotle from the school of his master.

ledge of all truths, and yet have to search for them, he says that truths may be *possessed* by us without our having them—even as a man may keep a number of birds shut up in a large cage without having them in his hands. And, as an illustration of this, he adduces the case of a man who knows arithmetic or the art of calculation. This art comprises under it all cognitions of numbers; and the use of it may not inappropriately be compared to a hunting after these cognitions. So long, therefore, as the man is limited to the possession of this art, he possesses, indeed, all the results obtainable by the calculation of numbers, but he has not those results actually: he possesses them in the same way that the owner does the birds, which fly freely to and fro inside the cage, and are not his except in so far as he has it in his power to catch them whenever he pleases. But let us hear Plato himself:—

'*Socrates.* Let us take as an example the art of arithmetic.

'*Theætetus.* Agreed.

'*Socrates.* Suppose this art to be a hunting after the cognitions of all numbers, even and uneven.

'*Theætetus.* Suppose it.

'*Socrates.* Through this art the arithmetician has under him, like so many servants, all the cognitions of numbers, and imparts them to others.

'*Theætetus.* Quite so.

'*Socrates.* And he who imparts those cognitions is said to teach them; he who receives them is said to learn them; but he who has them in his mind is said to know them.

'*Theætetus.* Nothing could be truer.

'*Socrates.* Now, take note of what follows from this. Seeing that the perfect arithmetician possesses in his mind all the cognitions of numbers, is it not true to say that he knows all numbers?

'*Theætetus.* So it seems.

'*Socrates.* And does not such a one sometimes calculate with himself the numbers of different objects, internal or external?

'*Theætetus.* Who can doubt it?

'*Socrates.* But to calculate is nothing else than to ascertain how great a given number is.

'*Theætetus.* Nothing else.

'*Socrates.* It seems, therefore, that this arithmetician seeks for what he already knows; because we have just confessed that he possesses all the cognitions of numbers. Do you perceive the contradiction?'

Now, Socrates by means of his system did away with the apparent contradiction, by explaining how it arose. The arithmetician *knows* all the results of his art, but he knows them only *potentially: actually* he does not know them, and therefore when he wants one or another of them, he must seek for it by making use of the art he possesses.

The ambiguity lies wholly in the word *to know.* As was afterwards remarked by Aristotle, to say that the arithmetician *knows* all the results of his art is not speaking with propriety. Properly speaking, it can only be said that he *can know* them, that he possesses the means or the art of arriving at them. It was this impropriety of language that occasioned the discredit of Plato's system. By using the word *to know* in the second of the above meanings instead of in the first, which is its only true and proper one,· he was led to assert that man *knew* everything from his birth, and hence that all ideas were innate in him.

Leaving aside, however, this impropriety of language, and the error it induced, and looking only at the spirit of the above dialogue between Socrates and Theætetus, everyone can see how

In very many places of his works the Stagirite referring to the child who, on being questioned by Socrates, gave replies which he had never learnt from anyone, and drew from within his own mind the solution of mathematical problems, finds fault with Plato for calling such performances by the name of *knowledge.* He very properly observes that what the child really knew were the principles of reasoning on which the solution depended, and whence he deduced it through reasoning. It is true that consequences are virtually contained in their principles, and that, therefore, he who knows the principles has also a *potential* knowledge of the consequences—has the power of knowing them ; but potential knowledge or the power of knowing is not as yet *actual* knowledge—knowledge in the true and proper sense of the word. Plato should not, therefore, have said that the child knew those mathematical truths, without qualifying the word *knew* by some such clause as 'under a certain aspect,' &c.—that is, potentially, or in so far as they were virtually contained in the principles of which he was cognisant.

Had Plato adopted this qualifying clause, the apparent contradiction suggested by him—that we learn what we

very near Plato came to the exact truth. In that dialogue it is irrefragably demonstrated that there must be an innate *knowledge*, which virtually comprises in itself all cognitions, in the same way that the arithmetical art comprises the knowledge of all numbers ; in short, a knowledge which contains the *art* of descrying and recognising the truth wherever met with. This knowledge, then, once granted, the power of acquiring cognitions, or the faculty of reason, follows as a matter of course ; for what is human reason but the *art of arriving at particular cognitions?*

Having come thus far, what else had Plato to do, in order to perfect his theory on the origin of ideas?

Simply to inquire in what this primitive art or this *original knowledge,* virtually comprising all cognitions, even as the arithmetical art comprises all the cognitions of numbers, could consist. He had already mastered the fact that to find out some particular conclusion respecting numbers, to solve

some arithmetical problem, it was necessary to possess the art of doing it, or, in other words, to possess certain principles, and to know how to apply them to the conclusions sought for. Now, what is true of reasonings relating to the limited subject of numbers is equally true of reasonings relating to everything else. Every use of our reasoning faculty is but the exercise of a *primitive art* innate in us, an art which cannot be learnt, whilst all other arts are learnt by means of it. If, then, we had not the ability to reason, it would be impossible for us to learn the art of reasoning. Now, Plato was, as we have seen, vividly impressed with the necessity of an innate knowledge for enabling us to make use of our faculty of reasoning. He had, then, only to go on to inquire into the nature of this knowledge, in order to discover the proper way out of the great difficulty and to the full possession of the truth.

already know—would have vanished ; for then the true and
genuine version of it would have been, as Aristotle puts it,
that by our investigations we 'come to learn what we were
in reality ignorant of, since we had only such virtual knowledge as was necessary to enable us to know it truly and
actually.'[1]

ARTICLE VI.

*Its defect notwithstanding, the reasoning of Plato contains an element
of solid truth.*

232. The remark of Aristotle was just, but it only told
against that part in which Plato's reasoning was defective,
leaving intact that solid substratum of truth which it contained.

The great Stagirite seems to have had the same misfortune as so frequently befalls thinkers of less weight than he.
When an author comes to discover some error in a theory, he
is apt to desist from all further examination and to reject it at
once as entirely false. He does not pause to reflect that the
error he has noticed is perhaps only a small part of the theory,
or even nothing more than a defect in the mode of its exposition, or a want of completeness in some portion of its fundamental idea. In looking, therefore, at the strictures which
Aristotle made on Plato's system, and considering how he
seems to have stopped as it were at the surface of it, I do
not find it difficult to understand why the Platonists, who
felt that in their master's teaching there still remained a
solid foundation of truth,[2] retorted on Aristotle by saying,
that the doctrine on ideas was much too high for his mental
grasp, so that he could neither comprehend nor embrace it.[3]

233. In fact, Plato's mistake consisted in having applied
his reasoning to deduced truths — as is, for instance, the
solution of a mathematical problem ; whereas it real force
and solidity manifest themselves in its application to the
primary or self-evident principles, and to these only.

[1] *Posterior.* i.
[2] Although even they did not know
how to distinguish and indicate it with
precision, and for this reason fell into
the opposite error of embracing Plato's
doctrine in its entirety.
[3] See the passage in Atticus, quoted
by Eusebius, *Præparat. Evang.* xv. 13.

By taking a deduced truth, and endeavouring to demonstrate that the mathematical conclusions elicited by Socrates from a child yet untaught in mathematical science must needs have been known to that child beforehand, Plato left himself open to the Aristotelian rejoinder, 'That it was sufficient if the child knew the principles whence those conclusions could be drawn, and was endowed with reason, or the faculty of deducing them.' This rejoinder admitted of no reply: the untenableness of Plato's particular contention stood completely exposed by the counter-proposition of his antagonist.

But if Plato was vanquished on that particular issue, the general drift of his argument still remained in undiminished force. Nothing was wanted except to present it in such a form as to make that force distinctly felt. Now, this is done as soon as one applies it, not to deduced truths, but to the primal and indemonstrable truth—that which virtually contains all truths, and is not itself contained by any anterior ones, because it is the first and most universal.

ARTICLE VII.

Aristotle does not seem to give an adequate explanation of universals.

234. On the subject of universals Aristotle leaves a void, or at least is obscure.

He fully grasped the distinction between primary and derived truths, and seems also to have reached so far as to reduce all primary truths to one only—the principle of contradiction.[1]

He accounts for the origin of derived truths, as I have said before, by means of *demonstration*, or deduction from the primary ones, and proves against Plato that derived truths are not innate in us.

But when he undertakes to account for the origin of *primary* truths, he no longer seems to feel the force of the Platonic argument, doubtless because Plato himself did not apply it to one class of truths more than to another. Hence,

---

[1] *Metaph.* iv,

having refuted Plato in regard to derived truths, he thought that there was an end of the whole subject in dispute.

Briefly stated, his explanation of the origin of primary truths is as follows.

These truths (so he argued with himself) are such that they cannot be obtained through deduction from anterior ones ; for were they so obtainable, they would not be primary, Therefore, they are by their nature incapable of demonstration. They must, therefore, be acquiesced in with implicit *faith*, without any demonstration ;[1] and in fact all men *do so believe* in them. Consequently, we must needs admit that there is in man a certain faculty in virtue of which he sees these truths by immediate intuition, and gives them his assent.[2]

235. This, then, is in substance Aristotle's way of explaining the formation of the primary notions of truths. He gives to man a faculty or power capable of forming them— a power very similar to Locke's *Reflection.*

---

[1] By *demonstration* is meant the deduction of one truth from another already admitted as indubitable.

Now, if primary truths are believed in without *demonstration*—that is, without being derived from other truths— does it follow that they are believed in without a *reason?*

To assert this would be tantamount to annihilating the human intelligence, and establishing a profound scepticism. Such, however, let me observe, is the inevitable issue of the system of those who place the criterion of truth in *blind common sense—i.e.* in the *dicta* of an authority unsupported by any reason. Of this new and most pernicious of all kinds of scepticism, the first seeds were, quite contrary to his intentions, sown by Reid, and then fully developed by Kant.

If, on the other hand, it be said that the primary truths are not believed in through *blind necessity*, but because they are *reasons* in themselves—lights whose brilliancy wins and as it were creates our assent—then it will be found difficult to reconcile the Aristotelian system, as commonly understood, with this *faith* which Aristotle says we yield to the primary truths without any assignable reason.

For if these primary truths are *reasons*, how could they ever be derived from the external things perceived by our senses?

In the external things sensibly perceived, those reasons cannot be found, because external things are not *reasons*, but *facts*, and facts are particulars, whilst reasons are universals.

Therefore, these reasons or primary truths in which we believe must either be communicated to us on occasion of our sensations by separated intelligences, as the Arabians maintained, or they must somehow exist in us *per se.* In the first case, their innateness would be denied to the human, only to be transferred to other intelligences ; and this would not explain how we derive them from the senses. In the second case, it would be through the implicit belief yielded to them that we are enabled to believe also in all derived ideas or truths, whose whole and sole motive of credibility they are ; and this would be equivalent to admitting that they are innate in us. In a word, we must either accept the sceptical theory or allow that some intellectual light visible *per se* is given us by nature.

[2] *Posterior.* lib. i.

As I have remarked elsewhere, these two philosophers seem to say to us: ' See if our explanation of the origin of ideas is not satisfactory. We admit a *faculty* capable of forming them, and what more do you require?' This is admirable so far as it goes; but, unfortunately, it gives no answer to the question that excites our curiosity—the vexed question of the origin of ideas. Of course, if we are simply to assume that man has in him a power, truly furnished with all that is requisite for forming or, better still, contemplating the primary ideas, I have nothing more to say. But the difficulty to be solved lies precisely in knowing how this power must be constituted, in order that it may serve for its purpose. Aristotle, after saying that the soul through the memory of many sensations forms a universal, adds immediately : but *let the soul be such that it can suffer this in itself.*[1] By this method it will be easy to dispose of any difficulty.

It is just the same as if I, on a certain perplexing question being put to me, were to content myself with the reply, ' This question will be solved provided we assume a *something* which will suffice to clear it up,' and then to congratulate myself on having done full justice to that question.

I think, therefore, that we still have a right to address both Aristotle and Locke thus: We do not for a moment deny that man has in him a faculty by which he can think, and thus acquire ideas. But we would wish to go further and to ask, If that faculty does not perhaps consist simply in the *power of making use of some notion or idea which man has in*

[1] *Posterior.* lib. ii. c. ult. The word to *suffer*, which Aristotle employs here to express the intuition of the understanding, and which he repeats in so many other places of his works, shows that he conceived that intellectual intuition as a *passion* wholly similar to that of sense. Indeed, he lays it down as a principle that, in order to explain aright the operations of the understanding, we ought to follow the analogy of the operations of the senses. See his books *De Anima*, especially the third. Conversely, to explain the operations of the senses, he often has recourse to the operations of the understanding. Hence he credits the senses with judgment, a function exclusively proper to the understanding ; and he credits the understanding with the passive perception of particulars, a function exclusively proper to the senses : or to speak more correctly, he attributes promiscuously to both these faculties the operations distinctive of each. In this way, the intellectual acts are no longer difficult to explain ; for, on the one hand, the sense is made to contribute the explanation, and, on the other, it is assumed to contain whatever is requisite for that end—a manifest ' begging of the question.'

him ab initio? if, in short, it is possible for any human thought to be anything else than either the vision or the application of a rule or idea? Now, if our philosophers should object to our pursuing our inquiry on this path, they would be very intolerant indeed, and their intolerance would be the commencement of their error; nor is it likely that men will be persuaded that the perfection of wisdom is not to be found except within the boundaries assigned to it by this *ipse dixit.*

ARTICLE VIII.

From some passages in the works of Aristotle it would seem that he did not sufficiently mark the distinction between sense and understanding.

236. Considering, then, that Aristotle limited his confutation of the innate ideas of Plato to the ideas formed through deduction, and therefore evidently acquired; and that as regarded the primary or, as he calls them, immediate ideas, he thought it enough to say that they originated from the senses through the use of a special *faculty* termed by him 'intellect,' which is ordained expressly *ad hoc,* and furnished with every requisite for the attainment of its end; we are justified in the suspicion that he did not sufficiently realise to himself the difficulty contained in the problem of the origin of ideas, a difficulty which presents itself in all its force, when one undertakes to explain the origin of the primary and most universal ideas. For this class of ideas cannot be syllogistically deduced from anterior ones, because there are none such, and all other ideas are deduced from them.

I am confirmed in this opinion by seeing that in some parts of his works Aristotle does not seem to have sufficiently marked the distinction between *feeling,* which belongs to the faculty of sense, and *thinking,* which belongs to the faculty of understanding.

237. He certainly knew that these are two different faculties; nor did he confound them together in the same way as did Condillac and others in our times;[1] but he only dis-

---

[1] The distinction drawn by Aristotle between sense and understanding is ac-   curately described by Sestus Empyricus in his 7th book *Against the Logicians,*

tinguished them through their objects, not perceiving that the *terms* of sense are not *objects*; and again that there is an essential difference in the manner of operating between the two faculties in question. To the corporeal senses he assigned as their proper objects *particulars*, and to the understanding *universals*;[1] he also allowed to the understanding the power of abstracting universals from particulars (*intellectus agens*), and of contemplating them when abstracted (*intellectus*

§ 217, &c. There, in expounding the doctrine of Aristotle and Theophrastes, he says that the *similitudes* of external things are received into our soul from the senses; but that these similitudes do not as yet constitute *thought*. For the production of thought it is necessary to suppose in the soul a certain *energy* or force entirely its own, by means of which the soul may from those phantasms of particular things *voluntarily* draw the idea, *e. gr.*, of *man in general*. Failing this intrinsic energy, it would be possible for the soul to receive sensations, and even have reminiscences as well as phantasms of them, but apart from *thought*. The word *voluntarily*, used for characterising the operation of the understanding in the formation of ideas, proves that Aristotle did not look upon it as a *blind* operation, but an operation accompanied with interior light, as are the acts of the will. Should anyone doubt this, he has only to take note of the way in which Sestus Empyricus had expressed the same thing a little before. He had said that in the formation of ideas the understanding acts in virtue of a *judgment*, and of *an act of election*. This would prove likewise that Aristotle had at least caught a glimpse of the very important truth that we cannot form an *idea* of any *determinate* thing, cannot make any special acts of thought, except through a *judgment*, and that to form ideas is nothing but to judge of our sensations. And if, as it would appear, Aristotle describes elsewhere the formation of ideas in a different manner, this simply proves that he was not always consistent with himself, and that, having once seen the truth above referred to, he did not afterwards realise its importance, nor follow it up steadily in its applications.
[1] In the passage I have alluded to

in the preceding note Sestus Empyricus, setting forth the doctrine of Aristotle, says that 'speaking generally the nature of things is twofold; some are *sensible things*, while others are such as to be perceived by the understanding.' Similar expressions are often found also in the works of Aristotle. But if these things are of two different natures, where is the passage from one of these natures to the other? Aristotle places it in this, that the *phantasms* of particular things are, to use his phrase, *potentially universal*. (*De Anima*, lib. ii. sect. 12.)

Now, I would ask, what do you mean by this expression? Or, how do you know that the particular phantasms have this *potentiality* in them? Doubtless from what you assume as a fact—*i.e.* that the understanding abstracts from them the *universal*; whence you infer that they must therefore have the capability of being so dealt with by the understanding as to yield to it the universal, which capability is precisely the *potentiality* you speak of. But in this case I must beg leave to observe that you give no answer to the crucial question, how the abstracting operation of the understanding takes place. You indeed assert this operation as a fact, but, instead of explaining it, you only treat us to a vicious circle; for it is nothing but a vicious circle to say that the reason why the particular phantasms communicate with ideas (the synonym of *universals*) is because they are *potentially universal*. It is the same as to say universals are drawn from phantasms because they *can* be drawn from them.

Your expression *potentially universal* is, therefore, only an obscure and mysterious way of affirming the very point which we ask you in clear and plain language to explain and prove.

possibilis). But this was not as yet seeing that intrinsic difference between the operations of the two faculties to which I wish here to call attention.

238. What makes it very difficult for us to perceive this difference is that, in consequence of our continually making use of the understanding conjointly with the sense, the operations of these two faculties become so intimately mixed up and as it were blended together, that they seem to us to be one and the same. Hence, without being aware of it, we attribute to the sense that which belongs to the understanding alone, and can hardly ever be said to form a true conception of this latter power.

239. From the same cause arises the inclination which we have to ascribe intelligence to animals, fancying that they proceed in their operations after the same manner as ourselves ; and likewise the inclination to attribute our own affections and thoughts to inanimate things. Being ourselves not merely material, nor yet merely sensitive, but a compound of matter, sense and intelligence, we find it extremely hard to get at a precise and genuine idea of what a *being* wholly *inanimate*, or purely *sensitive*, really is.

240. It would appear, therefore, that Aristotle fell, like Condillac (81–85), into the blunder of attributing to *sense* the faculty of making judgments [1]—a gross absurdity, inasmuch as to make judgments is the property of the understanding exclusively.

In fact, I argue thus : either a *judgment* is the same thing as a *sensation*, and in this case the proposition ' The faculty of sensation is capable of judging ' would be but a meaningless repetition, equivalent to this other proposition, ' The faculty of sensation is capable of having sensation ;' or else, a judgment is essentially different from a sensation, and then how can we attribute two operations which are essentially different to one and the same faculty, and say, ' The sense judges ' ? Is not this quite as preposterous as to say, ' The ear speaks,' or ' The nose sees,' or ' The hand sneezes,' or to

[1] See *De Anima*, Lib. III. cap. ix., *Metaph.* i., and many other places of his works.

formulate any other monstrous concept, whereby a faculty is unnaturally wedded to functions not its own?

241. Take the corporeal sense as it truly is ; do not associate with it anything foreign to its nature, and therefore any kind of *judgment*; and all that you will find remaining is a passive faculty, through which the sentient subject receives certain modifications (sensations)—*i.e. feels* differently from what it did before, and feels something other than itself. There is as yet no thought here, no act by which that subject has said to itself, 'This thing exists,' thus applying the most universal of all predicates, *existence*, either to itself or to something outside itself.

But, as I have said, to us who in this matter have not and cannot have any experience, because we are by nature at once sentient and intelligent—and are, moreover, continually in the habit of intimately conjoining what we feel with the judgment affirmatory of its existence, so that the two seem assimilated in one—it is most difficult to imagine a being which exists, indeed, and feels, but has no knowledge of what *existence* is, and, consequently, never predicates it of anything. Properly to distinguish these two operations, a very sustained abstraction, a most searching 'intellectual chemistry,' is necessary. By dint of long reflection we come at last to see most clearly, that to *feel* one's existence and to *think* of it or *affirm* it by a judgment are two things as different as can be. In the first, we descry an act by which the whole human subject exists simply as a sentiment,[1] and feels, therefore, the mode in which it exists ; while in the second we find an act whereby, not the whole human subject, but one of its faculties (the understanding), reflecting on the said *sentiment*, and at the same time being by nature possessed of the notion of *existence*, unites the two together, and says, 'I EXIST.' In this pronouncement, the subject (*Ego*) is judged, or, better,

[1] According to the author, the human subject consists in a *substantial sentiment*, which, when seen by the understanding in the idea of being, and consciously affirmed to exist, is called EGO. See this work, Vol. III. Part III. ch. iii. Art. 1—7; also *Antropologia in servigio della Scienza Morale*, Book IV. ch. iv. ; likewise *Psicologia*, Book I. ch. ii.-v., vii.-x. [TRANSLATORS.]

is the OBJECT of a judgment. On the contrary, the human subject as such, even when modified by sensations, is not the OBJECT of any judgment ; it is purely and simply a SUBJECT, one, undivided, without composition or decomposition of ideas, without motion and without action, except that of the primal act whereby it exists and immovably feels : in which state it could hardly be designated by the word *Ego*.

Such being the case, it is manifest that to credit the senses with the power of judging, as Aristotle seems to do sometimes, is an unjustifiable confusion of two very distinct faculties—*i.e.* the sensitive and the intellectual.

242. Of the insufficiency of Aristotle's distinction between sense and understanding a writer who had studied him deeply speaks in the following terms : 'According to the opinion of Aristotle, the sense and the understanding differ only in this, that the external things are *felt* in that same condition which they have outside the soul as particulars ; whereas the nature of things *cognised* is, indeed, outside the soul, but has not there that mode of being according to which the common nature (the *universal*) is cognised—*i.e.* apart from its individualising principles. Outside the soul, things have not this mode of being.'

This would mean, that the sense and the understanding differ only by their immediate terms. The sense perceives external things in their particularity ; while the understanding has only the power to perceive that which in those things is *common*, apart from all the rest.[1]

243. Now, in the first place, admitting all this, the diffi-

---

[1] What kind of power would this be ? If the understanding perceives only the universal while the sense perceives, together with the universal, the proper also, it follows that the understanding is merely a sense more limited, and therefore worth much less, than the corporeal ! On the other hand, considering that Aristotle, in so many places of his works, exhibits a thorough appreciation of the excellence of the understanding as compared with the sense, the thought naturally suggests itself, either that he did not see the consequences of this his theory, or that all this Aristotelian doctrine must be interpreted in a deeper and more recondite way than I have stated. I wish, therefore, the reader distinctly to understand that it is not my intention to censure directly the doctrine of the great Stagirite in so far as conceived by himself, but only what appears to be the most obvious meaning of some of his expressions, or at least the meaning in which they have been taken by so many of his commentators.

culty would always remain as to how the understanding can
make this abstraction without a universal to serve it as a guide
in the operation; for when anyone undertakes to separate a
number of objects into different classes, he must be possessed
beforehand of the universal idea which differentiates those
classes. That is, he must know that universal quality which
is to be the basis of the classification. In other words, in
order that the *intellectus agens* may distinguish and divide the
common from the proper, it must necessarily have in itself
some idea to direct it in that separation—to enable it to see
the greater or less degrees of universality belonging to the
various parts of the object on which it exercises itself for the
purpose of *purifying* it, if I may be allowed a metaphor
which has been so largely used by the ancients.

244. But, leaving this aside, and returning to our main
point, it was not enough to observe that it is proper to the sense
to perceive external things individualised by their respective
particularities; it was necessary furthermore to inquire
whether in such a perception man interiorly affirms something
to himself; whether, for example, he says, 'The thing which
I feel exists.' For if he does this, he pronounces a judgment;
and if he pronounces a judgment, is that judgment simply
synchronous with the sensation, or is it the sensation itself?
Here lies the whole knot of the difficulty.

The smallest degree of reflection upon ourselves will
suffice to show us that a sensation is felt in some external
part of our body—in the hand, in the foot, and so forth;
whereas the judgment which we make in consequence of
that sensation is a purely interior word, in no way connected
with any part of our body. This proves to evidence that the
act of *judgment* has nothing whatever to do with the *organic
sensation*; that the sense feels, indeed, but without pronouncing any judgment on what it feels;[1] that the act of judgment,

---

[1] From the sense proceeds the *instinct* causing us to seek certain things
and to shun others; but instinct is not
judgment: it is a passive inclination; it
belongs to *spontaneity*, and not to the
will. Nevertheless, we are always inclined to assume that what the animals
do by instinct is the result of knowledge
and judgment. This arises from our
habit of never performing consciously
any action apart from a judgment, because we are rational beings. Some-

different altogether from the act of feeling, is added by the understanding; and that, therefore, the difference between sense and understanding does not consist merely in this, that by the first a thing is perceived as particular, and by the second as universal; but also, and above all, in this, that the cognitive perception belongs exclusively to the understanding. The sense perceives only by way of *feeling*, but the understanding passes *judgment* on what the sense has so perceived, and thus *cognises* it.

ARTICLE IX.

According to Themistius's Paraphrase, it would seem that Aristotle did not properly understand the nature of the Universal.

245. The Philosopher of Stagira, then, did not sufficiently distinguish between *feeling*, which is passive as well as simple, and *judgment*, which is active, and composed of two terms— one of them, at least, a universal—from the union of which another composite apprehension is obtained. As a consequence of this slip, when he had to face the difficulty of explaining the origin of *primary ideas*, he thought that the way to get out of it would be by supposing the understanding to be a sort of sense which, when affected by universals, was obliged to perceive them in a passive manner,[1] similar to that in which the external sensories perceive the 'sensibles.'

But, seeing, on the other hand, that universals had no

---

times, however, that judgment is formed with such rapidity as wholly to escape our advertence.

[1] As I have already observed, Aristotle attributed judgment to the sense, and feeling to the understanding. Hence in his works we find *feeling* and *judgment*—two essentially different operations—predicated indifferently of each of these faculties (see *De Anima*, Lib. III. cap. vii.). As regards, however, the understanding, even this confusion shows that he caught a glimpse of a truth pregnant with important consequences, of which I should like to speak here, were I not deterred by the length to which this would carry me. I shall therefore content myself with pointing out how, by his improper way of speaking, Aristotle was clean overleaping the difficulty as to the forma-

tion of ideas. From the moment that sensation is supposed to be always united with judgment, the sense becomes a little intellectual faculty. Hence the real knot of that difficulty, which lies in explaining how the sense communicates with the understanding, no longer exists, and the whole question is transferred from the passage between sensation and judgment to the passage between one judgment and another— from a very thorny question to one so easy that it does not even deserve to be seriously proposed. This Aristotelian solution of the difficulty is about as much to the point as would be that exemplified in the following question and answer : ' How shall I best swim across yon river ? ' ' The best way for you to do it is by crossing over in a boat.'

existence outside the mind, he imagined this faculty to be possessed of the virtue of universalising particulars, through abstraction—that is, by taking from them all that was *common* (as if the *common* were not the *universal* itself) and leaving the rest. He forgot, however, to examine whether such an operation as this were practicable or even possible on the supposition that there was nothing innate in the human soul.

That Aristotle looked upon the abstraction performed by his *intellectus agens* as being nothing but the discovery in particular things of that which was already in them, seems clear from the exposition which has been given us of his doctrine by Themistius. If this exposition is correct, I do not see how we can reject the conclusion that the Stagirite did not rightly understand the nature of the universal. For the nature of particular things, in so far as it is universal, is not in them at all, and in so far as it exists in them, it is in no way *common*, but purely and simply (if I may so express myself) an act limited to their individual selves. The passage of the Paphlagonian philosopher to which I refer is as follows : —' This energy of the soul [*the abstracting energy*] consists in this, that even if the genera which fall under the sense were suddenly to fail and vanish, the soul would still have the power to draw from the sense their similitudes, and to retain them in the memory, and to discover and note whatever there is of common and universal in particulars. For EVEN SENSE PERCEIVES THIS. Indeed, whenever anyone by means of his senses knows Socrates, he knows also Socrates' humanity ; and he who sees this red thing or this white thing, sees also redness or whiteness. Nor is there anyone who would take Callias and humanity to be one and the same thing ; otherwise, as there is but one Callias, so there would be but one man in existence. But whoever sees Socrates, sees, in Socrates, all that there is of similar and common in other men also. Wherefore, in a certain way THE UNIVERSAL IS PERCEIVED BY THE SENSE, not, however, divided from the particular, but united with it, and by consequence.' [1]

---

[1] Themistii *Paraphrasis in Aristotelis Posteriorum Lib. II.*, cap. xxxv.   The real truth is, that the sense does not perceive the universal, either united

ARTICLE X.

To judge is more than to apprehend the Universal.

246. Nor can we wonder at Aristotle endowing the sense with power to perceive in the particular the *universal*, when we consider that he had granted to it the power of making *judgments.*

No one can make a judgment without some universal pre-existing in his mind, for to judge is to assign certain objects or qualities to a given class ; and a class cannot be formed except by means of something which is common to the things classified.

· Hence to ascribe judgment to the senses seems to be even more than ascribing to them the apprehension of that which the particulars have of common, in the way that Aristotle, as interpreted by Themistius, understands this apprehension—that is, embracing at once the common and the proper. For, in order to make a judgment, one must furthermore possess the idea of the *common*, apart from all that is proper, that it may be applied to the several particulars, and thus serve as a proper basis for their classification.[1]

---

with or divided from the particular. Hence, to attribute this perception to the sense is an absurdity. Even in the system of Aristotle, the word *universal* indicates the product of an intellectual operation, and has therefore no existence apart from the understanding in which it is acquired. How, then, can the sense perceive that which begins to exist only subsequently to its operation ?

[1] I have already observed, that the error of Aristotle may have simply arisen from impropriety of expression, the very fault with which he seems so fond of reproaching Plato. Possibly he takes *judgment* in a wider sense than belongs to it. Or he perhaps uses it in two significations which are essentially different—viz. (1) as meaning that *instinctive action* whereby animals tend towards certain things which we, on this account, qualify as good for them, or turn away from others which, for a contrary reason, we qualify as hurtful to them. This instinctive action is a sort of practical discernment between relative good and relative evil, and may easily be mistaken for a judgment proceeding from the faculty of reason. (2) As meaning the application which our understanding makes of a *predicate*, negative or positive—that is, of a *universal*—to some *subject*, either individual or at least less general than that predicate.

Only this latter operation is truly intellectual, while the inclination towards certain things, or the aversion to others, may be purely an effect of the animal instinct called forth by the sense. It should, however, be noted, that those things which the instinct seeks or shuns are not good or bad *per se*, antecedently to and independently of it ; but they are called good or bad solely in consequence of the opposite attitudes which it is seen to take in regard to them. In other words, their goodness or badness is purely relative to the disposition of that instinct. By means of this ob-

ARTICLE XI.

Absurdity of the doctrine expounded by Themistius.

247. Let us look once more at the proposition, 'The sense perceives the *common,* but in union with the particulars.'

servation it will be easy to see what a vast difference there is between *instinctive discernment and judgment* properly so called. *Instinctive discernment* precedes the goodness or badness of the things on which it bears, as the cause precedes the effect; *judgment,* on the contrary, does not precede, but follows. It is not the cause but the effect of the goodness or badness of the things it pronounces upon; for it pronounces them good or bad simply because it finds them such. In short, judgment is always based on a reason; instinct acts blindly—*i.e.* without seeing any reason. Judgment must conform itself to things as they are; instinct does not conform itself to things, but they conform themselves to it; and this accidental conformity is what we term their goodness. We, however, who are rational beings, when qualifying as good the things sought for by our animal instinct, make a judgment; thus uniting the *instinctive discernment* with an *act of reason.*

But what I have submitted as a conjecture respecting the abuse made by Aristotle of the word *judgment* turns out to be a certainty when we compare together other passages of this philosopher. For instance, in the third Book *De Anima* (cap. vii. et viii.), he lays it down that affirmation and negation belong to the understanding alone. He says that the sense, in apprehending sensible things, *judges of them after its own fashion*; and that when it feels them pleasurable or painful, it seeks or shuns them *as though it affirmed them* to be good or bad. He does not say positively that it *affirms them* such, because, as St. Thomas observes in his commentary, affirmation is exclusively an act of the

understanding; but it performs an operation which in its effects of *seeking* or *shunning* resembles the intellectual *affirmation*: 'Facere affirmationem et negationem est proprium intellectus; .... sed sensus facit aliquid simile huic, quando apprehendit ut delectabile et triste.' And a little further on, Aristotle —notwithstanding that he had previously attributed the function of judgment even to the *imagination* (*De Anima,* Lib. III. cap. iv. v.)—nevertheless takes away from it the power of *affirming* and *denying,* and hence also *knowing the truth,* which, as the Angelic Doctor explains, is proper only to the understanding : 'nam cognoscere verum et falsum est solius intellectus.'

The natural inference from this would be, that Aristotle imagined a species of judgment containing neither *affirmation* nor *negation,* neither assent nor dissent, nor pronouncement on the *true* or the *false.* In short, he retained the word *judgment,* but without the meaning in which it is commonly used. Of a truth I do not believe that in common parlance the word *judgment* signifies an act in which nothing is affirmed or denied— which has not the true or the false for its object. So far as I am aware, this kind of act is generally designated by the name of *sensation* or *instinctive motion,* and nothing more. This sensation or motion may very well cause the mere animal to do the same external acts which man performs as determined by the judgment of reason; but the apparent sameness of the effects does not in this case suffice to prove that their proximate producing cause is the same. (*a*) I shall, therefore, with the generality of men, reserve the term *judgment* to signify this cause in man in so far as he

<hr>

(*a*) How mere animals can imitate the effects of reason by means of sense and instinct alone has been explained at length by the author in his *Antropologia in servigio della Scienza Morale,* especially in chapter xi. of Book II. See also his *Psicologia,* Book V. [TRANSLATORS.]

Either this proposition is a contradiction in terms, or it means nothing.

The *common* in the *particulars*: what a strange expression this is, ' The common in that which is *not* common '! Can such a thing be? *Common* signifies not particularised, not limited to a real individual. If ten thousand individuals were mustered before me in succession, I should certainly receive in me as many impressions as are those particular units ; but I should not as yet have perceived anything *common*. Briefly, the *common* is nothing but a *relation* of individuals with an idea which is in my mind. After perceiving these individuals, I compare them together, and note their points of similarity or dissimilarity, always in so far as ˏthey are perceived by me—that is, I note that which in the perception of many individuals corresponds to one and the same idea, and that which corresponds to different ideas. That in which they are similar or correspond to the same idea is called

acts as a rational being, and the term *sense* or *instinct* to signify it in irrational animals.

But this is not all. Aristotle himself, in another place, where he comes back to the common manner of speaking, tells us that to *judge* is the same as to *predicate truth or falsehood* of anything (*De Anima*, Lib. III. cap. iv.). It seems, therefore, that he took the word *judgment* in its proper signification when using it in reference to the understanding ; but metaphorically when he applied it to the sense or the imagination.

This ambiguity of expression was one of the causes why the Stagirite failed to give a full and lucid explanation of the formation of ideas.

Owing to his abuse of the word *judgment*, the difficulty which it was necessary to overcome in this question could not be seen either by himself or by his disciples. Accustomed as we are to conceive a judgment as an act by which one *affirms* or *denies* a given predicate of a given subject, it comes to pass that, on hearing this word applied to the sense, we forget that the application must on no account be taken literally. Now, let the sense be once taken as a faculty which makes real

judgments, and there will no longer be any difficulty in explaining the acts of the understanding. Being told that the difficulty refers entirely to the understanding, we conclude that it has nothing to do with the sense, and therefore with judgment, because judgment in this case belongs to the sense. Behold the difficulty vanish from our sight. On the contrary, the reason why the difficulty refers to the understanding is precisely because the understanding has the power to make *judgments*. If, therefore, you give the same power to the sense, this difficulty is done away with. What can be easier for the understanding than to act through judgments, since it receives them ready-made from the sense? All that it will perhaps have to do will be to bring those judgments to perfection, to give them a regular form, to render them more explicit and clear ; and in this will consist that *affirming* or *denying* which is its exclusive attribute. Thus the knowledge of the true and the false will begin here by a sort of convention between the sensitive and the intellectual faculties. In fact, you have not explained the difficulty, but only confused and thrown it into the background.

their *common* nature (nn. 180–187). Now, the relation of many individuals with my ideas is in no wise found in any one of these individuals considered by itself and therefore outside of my mind. The existence of that relation is conditional on my seeing them together in one intellectual concept, and this is wholly beyond the province of the senses, which perceive only real individuals in their particularity—*i.e.* one by one, separately from the rest.[1]   In short, there must

---

[1] The doctrine of Aristotle was this : — There is in man something which judges of the sensations, and it is called common *sensorium*, because it could not judge of them unless it felt in its one self whatever was severally felt by all the other senses. Nevertheless, each particular sense also feels and judges of the various sensible things which fall within the sphere of its own perceptions. Hence the formula—rather vague it seems to me—' Each sense partakes to some extent of the virtue of the common *sensorium* ' ' sensus proprius participat aliquid de virtute sensus communis).' But how this participation of ' virtue ' took place was a mystery.

But it was also, in the system of Aristotle, no easy task—nay, a very hard one indeed—to explain l.y lucid and solid reasons how the common *sensorium*, its oneness notwithstanding, could possess different powers (the sensitive and the intellectual) and perform operations essentially at variance with each other.   And so he bethought himself of getting out of the difficulty by the easy and much smoother way of an argument by analogy. You have here (he said) the same case as is seen exemplified in a circle.   The centre of the circle is one and most simple, and yet all the rays terminate in it. The centre represents the common *sensorium*, and the rays represent the sensations received by it from the several senses. In so far as the common *sensorium* is variously affected by those sensations, it *feels*, and in so far as it is one, it *judges* (*De Anima*, Lib. III., cap. ii.).   This solution seems to have satisfied philosophers for a long time.   Nevertheless, it would have been easy to see that the simile broke down in more than one important particular.   The centre of a circle performs no operation, and although many

rays meet in it, they are not judged nor acted upon by, nor even so much as received into, it.   Nay, by its own self, it is not even a *centre* ; it is only a *point* ; and if that point is a centre, this arises solely from the fact that our thought refers to it all the lines which in this case we call *rays*.   Its existence as a centre, therefore, is purely relational, and the product of a mental act.

Therefore, even allowing for argument's sake the Aristotelian simile of the centre and the rays, there still remains to be explained how it is possible for our thought to originate this multiplicity of relations in a single thing, such as the centre of a circle is. Hence that which has been assumed in explanation of the way in which we think of universals—and the relations of things are all universals—is not more clear or better explained than thought itself, since it is only a particular case of thought.   Once explain how we come to conceive relations and universals, and you will have explained how it is that a certain point becomes for us a *centre*, where many lines end.   But this second explanation is impossible if the first has not preceded.   The simile therefore, is illusory ; it clears up the difficulty only in appearance ; it is of no use for explaining how a single faculty can feel the sensible things which are felt by the several senses, and at the same time judge of them—that is, compare them together, noticing their similarities and dissimilarities, and even judge them to be pleasant or unpleasant.   All these are real operations, and not mere relations added by understanding to the common *sensorium*, as happens when it considers the centre as the common meeting-point of many lines.   And even if it were easy to understand how a single thing could have many relations

needs be an interior faculty wholly different from the corporeal senses—a faculty which, after intellectually perceiving the

with other things, it would still be hard to conceive how one faculty, while *preserving its oneness*, could have many terms and perform many operations essentially different. And this all the more if it be true that a human faculty means a particular force of the soul, specialised and distinguished by the unity of its term, or of the operation characteristic of it. In truth, by the fact of allowing, as Aristotle does, that *sensation* and *judgment* are two essentially different operations, does not one admit that these operations belong to two different faculties? Is not the faculty of judging denominated from the act of judgment, as the faculty of sense is from the act of sensation? And if to feel a sensation and to make a judgment are essentially one and the same thing, why attribute *judgment* to the senses? Is not this an absurdity? Is it not to attribute to sense that which is not the attribute of sense? In that case the word *judgment* might well be abolished from human language, and the word *feeling* or *sensation* be substituted in its place, without the void being at all perceived—a thing evidently impossible.

But let us see by what line of argument Aristotle was led to give to the sense the faculty of judging. He says, ' We not only feel, but we also feel that we feel, and by so doing judge of what we feel. Now, either we feel that we feel through the same sense with which we feel, or through another sense. If through another sense, then I ask again, by what means do we feel that we feel what we feel with this sense? Is it through a third sense? If so, we should have to go on with a series of senses *ad infinitum*, because we should always have to repeat the same mode of reasoning. It is therefore necessary to conclude that the sense through which we feel that we feel is the very same as that with which we feel ; and hence that it is with this identical sense that we judge.' (*De Anima*, Lib. III., cap. ii.) This may appear an ingenious argument ; but, to mention only one of its defects, it rests on an erroneous supposition—namely, that in every

sensation there is necessarily included the sensation of the sensation. What, then, is the meaning of the words ' we feel that we feel '? This expression can only mean that the soul *reflects* on its own sensation. When the soul, reflecting on itself in order to ascertain its own state, finds that it has a sensation, we are then wont to say that it feels that it feels. But this turning of the attention of the soul upon itself is, properly speaking, a *thought*. Therefore in this case the soul *thinks* of its sensation, but does not *feel* that it has any. The *sensation* is the object of its thought ; the thought is the *act* terminating in that object. Let not, therefore, the object of the act be confounded with the act itself. The sensation, which is the object, is external and passive ; the thought by which the soul reflects on the sensation is internal, active and voluntary. When, therefore, it is said that we *feel that we feel*, the verb first occurring in this expression is used in a translated sense, in lieu of *we think* ; while the same verb as occurring in the last part is used in its proper meaning of *sensation*. Pure sense does not *feel that it feels* : it *feels*, and that is all. The sensation arises simultaneously with the change produced in the sensitive organ, but does not *reflect* upon itself. And if a sensitive organ, after being once stimulated by an external force, is again acted upon by the same stimulus, or by another, what takes place in it is not anything like *reflection*, but simply a new impression and sensation which our mind finds similar to and yet entirely separate in its existence from the first. With us human beings, however, who are endowed at once with the two faculties of sense and thought, it most frequently happens that we cannot have a sensation without at the same time thinking of it, although we may not advert to the fact or express it to ourselves. Hence it comes to pass that whenever *we become aware* of a sensation, that sensation is in us, not alone, but accompanied with the thought of it, and this thought is by a metaphor called ' feeling that we feel.'

single individuals, is able, by comparing them together, to find that they all correspond with, and are therefore thinkable through, one and the same idea. With this operation, but not before, does the word *common* begin to have a meaning, and to be used with propriety of language. To say that the senses perceive the *common* is to suppose this operation, whereby in the things which have acquired an existence in our mind we see that which is *common*, as already performed ; and, moreover, it is to suppose that this *common*, found by and in the mind, is the object of the senses.

248. Thus one becomes committed to the absurd opinion that the matter which falls under the senses is a production of the understanding ; and that the material part of thought is furnished, not by the sense to the understanding, but by the understanding to the sense. See how the wrong use made by Aristotle of the word *common* flings him from one extreme to its contrary, and binds him down to a proposition which is diametrically opposed to the fundamental principle of his system, and the starting-point of his whole argument— viz. that the senses supplied the matter of knowledge to the understanding.

ARTICLE XII.

Contradiction between two opinions of Aristotle.

249. Aristotle says that the *common* (the universal), abstracted from the particular, is the object of the understanding only.

Let us examine still better how far this proposition is reconcilable with the preceding doctrine of our philosopher.

Assuming that the *common* is not innate in us, abstraction is certainly the only means by which it could be obtained ;

Now, it is very easy for us to ascribe to beings purely sensitive that which we experience in ourselves ; and this appears to me to have been the case with regard to the reasoning drawn out as above by Aristotle. Having noticed that every time we become aware of the presence in us of a sensation, we also think of, *i.e.* reflect upon it, he supposed that it was an essential property of sense to reflect upon itself. Thus was he led to ascribe to the senses a function which is inseparable from judgment. I say *inseparable from judgment*, because, for me, to reflect that we feel is simply to say to ourselves, 'I experience a sensation,' which is to make a judgment, or to think.

for the term *common* simply signifies that which is similar in many individuals, and divided from that which is dissimilar, even as one nature is divided from another, and especially from its contrary.

Therefore, when Aristotle says that the *common* is the object of the understanding only ; when he tells us that universals have no existence except in the soul ; when he writes against Plato that 'The universal animal is either nothing or else posterior to the individual animal, and that the same must be said of every universal ; '[1] he well-nigh lays his finger on the true point of the difficulty to be grappled with in explaining the origin of universals ; but, as a consequence, becomes inconsistent with himself.

In fact, to say, on the one hand, that 'the object of the understanding is the *common*, in so far as common,' or, putting it in other words, that 'that object consists in the relations between subsistent and possible things ; ' and to say, on the other hand, that ' the *common*, in so far as *common*, does not exist in singulars but only in the understanding,' is one and the same thing.

But, if this is true, and if it is also true that the sense does not perceive universals as such, but only singulars in so far as singulars, it must be equally true that the term of the sense does not contain in itself the object of the understanding, these two things being, in fact, not merely essentially different, but the very opposite of each other. And, if so, how can Aristotle affirm that the understanding receives its object from the sense ?

Herein lay the whole difficulty proposed by the Stagirite, and the intelligent reader will see at a glance that it is the very same difficulty we have been all along examining, but presented here under a new aspect.[2]

---

[1] *De Anima,* Lib. I. cap. i.

[2] I say that it is the same, because the difficulty which we stated above was this : 'How is it possible for man to make judgments without an idea or a universal to start from, since the senses furnish him with particular sensations only ?' Whereas the difficulty presented here is this : 'The understanding has only ideas or universals for its object. But the senses supply it with nothing but sensations, which are purely particular. Will, then, the understanding form those ideas for itself by universalising the particulars perceived by the senses ? In this case it must, for such

ARTICLE XIII.

*The difficulty pointed out in this discussion was perceived by the School-
men, as is proved from a distinction which they invented in order
to meet it. That distinction is examined.*

250. The Schoolmen, perceiving that in this part of the
Aristotelian philosophy there was some confusion, endeavoured to present the thought of the Greek philosopher in the
most favourable light possible. For this end they devised the
following subtle distinction: 'The word *universal* is taken in
two significations. It means either the common nature
itself in so far as it falls under the intention of universality,
or the universal in itself.'[1] Hence they drew the con-

operation, have in itself some universal,
else it will never be able to add to the
perceptions of the senses, that universality of which they are entirely devoid.'
These, I say, are merely two ways of
presenting the same difficulty. According to the first way, the difficulty consists in explaining how man can begin
to *judge*, on the supposition that he has
no idea innate in him; according to the
second, the difficulty consists in explaining how man can begin *intellectually to perceive* anything—*i.e.* also on the
supposition that he has no idea innate
in him. That we have here two aspects of the identical difficulty will be
clearly seen when we consider that, as
regards real things—for instance, corporeal substances—to *perceive* them with
the understanding is the same as to
affirm or *judge* that they exist. What
is intellectually *perceived* constitutes the
term of a judgment; and in so far as
this term is judged, it is an *object* of the
understanding. It was not an *object*
before, but it becomes such in virtue of
the judgment. I cannot here stop to
explain how it happens that this judgment is sometimes more explicit and
sometimes less so, or that on some
occasions it is made with greater
advertence than on others; for this
would necessitate too long a discussion.
It is enough for my present purpose
that it be well understood that the intellectual perception takes place by
means of a judgment.

[1] In St. Thomas, however, we find

the difficulty presented in all its force.
Here are his words: 'As to the nature
which is subject to the intention of
universality—for instance, the nature of
man—we must say that it exists in two
ways: viz. one material, or that which
it has in so far as it exists in its natural
matter; the other immaterial, or that
which it has so far as it exists in our
mind. Now, in so far as it exists in its
natural matter, it cannot fall under the
intention of universality, because by the
natural matter it is individualised.
Therefore, the intention of universality
accrues to it only from this, that our
mind abstracts it from the individual
matter. But,' he observes, 'it is not
possible to abstract it from the individual matter in reality, as was asserted
by the Platonists. For man so far
forth as natural— that is, real—does not
exist except in this particular flesh and
in these particular bones. . . . . It
remains, therefore, that the nature of
man, considered apart from its principles,
has no real existence except in the
mind.' (*De Anima*, Lib. II. lect.
xii.) ['Universale potest accipi dupli-
citer. Uno modo potest dici universale
ipsa natura communis, prout subjacet
intentioni universalitatis. Alio modo
secundum se. Ista autem natura, cui advenit intentio universalitatis, puta natura
hominis, habet duplex esse: unum quidem
materiale, secundum quod est in materia
naturali; aliud autem immateriale, secundum quod est in intellectu. Secundum igitur quod habet esse in materia

clusion that the *universal* taken in the first sense—that is, the *nature itself,* not as actually universal, but as *capable* of

naturali, non potest ei advenire intentio universalitatis, quia per materiam individuatur. Advenit igitur ei universalitatis intentio, secundum quod abstrahitur a materia individuali. Non est autem possibile quod abstrahatur a materia individuali realiter sicut Platonici posuerunt. Non enim est homo naturalis, id est realis, nisi in his carnibus, et in his ossibus. . . . Relinquitur igitur, quod natura humana non habet esse præter principia individuantia, nisi tantum in intellectu.']

The meaning of this passage is: 'Some maintain that when the mind perceives a particular object it only perceives the identical thing which was perceived by the senses, and that the only difference is that the mind separates in the particular that which is common from that which is proper, and then fixing its attention exclusively on the common, perceives this by itself alone. Now, this way of explaining how the *term* of sense becomes an *object* of the mind would offer no difficulty if the separation supposed to be made by the mind were a real one ; if the mind could do in it what we do with a material substance—*e.g.* with a cake or a tart, when, cutting it in two, we put aside one half in order to use the other as we list. But we must remember that the separation here spoken of is quite another thing. It is called separation, not in a literal, but only in a metaphorical sense. The mind does not by any means abstract from a real being the *proper*, leaving there only the *common,* in the same way that true and real abstractions and divisions are made —as, for instance, when dregs are extracted from the wine, and the pure wine is left. Nothing of the sort. The understanding in perceiving a real being does not cause it to undergo any alteration whatever.'

Therefore, those who think that by simply telling us that the mind *abstracts* universals from particulars, they have explained how the mind perceives what the senses supply to it, are labouring under a mistake. Instead of an explanation, they have only given a very meagre analogy or similitude, and one quite inadequate to explain the

true nature of intellectual operations. The metaphor may satisfy superficial thinkers, but does not throw any new light on the question at issue.

When we have abandoned this *analogy* of abstraction and separation, which is not properly applicable to the particular supplied by the senses, because nothing is abstracted, nothing separated from it, what is left for us to say on the manner in which the understanding perceives things? All we can say for certain is, (1) that the sense-perceived particular suffers no alteration or division of any kind from the intellectual perception, and therefore that the word *abstraction* affords us no help towards explaining intellectual operations, if by them we are to understand operations by means of which we divide, in the particular perceived by the senses, the common from the proper, and fix our attention on the first apart from the second. (2) That a being in so far as it is intellectually perceived has a mode of existence which differs totally, and not merely in part, from that which the same being has in real nature. (3) That this mode of existence which a being has in the mind is characterised by *universality,* while that which it has in real nature is purely *particular.* And (4) that, therefore, any object whatever, in so far as it is *universal,* exists in the mind only; and hence that the object as perceived by the mind — that is, as *universal*—is entirely different from and has nothing to do with the terms of sense which consist exclusively of *particulars.* By these considerations the difficulty as to how the mind can receive its objects from the senses in the manner suggested by Locke or Condillac, is felt in all its force. So clearly was the difference between the terms of sense and the objects of the understanding seen by St. Thomas of Aquin, that, when confuting the error of those who placed the *intellectus agens* outside of man, and said that it communicated with him by means of the sensible phantasms, he could answer that this was impossible, for that the object of the *intellectus agens* was not in any way a part of these phantasms, as the word *abstraction* might lead one

being considered such (for this was the scholastic meaning of the phrase *intentio universalitatis*), was the term of the sensitive perception, while the *universal* taken in the second sense—that is, in so far as actually universal—was the object of the understanding only. It seemed that in this way the passing from the senses to the understanding could be explained—viz. that it could be shown how it happened that the term of sense became an object of the understanding.[1] For although the understanding could intue only the *universal*, nevertheless one appeared to see the possibility of this faculty receiving its object from the senses themselves, inasmuch as by means of the above distinction it might be said that the universal was perceived by the senses also.

But if the truth must be spoken, that distinction by requiring the word *universal* to be taken in a sense somewhat different from that which it had in reference to the understanding—viz. as meaning universal *in potentia* and not in act—was entirely defeating its own object. Indeed, if we examine it carefully, we shall find that the difficulties remain as before.

And first of all let us consider the expression, ' In so far

---

to suppose—that is, it was not anything taken out of them, but altogether free from phantasms, and therefore of a nature wholly different from theirs. Hence it followed that between the *idea* contemplated by this intellect and the *sensible phantasm* there could be no true communication. We see from this that the penetrating mind of the holy Doctor did not allow itself to be deceived, like the Arabians, by the metaphorical sense of the word *abstraction* (see the Commentary of St. Thomas on the third Book *De Anima*, lect. vii. x.).

[1] The difference between *term* and *object* has been explained by the author in his *Logica* (nn. 303-305), as follows : —

' No other faculty, except the understanding, has for its term an *object*. By *object* I understand a term seen or intued in such a way that the seer sees neither himself nor any relation with himself (*i.e.* as intueing subject). In that intuition, self as such remains for-gotten and excluded, while the term stands out by itself and presents itself as existing in an absolute mode. The said term appears simply as *being* (*essente*) ; and, although it is seen, nevertheless the seer cannot, by the mere act of looking at it, know or say that he sees it ; but in order to know this he must perform another act—I mean an act of reflection upon his intuition. This is the marvellous property of the understanding, that which distinguishes it from every other faculty, and especially from that of *feeling*. The faculty of *feeling* has for its term the *felt*. But the felt necessarily implies an immediate relation with the *sentient*, so that it is impossible to conceive that the felt exists, without implicitly conceiving the sentient and its act. Hence the felt is not *object*, but *term* only ; and the faculty of feeling has not the *property essential* to the faculty of understanding. [TRANSLATORS.]

as the common nature itself falls under the intention of universality, it is universal.'

I ask, can this nature be called *common*, even when considered apart from the aspect of universality under which it falls ? No one will say this, for if the aspect of *universality* be kept out of account, the nature no longer presents itself to us as *common*, but as *singular* only. When, however, we *in our mind* compare this *singular* nature with other natures also *singular* in themselves, but, like it, cognised by us, then we find, between it and them, the relation of similarity : and it is only by the addition of this *relation* that the singular nature acquires that *universality* which we express by the word *common*.

Now, the relation of which I speak is nothing but a mental concept, an idea. For a relation does not reside in either one or the other of the singular terms, or of the individuals between which it is found to exist ; but only in their union as effected by the mind comparing them together with a common species or idea contemplated by it.

If, then, a nature is always purely *singular* until it has been conceived by the understanding and considered in relation to a common idea, is it not an impropriety of speech to qualify that nature as *common* or *universal* independently of this mental operation—to attribute to the nature that which is in the understanding only, and is there posteriorly to that nature being perceived by the senses? If we wish to define the true limits of the capabilities of mere sense, we must exclude from our thought everything which is intellectually added to the sense-perceptions, and therefore that *intentio universalitatis* which, as Aristotle himself allows, is an addition made by the understanding. We shall then see that to call the nature as perceived by the senses *common* or *universal* is a clear misnomer.

In order that the proposition 'The nature perceived by the senses is common' should be brought within the truth, it would have to be translated as follows :—The sense perceives a nature as singular ; but when this nature has been perceived by the understanding, it becomes entitled under a certain aspect to the predicate of *common* or *universal*, because it is united to the idea which always possesses the character of universality. In fact, such predicate is only given to it to express that very relation with the idea under which the understanding perceives it.

Such being the case, it is manifest that the above distinction introduced by the Schoolmen avails nothing for the purpose of explaining how the term of sense can become an object of the understanding. The aim of the distinction was to show that such term even as that of the understanding can, in a certain way, be called *universal*; and that therefore it should not appear strange if the sense, although by itself incapable of perceiving universals, supplied to the understanding its object. On the contrary, from the remarks we have made it is quite plain that if the term of sense can in a certain way be called *universal*, this is only in consequence of our considering it relatively to the future operation of the understanding on it. But if such operation be excluded and we limit ourselves to considering the sensible term purely and simply in its relation to the sense, we can call it only *singular*, and, consequently, considered merely in this relation, there is nothing in it either really or potentially *common*. Whence, then, is the universal by means of which the understanding renders the sensible term common? The question remains just where it was, and the distinction is as good as if never made.

ARTICLE XIV.

The intellectus agens *of Aristotle does not account for the origin of Universals.*

251. The term of sense, then, and the object of the understanding are essentially different from, and the contrary of, each other. The sense perceives the *singular* ; the understanding adds to it the *universal.*[1]

---

[1] In a passage where Aristotle explains how the *objects of the understanding* are formed, we meet with a passing allusion to a *universal quiescent in the soul.* Having, in his attempt to show how all our ideas come from the senses, said that 'From the vestiges left behind by the *sensations* comes *memory*, and from our comparing many things stored up in the memory comes

Consequently, on the Aristotelian supposition that all ideas come from the senses, the difficulty proposed above as to how these which have nothing common or universal in themselves can supply the object proper to the understanding always remains in its full force.

Placed in this perplexity, the Stagirite, as we have seen, introduces an *intellectus agens* as a means of communication between the sense and the understanding. The office of this intellect is to take hold of the sensible phantasms (*singular* of course) and to transform them into universals; albeit as to how this functionary is to execute so important and honourable a commission, our philosopher does not think fit to tell us. It is, however, fortunate that the mysterious faculty which men in general call by the name of *intellect* or *understanding* goes on placidly doing its work, quite indepen-

experiment (experience), whence we deduce principles or ideas;' he, as though little satisfied with this *experiment* (which is of nothing but singulars), adds, ' from experiment *and from every universal quiescent in the soul.*' (*Analyt. Poster.* Lib. II. cap. ult.) Thus our philosopher, contrary to his premisses, feels obliged to admit, besides experiment, a something found in the soul itself. But be the sense intended by him in this somewhat obscure passage what it may, it is certain that St. Thomas in interpreting it could not have described the forming of our ideas in a manner more accurate and precise. To be able to describe accurately how this act takes place is already to be far advanced on the way to its explanation. The Angelic Doctor remarks that *experiment* stops at singular things; that therefore we must go further and deduce principles from a universal—*ulterius ex universali quiescente in anima* (a); and that this universal is formed by an operation through which the soul receives that which in reality is singular as though it were universal ('quod scilicet accipitur ac si in omnibus ita sit, sicut est experimentum in quibusdam'). Therefore, according to St. Thomas there is nothing universal outside the soul. It is the soul that adds *universality* to things

and receives as *universal* that which in itself is singular. Again, this *universalised* object is called by Aristotle *unum præter multa* (τοῦ ἑνὸς παρὰ τὰ πολλὰ), and on this St. Thomas remarks that, inasmuch as the specific *unity* of *many individuals* or singulars is not in, but outside of them (*præter multa*), it can only be added to them by the understanding. Hence this universal is not a portion of the individuals, a something really extracted from them, but an element independent of them; in short, it is an idea, and therefore of a nature quite different from that of real individuals, which are all *singular substances.* Hence it seems to me that when St. Thomas says that *there is nothing in the understanding which has not come from the senses,* he does not thereby mean to exclude from this faculty that *form of universality* which it adds to things, drawing it from itself, and in virtue of which it is an understanding. What that *form* is we shall see in its proper place. That such is the correct interpretation appears certain, and even evident, when we remember the *light* on which St. Thomas makes the existence of the understanding depend. Of this light more will be said elsewhere.

(a) Ἐκ δ'ἐμπειρίας ἢ ἐκ παντὸς ἠρεμήσαντος τοῦ καθόλου ἐν τῇ ψυχῇ· *Analyt. Poster.* Lib. II. c. 19.

dently of the speculations of philosophers, and of the laws which they would impose on it.

As for myself, had I the duty of teaching this *intellectus agens* how to perform the function entrusted to it by our philosopher—subject, however, to the express condition of not carrying within itself any idea whatever, but of having to draw all its ideas from the sensible phantasms—I own that I should feel greatly embarrassed.

252. In the first place, must this *intellectus agens* perceive the sensible and singular phantasms, or not?

If it does not perceive them, one would think that it cannot make them the subject of its operations, and thereby distinguish in them the proper from the common element.

But if it perceives them, then the perception of pure *singulars* belongs to it, even as it does to the faculty of sense.[1] And if so, the question arises, How shall it find in these singulars the universals which are not in them?

[1] In order to overcome this difficulty, the Schoolmen adopted the expedient of saying that the understanding perceived singulars *per quamdam reflexionem*. But anyone can see that the pronoun *quidam, quædam, quoddam*, however respectable in itself, and however often used by philosophers as a plank in shipwreck, has not always the virtue of satisfying the curiosity of minds in search of better reasons. The difficulty appears to me identical with that which I have had occasion to notice in reference to the common *sensorium*. Its solution is this. The sense and the understanding are two faculties of one and the same human subject ; the identical *Ego* which is modified by sensations thinks of them. There is no need, therefore, of supposing that the understanding perceives the sensations, as though these were perceived by two different faculties. Neither is there any need of supposing two species of phantasms, one similar to the other. This would be to multiply beings without necessity, and to necessitate a process of questioning *ad infinitum*. What we want is simply to realise to ourselves that unity of the *Ego* in which are found our sensations as well as our ideas and judgments. Aristotle supposed that the sensation felt in the external organ was one thing, and the sensation carried up to the common centre, another : hence two faculties, that of the *particular sense* and that of the *sensus communis*. The truth is, that in the external organ, considered as apart from the soul, there is no sensation at all, and that whatever sensation we experience, it is always and alone in the soul. There is, therefore, but one kind of sensations, and there are no other corporeal senses than the organic. But as it is only the soul which feels through all these sensories, so it is the soul which receives contemporaneously many sensations, under which aspect it might be called a *sensus communis* ; and it is also the soul which reflects on these sensations and thus thinks. The understanding is the faculty of thought, and does not, therefore, perceive the sensations in so far as singular. That which perceives them in this way is the soul, whereof the understanding is a special faculty. The function called *intellectual perception* consists, not in feeling the sensations, but in the judgment which the soul passes on them when felt. And in so far as the soul makes this judgment as well as others which follow after, it is said to be endowed with the faculty of *reason*.

As I have already observed, the reason why singulars, so long as they are such, contain no *universal*, is because the *universal* is nothing else than a relation which a thing has with other similar things, real or possible ; consequently it is an object of such a nature that the understanding alone can apprehend it, while the perceptions of mere sense lie wholly outside of it.

Now, if the universal is an addition made by the understanding, if it in no way exists in the terms of sense, where, I ask again, does the understanding get it from ?

253. Plato supposed that universals were innate in us, and that our soul added them to the singulars perceived by the senses ; and in so far as the soul carried within itself these universals (or ideas), it was called *intellect*. In other words, he supposed that we had in our minds from the first the exemplars of things, or, what comes to the same, the ' possibles,' to serve us as rules for correctly arranging the sensible realities into different classes. This undoubtedly solved the difficulty.

Avicenna had recourse to an *intellect outside of man*, but which communicates to him ready-formed all those ideas under which he afterwards classifies the realities perceived by the senses. This system also met the difficulty in some way.

But in Aristotle, at least as understood by the later interpreters, we find nothing of this.[1] His *intellectus agens* is represented to us outright as adding the universal to the singulars perceived by the senses (for this is, in ultimate analysis, what the understanding does in all philosophical systems) without either deriving that universal from the senses or having it in its own self!

[1] In the works of Aristotle we meet with passages indicating that he is little satisfied with his own system, and is on the point of embracing another, as the reader will see in the following article.

ARTICLE XV.

According to Aristotle the understanding communicates its own form to the things perceived by it. This, taken in conjunction with the denial of all innate ideas, is the foundation of modern Scepticism.

254. At times Aristotle strains every nerve to overcome a difficulty which impresses him forcibly, but, as I would almost venture to affirm, more on the side of his feelings than on that of his reason.

For instance, he will tell you that, 'Whatever is received, is received after the manner of a recipient ; hence as when you pour a liquid into several vessels, that liquid adjusts itself to their various shapes, so must it be with whatever is received into our sense, or into our understanding. These faculties are like two vessels which give to one and the same thing different forms. The form given it by the sense is that it remains just as it was, a singular, and the form given it by the understanding is that of *universality*, the only form under which this faculty can conceive.'

It is easy to see in these doctrines a clear trace of Kantism, for they lead us to infer that the human understanding has a certain *form* to which the things perceived by it must adapt themselves without our knowing why.

Now, either we admit that this form consists in the exemplar or essence of truth, and in this case we must say that the exemplar or essence of truth is known to us by nature, as I maintain ; or we admit nothing of the kind, and then we shall be bound to say that the understanding, limited and determined as it necessarily is, will give to the things perceived a form purely subjective, which is precisely the foundation whereon modern Scepticism and the *Critical Philosophy* have been reared.

255. But in the latter supposition the whole of this huge fabric of error would, obviously, rest upon nothing better than a material analogy—the analogy of a recipient.

Now, I can well understand how a liquid may be poured into a vessel without having previously that form which it is gradually made to take by the pouring process; but I am utterly at a loss to conceive how it is possible for *singulars* to make their way into the mind, which, according to Aristotle himself, apprehends only *universals* ; or how, even should they succeed in entering into it, they must necessarily be changed there into universals.

If the *singulars* do not enter into the understanding, they cannot receive that configuration which this faculty will give them, just as the liquid cannot conform itself to the shape of the vessel if it does not enter into it.

But if they do enter, then the nature of the understanding is no longer such as absolutely to disqualify it from apprehending anything except under the form of *universality.* If the understanding has that form and no other, it cannot operate otherwise than in accordance with it; therefore, on this supposition the presence of a mere singular in the understanding is simply inconceivable.

In the liquid referred to we distinguished two successive forms—viz. that before its infusion into the vessel, and that after the infusion. But the liquid under the latter form is the self-same liquid as before. No change has been made in its nature. That form is purely accidental to it.

Not so with the *common nature.* In so far as *common*, it retains nothing of the singular; it is an object wholly different from what the senses have perceived ; it did not exist to us before the understanding apprehended it ; its existence for us began with the act by which we came to know it.

On the other hand, if the object of our understanding has its form as *object*, simply because the mind has given it such form from its own subjective self, Scepticism would, as I have said, be inevitable, for the truth would no longer be essentially objective and absolute ; it would be nothing but subjective truth, which is the same as to say *not truth* ; and this is exactly the sort of truth that the system of Kant offers to us—a system which in reality is nothing but the Aristotelian analogy of the recipient, developed and cleverly carried out to its conclusions.

ARTICLE XVI.

An Aristotelian self-contradiction.

256. At other times, to escape from the rock of Scepticism, Aristotle sets aside his simile of the recipient which alters whatever is admitted into it by making it adjust itself to its own limited form.

Thus we hear him speak as follows:—'The *intellectus agens* changes nothing; it only separates; it divides in things the *common* from the *proper*. This separation made, the *passive intellect* apprehends the *common* only. But by simply *apprehending* a part of a thing we do not apprehend the thing as changed, and therefore falsely. The apprehension is partial, yet truthful.'

In thus explaining his mind Aristotle would seem to convey that he imagines the *intellectus agens* as a sort of prism naturally endowed with the property of refracting light and separating the colours, and this would be the same as to intimate that the mental separation alluded to is the effect, not of a voluntary action, but of a certain *blind* necessity, obliging the understanding to act in this way and no other.

257. To borrow a comparison from the senses, one might say that the understanding separates in things the common from the proper in the same manner that the eye and the ear separate light and sound, inasmuch as these organs take each what belongs to itself. But, however ingenious this way of explaining the separation between the *common* (supposed to be in things) and the *proper* may appear, it is not less futile or more admissible than the others.

In the first place, it rests upon an evidently erroneous supposition—viz. that the *proper* and the *common* enter into the external thing as its component parts, even as the various colours combine into one ray of light; or, again, as the waves of light and sound, although striking the eye and the ear simultaneously, produce the sensation only in that one sense which is suited to each of the waves respectively. That this is an error I have already shown. The *common* does not exist in the singular things themselves, but is added to them by the understanding through its considering them in relation with an idea.

To say, therefore, that the understanding apprehends the *universal* or *common* by separating it from the *proper*, is to suppose that the *universal* or *common* exists antecedently to the intellectual act. On the contrary, the question to be answered is: How does the understanding come by the *universal*, seeing that this is not to be had from the natures of things, which are purely singular and individual?

Consequently, when Aristotle replies that the understanding obtains the universal by separating it from that which is proper in things, he does not solve the question of the origin of universals, but begs it, and in so doing contradicts himself.

ARTICLE XVII.

According to the system just expounded, the understanding would operate blindly: absurdity of this.

258. Moreover, is it possible to imagine in the understanding a blind operation, such as we see in physical things— *e.g.* in the elective function whereby the food distributes itself through its diverse channels during the digestive process, or in the division of colours effected by a prism?

Such a belief may happen if one considers the understanding merely in a general and abstract way, but not if one reflects on what the understanding really and truly is.

The understanding is the faculty of knowledge; therefore its acts cannot be blind. They must be essentially cognitive; for we here speak of the very source of that intellectual light which informs all our cognitions.

And to come closer to the point, let me ask: Does the *intellectus agens*, when making in things this supposed separation of the *proper* from the *common*, know the difference between these two elements in order to reject the first and retain the second? If it discerns that difference, it does not operate blindly, but with knowledge of cause. But in this, the only case conceivable in which the understanding can

make such a separation, it must be possessed beforehand of
some ideas to guide it in its work ; for to think ' This nature
is common ' is the same as to say to oneself, ' An infinite
number of individual natures similar to this one is possible;'
and this presupposes the *idea* or the *simple apprehension of
that nature*—an idea or apprehension which is wholly independent of time, of place, or of an individual circumstance :
is a mere *possible*, in short a *universal*.

Thus, the more I consider the matter, the less am I able
to understand how the function assigned by Aristotle to his
intellectus agens, of transforming singular sensations into ideas,
with the condition of not having in itself anything innate, can
possibly be accomplished.

ARTICLE XVIII.

Aristotle catches a glimpse of the true doctrine.

259. But Aristotle himself in some of his happier moments,
and when, perhaps, less pre-occupied by the thought of com-
bating Plato, betrays some suspicion or misgiving as to the
justice or even the possibility of the hard condition imposed
by him on his *intellectus agens* in the performing of its appointed task.

Hence he seems sometimes inclined to grant to this intellect a universal of some sort, by applying which it may universalise the perceptions of sense. For their universality, as
I have repeatedly observed, consists simply in their relation
with a *universal* (an *idea*), and from this alone are they afterwards called *common*.

On this point, however, the utterances of the Stagirite are
so scanty that I am not sure whether we can form from them
a very clear conception of his meaning. He says that the
intellectus agens is *substantiâ actu ens* [1]—three words, and that

---

[1] Καὶ οὗτος ὁ νοῦς χωριστὸς καὶ ἀπαθὴς
καὶ ἀμιγὴς τῇ οὐσίᾳ ὢν ἐνεργεία. *De
Anima*, Lib. III. cap. vi.

Of this intellect, which is by its
very substance or essence (τῇ οὐσίᾳ) in
act, St. Thomas says in his commentary

(*De Anima*, Lib III. lect. x.) that
it always and necessarily *understands*,
because its nature *consistit in ipso intelligere*. Taking this in connection with
the scholastic axiom, *objectum intellectus
est ens*, the reader will see that St.

is all. By these words he appears to say that the reason why this kind of intellect can draw ideas or universals from the singulars perceived by the senses is because it has in itself an *act*; and that this act must be substantial to it, else it could not perform that operation.

Interpreted in the light of the usual principles of our philosopher, this would seem to be resolvable into the following argument: 'The sensations, or rather the phantasms which the sensations leave in our soul, are not, as such, objects of the understanding: that is, they are not ideas except *in potentia*, because they are singular, and the understanding can only apprehend universals. We must, therefore, admit in the soul some sort of faculty endowed with the virtue of rendering these phantasms or ideas *in potentia* ideas in act; and this faculty is called *intellectus agens*. But in order that a thing may cause another to pass from potentiality to act, it must itself be in act. Thus, according to the principles of our philosopher, one body cannot move another unless it be itself already in motion. Therefore, the *intellectus agens*, in order to convert the phantasms received from the senses into actual objects of knowledge, must by its own nature be itself in act.' [1]

Here Aristotle stops; and I am not aware that in any part of his works he explains more clearly the meaning attached by him to the word *act* as used in this place.

260. Supposing, however, that Aristotle meant that this intellect in act is coeval with and connatural to man, and not coming into existence on occasion of the phantasms themselves, it may be affirmed that, by establishing the above proposition, he made a step further than Locke and the modern Sensists educated in his school.

These philosophers, though admitting a faculty of thought, never even dream of the necessity of ascertaining how it is constituted. They rest content with the supposition that, no matter what its nature may be, it is good enough for its

Thomas's is the identical doctrine which the author holds on the nature of our intellectual faculty, placing it in a primal and abiding act of intellection or vision of *being in general*. [TRANSLATORS.]

[1] *De Anima*, Lib. III. cap. vi.

purpose. Aristotle does something more than this; for, by adding that the faculty considered by him as capable of abstracting universals from singulars must be in act, he, if nothing else, takes us to the very threshold of the great and difficult question as to whether there be not something innate in the human understanding. Since, according to him, that act is *substantial* to the faculty itself, we can at least infer that it must be innate. However wrapped up in mystery, however vague and much too laconic, this expression evidences, nevertheless, the progress made by his mind in its inquiries, and justifies the belief that he had at least some inkling of the difficulty of which we speak, concerning the origin of ideas.

ARTICLE XIX.

The hint of the true doctrine given by Aristotle is explained.

261. I will add that if the fugitive hint thrown out by Aristotle as above be taken in a reasonable spirit, it is susceptible of such an interpretation as may perhaps bring us very near the true doctrine.

What can the *act* constituting the faculty of knowledge be ? Such an act is not conceivable otherwise than as infusing a knowledge of some kind into the faculty constituted by it.

Wherefore by saying that the *intellectus agens*, in order to form universals—that is, intellectual cognitions—must be itself ' in act,' Aristotle seems to insinuate that this intellect has by its very nature some sort of knowledge which enables it actually to produce its other cognitions when the occasion is given to it by the sensible phantasms. As to his not proceeding to inquire into the difficult question respecting the nature of that *innate knowledge*, this may possibly have been due to a fear lest by so doing he might be obliged either to contradict himself, or to say things too favourable to the system of his adversary Plato.

It might also be, as happens sometimes, that after this casual flash of light by which he saw that the intellectual faculty must have in it an innate act—equivalent, as we have seen, to some kind of innate knowledge—other thoughts took his attention away from so happy an idea, which if followed out by a man of such marvellous abilities might have been most fruitful in excellent results.

ARTICLE XX.

Aristotle acknowledges that the human understanding carries with it by nature a light, as attested by mankind generally.

262. Concerning the above statement of Aristotle, the commentators have said but little, although, its brevity notwithstanding, it is one of the most remarkable in all his writings.

Nevertheless, the remarks made on it by St. Thomas are such as to confirm me in the view I have just submitted.

Seeking to ascertain the sense of the expression, 'An intellect substantially in act,' the holy Doctor begins by observing that the Stagirite could not have meant by it that this intellect has, innate, the ideas of all things, (1) because this would be that very doctrine of Plato which he combats in so many places, and (2) because if this intellect were such as to be able to know all things by itself, a death-blow would be struck at another principle constantly taught by Aristotle himself, and confirmed by experience—viz. that the thoughts of our mind are conditional upon its receiving from the senses the phantasms of external things.

Having excluded this interpretation, St. Thomas goes on to inquire what can be the nature of an intellectual faculty which, without actually having in itself the ideas of all things, is nevertheless *in act.*

It would seem that such a faculty can only be something holding an intermediate state between having all ideas and having none at all.

Here are the words of this most shrewd commentator :—
' To knowable things the *intellectus agens* stands in the relation of an act in this sense, that it is an energy immaterial, active, capable of rendering other things like to itself—that is to say, immaterial : and it is thus that the things which in themselves are knowable only potentially, are made by it knowable in

act.'[1] And now I beg of the reader to note the simile by which St. Thomas explains this :—' For,' he adds, ' in the same way does the light cause the colours to be in act, although in the light itself the colours are not found severally distinct.'[2]

263. This Aristotelian simile is admirably adapted to the subject in discussion.

For although the light does not, as pure light, contain all the colours in a state of division, yet it is susceptible of such division by means of a refracting and reflecting medium.

Therefore, according to this simile, the theory of ideas would have to be the very reverse of what it was represented above. There the operation of the *intellectus agens* was said to consist in separating in sensible things the common from the proper, it being erroneously supposed that the common exists in things independently of the operation of our mind. The things were compared to a ray of light made up of different colours, viz. the common and the proper ; and the mind was compared to a prism capable of separating these colours. Here, on the contrary, what is compared to the light are not the sensible things, but the *intellectus agens*, or rather the act substantial to it—or, still better, that in which this act terminates ; while the prism, the medium which divides the colours composing the ray, are the sensible things. Thus the *common* would be in the mind and not in the things, and would be singularised and individualised through the things on which the mind brings it to bear. The singularising and the individualising would correspond

---

[1] It should be observed that, according to St. Thomas, that which is *immaterial* is knowable or intelligible *per se*. It follows from this, that the word *intellectus* as used by him is taken in an objective sense—viz. not as that which *understands*, but as that which is *understood* : otherwise the argument would have no force.

[2] This simile of the light, so appropriate for explaining the innate element existing in the human mind, has always been in use. We find it in all philosophical schools as well as in all languages. [The original passage of St. Thomas runs thus :—' Comparatur igitur (intellectus agens) ut actus respectu intelligibilium, in quantum est quædam virtus immaterialis, activa, potens alia similia sibi facere, scilicet immaterialia. Et per hunc modum, ea quæ sunt intelligibilia in potentia facit intelligibilia in actu. Sic enim et lumen facit colores in actu, non quod ipsum habeat in se determinationem colorum.'—*De Anima*, Lib. III. lect. x.]

to the colours, and the common to the *light* pre-existing in the mind. In this latter supposition many difficulties would be cleared away, for although our mind would descry no separate colour except in so far as divided by the action of the external prism of sensible things, yet it would have the light innate in it: in other words, although it would not have any knowledge of the singular and determinate,[1] it would have, innate in itself, a most elementary notion or idea, an intelligible form not determined in this or that way until the sensations come to determine it. Or, to express the same thing in another manner, our mind would not possess any one derived idea, as Plato, if we are to believe his rival Aristotle, asserted ; but it would have innate *ab initio* the first and most universal idea of all. No deductions would be innate, but the principle of all deductions would ; for (as we shall see in its proper place) the first and most universal of all notions or ideas, when variously applied to objects of less extension than itself, assumes those forms which we know under the name of *principles* ; and principles are recognised by Aristotle himself as indemonstrable.

264. Wherefore, St. Thomas, explaining how the light innate in our mind can come to it, concludes with these words : 'The active energy of which I speak is a certain participation of intellectual light coming from substances outside of our mind ;'[2] that is, according to his own doctrine, from God Himself.[3]

---

[1] On an attentive perusal of St. Thomas, it will be seen that where he denies the existence of innate ideas, he never intends to speak of other than determinate ideas or species : 'Anima intellectiva,' he says, 'est quidem actu immaterialis, sed est in potentia ad determinatas species rerum.' 'The intellectual soul itself is indeed immaterial in act, but it is potentially so in reference to the *determinate species* of things' (*S.*, P. I. q. lxxix. art. 4, ad 4tum). This is precisely what I hold. I deny that the human mind has by nature any determinate ideas or species; but I say that it has one idea *indeterminate* in the widest sense of the word ; the very same which St. Thomas calls a *light* and which constitutes the mind *actu immaterialem.*

[2] 'Hujusmodi autem virtus activa est quædam participatio luminis intellectualis a substantiis separatis.'—*De Anima*, Lib. III. lect. x.

[3] 'Intellectus separatus secundum nostræ fidei documenta est ipse Deus.' *S.*, P. I. q. lxxix. art. 4.

ARTICLE XXI.

The Arabians, by denying the existence of a light innate in man, fell into the erroneous doctrine that the intellectus agens *was outside of the human soul.*

265. The passage last quoted from St. Thomas is directed against another school of commentators of the Stagirite—I mean Avicenna and his followers.

Reading in Aristotle, on the one hand, that man has no innate knowledge, and that his intellect is a mere potentiality, and, on the other, that the *intellectus agens* is not a mere capacity for knowing, but something substantially in act (*substantiâ actu ens*)—·for if it were not itself in act it could not convert the things perceived by the senses into actual objects of knowledge, or, in other words, furnish the *intellectus possibilis* with *ideas*, which are all by their nature universal— these philosophers were unable to reconcile the two statements together. Hence they took to the expedient of supposing that by *intellectus agens* Aristotle meant some mind other than man's own—viz. either the divine or the angelic. A mind like that, being in act, and therefore in actual possession of the ideas of all things, would be able to exercise an influence on the human mind (the *intellectus possibilis*, a simple capacity of knowing), and communicate to it on occasion of the sensations that universality which, when joined to the sensible phantasms, furnishes the *ideas* of external things.

266. This interpretation, however, is utterly repudiated by St. Thomas, both as being an error in itself and as contrary to the mind of Aristotle. The contention of the holy Doctor is in substance this, that the *intellectus possibilis* and the *intellectus agens* mentioned by the Stagirite are two faculties of one and the same human mind, but considered under two different aspects. The *intellectus possibilis* is the mind in so far as capable of having cognitions ; and the *intellectus agens* is the mind in so far as always in act, not because brought out thereunto by the sensible phantasms, but because of the

activity essentially inherent in its nature. And certainly if I had to interpret Aristotle in the most favourable way by restricting myself to some of his happier expressions, I think I should not perhaps be wide of the mark were I to describe what he said in a passing way as follows :—' Experience tells us that we have not the ideas of external things before we are affected by sensations ; consequently we should beware of assuming the innateness of such ideas ; because if we really had them in us, we should know that we had them.[1] On the other hand, it is equally certain that sensations are not ideas ; for sensations terminate in the singulars by which they are severally produced, and therefore are essentially singular, while ideas, being exemplars of all the individuals similar to one another, are necessarily *common* or *universal.* We must therefore suppose that the same human being who experiences the sensations has in him the faculty of universalising. But as universality is not found in the sensations, it follows that, in order to be able to attribute universality to them, this faculty must already have it in itself. Thus the sensible phantasms, or ideas merely *in potentia,* when seen by the mind in union with the universal form which belongs to it, will become actual ideas.[2] Therefore, to convert the

---

[1] This is not a legitimate deduction. We might have ideas without being conscious of them, as has been so justly observed by Leibnitz. Such, however, is the usual argument of all those who deny the existence of innate ideas. Aristotle makes use of it in *Analyt. Poster.* Lib. II., cap. ult.

[2] In his second book *De Anima* Aristotle calls *phantasms* ' cognitions *in potentia,*' which is the same as saying that they are not cognitions, and that therefore it is necessary to explain by what operation of our mind they become cognitions, universal conceptions, ideas. Nevertheless, in the same place, Aristotle goes very near the truth ; for, wishing to point out the difference between sense and mind, he places it in this, that while ' the active part of the sensitive operation is outside the soul, the active part of the intellectual operation is in the soul itself.' By these words he means that

sensations are the effect of an action exercised on us by external bodies ; but that intellectual perceptions, in which ideas are contained, proceed from an internal activity essentially inherent in our soul. Now, on the strength of this observation we might proceed further, and argue thus : ' The universality characteristic of intellectual conceptions is either *created* by the mind, or, being innate in the mind, is only *added* by it to the phantasms. Now, to attribute to the mind a creative force is certainly much more than to attribute to it the power of simply adding one thing to another ; and this reason alone would be enough to make us decide in favour of the latter alternative. But besides this, by observing and analysing what the mind does when forming its conceptions, we find that that operation is not by any means productive of anything new, but only a *seeing* of that which is already produced. To under-

sensible phantasms into *actual ideas* is nothing else than to universalise them ; since it is by being universalised that they receive that *actuation* which entitles them in a true sense to the name of *ideas.* But inasmuch as one thing cannot cause another to come into act unless it be itself already in act, it follows that this faculty which has the virtue of producing actual ideas must be itself actuated accordingly—*i. e.* there must be in it that which constitutes that universality which it adds to the sensible phantasms.'[1]

ARTICLE XXII.

St. Thomas refutes the error of the Arabians.

267. But let us return to the Angelic Doctor. He shows that the *intellectus agens* cannot be a substance outside of us, for the reason that it would be an absurdity to suppose that human nature has not in itself all that is necessary for the performing of that act for which it is essentially ordained, viz. the act of cognition.

'Man's nature,' he says, 'would not be fully constituted if it had not in itself all that was necessary for accomplishing the operation proper to it. Now, that operation consists in knowing, and this cannot be accomplished except through the two intellects combined—*i.e.* the possible (*possibilis*) and the active (*agens*).'[2]

268. Then, to prove that Aristotle by *intellectus agens* meant a faculty inherent in the human soul, he observes that

stand is simply to *see* ; but to see is not to produce : therefore, the mind does not create the ideas of things—it looks at them.

[1] Reflecting on the history of the thoughts which passed through Aristotle's mind as set forth in his writings, it seems to me probable that, in treating of human ideas, he often restricted his attention to the ideas of sensible things. Hence his inability to recognise the existence of any idea in man prior to his thought being determined by those things to something real. That man could have the idea of *indeterminate being* was to him inconceivable ; for him this was

a light, but not yet an idea. And if the word *idea* were reserved for denoting some universal conception of a determinate kind, I also would say that there is no innate idea in us, but only a *light.* My contention is not about words, but about things.

[2] 'Non enim homo esset a natura sufficienter institutus, si non haberet in seipso principia, quibus posset operationem complere, quæ est intelligere : quæ quidem compleri non potest, nisi per intellectum possibilem, et per intellectum agentem.'—*De Anima,* Lib. III. lect. x.

the philosopher calls this faculty 'as it were a habit, or a light ; ' an expression, says the Angelic Doctor, which would not be correct if the *intellectus agens* were a substance separate from man. We see, therefore, that St. Thomas, although allowing that the actuation intrinsic to the nature of the *intellectus agens* comes from the influx of a higher mind, is totally opposed to the view of the Arabian thinkers.

ARTICLE XXIII.

Credit due to Aristotle for having seen the necessity of an innate primitive act in the human understanding.

269. However we view it, the mere fact of Aristotle having discovered that our cognitive faculty is not a mere potentiality, but something essentially in act, seems to me a very great deal, notwithstanding that he omitted to inquire into the nature and extension of this act.

It is possible that our philosopher, having once rejected the Platonic system because he saw, or thought he saw, errors in it, took up an entirely contrary attitude, and, as it happens with those who have not as yet sifted a question thoroughly, he felt confident at first of being able to account for the operations of the human mind without conceding to it any such thing as an innate knowledge; but on subsequently going deeper into this thorny question, he found that some compromise was necessary, and that the faculty which produces ideas must be admitted to have in it by its very nature a light of some sort, or, which is the same thing, some primal idea, to serve both as a means and a rule for the forming of all the others.

270. What inclines me to this opinion is to see the hesitating manner in which Aristotle speaks in so many places of his works, and those grammatical particles which he so frequently introduces into his argument by way of correctives. Half-expressions like these, while saying nothing decidedly clear or precise, are very significant—indeed, much more so than he who employs them would wish ; for they clearly show that our philosopher, hanging as it were between

two sides, would fain speak his thoughts out fully and unconditionally, but dares not for fear of the consequences ; or at least, they indicate that his reason, his conscience, is still in some doubt, some perplexity, respecting the doctrine he expounds.

For example, in the passage now under consideration, speaking of the substantial act of the *intellectus agens*, he declares openly that it is not by any means like the *intellectus possibilis*, 'which sometimes understands and sometimes not ;' and then he adds that it is '*as it were* a habit, *as it were* a light*' (ὡς ἕξις τὶς, οἶον τὸ φῶς)* [1] without having the courage to say positively that *it is* a habit, that *it is* a light.

271. In confirmation of my view I beg leave to refer again to the passage which I quoted on this matter from the latter part of the second book of the *Posterior Analytics* (see note to n. 251), where Aristotle asks himself the question as to 'How we come to the knowledge of *first principles.*' After laying it down that these principles are neither obtainable by means of demonstration nor innate in us, he engages to account for their origin by means of the senses, thus : '*Sensations* leave *phantasms* in the soul ; phantasms produce *memory* ; from many of these memories compared together comes *experiment* (experience) ; and from this experiment we deduce the universals which become the principles of the sciences and the arts.' [2]

---

[1] *De Anima,* Lib. III. cap. vi.

[2] A great hindrance to the finding of the truth in debated questions arises from the want of clearness in the ideas which are sometimes mixed up with those questions ; and in order to master well the history of the errors into which an author has fallen, it is necessary to know precisely where the obscurity and confusion of his ideas lies. This is why, in examining the reasonings of Aristotle, I have repeatedly called attention to those passages in which he did not seem to have formed a clear and exact conception of what he was speaking about. I will give here another example of it. The whole difficulty respecting the origin of ideas consists in explaining how we can come by the knowledge of *universals,* seeing that whatever we get from the senses – viz. sensations and sensitive perceptions—is singular. If we can only explain the formation of *one* universal, *one* idea, the difficulty is solved. It should never be forgotten that the very first of our judgments presupposes in us the knowledge of some universal ; for without an idea no judgment is possible. Consequently the whole knot of the difficulty lies in the first step taken by our reason, in the first and simplest of our judgments.

On the contrary, what did those philosophers do who failed to perceive that this was precisely what had to be explained? They simply passed it by, and began their explanations, not at our first intellectual operations, but at those which come last—*i.e.* at the reasonings whereby we establish scientific principles. Their whole aim was to describe the foundation of these principles, and,

Now, after hearing our philosopher so easily explain the knowledge of the first and most universal principles, you

it must be confessed, they succeeded entirely; for all that was really hard to explain—viz. the first step taken by human reason—was, as I have said, assumed by them. Now, to this kind of deception Aristotle himself falls occasionally a victim. To him also the knot of the difficulty sometimes presents itself, but out of its right place—in the last step instead of in the first. The passage which I have just quoted from him in the text proves this to evidence. He there strains every nerve to explain how *the principles of the sciences and the arts* are formed, as if the difficulty consisted in this, and not rather in explaining the origin of those primary ideas, common to all men, whence all human reasoning starts. The truth of what I am saying is seen still more openly in the paraphrase which Themistius makes of that passage. ' The universal,' says Themistius, ' is the work of the mind, and is formed by it.' I ask, ' How is it formed?' This is the problem you have to solve.' He answers, ' By an induction; for it is the property of the mind to unite, to gather together, and, as Plato says, *to give determination to things indeterminate.*' (Upon this passage I beg leave to note in passing how Aristotle seems therein to agree with Plato in admitting that it is the proper function of the mind to *determine* that which pre-exists in it in an *indeterminate* form; which would confirm the conjectures I have expressed concerning the *intellectus agens* of Aristotle.) Now, as regards this induction by means of which the mind gathers the singulars together and unites them into universals, how is it described by Aristotle, according to the paraphrase of Themistius? Let us hear the whole passage: ' This induction is not accomplished in a short time. Between our receiving the perceptions of the senses, and our uniting them together, there passes a considerable interval. For the senses begin at once to produce phantasms; but it is only after they have long been exercised in this that the energy of the soul which we call *mind* is brought out into full play, and adds the conclusion (the *universal*). To bring this about, however, many

years and much knowledge are required; for that which is scattered and divided cannot be gathered together and joined into one except after a lengthened period of time.' (*In Poster.* Lib. II. cap. xix.) Thus all the difficulty which is encountered in explaining how the mind forms universals is thought by this philosopher to consist in the formation of *scientific* principles; and doubtless these are only formed by means of repeated and long-protracted observations. For instance, in order that men cou'd arrive at the universal principle, ' Peruvian bark is a febrifuge,' it was necessary (1) that those who occupied themselves with this discovery should have attained to the use of reason; (2) that they should repeat their experiments a very great number of times, and then form by induction the universal proposition, ' The Peruvian bark is a febrifuge.' Aristotle illustrates his thought by an example similar to this, taken from medicine.

Now, to all this reasoning the advocates of innate ideas have no exception to take save this, that it is wholly beside the question. The reasoning assumes that the difficulty consists in explaining how scientific principles are deduced, whereas it consists in explaining the *source* whence that deduction originates, *i.e.* the *universal* itself, even the most common and seemingly most obvious. In fact, before a man can, for instance, arrive at the universal proposition, ' The Peruvian bark is a febrifuge,' what does he require? Most assuredly he requires the pre-existence in his mind of many other universals. Every one of the terms of that proposition expresses a universal. The word *Peruvian bark* does not signify this or that material piece of bark, but it signifies the *species*— *i.e.* it is equally applicable to all possible individual samples of that species. Consequently, it expresses a *universal*. In like manner the word *fever* does not denote the particular fever caught by Sempronius, or by Caius, but that *species* of illness which is called *fever*. Now, the question, ' What is the relation between the two universals designated respectively by the words *Peruvian bark* and *fever*?' differs entirely

would naturally expect him to conclude that there is, therefore, no knowledge even of an habitual kind innate in us.
Not at all, he wavers in his conclusion ; he lets you see that
his explanation has not entirely satisfied him ; he ends by
saying, not that there are absolutely no innate habits in our
soul, but only that there are no *determinate* habits innate
(ἀφωρισμέναι αἱ ἕξεις).[1]

from this other question, 'How can
man form the ideas designated by the
words '*Peruvian bark* and *fever*?' The
first is a *medical* question, which is
solved after much experience through
an induction more or less protracted
and therefore more or less likely to
be true. The second, on the contrary,
is an *ideological* question, having for its
object to explain, not a scientific fact,
but a plain common fact, that of the existence in men's minds of the ideas signified by the terms *Peruvian bark* and
fever. The forming of these ideas does
not require a long time, nor much experience, nor any extensive process of in-
ductions. It takes place as soon as
children come to the use of reason, or
at least as soon as they begin to speak.
Hence, you will hear a child freely
make use of the words *fever, bark*, or
the like substantive nouns expressive
not of mere individuals but of *species.*
The question, therefore, is, 'How does
this child, from the particular individual and subsistent things which it
perceives with its senses, pass so quickly
to the species or ideas, without which
it could not converse at all ?' This, I
say, is the question. Now, Aristotle,
or Themistius eschews this question
about the origin of the *first universals*,
and instead treats that of the formation of
scientific principles or the *last universals*
which suppose the first already formed,
since they are only a combination of
those. Therefore, he is not right in
concluding the explanation of the question he had proposed to himself, viz.
'How man forms the universal?' with
these words : 'But this induction' (by
which we arrive at scientific principles)
'is formed in a manner so gradual and
insensible that its very continuity prevents our being able to say for certain
where it begins or where it ends.
Hence, many persons think that man
has in him ideas by virtue of his very
nature, that is, requiring neither study

nor a mind to produce and awaken
them ; which is an error.' Here we see
the usual expedient of those who pretend to derive all human knowledge
from the senses. Finding it impossible
to explain how the universal can come
from singulars, they take refuge in the
allegation that this transition happens
so slowly and insensibly as to elude
observation ; whence many imagine
that the universal is innate in man.
Thus it is sought to establish a system
by throwing darkness around it.
These philosophers tell us that all ideas
come from the senses ; and when we
ask how, they answer: In an imperceptible way, by a progression which
escapes notice. But if so, then the
progression would be infinite, for from
the particular to the universal the distance is infinite. The universal as such
has no limit, while the individuals, no
matter how much they be multiplied,
either simultaneously or in succession,
can never absorb or exhaust a *species.*
Accordingly, to explain how *ideas* come
from *sensations*, we should have to suppose that an infinite progression, the
ultimate term of which would be the
ideas, is actually possible. But it is
not possible, for if the progression were
to reach that term, it would end there,
and consequently would not be infinite.
Therefore the ideas would never be
produced. In short there is, between
sensations and ideas, a difference not
merely of degree, but of kind ; and
thus a gradual passage from the former
to the latter is simply impossible. But
to return to our subject, Aristotle speaks
unreasonably when he says that 'there
are no innate ideas, because scientific
principles come from ideas by means of
an induction.' This is just as if one
were to say, 'stones are not the work of
nature, because man builds houses with
them.'

[1] *Posterior.* L. II. ch. xix.

272. And here I would invite the reader to note how completely this expression by which *determinate habits* only are excluded from being innate in man, agrees with my way of thinking and of speaking.[1]

I find the error of Plato in having supposed innate the ideas of special beings, viz , *determinate* ideas, corresponding in every respect with subsistent realities. I say, on the other hand, that his system is in part true, viz., if it be limited to admitting as innate some idea, expressive, not of any individualised beings, but of some universal essence, some idea perfectly *indeterminate*, and of this kind of ideas a number not less and not greater than is found necessary for explaining the formation of all other ideas ;[2] in fact, some such idea as Aristotle himself seems to have felt to be necessary when, not daring to deny the innateness of *all habits* indiscriminately, he restricted that denial to *determinate* ones only ; in other words, when he excluded, not the light as such, but the light as already divided into colours.

[1] The two opposite systems of Aristotle and Des Cartes, when taken in a spirit of moderation, may be brought very near each other. Thus Aristotle discards innate ideas ; but admits some kind of innate *habits*. Now some amongst the followers of Des Cartes admit innate ideas ; but in defining what they mean by innate ideas, they say that they are like innate *habits*, and this brings the two systems very near each other. Galluppi expounds the mind of the Cartesians thus : ' Some of them compared innate ideas to the *habits* of the will. In their opinion, when a dominant passion has possessed itself of the human heart, it continues to operate in it, even in those moments in which one has no consciousness of its acts. An ambitious man, for instance, who has conceived an intense desire of obtaining a certain post, even when not advertently thinking of that post, does not cease to harbour the desire in question, insomuch that we may truly affirm that he is even then coveting the post. Now, what is this habitual feeling, living in the heart of the ambitious man, even when not actually conscious of any distinct act of ambition ? According to these philosophers, it is nothing but the passion itself permanently in act, though not consciously so. The privation of this habitual passion is precisely what distinguishes it from those distinct coveting acts of which the ambitious man has consciousness. In the same manner the *a priori* and innate notions are really and continually in our minds, but disjoined from the act of consciousness until the sensible ideas awaken in us the consciousness of them. It is thus that, not to speak of others, the anonymous author of the *Treatise on the Nature of the Soul,* directed against Locke and his followers, expresses the nature of innate ideas' (*Saggio Filosofico sulla Critica della Conoscenza,* vol. iv. pp. 2, 3).

[2] One idea alone is sufficient to explain the production of all the others, as I shall demonstrate in its proper place ; nor, indeed, could there be more than one absolutely indeterminate idea.

ARTICLE XXIV.

*According to the interpretation of Egidius, the indeterminate habits
hinted at by Aristotle are innate in the human soul.*

273. I shall conclude these observations on Aristotle by
quoting a remarkable passage from Egidius, the *doctor funda-
tissimus*, about the reasoning of the Stagirite referred to above.

The passage appears to me worthy of notice, because it
shows how this acute commentator saw reason for believing
that Aristotle (willingly or not) really admitted the innateness of *indeterminate habits* in the human soul, and moreover
that it is precisely by this kind of habits that the *intellectus
agens* is constituted. And this lets us in some way into the
secret of Aristotle's meaning, when he said that an *act* must
necessarily be inherent in the human mind, to enable it to
obtain determinate habits or ideas ; that act consisted in
indeterminate habits or ideas.

Here, then, are the words of Egidius :—

' We must also consider that the habits of the principles
of reason are not in us in a *determinate form*—that is, they are
not *completely innate*, for that is called *determinate* which has
a term, and reaches that term fully. Now, the knowledge of
the principles has not been infused into us by nature in a
formally complete state. Nevertheless, we have in us something which relates to the knowledge of principles in an
effective as well as final and dispositive way, inasmuch as
there is in us, inserted by nature, *the light* of the *intellectus
agens*, by virtue of which these principles become known to
us as soon as we understand the terms of the proposition.' [1]

ARTICLE XXV.

Conclusion on Aristotle.

274. The favourable interpretation I have endeavoured to
give to some passages of Aristotle might be continued still
further.

[1] This passage is given by Dominic of Flanders, in the questions which he wrote on St. Thomas's *Commentaria* on the books of Aristotle's *Posterior Analytics.*

But in order to show how nearly that system on the origin of ideas, which I believe to be the true one, was approached by this extraordinary man, for so many ages held and proclaimed, to use Dante's words, as 'the master of them that know,' it would be necessary for me to premise an exposition of the whole system itself; and this does not enter into the plan of the present work.

I cannot, however, refrain from saying, that if other passages of the same author were also taken into account, he would have to be charged with many more blemishes not less serious than those which have been pointed out in these pages, and, all things considered, we should perhaps have to conclude, that if he is marvellous for the *subtlety* of his mind, he lacks nevertheless the *sublimity* characteristic of the genius of Plato.[1]

ARTICLE XXVI.

Two kinds of doctrine in Plato.

275. But it is high time for us to return to Plato.

In the foregoing remarks on the defection of Aristotle from the Platonic school, I have sought to prove that one of its causes was the imperfect manner in which Plato had set forth his reasons for believing that ideas are congenite with man, as well as the undue extension he had given to his doctrine, or at least the want of scientific precision in his exposition of it.

I will now mention another reason of that sturdy opposition of which the Platonic system has never ceased to be the object, without, however, being on that account altogether discarded or obliterated from the memory of men, as is the

[1] *Aristotle and Plato.* We have already remarked in the Preface that Rosmini's character and education led him to give the most benign interpretation to the philosophers he studied. Accordingly, in his important work, *Aristotle examined and explained*, written but two years before his death, and containing his most matured convictions on the doctrines of the two greatest thinkers of the old world, whilst declaring his belief that they cannot be fully reconciled, he shows that they have a great many points of contact, particularly in their views on the nature of knowledge and universals. He there collects a great number of passages from the several works of Aristotle, which prove how this subtle genius had a most penetrating insight into the true nature of intelligence, and of the intellectual light. [TRANSLATORS

case with opinions that have been demonstrated absolutely groundless and false.

The history of Platonism has two parts. On one side we see this philosophy constantly impugned, and very often with so formidable a force that it seems as if it must have been entirely prostrated and forgotten ; and, on the other, a continual reaction in its favour, which shows it to be possessed of a tenacious and inextinguishable life. Even in those periods in which the opposition to it was fiercest, we cannot say, that the substance of its doctrine was ever condemned by the really unanimous voice of mankind. The many who denounced it, always did so with a certain degree of hesitation. They never spoke with that security which characterises a judgment about which not the shadow of a doubt exists. Though ridiculing it as a piece of folly, they still betrayed symptoms of some secret misgiving. Then, when least expected, the derided doctrine found new and most ardent defenders against a multitude of others who felt indignant at seeing, as they thought, the world retrograde, instead of doing their bidding and going forward. A protest so vigorously maintained in defiance of the crowd of scoffers, can only be explained on the supposition that Platonism has in it a foundation of truth ; as, on the other hand, the constant opposition made to it is inexplicable, unless by supposing that in some part it is either erroneous or inexact, or at least obscure, or not stated with sufficient precision of language.

Plato has been accused of obscurity,[1] and many declare his system erroneous, whilst gravely assuring you that they do not understand it ! What can be said for certain is, that the greatest opposition came from a crowd of philosophasters who depicted Plato just as their poor minds had imagined him.

---

[1] Laertius says, that Plato is 'wont to make a display of terms in order that his works may not be understood by the unskilled and untutored.' But I do not think him equally correct (except perhaps in a partial sense) in the other remark which he makes, to the effect, that Plato ' takes the same words in different meanings, and moreover uses words of contrary meaning to denote one and the same thing.' When we go beyond the surface and penetrate into the inner spirit of the Platonic philosophy, we find that the defect mentioned by Laertius is more apparent than real.

But amongst these plebeian sophists rather than philosophers, of whom France alone gave birth in the last century to perhaps some hundreds, we must by no means place Aristotle, who, if he ranged himself against his master—possibly from some feeling of ambition and emulation—had also, as we have said, a mind capable of noting where the Platonic teaching was at fault.

276. Now, even independently of this imperfect or erroneous portion of Plato's system, its varying fortunes may be accounted for by the following circumstance.

There are, in the writings of the great Athenian, two doctrines blended together—the one *positive* and *traditional*, the other *rational*.

The distinction of these two sets of doctrines can be observed in all antiquity, and is as it were the key to the full understanding of ancient philosophy. Aristotle himself notices it very clearly; and he makes mention of two classes of wise men as being universally acknowledged—that is to say, the *Theologians* and the *Philosophers*.[1] By *Theologians* he must have meant those who occupied themselves in collecting those truths which, having been divinely communicated to men at the very beginning, had never been entirely lost, but were handed down traditionally from generation to generation. By *Philosophers*, on the contrary, he must have meant those who, not being satisfied with tradition and authority, and oftentimes paying little attention to either, applied themselves to the study of truth under the guidance of their individual reason alone.

It seems to me that by considering somewhat attentively

---

[1] *Metaph.* lib. iii. c. 2. Aristotle showed almost invariably but little regard for the *traditional* philosophy and its teachers, whom, as may be seen from the passage of his *Metaphysics* here referred to, he was accustomed to ridicule. And in part he was right; for the representatives of Theology were poets who had disfigured it with endless fables. It may be asserted that from Anaxagoras to Plato the rational philosophy had a tendency to join itself with the traditional. This tendency manifested itself more than ever before in Socrates, and received from Plato its ultimate development. Aristotle moved in the contrary direction, whereof Thales had been the originator; but at the same time he remained under the influence of the original tradition, which had been previously accepted, so to speak, as a guest by philosophy. A reference to his work, *De Cælo*, would be enough to prove this.

the distinctive characters of the two celebrated schools of antiquity, the Italic and the Ionic, we may easily discover in what their fundamental difference consisted. For we shall then see that Pythagoras, the founder of the former school, took as the basis of his philosophy the *traditional* and *symbolical doctrine*, while Thales, the founder of the latter school, grounded all his inquiries on pure reason, and thus produced a doctrine purely *rational*. Hence, Pythagoras was inclined to adopt the analytical process, and Thales the synthetical. The first started from the whole, and by decomposing came to the parts, always with a view to return to the whole, which was the object of his thoughts. The second set out from the parts, and by composing aimed at ascending to the whole; but in the interminable journey he broke down, ever falling back on the parts, which were in reality all that his mind could grasp. The first began from God, the second from Nature. The first travelled freely along the lofty regions of pure spirituality, while the second was trying hard, though in vain, to disentangle himself from the trammels of matter.

Plato united in himself both these kinds of doctrine. He may be said to have descended at once, through Architas, from Pythagoras, and, through Socrates, from Thales.

The valuable feature of the Pythagorean School lay in its intention to collect together the salutary doctrines consigned from the very beginning by God to men,[1] and preserved by society. The valuable feature of the school of

---

[1] In my *Teodicea* (*nn.* 94–124) I have pointed out that God communicated to our first parents (1) a certain number of positive truths; (2) the use of speech to set in motion their reasoning faculty, which would not have been able to come forth into exercise by itself, but required for that purpose some stimulating principle from without. From these two things received by man from the first moments of his existence proceed, as from their origin, the two doctrines which I have distinguished. Out of the *positive truths* arose the *traditional doctrine* which men had the duty of faithfully preserving in their memory; and from the impulse communicated to their reason sprang the *rational science* which man was destined to develop by means of reasoning, or the application of the abstract principles received through language to either the positive data of revelation or to the sensations produced in him by the beings which composed the material world. Thus both branches of human knowledge are finally reducible to the First Cause. They come from God, and man oftentimes adds to them nothing but his own aberrations.

Thales lay in the encouragement it gave to the active exercise of human reason.

Plato's travels for the purpose of collecting the doctrines of Pythagoras are well known. From Socrates, on the other hand, he had learnt the method of philosophising, or making use of his own reasoning powers. Indeed, it may be said that the whole teaching of Socrates reduces itself to the method of reasoning well on everything that is presented to our consideration. It was therefore the perfect fulfilment of the intention of Thales, the first in Greece who, leaving the *dicta* of schools aside, began to think for himself.[1]

Socrates, however, did not content himself with bringing the method of Thales to perfection;[2] he also carried it a step further in its application. Up to the time of Archelaus, Socrates' master, philosophical reasoning was scarcely applied to any but physical things;[3] and between the

[1] That is, he gave to human reason the same kind of hardihood which, in modern times, Des Cartes was seen to give it, who bound himself on principle (one of his principles of *method*) not to accept a single truth from other men before submitting it to a rigorous scrutiny. Hence, also, his errors; hence the imperfection of his philosophy. Hapless and impotent human nature! This was the noblest effort made by it with that reason which constitutes it supreme in this visible universe; and yet the effort only served to plunge it into a maze of errors, or else to force it to acknowledge its boundless ignorance!

[2] Be it observed that the method of Socrates is precisely the one adapted to the investigation of truth, the sole aim of the Ionic school, which was essentially inquisitive and sagaciously critical. This method starts with observation, and from singulars ascends to universals. Those who from childhood have had their minds prejudiced against the philosophy of Plato—gainsaid in times near our own, not because convicted of error, but because thought to be conjoined with something elevated and spiritual—imagine that it follows a contrary method, and bases its explanation of facts on purely arbitrary hypotheses. But the truth is exactly the

other way. It is they—I mean, the Sensists—who invariably begin by some preconceived hypothesis of their own, and then judge of the facts in accordance with that hypothesis. I will take it upon myself to affirm that so far as regards the method of reasoning, that which we find in the Dialogues of Plato is infinitely more rigorous and exact than that employed by Aristotle. Now whence this hallucination which makes the Sensists fancy that the art of observing nature and of being good reasoners is their exclusive privilege? Simply from this, that they, before all things, look at the *results* of the two philosophies. Their own philosophy does not go beyond mere matter: the contrary philosophy issues in the admission of spiritual beings. But the foregone conclusion of the Sensists is, that the existence of spiritual beings is a pure dream, or at least is impossible to prove by reasoning. That is enough; every one who proves it must be wrong; he has a bad method of reasoning.

[3] Nevertheless great progress had evidently been made. Although the inheritors of the doctrine of Thales professed nothing but the science of nature, the third in their order of succession, Anaxagoras, had already receded from the materiality of his master, Anaximenes, and had felt the

inauguration of the method by Thales and the transferring of its use from physical to moral things by Socrates, there intervened the space of over a century. However, when Socrates said that 'the things that are above us have nothing to do with us,'[1] he revealed the source whence his ideas had been derived. There was in this short sentence a clear trace of the Ionic school, which by laying on man the duty of finding the truth by his own investigation alone, obliged him to start from sensible and natural things, and thus threw him on a path slow, wearisome, and full of dangers. Hence the mere passage from physical to moral things was regarded as a miracle, and taken for the foundation of a new school ; because in fact such a passage had not been made, and could not be made by degrees, but only by a leap, *i.e.* through a man altogether extraordinary, as Socrates was. Nor did Socrates himself perform the great achievement as a result of his own independent thoughts, but driven to it, so to speak, by the evident needs of a society for which, in consequence of its having attained to a more adult growth, the Ionic philosophy had become too poor and cold. For the more society progresses the greater is its need of moral truths, that it may exist. However, the effort of Socrates was so great that, his

need of admitting the existence of purely spiritual beings. Socrates in his youth had heard the lessons delivered by Anaxagoras, then an old man.

[1] Socrates himself complained of Plato as having introduced into his philosophy doctrines alien to its spirit —meaning those of Pythagoras. See Brucker, *Hist. Phil.* part iii. ch. 2. Xenophon likewise found fault with Plato, 'because abandoning the sober philosophy of Socrates, and investigating too curiously the nature of the Gods, he made an ambitious display of many unseasonable and useless doctrines, and from a love for τερατολογία, and the portentous wisdom of Egypt and of Pythagoras, he, supercilious professor of wisdom that he was, vented ridiculous things.'

Such was the testimony which the greatest philosophers of antiquity, such as Socrates and Xenophon, rendered to the absolute impotence of fallen humanity ! The highest gift which this nature could boast of was intelligence ; but this intelligence, when raised to its highest perfection, put limits to its own self, and thought it wrong to inquire into that which, after all, ranks first in excellence and sublimity. And why so ? Because it foresaw that the result of such an attempt would probably be much more disastrous than ignorance itself. For error is worse than ignorance. Now that which Xenophon called the *sobriety* of the philosophy of Socrates, is in reality a great humiliation for human nature. Man's revolt against his Creator has reduced not only the individual, but the species itself, to such a low state that the loftiest point to which human genius abandoned to itself could ever reach in all antiquity was the converting of ignorance into a virtue and the including of all wisdom in the saying, 'All I know is that I know nothing.'

stupendous genius notwithstanding, he seemed so wearied
and so exhausted by it as to stop half way ; and in order not
to impose a burden too heavy for human strength to bear, he
took the resolution of excluding from his philosophy, first,
every kind of physical research, and then, as far as possible,
all such metaphysical speculations as seemed to him not
imperatively demanded by the daily necessities of human life.

277. Plato, then, while treating his subjects by philosophical
reasoning, added to this latter the positive and traditional
doctrines also.   But these could not but have suffered many
alterations.   The multitude, amongst whom they were dis-
persed, are never the faithful custodians of a doctrine ; for
they can never say the same thing twice over without either
adding or subtracting, exaggerating or extenuating, according
to the state of their ever-changing fancy, and of their only too
inconstant passions.

Nevertheless, these popular doctrines, though strangely
disfigured by absurdities, served Plato for the double purpose
of embellishing his incomparable eloquence to which he devoted so much attention, and of ingratiating his teaching all the
more easily with the masses.   But in the meantime the fables
unadvisedly mixed up with his philosophical reasonings, in
order to make them more acceptable, were a great cause of
the war waged against his system.   Those who could prove
the unreality and absurdity of these accessory embellishments
or props introduced by him, considered that they had sufficient reason for condemning the system wholesale.   Such was
the price which Plato, a man subject to error like all of us,
had to pay for his overweening confidence in attempting the
impossible—that is, to win at once the approval of sages and
of the corrupt society in which he lived.

The distinction between the two species of doctrine manifests itself very plainly in the *Meno,* and in reference to our
very question on the origin of ideas.   For, having stated the
difficulty concerning this question in the way we have described
—that is, having shown that in order to arrive at a truth we
want to know, it is necessary that we should have some notion
of it beforehand, else we could not on its presenting itself to

us recognise it for the one we are seeking—Plato does not content himself with solving the question by means of reasoning, but calls in the positive and fabulous doctrine to his aid.

The separation of this second species of doctrine from the first is unmistakably visible in his own words. So long as he is expounding the rational doctrine, he makes use of reasoning as usual; but when he comes to the traditional, he at once refrains from reasoning and has recourse to authorities of a higher order. Let us see. 'This,' says Socrates, 'I learnt in time past from men and women skilled in divine things.'

To whom *Meno* replies: 'What was it they said?'

Socrates: 'True and very excellent, as I think.'

Meno: 'Pray recount it to me; and who were they that spoke thus?'

Socrates: 'They were holy men and holy women, persons who could for certain give a good reason of the doctrines they professed. Moreover, Pindar and as many of the poets as are known to be divine, have handed down to us some other things to which I pray thee to attend, that thou mayest tell me whether in thy opinion they are true. For these sages maintain that the soul of man is immortal, and that it sometimes departs hence (which is called " to die "), and sometimes returns hither again; but that it never perishes. Wherefore they admonish us to live most holily; for those who have already paid the penalties of the former misery to Proserpine, receive their souls back from her every nine years, and are sent up to the Sun until they become kings, excelling in glory, in sagacity, and in prudence. Then they are called by men holy heroes. For the soul being immortal and having many times gone from this life to the other, and come back from the other to this, and therefore having repeatedly seen the things which take place in both, and perceived them all, has at last nothing further to learn. Hence it is no wonder if man can remember all that appertains to virtue as well as to other things, since he knew them once. For all nature is cognate and consonant with itself, and as the soul has learnt all things, so it comes to pass that when a man has had some one thing brought to his memory (which we call " discipline ") he is able to recall all the rest, provided he be earnest and persevering enough in his inquiries. Therefore to investigate and to learn is a reminiscence.'[1]

We see from this how the traditional doctrine, although corrupted by the popular as well as the poetical fables, was invoked by Plato in support of his system regarding the innateness of ideas. He thought it would do him good service in bringing that system into credit with the public, for the great majority of whom it would have been hard to conceive how a man could be possessed of any ideas prior to the experience of his senses. Hence his use of a popular fable, to suit the popular comprehension. The attempt, however, had the contrary effect to what he intended, and in course of time it did most serious injury to his system. For time destroys falsehoods, though sometimes the fall of these involves also the temporary fall of those truths which a mistaken calculation had joined with them. But the moment comes at last when the truths being wholly disencumbered from false accretions, and made to stand by themselves alone, are seen in their own native genuineness and endure perennially.

Indeed, the fabulous explanation given by Plato of the way in which ideas enter the human soul, is one thing, and his philosophical system as made out on purely rational grounds is another. The greatest adversaries of Plato, on the contrary, think it enough to direct their attacks against the fabulous part of the system ; and having shown up the baselessness, falsehood, and impiety of believing that human souls, before entering into their bodies, were in the stars, and that, having once dropped down into this sublunary world, they are through death made to go backwards and forwards over and over again, no one knows how often, they conclude that Platonism is a vain dream and an irreligion to be shunned ;[2] as though

---

[1] I have already observed that Plato's belief in the necessity of considering all human ideas as innate arose from his not having distinctly perceived how one originates in and flows from the other. From this passage, however, it appears that he noticed the existence of a connection and mutual dependence between ideas. But if this knowledge sufficed him for explaining the *association* and *reminiscence* of ideas, it did not go far enough to make him realise the fact that the formation of them all is traceable to one *parent idea*.

[2] Not so the Fathers of the Church, especially St. Augustine. He separates

the system consisted in that accessory, which Plato added to it by way, as he thought, of embellishment, and to render it more attractive, and particularly to a people so fantastic as the one in whose midst he was writing.

in Plato the false and fabulous from that which is philosophical and even true. He combats the first part by opposing to it the authority of Christian faith or divine revelation ; but with the philosophical part he deals argumentatively ; thus meeting each with weapons suitable to itself.

CHAPTER II.

LEIBNITZ.

ARTICLE I.

The difficulty to be overcome in accounting for the origin of ideas was seen by Leibnitz.

278. Leibnitz, a fair-minded and reasonable man, and full of conciliatory spirit, finding himself obliged to dissent from Locke, took a most amicable and generous attitude in dealing with him, and instead of exaggerating the divergence of their views, he smoothed it down as much as possible. He thus stood before his adversary in that position in which two men of different opinions ought always to be, when they are actuated, not by vanity—that prolific mother of enmities—but by a sincere desire to come to an understanding, and to arrive together at the truth.

As I have already remarked (n. 235), so long as Locke says, ' I admit in man a faculty of thinking, of passing from sensations to ideas, and even of forming judgments and reasonings,' no one can reasonably contradict him. This admission ought therefore to be accepted as common to both sides, and as a starting-point whence to proceed to the further inquiry, how the faculty of thinking must be constituted in order to be capable of performing the operations which Locke himself attributes to it ; and whether it be not perhaps necessary to concede to it something innate in such a way that its existence depends essentially on this innate element. Thus, instead of opposing Locke in the general principle of his system, one simply invites him to prosecute his investigations on the human understanding ; and this is what Leibnitz did, in language as courteous as it was true and forcible.

279. In his *New Essays on the Human Understanding,* which were published only after his death, we find *Philalethes* who defends the opinion of Locke, granting to *Theophilus* (*i.e.* to Leibnitz himself) that the faculty of thinking is innate in man. Theophilus accepts the concession, with only this one remark, that 'a true faculty is never a mere potentiality, but has always in it some real tendency and some action.' [1]

And inasmuch as Locke placed the faculty of thinking in the power of reflecting on one's own sensations and on the acts of the soul, Leibnitz joins hands with him, and deftly entering upon an analysis of this 'reflexion,' finds that by admitting it, one does not as yet contradict the theory of innate ideas rightly understood, but rather draws near to it. Let us hear himself :—

'Peut-être que notre habile auteur ne s'éloignera pas entièrement de mon sentiment. Car, après avoir employé tout son premier livre à rejeter les lumières innées prises dans un certain sens, il avoue pourtant au commencement du second et dans la suite, que les idées qui n'ont point leur origine dans la sensation viennent de la réflexion. Or la réflexion n'est autre chose qu'une attention à ce qui est en nous, et les sens ne nous donnent point ce que nous portons déjà avec nous. Cela étant, peut-on nier qu'il y ait beaucoup d'inné en notre esprit, puisque nous sommes innés à nous-mêmes, pour ainsi dire, et qu'il y ait en nous être, unité, substance, durée, changement, action, perception, plaisir et mille autres objets de nos idées intellectuelles ? Ces mêmes objets étant immédiats et toujours présents à notre entendement (quoiqu'ils ne sauraient être toujours aperçûs,[2] à cause de nos distractions et de nos besoins), pourquoi s'étonner que nous disions que ces idées nous sont innées, avec tout ce qui en dépend ?[3]   Je

---

[1] Book II. ch. i.   This observation of Leibnitz is something, but it is not all.   The *tendency to action* does not go beyond the sphere of simple *subjectivity.*   The great man did not ascend high enough to catch sight of the *object* of the intellect.

[2] Leibnitz distinguished *perception* from *apperception.*   By the former term he meant a modification effected in our soul without our being conscious of it ; and by the latter, a modification joined with consciousness.

[3] My object in referring to this passage is simply to point out on what side the German philosopher took his adversary.   It seems to me, however, that Leibnitz is faulty in this, that he uses the expression *innate ideas* in different meanings.   In fact, this passage would

me suis servi aussi de la comparaison d'une pierre de marbre qui a des veines, plutôt que d'une pierre de marbre tout unie, ou de tablettes vuides, c'est-à-dire de ce qui s'appelle *tabula rasa* chez les philosophes ; car si l'âme ressemblait à ces tablettes vuides, les vérités seraient en nous comme la figure d'Hercule est dans un marbre quand le marbre est tout à fait indifférent à recevoir ou cette figure ou quelque autre. Mais s'il y avait des veines dans la pierre qui marquassent la figure d'Hercule préférablement à d'autres figures, cette pierre y serait plus déterminée, et Hercule y serait comme innée en quelque façon, quoiqu'il fallût du travail pour découvrir ces veines et pour les nettoyer par la politure en retranchant ce qui les empêche de paraître. C'est ainsi que les idées et les vérités nous sont innées comme des inclinations, des diposi-tions, des habitudes ou des virtualités naturelles, et non pas comme des actions, quoique ces virtualités soient toujours accompagnées de quelques actions, souvent insensibles, qui y répondent.'[1]

Further on he expresses the same sentiments in these other words : ' On m'opposera cet axiome reçu parmi les philo-sophes, qu'il n'est rien dans l'âme qui ne vienne des sens, mais

lead us to understand by *innate ideas* merely the *matter* of our ideas, or else ideas acquired from the first instant of our existence. For the drift of it ap-pears to be, (1) that we carry with us the matter of our ideas ; (2) that we also possess from the first moment of our existence the intellectual faculty ; (3) that this faculty, having always its mat-ter manifestly present to it, cannot remain inactive. Hence it follows that it must likewise receive all these ideas from the first moment of its existence. But, on the other hand, in many other places it seems that by *innate ideas* Leibnitz means ideas essential to the understanding itself, so essential that without them the very concept of *un-derstanding* would vanish ; and it is in accordance with this that he describes them here as active virtualities of the understanding. Now, it is very necessary to keep these two significa-tions perfectly distinct, for by using the same expressions in different mean-

ings, different questions are confused together. In fact, to ask if there are *innate ideas* in one sense is a very dif-ferent thing from asking if there are *innate ideas* in another sense. The question whether, as soon as our under-standing exists, it has also a matter on which to exercise itself, and thus form ideas at once, although there would be no absurdity in imagining it without them, at least by an abstraction, is a question relating to a fact more than anything else. On the contrary, the question as to whether the understand-ing itself be nothing but the actual in-tuition of some idea, and the power of making use of that idea for the purpose of reasoning, so that to deny all innate ideas would be to destroy the under-standing, is a question turning not on a mere fact, but on the nature of this faculty.

[1] *Nouveaux Essais,* &c., *Avant-propos* (*Œuvres de Leibnitz,* Paris, 1842, vol. i. p. 5).

il faut excepter l'âmc même et ses affections ; *nihil est in intellectu quod non fuerit in sensu; excipe, nisi ipse intellectus.* Or l'âme renferme l'être, la substance, l'un, le même, la cause, la perception, le raisonnement, et quantité d'autres notions que les sens ne sauraient donner.[1] Cela s'accorde assez avec notre auteur de *l'Essai* (Locke), qui cherche une bonne partie des idées dans la réflexion de l'esprit sur sa propre nature.'[2]

From these passages we see quite plainly that the difficulty to be surmounted in explaining the origin of ideas was, though somewhat confusedly, perceived by the German philosopher. His argument went to prove that a faculty of thinking wholly devoid of the ideal element would be a faculty only in name, a power that is not a power, a contradiction in terms. He was, in substance, saying to Locke : ' If you reflect carefully on what that faculty of thinking, that intellect, which you admit as innate in man, really is, you will see that it must necessarily have in it some innate notion or idea, since without this the intellective soul could not exercise its power of reflection either on the sensations or on itself.'[3]

ARTICLE II.

Leibnitz was led to perceive the difficulty by the analysis, not of the intellectual faculty in particular, but of powers in general.

280. But although Leibnitz was clear-sighted enough to see that it would be impossible to explain how the soul could perform acts of thought unless some innate notion or idea were presupposed in it ; nevertheless he did not come to this knowledge by an accurate analysis of the nature of the intellectual faculty itself. He deduced it from a very abstract

[1] Here also the reasoning of Leibnitz is not sufficiently exact. For if he speaks of the idea of *being*, of *substance*, &c., in general, our soul could not furnish it to the understanding any more than could the senses ; because the soul is but a particular being, substance, &c., like bodies ; hence *substance in general*, being an object of the intellect, has in it something not to be found

either in bodies or in the soul, and this something is its *universality.*
[2] *Nouveaux Essais,* &c., liv. ii. ch. I, p. 59.
[3] In the passages I have quoted from Leibnitz this thought also is expressed, and I have selected it by preference as the best thing they contain, although it is stated confusedly, because mixed up with other matters.

principle, from the nature common to all powers generally, which he believed he thoroughly understood. He says :—

'On me répondra peut-être que cette *table rase* des philosophes veut dire, que l'âme n'a naturellement et originairement que des facultés nues. Mais les facultés sans quelque acte, en un mot les pures puissances de l'école, ne sont aussi que des fictions que la nature ne connaît point et qu'on n'obtient qu'en faisant des abstractions. Car où trouvera-t-on jamais dans le monde une faculté qui se renferme dans la seule puissance sans exercer aucun acte ?[1] Il y a toujours

---

[1] The high esteem I entertain for Leibnitz causes me to be severe with him. Every slip in his reasoning ought to be noted, in order that it may be seen how even a very slight inadvertence suffices to induce error ; how an error, however small it may be, nay almost imperceptible, invariably begets a progeny like itself, which in more logical minds is very rapidly developed.

Here, then, our philosopher, after having said that bare faculties (*facultés nues*) are only an abstraction, suddenly appeals to facts by asserting that there is not in the whole universe a single power in a state of total inaction. This is too precipitous a transition. He was speaking of faculties considered in themselves, and telling us that their nature is such as always to be conjoined with an act of some sort. It was a metaphysical speculation. The question, 'Whether a power devoid of all action was possible,' took the reader into the world of possibilities. Now, to prove the impossibility of a power like that by appealing to the fact and asking, 'Where in the entire universe do we find a power wholly without action, is to change the question, to descend to the world of realities, to refer to experience in order to know with absolute certainty what is possible or is not possible. But experience witnesses only to matters of fact, it only informs us of that which is or is not, and therefore has no force in determining what *can* be. And even if it had, who will ever be able, on the ground of experience alone, to affirm with truth that there is not in the whole universe a single power which remains in a state of absolute inac-

tion even for one instant, or that such a thing is impossible? Who will be able to examine all powers without exception, to observe every one of them in every instant of their existence ? The most that observation could fairly supply would be a conjectural argument of analogy, sufficient, indeed, to prove a fact, a general fact if you will, but not yet apodeictically necessary. Now, this mixing up and confounding together of the two worlds, the real and the possible, occurs frequently in Leibnitz. And since, in his philosophy, this confusion is of great relevance, I hope I may be pardoned for quoting another passage where a similar want of distinction between *fact* and *possibility* is exhibited, and the first is adduced for demonstrating the second. He says, therefore, 'I maintain that, naturally, a substance could not be without action ; ' and then he immediately adds, 'Not even bodies are ever found without motion' (*N. Essais*, &c., *Avant-propos*, p. 7). Now, the first of these two propositions is abstract, but the second, by referring us to bodies, becomes concrete, and is not therefore intrinsically *necessary* like the first. Had he contented himself with saying, 'Bodies must always be in action, because they are substances,' the argument would have been all right, *i.e.* on the supposition that he had previously demonstrated that bodies are substances, and that every substance must always act. But to affirm that all bodies move because 'experience tells us so, and to be persuaded of this we need only consult the work of the illustrious Mr. Boyle against absolute rest,' is a reasoning which will not hold.

une disposition particulière à l'action, et à une action plutôt qu'à l'autre. Et outre la disposition, il y a une tendance à l'action, dont même il y a toujours une infinité à la fois dans chaque sujet, et ces tendances ne sont jamais sans quelque effet. L'expérience est nécessaire, je l'avoue, afin que l'âme soit déterminée à telles ou telles pensées, et afin qu'elle prenne garde aux idées qui sont en nous ; mais le moyen que l'expérience et les sens puissent donner des idées ? L'âme a-t-elle des fenêtres ? ressemble-t-elle à des tablettes ? est-elle comme de la cire ? Il est visible que tous ceux qui pensent ainsi de l'âme la rendent corporelle dans le fond.' [1]

281. Thus does Leibnitz point out the danger of all these analogical ways of speaking of the soul—the very ways by which the followers of Locke try to explain their system. And yet they claim for themselves the credit of being the only philosophers who adhere to a strictly rigorous method of reasoning ! As to all their adversaries, these, in their opinion, substitute imagination for argument ; and this simply because they differ from them, and refuse to be satisfied with the material similes so common in their writings. Leibnitz, on the contrary, exhorts them to exclude these gross analogies, of windows of the soul, of wax, of a *tabula rasa*, and to consider the human understanding as it really is, viz. a mere power of knowing. He reminds them that if they do this they will upon careful reflection find that the intelligent soul must of necessity be endowed with some act, because there is no power without some act inherent in it. And whereas this

It is to exchange the facts of the real world for the immutable and eternal relations of the world of ideas.

This is all the more deserving of attention, inasmuch as in the ideas of our author there is sometimes a manifest vicious circle. Thus, to prove that the human understanding always thinks, he has recourse to the necessity which exists of every faculty having an act of some kind ; and then to prove the principle that every faculty has an act of some kind ; he alleges a fact and says, 'Experience shows that there are no powers in nature without action ; ' whereas the question, 'Whether the understanding always thinks,' when put in this form, is precisely as to whether 'there be in point of fact any power destitute of all action.'

How Leibnitz came to make this confusion of the *real* with the *ideal* world, will be explained further on.

We shall there see that the cause of his not grasping sufficiently so important a distinction as that between these two worlds lay in the very nature of his philosophy.

[1] *Nouveaux Essais*, &c., liv. ii. ch. 1, pp. 58-9.

act must accord with the power to which it belongs, they will see that the act of the faculty of knowing must consist in a knowledge of some kind, in some innate notion or idea which constitutes its natural term and object. This reasoning by which Leibnitz became convinced of the necessity of admitting something innate in the human soul, was similar to the argument by which Aristotle proved that to explain the origin of human cognitions we must admit in man an *intellectus agens*—that is, an intellect originally and naturally in act. 'As a motion does not naturally arise except from another motion, so a perception does not naturally arise except from another perception.' Such are the words in which Brucker formulates the doctrine of Leibnitz, and they would seem to be the words of Aristotle himself.[1]

ARTICLE III.

Leibnitz saw the difficulty imperfectly because he deduced it from principles which were too general.

282. Nevertheless, between Aristotle and Leibnitz there is the following difference : Aristotle inferred the necessity of his *intellectus agens* from studying the nature of the intellectual faculty in particular, and finding it impossible to explain how it could actually form ideas unless it were itself in act from its very beginning ; Leibnitz, on the contrary, deduced the necessity of admitting some primitive act in the human understanding by examining the nature of powers in general, which, according to him, could not exist without being in some way always in act.

But to deduce the said necessity in this second way was to take the thing from too high a stand-point. The argument did not exactly close with the real question at issue, 'Whether the formation of human cognitions is conceivable, or possible to explain otherwise than by presupposing some intellectual element innate in the soul.' It did not go straight to the heart of the difficulty itself, but sought its solution in a principle external to it. The proceeding was a very dangerous

[1] Period III., Part II., Bk. I., ch. 8.

one, and, as we shall see, it produced the imperfections of the
Leibnitzian system.

The German philosopher, then, saw the difficulty, but only
in a general way. He saw that to make the formation of
ideas possible, some antecedent idea was necessary, but he did
not view this necessity in that proper and particular form in
which I have endeavoured to present it to my readers. In
short he did not see, at least not clearly, that the faculty of
forming ideas is such that it must have from its very beginning
some idea which enables it to form judgments, and, through
judgments, all other ideas.

ARTICLE IV.

Leibnitzian solution of the difficulty.

283. Here, then, are the Leibnitzian pronouncements :—
The senses cannot produce the primitive perceptions of
the soul. It is impossible for the body to exercise any
action on the soul.[1] In general, it is impossible for a created
being to exert a true action on another created being ; and
for the power of these beings to break through the individual
sphere belonging respectively to each, and therefore to enter
into others with its action. All the changes to which a being
is subject proceed, therefore, only from a principle internal to
it, and endowed with the force necessary for evolving itself
through a determinate series of changes. God having so
ordered the universe that the changes of each being shall proceed constantly in harmony with those of the others, it comes
to pass that such changes as constantly precede, and such as
constantly follow, are believed by men to be related to one

---

[1] And this not because the nature of
the body differs essentially from that of
the soul ; since, according to Leibnitz,
the body was nothing but an aggregate
of simple monads each having its own
perceptions, so that he sometimes says
that these monads may, in a certain
sense, be termed souls. He excluded
physical action between the body and
the soul simply on the general principle
adopted by him, that 'no created being
could exercise a real action on another
and produce a change in it,' and consequently that all changes which take
place in any being must be ascribed to
a principle internal to itself. Such was
the conception he had formed of the
power of acting. Nevertheless, he seems
sometimes to forget his general principle—the foundation of his whole system—and to lay stress on the different
natures of body and of soul.

another as *cause* and *effect*, whereas, in point of fact, they are only *co-existent.*

Such, in a few words, is the celebrated doctrine of '*pre-established harmony.*'

The principle that every change which takes place in a being arises simply from a force internal to it and gradually develops itself into a determinate series of motions, was applied by Leibnitz to explain the genesis of our ideas. In his opinion these ideas are nothing but a series of modifications or changes undergone in due succession by our understanding. They were all contained in it from the beginning and by its very nature, but in a manner so imperceptible that we had no consciousness of them. To these he gave the name of *perceptions*, to distinguish them from *apperceptions*, which were the selfsame ideas, but after the consciousness of them had been awakened in us.

284. Accordingly he said that ideas differ from thoughts, and can therefore be in the soul without any actual thought— *i.e.* without any advertence being given to them : ' Pour que les connaissances, idées ou vérités soient dans notre esprit, il n'est point nécessaire que nous y ayons jamais pensé actuellement ; ce ne sont que des habitudes naturelles, c'est-à-dire, des dispositions et aptitudes actives et passives, et plus que *tabula rasa.*' [1] To the usual objection of the followers of Locke, represented by Philalethes, 'Mais n'est-il vrai que l'Idée est l'objet de la pensée ?' Theophilus replies, ' Je l'avoue, pourvû que vous ajoutiez que c'est un objet immédiat interne, et que cet objet est une expression de la nature ou des qualités des choses. Si l'idée était la *forme* de la pensée, elle naîtrait et cesserait avec les pensées actuelles qui y répondent ; mais en étant l'objet, elle pourra être antérieure et postérieure aux pensées.[2] Les objets externes sensibles ne sont que médiats, parce qu'ils ne sauraient agir immédiatement sur l'âme. Dieu seul est l'objet externe immédiat. On pourrait dire que l'âme même est son objet immédiat

---

[1] *N. Essais*, &c., liv. i. (ch. iii. p. 55).
[2] If the word *thought* (*pensée*) is reserved to indicate a reflex act, I agree with Leibnitz ; but an *idea* without *intuition* is inconceivable to me.

interne ; mais c'est en tant qu'elle contient les Idées ou ce qui répond aux choses, car l'âme est un petit monde où les Idées distinctes sont une representation de Dieu et où les confuses sont une représentation de l'univers.'[1]

285. Hence it appears that Leibnitz admitted two things as innate in the soul : (1) the imperceptible ideas of all things ; (2) certain instincts which prompt us to reflect on these ideas, to think of them actually, and thus to acquire the consciousness or *apperception* of them. And as these instincts are different in each individual from his origin, so they produce in each a series of thoughts different from those of his neighbours, by determining him to reflect on some rather than on others from among all the innate ideas which lurk in the inner recesses of his soul : ' Il faut bien,' he says, ' que dans cette multitude de nos connaissances nous soyons déterminés par quelque chose à renouveler l'une plutôt que l'autre, puisqu'il est impossible de penser distinctement tout à la fois à tout ce que nous savons.'[2] In a word, he imagined each idea as, so to speak, a little power standing by itself, as a being possessed of the virtue of drawing to itself the attention of the understanding. For this reason he also on many occasions designates ideas by the names of *instincts, aptitudes, dispositions,* &c., as though they were vieing with one another in an effort to acquire in the understanding a more lucid state, and to wake out of slumber by producing in man an actual consciousness of them. And since, as we have seen, the activity of these instincts varies with different individuals, it was but natural that each individual should feel interiorly impelled towards some kinds of thought rather than towards others, and to give actual advertence to some ideas in preference to all the rest.[3]

[1] *N. Essais,* &c., liv. ii. ch. 1 (pp. 57–8). In this place Leibnitz says that the soul is the object of the understanding in so far as it contains ideas, because ideas are the proximate object of the understanding. Agreed : but this is a very different thing from saying, as he does elsewhere, that the understanding forms the ideas of being, of substance, &c., because it perceives the soul which is all these things. The soul is the *real* object of the understanding, even as all the corporeal things which it knows, are its real objects. As I have said, this mixing up of realities with pure *ideas* is an inaccuracy frequent in the writings of our philosopher.

[2] *N. Essais,* liv. i. ch. 1 (p. 30).

[3] ' Tout sentiment est la perception d'une vérité, et le sentiment naturel est la perception d'une vérité innée, mais bien souvent confuse.'—*N. Essais,* &c., liv. i. ch. 2 (p. 45).

According to Leibnitz, then, all ideas issue out of the depths of our soul. But let us now see how he accounted for the fact of some ideas being included in others, and again of our being able to pass to the distinct consciousness of new ideas by the development of a single one.

ARTICLE V.

How innate ideas, as understood by Leibnitz, are made successively to pass from a confused to a luminous state.

286. In the first place we must call to mind another principle of Leibnitz, drawn from his meditations on the nature of powers in general. It was, that no power and, generally, no being could exist except as altogether simple, and therefore without parts.

But as, on the other hand, every being must be different from the rest, he could not imagine in simple beings any diversity save that of their perceptions.

He held, therefore, that each of these simple beings, called by him *monads*, had its own perceptions, though not all were conscious of them.

287. Conformably to these views, he describes the original link of union between human ideas in the following way.

The soul had from the first the perceptions of those simple beings or monads of which its body is the compound result, and which we may designate by the capital letters A, B, C, D, &c. But the soul could not have the perception of A without at the same time representing to itself all the perceptions proper to A, because it is by these perceptions that A is determined and individualised. Therefore, in perceiving A, the soul perceived all the perceptions of A.

Now, let us suppose that the perceptions of A consist in perceiving the monads called by the small letters *a, b, c, d,* &c. It is clear that in the representation which the soul has of A there will necessarily be included the representation of this series of monads also. Apply the same mode of reasoning severally to B, C, D, &c., and you will in each case have a similar result.

But, on the other hand, each of the monads *a, b, c, d,* &c., has in its turn the perception of other monads ; hence the identical reasoning holds good also in respect of each of them. By following up this line of thought you will be able to run through all the monads of the universe, and will thus discover that the perceptions of these monads are all included the one in the other, in the same way as seeds appear to be involved and wrapped up indefinitely within one another. Consequently the soul which perceives A, B, C, &c., perceives *ipso facto* the whole universe.

Such is the representation of the universe which Leibnitz attributed to all his monads, and from which in process of time there come out into clear light such among the perceptions as have a greater instinctive efficacy or force to draw to themselves the attention of the soul, to cause it, as it were, to fix its eye on them in particular.[1]

This indistinct representation of the universe was called by Leibnitz the *schema* of the monad, and, as may be gathered from what has just been said, it varied with each monad ; because the original perception proper to each, and therefore the order in which the other perceptions were contained and involved in it, were in each case different from those of the other monads. Hence, ' Even as a city, seen from different points of view, does not seem to be the same city, but is, as it were, multiplied according to the different aspects it presents to the eye, so, owing to the countless multitude of simple substances, it comes to pass that there are, so to speak, as many different worlds, which, nevertheless, are but one and the same world, variously represented according to the different aspects in which it is viewed by each monad.'

ARTICLE VI.

Merit of Leibnitz in this question.

288. One of the facts which escaped the observation of Locke was that of *small perceptions,* or, to speak more accurately, perceptions without advertence.

[1] See the *Theses* for Prince Eugène, published by Leibnitz in 1714.

This fact was, on the contrary, noticed very particularly by Leibnitz, and it became in his lofty intellect most fruitful of consequences ; and this seems to me his principal merit relative to the question of which we are speaking.

To such a degree does Locke forget that there are in us sensations and ideas of which we have no consciousness, that he would even exclude from the soul every kind of virtual knowledge. ' This,' says Leibnitz, ' is such a paradox that one can hardly believe that Locke took the thing in a rigorous sense. The recollection of things forgotten which is aroused in us on some trivial occasions is a matter of everyday occurrence with all of us, and quite sufficient by itself to prove that those ideas were virtually in us before.' [1]

289. The existence of perceptions unaccompanied by advertence is established by our philosopher in the following passage :—' Outre que nos adversaires, tout habiles qu'ils sont, n'ont point apporté de preuve de ce qu'ils avancent si souvent et si positivement là-dessus, il est aisé de leur montrer le contraire, c'est-à-dire, qu'il n'est pas possible que nous réfléchissons toujours expressément sur toutes nos pensées ; autrement l'esprit ferait réflexion sur chaque réflexion à l'infini, sans pouvoir jamais passer à une nouvelle pensée. Par exemple, en m'apercevant de quelque sentiment présent, je devrais toujours penser que j'y pense, et penser encore que je pense d'y penser, et ainsi à l'infini. Mais il faut bien que je cesse de réfléchir sur toutes ces réflexions, et qu'il y ait enfin quelque pensée qu'on laisse passer sans y penser ; autrement on demeurerait toujours sur la même chose.' [2]

290. This argument proves not only the existence of the fact, but also its necessity, if we are ever to bring any thought to completion. In further proof of his doctrine Leibnitz appeals to observation, and strengthens his case by some remarks which I think it well to quote. For the fact here alluded to very easily escapes attention, while it is of the greatest importance in all the philosophy of the human mind, and therefore can never be too much insisted upon. He

---

[1] *N. Essais*, &c. (*Avant-propos*, p. 6).   [2] *N. Essais*, &c., liv. ii. ch. 1 (p. 65).

writes thus :—' Il y a mille marques,[1] qui font juger qu'il y a à tout moment une infinité de perceptions[2] en nous, mais sans aperception et sans réflexion ; c'est-à-dire, des changements dans l'âme même, dont nous ne nous apercevons pas, parce que ces impressions sont ou trop petites[3] et en trop grand nombre, ou trop unies, en sorte qu'elles n'ont rien d'assez distinguant à part ; mais jointes à d'autres, elles ne laissent pas de faire leur effet et de se faire sentir dans l'assemblage, au moins confusément. C'est ainsi que la coûtume fait que nous ne prenons pas garde au mouvement d'un moulin ou à une chute d'eau, quand nous avons habité tout auprès depuis quelque temps. . . . . . . Pour juger encore mieux,' he says a little lower down, 'des petites perceptions que nous ne saurions distinguer dans la foule, j'ai coûtume de me servir de l'exemple du mugissement, ou du bruit de la mer, dont on est frappé quand on est au rivage. Pour entendre ce bruit, comme l'on fait, il faut bien qu'on entende les parties[4] qui composent ce tout, c'est-à-dire, le bruit de chaque vague, quoique chacun de ces petits bruits ne se fasse connaître que dans l'assemblage confus de tous les autres ensemble, et qu'il ne se remarquerait pas si cette vague qui le fait était seule. Car il faut qu'on soit affecté un peu par le mouvement de cette vague et qu'on ait quelque perception de chacun de ces bruits, quelque petits qu'ils soient ; autrement on n'aurait pas celle de cent mille vagues, puisque cent mille riens ne sauraient

[1] N. Essais, &c. (Avant-propos, p. 7).

[2] In the philosophy of Leibnitz the term perception has a very wide meaning, and embraces also every kind of thought.

[3] Speaking of ideas, this is not because they are too small, but because they are not adverted to. Sensations can be small, but ideas cannot, although they may be in us without advertence, or without being gazed at by the mind with an intense and recollected attention.

[4] Leibnitz supposes, then, that each of the little noises through which we come to perceive distinctly a full sound, are heard by us ('il faut bien qu'on entende les parties'). It seems, therefore, from this and other passages in which he describes perception as a true sensation, that he is in open contradiction with himself. But granted that the perception is really felt by us without our reflecting on it, then I say that sometimes this perception may very well result from a great, though never infinite, number of minor perceptions, as will appear from what I shall say in the following note. In that case the act by which the soul perceives would be simple, but terminating in the manifold ; or, which is the same thing, the manifold would be perceived in the simple ; or, again, the many would be perceived by one. There is no more difficulty in admitting this fact than in admitting that two different terms are joined together in a judgment.

faire quelque chose.[1]   D'ailleurs on ne dort jamais si pro-
fondément qu'on n'ait quelque sentiment faible et confus ; et

[1] This reasoning of Leibnitz does not appear to me exact. There is certainly no absurdity in supposing that in order that a sensation may be produced in us, our organs must be impressed with a certain degree of force, failing which, the sensation would not arise. For we must not confound the impression made on the bodily organ with the corresponding sensation or sensible perception which takes place in the soul. That even the smallest external force produces in our bodily organs, when properly applied to them, some physical impression, seems indubitable. The very expression ' external force applied' imports a something which acts, much or little, according to the greater or less degree of its impressiveness ; and therefore, when it is applied to a fit and proper subject, doubtless it will produce some effect. But it does not follow that every action, however slightly exercised on our external organs, always produces a sensation in the soul. What necessity is there for believing it ? For instance, I have no manner of doubt that even the least wave of the sea in motion produces slight undulations in the air, and that these make their impressions on my ears. Nay more, I am willing to believe that, not only every wave, but also every drop of which a wave is composed, by being set in motion, causes the air proportionately to move, and in such a manner as not to stop until that gentle undulation has communicated itself to the whole atmospheric body, so that not my ears alone, but the ears of those living at the farthest distance, will, in an ever-decreasing proportion, be touched and affected by it. But what of this ? Will that affection of my ears cause a sensation, a perception in my soul? Experience proves that it is not enough that the impression of external things upon the sensitive parts of our body be made in the outer extremities of the nerves. The vibration or shock must be transmitted to the brain, else there will be no sensation. Now, is it quite certain that every impulse, no matter how feeble, given to the outer extremities of the nerves, will suffice to produce in

them that continuity of vibration which is necessary for exciting a sensation ? May it not be that, for this vibration to be propelled as far as the brain, the impression on the sensories must have a certain degree of strength ?

But leaving this aside, whence did Leibnitz derive the opinion which I am now confuting ? From an application of the *law of continuity*, of which he was very fond of making use. It is not, certainly, my intention to enter here on an examination of this law, or to define its precise limits. To show how mistaken was the application which the great philosopher of whom I am speaking made of it in the present case, the following remark will suffice. I ask : What relation is there between the *impression* produced in the bodily organs, and the corresponding *perception* of the soul ? According to his philosophy, these are two things of quite a different nature; nor can the one be the cause of the other : one comes, indeed, after the other, but this is a conjunction, not a relation of cause and effect. Why, then, shall I be obliged to *perceive* every least *impression* made on my external organs ? Certainly not by the law of continuity, since between the *impression* and the *perception* there is no communicating link. The two are as completely divided by origin as they are by nature. Therefore, even if the law of continuity were applicable here, this could only be with reference to the series of *impressions* on the one hand, and to that of *perceptions* on the other. I mean that, pursuant to the said law, it would have to be laid down that there can be no strong impression except on condition of its having been preceded by a proper series of weaker ones ; and likewise that there can be no vivid perception until one has had that same perception in all those lesser degrees which were necessary before it could reach its present intensity. That law, then, could at the most apply to each of the two things separately ; but it could never be of any use for explaining the passage from the one to the other. Such being the case, there will be no absurdity in supposing that the series of *perceptions* begins only when the

on ne serait jamais éveillé par le plus grand bruit du monde, si on n'avait quelque perception de son commencement, qui est

series of the degrees of strength in the *impression* has already made some progress, and our organs are stimulated with a certain degree of force. This is a law of nature which cannot be discovered by guessing, or deduced *a priori*, but which must, if possible, be ascertained by diligent observation only. And I must say that, so far as my own observation extends, I am persuaded that it is not every kind of impulse applied to my bodily organs that will cause a perception in me. To be actually felt, the impulse must come with a certain amount of power; and perhaps this amount of power must vary according to the diverse degrees of delicacy in the texture of the organs of different individuals. I grant that there may be in us a perception without our adverting to it: indeed, there are continually in us perceptions to which we do not advert, because our attention is taken up with other things. Nevertheless, it is necessary that we should be able to advert to them by directing our attention thereto; for if we could not in any way advert to them, we should have to say that they do not exist in us, or at least we could not say that they do exist. Thus, for example, if after having deliberately tried over and over again to smell a flower, I perceive no smell, all I can say is, either that the flower has no smell, or, if it has, that the action of my olfactory nerves is suspended by reason of a cold or of some kind of torpor; so that although my nostrils can always receive the external impression, they, on their part, are not always so fit to receive it that my soul must have the perception of smell. At all events, I should at least have to consider this as a strong probability; because, after all, it might really happen that I did not know how to direct my attention to that perception; for experience shows that in order to direct our attention to what takes place in ourselves, we must have acquired the ability for it. And in point of fact this ability to turn their attention on themselves and to direct it as they like best, varies very much in different men. It is not everyone who knows how to observe human nature well. Only very few are vigilant and quick-sighted enough to seize upon that which passes within them, sometimes in a most fugitive way. To the greater number this is an unknown art; hence the difference between philosophers and men in general, and, again, between philosophers and philosophers. But, apart from all this, among the circumstances which make it difficult for a man to turn his attention at pleasure to anything which takes place within himself, one of the most important is precisely the minuteness and faintness of a sensation. Very vivid sensations draw our attention to them, so to speak, violently, and take it away from those which are less vivid. On the contrary, in order that we may turn our reflection in particular to very slight sensations, we must put forth the spontaneous energy of our soul in a degree all the greater the feebler those sensations are. This is why it is so very difficult to fix our attention on the most minute of our sensations, and why those who wish to lessen that difficulty find considerable assistance in isolating themselves from objects which act powerfully on their external senses—for instance, shutting themselves up in a dark and perfectly still place, where nothing will cause distraction. It will be seen by these remarks that we can never absolutely affirm that we have not at this present moment the little sensations, say, of sounds coming from very far away, because we and those around us cannot by any stretch of attention become aware of such. In a matter like this there is always some room for doubting.

To conclude: the whole object of this long note is to invite attention to the difference (1) between sensations *without advertence*, and (2) *little* sensations. Leibnitz speaks now of the one and now of the other kind, as if they were all one and the same. But they should be most carefully distinguished; for from this distinction spring some of the noblest consequences in the philosophy of the human mind, which, however, it would take me too long to detail here.

The reason, then, why we are not

petit ; comme on ne romprait jamais une corde par le plus grand effort du monde, si elle n'était tendue et allongée un peu par de moindres efforts, quoique cette petite extension qu'ils font ne paraisse pas.[1]

291. The objection, therefore, which Locke prefers against innate ideas on the ground that, if we had any, we should know it from our earliest infancy, because nothing can exist in our soul virtually and without our being aware of it, is simply frivolous. It vanishes before the obvious and indisputable fact noticed and cited by Leibnitz—*i.e.* the existence in us of perceptions of which we have no actual consciousness. Such are those ideas which, although they do not occupy our attention now and here, can still be recalled by us at pleasure, or else can come before us of themselves, through their association with some fortuitous occasion which is connected with them. Likewise we have, and continually receive, perceptions which, either owing to their faintness and littleness, or to their multitude, or to some other cause, escape our attention, and pass away from us unheeded. In a word, it is one thing for an idea or perception to *exist* in our soul, and another thing for us *actually to think* of it. Sometimes we have it and do not know that we have it, and therefore cannot say anything about it ; nay, unless we are on our guard, we may be apt to believe and to affirm that we have it not.

aware of having certain sensations, whether great or small, is because we *do not reflect* upon them, do not turn our attention to them. But they may be in us for all that, although, owing to our not adverting to them, we are ignorant of their existence, and therefore are very apt to deny that we have them.

But the *littleness* of a sensation is only one of the many circumstances which often hinder us from adverting to it. Hence there may be in us sensations of which, their littleness notwithstanding, we are distinctly conscious. In some persons this is more the case than in others ; and it depends on the greater or less proficiency of each in the art of self-observation. Although *little* sensations do not always nor necessarily remain in us unobserved, and consequently in a state in which we are unable to speak of them, yet they often remain so, and for this reason it is easy to confound them with *non-reflex* sensations—an error against which even so great a man as Leibnitz did not sufficiently guard himself. But even very strong and vivid sensations are in us sometimes without advertence—that is, when our attention happens to be wholly engaged by another object yet more interesting and attractive to us. Thus Archimedes of Syracuse, being profoundly absorbed in the solution of a problem of his favourite science, was quite unconscious of the terrible noise caused by the irruption of the beleaguering Roman host into the captured city.

[1] *N. Essais,* &c., *Avant-propos* (p 7–8).

It is thus, says Leibnitz, that the ideas of things are originally in us. They lurk in us as *insensible perceptions.*[1] Imagine to yourself a block of white marble intersected with very minute veins of faint red or yellow, or some other colour, in such a manner as to delineate a statue. The marble represents the soul, and the veins represent the ideas. As, in order to produce the statue, the sculptor would only have to follow with his chisel the traces already marked out by the veins, even so it is with man's intellectual development. By reflecting on the ideas sketched as it were in his soul, he becomes aware of their existence, brings them out actually to view, and is thus able to discourse about them.

292. On this stock of faint perceptions congenite with us, Leibnitz draws very largely for the purposes of his philosophy ; indeed, he derives from them the explanation of almost all the facts of the soul. ' Ce sont elles, qui forment ce je ne sais quoi, ces goûts, ces images des qualités des sens, claires dans l'assemblage, mais confuses dans les parties ; ces impressions que les corps qui nous environnent font sur nous et qui enveloppent l'infini ; cette liaison que chaque être a avec tout le reste de l'univers. On peut même dire qu'en conséquence de ces petites perceptions le présent est plein de l'avenir et chargé du passé, que tout est conspirant (σύμπνοια πάντα, comme disait Hippocrate), et que dans la moindre des substances, des yeux aussi perçants que ceux de Dieu pourraient lire toute la suite des choses de l'univers : *Quæ sint, quæ fuerint, quæ mox ventura trahantur.*' [2]

---

[1] We have seen that the perceptions which Leibnitz here calls *insensible* are described by him elsewhere as being *felt*, though not *apperceived*, by us. Do not the two statements seem contradictory ? Be this, however, as it may, we must never forget that *sensation* is one thing and the *thought* of it is another. It is only by *thinking* that we become aware of the presence of a sensation. Failing the thought, we should have in us the *sensation* (quite a different thing from the external *impression* made on our bodily organs), but we should not know that we have it. Animals have sensations, but they do not *think* of them.

[2] *N. Essais,* &c., *Avant-propos* (p. 8).

ARTICLE VII.

Leibnitz admits less of the innate than Plato.

293. Leibnitz tells us that he admits in the human soul something more of the innate than was admitted by Plato: that is, not *reminiscence* only, but *presentiment* as well.

This statement, however, must not be taken strictly to the letter. For, as regards the presentiment of things to come, it does not arise more from the insensible perceptions of Leibnitz than it does from the ideas of Plato. Indeed, there have been Platonists who deduced from these ideas not merely presentiments, but prophecy, divination, and enthusiasm.

294. Wherefore, considering the two systems in themselves, and setting aside their respective consequences, I think I am justified in saying that Leibnitz admits less of the innate than Plato.

Plato maintained that all ideas were in us from the beginning of our existence, like those things which a man has learnt but does not now remember. This implied that these forgotten ideas were in our mind full and complete, and required nothing but to be recalled to memory. Leibnitz, on the contrary, compares ideas to exceedingly slight veins running through a block of marble, or to cracks marked in a tablet, so minute as hardly to be visible. Hence his innate perceptions are outlines of ideas rather than ideas in the proper sense of the word.

It is the instinctive activity of the soul that brings them into being and perfects them, and for this something more is required than for merely awakening a remembrance.[1]

---

[1] In the work of Leibnitz quoted above, Philalethes objects to Theophilus, that in order that we may reasonably admit innate ideas we ought to have proofs drawn from sensible experience. To this Theophilus replies:—'On la décide comme l'on prouve qu'il y a des corps imperceptibles et des mouvements invisibles, quoique certaines personnes les traitent de ridicules. Il y a de même des perceptions peu relevées, qui ne se distinguent pas assez pour qu'on s'en aperçoive ou s'en souvienne ; mais elles se font connaître par des conséquences certaines.' (*N. Essais*, &c., liv. ii. chap. 1 [p. 60].)

ARTICLE VIII.

To explain the existence of our ideas Leibnitz assumes more of the innate than is necessary.

295. Had Leibnitz concentrated his attention on the fact of ideas, and contented himself with offering an explanation of that fact, I feel confident that so acute an intellect as his would surely have hit the true mark.

But instead of stopping at the acts of the intellectual faculty, he launched out into the consideration of the nature of powers generally; and this led him to concede to this faculty more of the innate than was necessary.

Not having sufficiently grasped the nature of the mind and of ideas, he could not utilise that intimate connection which exists between one idea and another, and in virtue of which one naturally flows out of the other; so that it is quite unnecessary to admit as congenite with us the traces of all ideas, as he felt bound to do, but it suffices to admit as such that one idea whence all the others originate.

It will be remembered that the difficulty proposed by me at the commencement lies in explaining how we begin to make judgments. Now, one idea is enough for this purpose, since by making use of that idea we can form as many judgments as we have occasion for; and these judgments will supply us with other ideas, which will in their turn serve us as materials for other and other judgments, and hence for other and other ideas. It is therefore necessary to examine well the genealogy of ideas. This examination will show us that they all descend from a common stem, a first idea, the *essence of ideas*, through which alone our faculty of judgment is fully constituted. With this kind of investigation Leibnitz troubled himself but little, and the consequence was that he could not see how to reduce innate ideas to one, the foundation and origin of all the rest.

I do not mean to say that our philosopher did not know that ideas derive one from the other; what I mean is, that he did not make of this fact all the use he could have made.

Had he done so, he would never have thought of assuming as innate in our soul the perception of the universe and of all the particular things therein contained, the multitude of which, according to him, is infinite. For he would have seen that one idea, taken conjointly with the sensations, was sufficient to produce all other ideas and cognitions.[1]

ARTICLE IX.

Other errors of the Leibnitzian theory.

296. But, let me say it again, Leibnitz could not see the truth of what we have just stated, because he occupied himself more with the principles of general metaphysics than with man himself to whom these principles had to be applied.

This was, in my opinion, the reason why he did not sufficiently master the great distinction, so difficult to be well understood, between *sensations* and *ideas.*

Having laid down the principle, that it was impossible for the body to exercise a true action on the soul, he felt logically bound to attribute ideas as well as sensations to one and the same internal energy of the soul. After this it was

[1] Leibnitz, to express that which he considers to be innate in our soul, uses sometimes the phrase *virtual knowledge.* It would seem from this that by 'innate' he meant only such knowledge as lies included in some principle; since consequences are said to be *virtually* contained in their principles, for the reason that they are deducible from them. But in other places he speaks in such a way as clearly to indicate that he looked upon his innate cognitions as existing, not *virtually* or as included in others, but in themselves. Take for instance the following passage, where, alluding to the more difficult sciences, he delivers himself thus:— 'Leur connaissance actuelle n'est point innée, mais bien ce qu'on peut appeler la connaissance virtuelle; comme la figure tracée par les veines du marbre est dans le marbre avant qu'on les découvre en travaillant.' (*N. Essais,* &c., liv. i. ch. 2 [p. 39].) The reader will not fail to note how different the meaning attached here by Leibnitz to *virtual knowledge* is from that in which the same expression might be understood at first sight. If the sculptor, instead of having the statue delineated by the veins in the marble itself, had only a mechanical principle, expressed, say, by a mathematical formula, to guide him in his work, without himself knowing what sort of statue should come of it, he would in this case have a *virtual knowledge* of the statue, since this is *virtually* contained in that principle; for although the statue and the principle are two entirely different things, he can nevertheless, by perfectly carrying out the latter, produce the former perfect in every particular. Now, it is not in this sense that Leibnitz understands *virtual* knowledge. He means by it a knowledge *in outline,* like the statue traced out by the veins in the block of marble. It is a purely *analogical* allusion, not very happily chosen, if the truth must be spoken, and it led the great man astray.

an easy matter to confound them together, or at least to be
wanting in the care necessary for drawing an exact line
between their entirely different natures.

297. '*C'est sensation*,' he says, 'lorsqu'on s'apperçoit
d'un objet externe'[1]—that is to say (according to his manner
of speaking), when we not only *perceive* the object, but *know
that we perceive it.*

But although the sensation has a *term*, it has not an
object. To have an object belongs, not to the sensitive, but to
the intellective faculty alone. Therefore, he here confounds
together the two orders of sense and understanding.

298. Besides, how do we become aware of a perception
except by thinking of it? If, then, *sensation* consists, not in
the perception, but in our knowing that we have the perception, clearly sensation is the same as *thought*. Here we see
again the *order of real things* confounded with *that of pure
ideas.*

In fact, sensation refers to a real thing; but *thought*
reflects on that real thing by confronting it with an idea.[2]

---

[1] *N. Essais*, &c., liv. ii. ch. 19. If,
as Leibnitz says here, sensation consists
in *apperception*, it follows that, according to him, where there is only *perception*, there is no *sensation*; which is in
direct contradiction to what he has said
elsewhere. In this opinion I could not
agree with him. To me, a sensation
not *thought of*, not *adverted to*, is a
perception in so far as it takes in an
extraneous term. If it is thought of or
adverted to, the name of *apperception*
may fittingly be applied to it.

[2] As I have said in the text, Leibnitz
himself tells us that 'sensation is when
we *apperceive* an external object.' Now,
concerning this, I beg the reader to bear
in mind the remarks I have already
made. We cannot become aware that
we have perception of an external
object without making an interior
judgment whereby we affirm to ourselves
that that object *exists*. Now, to make
this judgment is the same thing as to
assign the object which we have perceived with our senses to the class of
beings—in other words, to predicate
existence of it; and to predicate existence of a thing which has fallen under

our senses is nothing but to compare
that thing with a universal—nay, the
most extensive of all universals. Until
I judge that the particular thing which
comes in contact with my senses, although different from myself, exists
even as I exist—belongs, like myself, to
the universal class of beings—I cannot
be aware of having perceived an external
object; since this *apperception* supposes
that I know that object to be something; and to know that it is something is to consider it as one of the
things that can exist, and of such and
such a nature. Without this, I could,
indeed, have *sense-perception*, but not
know that I have it; for I should not
know what I, or the sensible perception,
or its term is. Undoubtedly, for us
who are endowed with reason, and
therefore regularly accustomed to con-
join our sensations and their terms with
a cognitive act, it is a most difficult
thing to imagine a state of the soul with
sense-perception alone, detached from
all thought; but, unless we master this
difficulty, and completely separate in
our mind the sensible from the knowable, we can never hope to make any-

Hence in every thought there is always an element of universality ; whereas in sensation there is nothing universal, all is particular and concrete.

299. We can thus see how it is that Leibnitz so often mixes up unconsciously the world of realities with the world of abstractions, and goes indifferently from one to the other without properly adverting to the infinite distance which divides them.

Of this kind of inaccuracy I have given some instances in the note to n. 280. Here is another :—

Leibnitz, after making the usual distinction between necessary and non-necessary truths, does not perceive that the former can be nothing but universals (that is, truths relating to mere possibilities, with the sole exception of God, who is the only necessary real being). Hence, wishing to prove that necessary truths cannot be derived from the experiences of the senses, he argues as follows :—

' Si quelques évènements peuvent être prévus avant toute épreuve qu'on en ait faite, il est manifeste, que nous y contribuons en quelque chose de notre part.' [1] Underneath this argument there lies a precious truth ; but there is also in it an error. Our philosopher knew that the imagination cannot extend to things which have not previously fallen under the senses ; therefore he immediately adds :—' Les sens, quoique nécessaires pour toutes nos connaissances actuelles, ne sont point suffisants pour nous les donner toutes.' [2] But then he proceeds to ask the question, whether among the things of which our sensible experience has actually awakened in us the idea, there is ever a case in which we can foresee as a matter of certainty and necessity that such or such a thing, such or such an event, will happen. If, says he, we can have a prevision like this, it cannot be due to the senses ; because the senses supply us only with particular examples and cases,

thing like fair progress in this philosophy of the human soul.

[1] *N. Essais*, &c., *Avant-propos* (p. 3). The argument is excellent if we consider that even a merely conjectural prevision, like every comparison of one thing with another, requires universals in the mind ; for what is common in many things is always a universal, an idea.

[2] *N. Essais*, &c. *ib.*

and consequently with an argument of induction or analogy, which never constitutes necessity.

Now, it is certain, he continues, that we possess the faculty of sometimes foreseeing as necessary certain events; there must, therefore, be in us something innate whence this necessity, which is not derived from the senses, can be drawn. Very well; but how does he prove that we have this faculty of foreseeing events with apodeictic certitude?[1]   By quoting

[1] On this subject Leibnitz observes (1) that animals are easily caught, because they have not the faculty of drawing universal and necessary conclusions from the things around them; (2) that empirics are liable to many errors, because they trust to experience alone; that similar errors have happened to statesmen and to commanders of armies, owing to their having placed too much reliance in their own experience; and that the wisest men, besides making use of experience, always endeavour to penetrate, if possible, into the reason of the fact, in order to be able to judge whether or not exceptions ought to be made. Then he subjoins : ' Car la raison est seule capable d'établir des règles sûres et de suppléer à ce qui manque à celles qui ne l'étaient point, en y faisant des exceptions, et de trouver enfin des liaisons certaines dans la force des conséquences nécessaires ; ce qui donne souvent le moyen de prévoir l'évènement sans avoir besoin d'expérimenter les liaisons sensibles des images, où les bêtes sont reduites, de sorte que ce qui justifie les principes internes des vérités nécessaires, distingue encore l'homme de la bête.' (*N. Essais*, &c., *Avant-propos* [p. 5].) On all this reasoning of Leibnitz I wish to submit the following observations :—

In the first place, the prudential rules which a wise man follows in his actions are, indeed, based upon the prevision of certain events, but that prevision is not absolute, or, as philosophers say, *apodeictically* necessary, but necessary only relatively or hypothetically. For example, knowing that it is of the nature of the sun to shine, I predict that it will shine to-morrow. But this prediction, although founded on the knowledge of the nature of the sun, has no intrinsic necessity. Its

fulfilment is conditional on the supposition that the revolution of the sun will continue, and that no change will occur in it, the contrary of which is not impossible, since it involves no contradiction. Leibnitz, therefore, confounds *apodeictical* with *hypothetical* necessity. Now, it is only by apodeictical necessity that the power of human reason is fully manifested, because as regards this kind of necessity human reason is in no way indebted to the senses, but owes it all (to say it in passing) to the infinite force of an uncircumscribed and super-sensible truth.

Pascal fell into a somewhat similar error when, as I have observed elsewhere, he classed among the first principles of reason such things as *space, time, motion,* and *matter,* maintaining against the Pyrrhonists that the knowledge of these things is as certain as any that we obtain through abstract reasonings. (See *Teodicea,* note to No. 146.) Space, time, &c., are not *principles* of reason at all; they are merely positive *data* of experience. The principles of reason are intrinsically necessary ; in the *data,* on the contrary, there is something *arbitrary,* since they depend in great part on the will of the Creator, if not always for existing in one mode rather than in another, certainly for existing or not existing, and for such or such of them being submitted to our experience rather than others. In a word, the necessity of the *principles* of reason is apodeictical, while, on the contrary, the necessity of the *first data* of experience is hypothetical—*i.e.* they are the materials of the reasonings which we make on certain kinds of things, not, indeed, in virtue of their very nature, but simply because they happen to be given to us as such materials.

If it were desired to institute a com-

the example of Euclid, who from mathematical axioms deduces necessary consequences. I ask if this is not to confound the world of abstractions with the world of realities. What else are Euclid's books but a continuous series of abstract truths deduced from abstract principles? But future events belong to the real world, and the possibility of foreseeing them with absolute certainty cannot be inferred from the possibility of so deducing the truths of pure geometry from their principles.

Leibnitz, therefore, widened the force of *a priori* reasoning beyond its just limits. By assuming as innate in the human

parison between the error of Pascal and that of Leibnitz, the result would be as follows :—

I. First of all, three things must be premised—namely, (1) there are the primary or absolute principles of reason, such as the principle of contradiction, &c; and these have apodeictical certitude.

(2) The principles of reason, when applied to certain classes of contingent things, produce other principles characterised by hypothetical necessity ; and these it would be more accurate to call by the name of *first data* : such are *space, time, motion,* &c.

(3) By means of *principles* and *first data*, other consequences are deduced of a necessity which is *doubly hypothetical*, because dependent upon two suppositions—*i.e.* the *data* of *space, time,* &c., and the *datum* of *bodies,* &c.

Now, Pascal confounded the apodeictical necessity of the first principles of reason with the *hypothetical necessity of the first data.* Leibnitz descended a step lower by confounding the *apodeictical* necessity of principles with the *necessity doubly hypothetical.*

II. Moreover, the argument of Leibnitz is directed to prove that we cannot derive from the senses all our cognitions, because the senses never give us necessary and universal cognitions, which must therefore be drawn from the depths of our own reason. Now, this can be proved by means, not only of apodeictical, but also of hypothetical necessity, of whatever degree ; for no necessity of any kind can ever be furnished to our reason by the senses. The argument of Leibnitz, therefore, is correct when taken as a whole ; but we

may note in it a partial inaccuracy. He confounds the action of animals with that of empirics ; I maintain that this is incorrect, and that even the action of empirics is grounded upon a reason, a principle which, in its way, is universal and necessary, and therefore cannot, in this part, be derived from the senses. In fact, empirics frame their practical decisions on the rule of 'similar cases, similar results.' They start, therefore, from the universal principle of *analogy*, which, although frequently misleading, is always universal in itself, or at least is so taken by them. Their errors arise simply from crediting experience with more than it can fairly claim: 'It was so ere now, therefore it will be so again.' But even this undue extension given by them to the results of experience, this universalising of the import of similar cases, would be impossible to them if they limited themselves exclusively to the testimony of the senses. Their reason alone supplies that *universality* and that *necessity* which the facts as experienced by the senses do not contain. True, in this they commit an error ; nevertheless, their very error shows that they go beyond the sphere of the senses, and have the conception of the *universal* and the *necessary* in their mind. With the animals the case is very different. They have no intellectual rule or principle by which to guide themselves. Their inclination to repeat certain actions, to do some by preference, and to shun others, is merely the effect of instinct or of habit. Therefore, the action even of an empiric cannot be confounded with that of the brute beast.

soul the representation of all things in the universe, he supposed that this soul had in it by nature not only the *ideas*, but also the *perceptions*, of all real things. Hence it was natural for him to suppose that the soul drew from within itself (*de son propre fond*) the concrete as well as the abstract truths ; and this is the origin of the *Leibnitzian presentiment*.[1]

ARTICLE X.

Conclusion as to the theory of Leibnitz.

300. The outcome of all we have said on Leibnitz is, that he erred by excess :—

(1) In assuming as innate in our soul all ideas, and even the perceptions of real things ; whereas one idea, assisted by the data of sense, is enough to account for the formation of all other ideas, as we shall see better in its proper place ;[2]

(2) In exaggerating the force of *a priori* reasoning—*i.e.* not limiting, as he ought to have done, the validity of its conclusions, to absolute certainty within the domain of abstract truths, and to probability within that of real things ; but claiming also for it the power of descending to real and contingent events in such a manner as to predict them sometimes with infallible certainty, even without any need of experience.

The excess, then, applies to both *reminiscence* and *presentiment*.

To *reminiscence* : for although the Leibnitzian reminiscence does not, like the Platonic, consist in a simple recalling of ideas, but furthermore in an interior energy which, by giving them additional light, perfects and completes them ; nevertheless, it never amounts to more than the power of bringing

---

[1] If Leibnitz had restricted himself to allowing to human reason the power of giving an *a priori* demonstration of the existence of God, he would have been right. God being the NECESSARY REALITY, there is no absurdity in the notion that there may be in human reason a necessary principle whence to deduce the existence of that Reality. As to the existence of contingent things, there could only be a *moral* necessity, which I verily believe was what Leibnitz had in his thoughts. But more of this in another place.

[2] It would appear that Leibnitz looked upon the organic sensation as being merely an occasion of making us advert to the idea, which we already had in us, of an external being, by calling forth into exercise that instinctive energy of the soul which our philosopher added to ideas.

out into greater relief that which already exists in the soul; while, on the other hand, it seems manifest even at first sight, and it becomes more so the more we reflect on it, that our faculty of reasoning consists also in the capacity of generating new ideas and concepts, through judgments made, in the first instance, on our sensations. Now, these judgments are possible from the moment that the reasoning faculty is supposed to be possessed of only one idea, the most universal of all; since that idea will serve as an exemplar or standard whereby to judge of whatever the sensations set before it; nor, consequently, will there be anything more required for explaining that wonderful intellectual fact which we call *reasoning.*

To *presentiment*: for no future contingent event can ever be deduced except by way of conjecture, or subject to certain conditions: for instance, I foresee that if the sun rise to-morrow, and nothing interferes with its action, it will shed its light upon the earth.

.

CHAPTER III.

KANT.

ARTICLE I.

Kant, without any examination, takes for granted the principle of Locke, that all human knowledge comes from experience.

301. Kant entered the philosophical arena at a period when modern philosophy had already made some steps towards improvement.

To a most penetrating mind he joined an intense study of the philosophers who had preceded him ; and while in part opposing himself to all, he also in part endorsed the opinions of all.

Nevertheless, he clothed his eclecticism with such originality of expression, and arranged it in so symmetrical a form, that it seemed quite a new system, as remarkable for the connection of its parts as for the diligence with which it had been elaborated.

The spirit of his age had a tendency to the philosophy of Locke, and he felt all its influence. This philosophy had undergone diverse modifications, and encountered diverse kinds of opposition ; he went with the times, and made a step further in the same direction.

302. Having now to give a brief exposition of his system, I shall begin by observing that he, without any examination, conceded Locke's principle that all our knowledge comes from experience. [1]

[1] It is singular to see how Kant accepted this proposition gratuitously, as though it did not require any proof. He rests on it the whole of his philosophical edifice, saying, 'That all our knowledge begins with experience there can be no doubt.' (a) Such are the opening words of his *Critique of Pure Reason.*

(a) This and the following translations of passages in Kant are taken from that of T. M. D. Meiklejohn. London edition, 1872. [TRANSLATORS.]

' But,' he added, ' if all our cognitions come from experience, it is the duty of philosophy (1) to examine the nature
of these cognitions, as well as their different species; (2) to
see how experience is able to produce them all.'

Of this fundamental principle he never
gives any other reason except that which
is contained in the interrogation immediately following, and which, as everyone can see, so far from being *critical*,
is in a very high degree *dogmatic*. Let
us hear it: ' For how is it possible
that the faculty of cognition should be
awakened into exercise otherwise than
by means of objects which affect our
senses, and partly of themselves produce
representations, partly rouse our powers
of understanding into activity, to compare, to connect, or to separate these,
and so to convert the raw material of
our sensuous impressions into a knowledge of objects which is called experience?' After which interrogation he
peremptorily concludes: ' In respect of
time, therefore, no knowledge of ours
is antecedent to experience, but begins
with it.' Thus that philosophy which
distinguishes itself by the name of *critical* has started from a principle that,
instead of being submitted to any *criticism*, was received just as prejudices
are received. Should this first proposition, therefore, prove on examination
to be destitute of solidity, all the vast
fabric raised on it would necessarily fall
to the ground.

All I need say for the present is,
that the reason adduced by Kant on
behalf of his principle is not sufficient
to prove it. In fact he asks, ' Is it
possible that the faculty of cognition
should be awakened into exercise otherwise than by means of objects which
affect our senses?' Now, by this
question he evidently presupposes (1)
that there are external *objects* independently of our faculty of knowing; (2)
that all our cognitions are formed through
the exercise of this faculty; for if there
were any cognitions innate in us, there
would be no need of the said faculty
being stimulated to their formation.
He assumes, therefore, the very thing
which he intends to prove. Again, in
this assumption he is at once opposed
by many, and in the first place by Des
Cartes. The latter, by the fact of holding that it is of the very essence of the

human understanding to be in action,
and that, therefore, it *always thinks*,
denies that this faculty, in order to think,
requires to be excited by external things.
Then he is contradicted point-blank by
Leibnitz, who will furthermore tell him
that it is impossible that sensible things
should excite the soul to thought, because
between these things and the soul there
can be no true communication; and
that every operation of the soul proceeds
from an energy intrinsic to it, from instincts which are, of their own nature,
subject to a determinate mode of development. So, again, he is contradicted
by Malebranche, and by all those philosophers who derive our ideas from an
immediate action of God on our soul.
To treat all these opponents as if they
were not worth noticing is rather too
much, nor does it well agree with the
method of the author of the *Critique*
himself, who in his works stops to refute
the opinions of these writers on points
of far less importance than the one here
spoken of. On the other hand, if the
above first proposition does not require
proof, neither will the *Critical philosophy*
require any; since in that proposition
the whole of this philosophy is virtually
included. Assume, then, that the proposition is certain, and you will be
bound to say that ' Des Cartes, Leibnitz,
Malebranche, and all who look upon
ideas either as being innate in us, or as
produced otherwise than by sensible
things, are certainly in the wrong;' and
that for a proper account of the origin
of human cognitions you must rely on
Kantism. Thus our author begins by
gratuitously laying down a principle
which will make the acceptance of his
system obligatory on you. Indeed, this
is an error very frequent among philosophers. They start with a proposition which seems evident, and implicitly
contains their theory, and this proposition they dispense themselves from
proving. Then they draw out the theory,
and declare it true; and so it would be,
provided the fundamental principle from
which it has been deduced were true.

And so far he was right. Locke had begun his work straightway by explaining the origin of our cognitions. This was an error in philosophical method, a jumping at the cause before knowing and examining the facts. The facts were the human cognitions; he should therefore first of all have examined well these cognitions, thoroughly mastered their nature, analysed them, ascertained the elements of which they are composed, and classified them into their different species. For to explain the origin of human cognitions is nothing but to assign a fit and proportionate cause whence they do, or at all events can, come. But in order to be able to assign a fit and proportionate cause, we ought, before everything else, to occupy ourselves with the effect ; nor can we begin inquiring into the former until we have made ourselves sure of the qualities and parts of the latter. Locke forgot this obvious rule of method, and instead of commencing his investigations at their natural beginning, plunged headlong into the middle. Thus he undertook to do the impossible—*i.e.* to account for what he did not as yet know, because he had not examined it.

ARTICLE II.

In his opposition to Locke, Kant imitated Leibnitz.

303. By assailing Locke as above stated, Kant was but imitating Leibnitz.

Leibnitz had taken for his ground of attack the *faculties* of the soul ; Kant took that of the *cognitions* produced by those faculties. But, this difference notwithstanding, their modes of reasoning were similar. Leibnitz had said to Locke: 'I allow, that by conceding to the human soul, besides sensitivity, the faculty of reflection, all human cognitions can be accounted for ; but it remains to be seen whether this faculty of reflection can exist on the supposition that there are no ideas whatever innate in the soul.' Kant said : 'I allow that all human cognitions come from experience ; but it remains to be seen whether an experience capable of producing all these cognitions is possible on the supposition that the soul has nothing but sensations to draw upon.'

Kant was thus directing attention to the fact that to say that 'all our cognitions come from experience' is one thing, and to say that 'all our cognitions come from the senses'[1] is another. Undoubtedly he said, before we form experience—that is, before we bring our faculties into exercise—we have no cognition ; but does it follow from this that our experience is formed by sensitivity alone? This is quite another question, and the only way to decide it is by examining in what the product of our experience (the cognitions) consists, and seeing whether this product can come from sensitivity alone.

ARTICLE III.

Two species of knowledge, the one a priori and the other a posteriori, admitted by all philosophical schools.

304. The philosopher must, then, make two researches. He must, first, investigate the different species of human cognitions ; and then (supposing that they all come from experience), ascertain on what conditions an experience capable of producing them all is possible.[2] We shall treat of both.

---

[1] Kant does not always seem to be consistent with himself in the meaning he attaches to the word *experience*. When he says, 'Though our knowledge begins with experience, it by no means follows that it all arises out of experience' (*Critiq. of Pure Reason*, Introd. I.), he takes *experience* for the use of our senses. On the contrary, when he asks, 'Whence could our experience acquire certainty if all the rules on which it depends were themselves empirical?' he seems to consider *experience* as the fount of all our cognitions, and to distinguish it from the senses : he then takes *experience* to mean the acts of our spirit, which are a compound of sensitivity and intelligence Generally speaking, however, it is in the first of these two significations that he employs the term *experience* ; but I prefer to take it in the second, because to me this seems to be better calculated to make us penetrate into the spirit of the *reflection* of Kant. Here, therefore, I depart somewhat from his more

usual way of expressing himself, although not from the substance of his philosophy. Should any of my readers not feel satisfied with this, he is already advertised of it, and can correct my expressions by himself.

[2] Modern philosophers generally hold that all human knowledge comes from experience, but they do not trouble themselves with the question as to what experience is.

Does experience consist in the facts considered by themselves, apart from our knowledge of them? Certainly not ; for so long as the facts are not known to me, they are, so far as my knowledge is concerned, as though they were not.

Are we, then, by *experience*, to understand the facts as known to us? If this is the meaning of the term *experience*, it becomes necessary to ask of what kind of knowledge one speaks. Does *experience* mean the facts known by us with the senses alone? This would be an absurd question. The

Prior to Kant, all philosophers had observed, and admitted as a patent fact, that our cognitions are of two species, which they called respectively *a priori* and *a posteriori*. This division has come down to us from the Schoolmen, who received it from the philosophical schools of antiquity; hence we may safely say that it has the sanction of all ages.

305. Suffice it here to observe that it has been admitted by modern philosophers, however divergent their views might be on other points.

Des Cartes admitted an *a priori* knowledge, and in this alone found the basis of human certainty.

Locke recognised the same distinction. He says, ' If the ideas are abstract whose agreement or disagreement we perceive, our knowledge is *universal*; for what is known of such general ideas will be true of every particular thing in which that essence [1]—*i.e.* that abstract idea—is to be

senses, taken by themselves, can give *sensations*, but not *knowledge*. By saying that I know a fact with my senses alone, I detach that fact from every thought I have of it. In this state, facts are sensations and nothing more : there is no comparison made between them, no relation of any sort. These facts known (as is so improperly said) with the senses alone, can neither be written nor spoken of, because language has not individual words fit to express them, and also because, in order to connect them with some sensible sign whereby to render them capable of being expressed, I should have to bestow some reflection on them, which is against the hypothesis that I know them with the senses and nothing else.

Therefore, experience will consist in the facts as known in the true sense of the term. Now, here the action of the understanding necessarily comes in, to place some universality in them by considering their individuality in relation with *being* and, in *being*, noticing the relations which exist between them, and distinguishing them into classes or species. Certainly, an experience like this can and does produce our cognitions. But if this be what we mean by saying that all our cognitions come from *experience*, then the question at

once arises, In what does the intellectual cognition of facts consist? What is this understanding by which we form, or at least complete, experience? How must this faculty of knowing be constituted in order to be capable of producing such an experience? And to inquire how this faculty is constituted is the same as to inquire whether there must be some innate element in it, and if so, what that innate element is; and this again is the same as to ask, ' What conditions are required to make the experience of which we speak possible?'

[1] Here Locke uses the word *essence*, while in other places he maintains that of what is called *essence* we have no knowledge whatever. This is the perpetual and necessary self-contradiction of all those philosophers who attempt to eliminate from human knowledge something without which it could not exist. What they professedly exclude, declaring it an object outside the field of philosophical inquiry, they introduce indirectly and unconsciously into their subsequent reasonings. Nor can they help doing so, for otherwise it would be impossible for them either to reason or to speak. The essences of things are elements of all human thoughts; and language, being formed on the first principles of common sense,

found, and what is known of such ideas will be perpetually and for ever true.' And the consequence which he draws is very noteworthy. Let us hear it : 'So that as to all general knowledge, we must search and find it only in our own minds and 'tis only the examining of our own ideas that furnisheth us with that.'[1] Does it not seem incredible that after having observed that some of our ideas are universal, and that this universality cannot be found outside the understanding, he should not have perceived the necessity of admitting in this faculty something more than is furnished to it by the senses? Such, however, is man. Sometimes he is divided from truth by, so to speak, a mere hair's-breadth, and yet that hair's-breadth is too much for him![2]

Condillac, in his *Cours d'Etudes*, says that the distribution between *a priori* and *experimental* truths is a real one. From the former truths he derives the *evidence of reason*, and from the latter the *evidence of sense* and of fact.

A similar observation is made by Leibnitz; only that he goes further and demonstrates that the certainty of our knowledge can in no way be derived from sensations, but must come from the understanding itself.

The existence, then, of these two species of knowledge seems a fact equally recognised by all, even the most opposite schools. From this fact, therefore, as from a firmly-

reduces itself principally to the expressing of essences, nor can a single word be uttered without indicating them or making allusion to them.

[1] *Human Understanding*, book IV. chap. iii. § 31.

[2] Locke says : 'General ideas can be in our own mind only, and reflexion furnishes it with them.' But, I ask, how can reflexion furnish our mind with them? 'By the abstraction,' he answers, 'which it exercises upon the particular ideas received from the senses.' But pray what does abstraction do? It separates, divides; it does not add nor create anything. You suppose, then, that a particular idea contains a universal element. You are therefore still bound to explain how this element comes to be in it. To make such a thing possible, there must intervene, between your 'sensation and reflexion,' an intellectual perception—*i.e.* a mode of perceiving, not merely passive like that of the senses, but endowed with a special energy of its own : an energy which to the terms of the sensations adds *universality*, and thus composes particular ideas from two elements—the particular or *sensible*, and the universal or *abstract*. When particular ideas have thus formed, your 'reflexion' can come in, to decompose them into their two elements, and then to compose them again into any groups or combinations it pleases. But without this intellectual perception there is no material for your 'reflexion' to exercise itself upon.

settled point, we can with all good reason start in the inquiries now before us.

ARTICLE IV.

The characteristics of a priori [1] *and of* a posteriori *knowledge.*

306. The characteristics recognised both by Leibnitz and by Kant [2] as belonging to *a priori* knowledge, are *necessity* and *universality.*

The experience of our senses shows us *that which is*, but it cannot show us that which *must be*. Because a fact has happened in a certain way once, twice, or a hundred times, it does not necessarily follow that it must happen in the same way the hundred-and-first time also. If, then, the experience of the senses gives us only the knowledge of the contingent, this knowledge is not *necessary*. Consequently, the knowledge of the contingent is *a posteriori*. *Necessary knowledge*, on the other hand, may be purely *a priori*; but in no case does its necessity spring from the senses, but always from an intrinsic reason seen by the understanding. This seems manifest beyond the possibility of doubt. [3]

---

[1] Kant, in order to prevent ambiguities in the course of his reasonings, took care to define accurately the meaning of the phrase '*a priori* knowledge.'

He remarks that this expression is used in two different significations.

(1) Sometimes a judgment is called *a priori* because it is made before the occurrence of the event which forms its subject-matter, although the rule on which that judgment depends has been supplied by experience. For instance : I see that a house is being undermined, and before the house has fallen, I judge that it will fall. Why ? Because experience has taught me that a house without a foundation falls.

(2) Sometimes, on the contrary, a judgment is called *a priori* because it rests on a rule, not supplied by experience, but apodeictically necessary. For example, a certain fact happens, and I judge that some cause has produced it, without having seen that cause ; and I do this, not because I have found on previous occasions that facts had an adequate cause, but be-cause I know that no fact can exist without a cause. (*Critique of Pure Reason*, Int. i.)

Now, it is in this second meaning only that the expression '*a priori* knowledge' is employed by Kant.

[2] Not that other philosophers did not see these characteristics ; but Leibnitz and Kant are those who in modern times have laid particular stress on them, and have been more vividly impressed with their importance. It is almost invariably in this that the special merit of great thinkers consists. They bring into prominence the metaphysical truths already known but not grasped with that distinctness and vividness which are necessary to bring their great fecundity to light, and to give them their proper place in the genealogical tree of ideas, in the human mind, and in the account made of them.

[3] Even the sceptical Hume acknowledges that the truths consisting of relations between ideas are characterised by *necessity*.

For example, we see the sun rise each morning, and hence we conclude that it will rise to-morrow. But this, after all, is simply a conjecture founded on analogy. No one could prove that it is intrinsically impossible for the sun not to rise to-morrow, since the Almighty could, if He pleased, stop its course. On the other hand, to say that 'the part can be greater than the whole' would be a proposition so absurd that no man in his right senses could assent to it ; and this, not because he has never seen a part greater than the whole, but because he feels that the thing cannot be. Suppose that my opinion were asked as to whether or how a certain event, of which I never had any experience, will happen ; the most I could say would be that 'I do not know.' But the mere fact of my never having seen anything of the kind would not warrant my setting down that event or the mode of its occurrence as impossible. To justify me in doing this, the thing must present to my mind nothing short of a self-contradiction.

Therefore, the *a posteriori* knowledge—the knowledge of facts which fall under the senses—is accidental ; and, besides it, there is a necessary knowledge which we denominate *a priori*, for the reason that it has for its foundation an intrinsic necessity given by pure reason, and not in any way by the senses.

As the knowledge derived from sensible experience is devoid of *necessity*, so is it devoid of *universality*.

Our experience is always limited to a certain number of cases. For example : do we wish to know whether all the flowers of the jessamine smell alike? We walk into our garden ; we pluck a number of these flowers—ten, twenty, fifty ; we leisurely smell every one of them in succession. Now, what do we really know by this? Unless we wish to attribute to experience more than belongs to it, we shall have to confess that the knowledge thus gained by us is neither more nor less than this, that the ten, twenty, or fifty flowers, whose odours we have inhaled, have the same kind of fragrance. Whatever we know beyond this lies outside the bounds of experience.

Mere experience would not even authorise us to affirm that the same flowers, if similarly tested again, would emit precisely the same odour as before. It is only by the law of analogy that we can say this; and the law of analogy carries our mind further than the narrow circle of experience could ever justify.

If, after the fifty trials of which I have spoken, we, on seeing that the numerous tiny flowers left behind on the trees resemble the former ones in colour, form, and every other particular, imagine or conjecture that they also would, if tested in the same way, affect our nostrils with a like fragrance, then, instead of keeping within the bounds of experience, we rely upon analogy on a wider scale. Without any experiment, but purely on the strength of an *a pari* argument, we attribute to this new multitude of flowers the same odoriferous quality which we found in the fifty. Nay, we go further, and extend the same rule to all the countless jessamines which exist in other gardens also—in fact, everywhere in the whole world.

Nor is this all; for however immense may be the number of jessamine flowers in actual existence,[1] our thought can freely expatiate abroad so as to embrace all *possible* jessamines, and apply and attribute the very same odour to every one of them also. And it is on this account that writers on botany speak straightway of that odour as characteristic of the plant considered as a *species*.

Clearly, then, the cognition supplied by sensible experience neither is nor can be possessed of *universality*. It is only particular, though more or less extensive, according to the opportunities one has had of making experience, and therefore always infinitesimally small as compared with a cognition characterised by *universality*; for this, to be truly such, must, and really does, apply to all the possible individuals of a species whose number is endless.

---

[1] Our experience of anything, how often soever repeated, is always exceedingly, nay infinitely, small, as against all possible cases of that thing; and yet all possible cases are essentially embraced by a universal and necessary idea.

307. The universality of *a priori* knowledge flows from its *necessity*.

In truth, that which is necessary can never be otherwise than it is. On the contrary, when I, reasoning by analogy, expand the results of my experience into a universal proposition, this universality is not rigorously true. According to the expression of Kant, ' it is only an arbitrary extension of validity from that which may be predicated of a proposition valid in most cases to that which is asserted of a proposition which holds good in all.'[1]

308. But what deserves the greatest attention is that, were we to restrict ourselves to the depositions of the senses alone, even such universality as we obtain from analogy, imperfect as it is, could never be imparted to our cognitions ; indeed, no universal conception of any sort would be possible to us.

Suppose I have perceived six objects ; I could not extend my thought to a seventh, because this has not fallen under my perception. Much less, then, should I be able to extend it to all similar objects that exist, in respect of which the number

---

[1] *Critique of Pure Reason*, Introduction ii.

Hence when we universalise some particular proposition derived from sensible experience, we cannot be absolutely certain of its universality. As an illustration of this, take some part of the human body—for instance, the liver. The dissection of numberless dead bodies has shown this result, that ' the liver is on the right side of the heart.' Now, let us try to universalise this fact so many times attested by experience, and say absolutely, 'In the human body the heart is always on the left, and the liver on the right.' Can we be absolutely certain of the truth of this proposition? No, because there is no intrinsic necessity in it. How do we know but that there may be some exception to the ordinary rule? Even independently of any experience to this effect, we may conceive the possibility of such exception. Then even experience may come to decide the point. In fact, as Leibnitz tells us, in a dead body dissected at Paris, the heart was found on the right and the liver on the left.

But that there may be no ambiguity in this matter, let me observe that when I universalise the result of my experience, I conceive that result either as accidental or as essential to the thing experienced. It is essential when it ' relates to that which constitutes the very essence of that thing.' For example, the proposition ' Man is a rational being' expresses the essence of man. Hence when experience gives me this proposition, I receive it as necessary, inasmuch as I do not conceive man except as a being endowed with reason. Consequently, every man must, by the hypothesis, be possessed of this faculty, else he would not be what I mean by the word *man*. From this we can see that *necessity* and *universality* are founded on the knowledge of *essences* ; and therefore Locke was again in contradiction with himself when he admitted a knowledge truly universal, and at the same time denied that we know anything of the essences of things. But the knowledge of essences is not given us by the *experience* of the senses, which is now the subject in discussion.

I have seen is perhaps but a most insignificant fraction ; and much less still to all that exist only potentially. It is to this last kind of extension that the universality conceived by our mind is always necessary—I mean the conception of the possibility of an indefinite number of individual objects which cannot affect the senses, because they are not as yet in existence.

309. Hence even such *universality* as can be gathered by reasoning from analogy, although devoid of strict necessity as well as certitude, presupposes in our mind a knowledge *a priori* in no way derived from the senses. If necessity imports an *actual universality*, analogy supposes a *potential universality*. *Necessity, actual universality, potential universality,* are conceptions transcending all sensible experience, and impossible to explain otherwise than by means of a power inherent in our mind itself.[1]

[1] As I have already remarked, the function called *abstraction* was not correctly described by Locke ; and from this inaccuracy arose his errors. His description of that function amounts in substance to the following: 'I see a certain tree in my garden. By comparing it with the other trees there, (1) I notice something which the tree I am looking at has in common with them all ; this something common to all alike gives me the idea of the *genus*, which I express by the word *tree*; (2) I notice that the tree I am looking at has, furthermore, something in common with a certain number only of those trees ; and from this element, limited to trees of a certain class, I form the idea of the *species*, to which I give the name, for instance, of *pear-tree.* Lastly, I notice that, besides the features which this tree possesses in common with all trees generally, and with pear-trees in particular, there is in it something proper to itself exclusively, and from this I have the *particular idea* of it, to which I do not give a name, because I do not feel any need of naming this tree individually.'

Now, leaving aside here the inaccuracies contained in this description of how a particular idea comes to be formed, I say that if my generic idea of *tree* represented nothing but the quali-

ties common to that determinate number of trees which I have examined, and, in our case, to the trees in my garden, this idea would not include a single tree beyond that number, and therefore I could not apply the name of *tree*, either to such trees as are only possible, or to the subsistent trees which I have never seen, but only heard mentioned by some one. Now, this is certainly not the way in which the terms expressive of a genus are usually understood. Clearly, when I say *tree*, I designate something which is common, not to ten or twelve, &c., particular trees, nor yet to every tree in actual existence, but to all imaginable, and therefore all possible trees. Hence in a generic idea, signified by a common noun, there is always comprised a *notional element* applicable to an *infinite* number of individuals—I mean, the idea of their *possibility*, which transcends all the bounds of experience.

Moreover, the extension of a *generic* idea is independent of the number of the individuals which have been submitted to the experience of my senses. A man who had examined in succession all the trees in the world would have an idea of the *genus* tree more exact, perhaps, but certainly not more *extensive* than that formed by another man who had never left home or gone beyond the small enclosure of his garden. Both

ARTICLE V.

Hume, by discarding a portion of a priori *knowledge, induces Scepticism.*

310. Locke had laid down this principle, ' All ideas come from sensation and reflexion.'

At the same time, he had admitted this fact, ' Human knowledge is of two species, the one *a priori*, and the other *a posteriori.*'

He had not perceived that these two propositions could not hold together, so that if one was true, the other must necessarily be false.

Had he taken note of this, he would either have corrected his principle [1] or denied his fact, even as he denied the fact that we possess the idea of substance,[2] because he found it stained with the crime of not being reconcilable with his theory.

311. But no error, be it ever so small and unperceived at the beginning, can long remain concealed in a philosophical

of them would speak of *tree* in general, attaching to this word an idea fully as extensive as is that of *possibility*, which has no limits of any sort ; both would apply the word *tree* not only to all the trees which God has created, but moreover to all those which He *could* create. The same observation holds good in regard to *specific* ideas ; and this will show that these ideas also have an extension infinitely greater than could ever be supplied by any amount of sensible experience, and that therefore it is necessary to admit that they come from another source, a source sufficient to account for that idea of possibility which is mixed up with all generic and specific ideas, and constitutes their great extension, and cannot possibly originate in the senses.

[1] According to Locke, reflexion is the applying of our attention to sensations and the other operations of our soul. This faculty, therefore, simply adverts to that which already exists in the soul. Here lies his error. Had he spoken of reflexion without defining it, one might have exculpated him by giving him the benefit of the more favourable interpretation, as Leibnitz, for example, tried to do.

[2] I have already shown that the impossibility of drawing the idea of substance from sensations arises from the fact of its containing the idea of *existence*—the most universal of all ideas. Therefore the impossibility of accounting for the idea of substance by means of the senses is the same as that which is found in attempting to derive from them universals in general. Again, as I have also observed (305-306), it is from universal ideas, especially that of essence and of substance, that the necessity of propositions arises. But Locke, having overlooked all this, denied the idea of substance, because he found it irreconcilable with the fundamental principle of his system on the origin of ideas ; while, on the other hand, he admitted that we possess necessary and universal ideas, as well as *a priori* knowledge, because he did not see that the difficulty of explaining the origin of them both was the same.

system. Like truth, error develops itself, and, when fully developed, exhibits all its deformity, working mischief according to its nature. There is nothing hidden but will come to light. And this revelation of the evil fruits of error is necessary in order that the error may be vanquished and eradicated ; even as it is often necessary for the purifying and the health of the human body that its bad humours should come to a head somewhere and burst, ugly as the sight may be.

Hume imbibed the philosophy of Locke with his education. It had become the philosophy of the time, and even men of seemingly most independent minds feel the influence of the opinions of the world around them. Hume accepted, therefore, on the authority of his teachers, as a truth past questioning, the Lockian dictum, 'We have no knowledge except what comes to us from the senses.'

With this principle fixed in his mind, he began to examine the other proposition, also of Locke, 'There is an *a priori* knowledge,' [1] and he was not slow to observe that it was simply incompatible with the fundamental principle of that philosopher.

312. Let us take, said he, one of the most celebrated *a priori* propositions, 'Every effect must have a cause.' Can the *necessity* expressed in this proposition be derived from the experience of the senses ? Assuredly not.

In the first place, sensible experience presents to us nothing but *facts*, each totally distinct from the others. A certain fact may, indeed, be seen to follow another again and again in a uniform manner, as, for instance, warmth follows light when the sun rises. But what is this ? Simply a *conjunction* of two facts, a distribution of them in the order of time. Now, who assures me that these facts are also *connected together* as cause and effect ? Because one fact precedes and another follows, am I therefore bound to believe that the first is the cause of the second ? It is evident that the successive

---

[1] Nevertheless, he only examined a portion of the *a priori* knowledge— namely, the principle of *causation*. Had he been consistent he could not have saved the least fraction of it. His reasoning annihilated it entirely.

order of two things gives me no right to say, *post hoc, ergo propter hoc.*[1]

Again, supposing that by an impossibility I could with my senses perceive that two facts are *connected together* as cause and effect, why should I from this conclude that the thing *must* be so and cannot be otherwise? The senses tell me that which *is*; they cannot tell me that which *must* be. Consequently the *necessity* expressed by the proposition 'Every effect MUST have a cause' is not derived from the senses.

In the third place, even if I could with my senses perceive (1) that many of the facts seen by me have a cause, and (2) that they *must* have it, would that imply that the thing must *always* be so, even in those facts which I have never seen—nay, in all the facts that are merely possible? No; such universality as is conveyed by the proposition 'Every effect must have a cause' could not in any way come to me from the senses; for universality is not a thing that can be seen by the corporeal eye or touched by the hand. Not even all the facts actually existing are examined, and, as regards merely possible ones, sensible experience is altogether out of the question.[2]

Such were the conclusions at which Hume arrived by comparing the principle of causation with the capabilities of the senses.

313. But Locke's principle that 'All our knowledge comes from the senses' had been irrevocably embraced, and no thought of a compromise could be entertained. What was therefore to be done?

Nothing but to adopt the method of reasoning which Locke had used in reference to the idea of substance. This idea, Locke had said, is utterly inconsistent with my principle; therefore, it does not exist. The principle of causation, said Hume, because necessary and universal, can-

[1] Every *fact* which falls under our sensible experience, is simply an *effect*; the *cause* lies beyond the reach of the senses.

[2] I here express Hume's argument more forcibly, perhaps, than he does himself; but its drift remains substantially the same.

not possibly come from the senses; therefore, the proposition which affirms it is gratuitous.

314. But whence is it that men are thus deceived? That they always take this proposition as true, and continually resort to it in their reasonings?

From *habit*, replied Hume. The idea of *conjunction* is so akin to that of *connection*, and a fact which is seen constantly to precede looks so much like a *cause* in respect of another which constantly follows it, that 'men are most easily induced to take the one thing for the other, and so instead of saying, as they ought, 'This usually comes after that,' they say, 'This is the effect, and that is the cause.'

Moreover, if this erroneous judgment were restricted to those things which men actually experience, the proposition could never be taken as universal. It is, therefore, by arbitrarily extending the limits of actual experience, that they give it universality. Finding so often that certain facts happen in succession, and seem to be dependent on each other, they conclude that this will *always* be so, that it is so also with the facts they have not seen, and even with such as exist only potentially. This is how they, first invent, and then implicitly believe in the universal proposition, '*Every* effect has a cause.'

But this proposition, which the imagination has *universalised*, would not as yet be *necessary*. Therefore, continued Hume, the imagination sets again to work and perfects the axiom, persuading men that an effect without something to produce it would be an impossibility. Hence the solemn enunciation, 'Every effect *must* have a cause.'

315. Thus a universal and necessary principle which has been admitted always and everywhere—and which is the starting-point of nearly all human reasonings, the basis of all the highest truths, of all religious beliefs, and of all moral teachings—was coolly set down as valueless by modern science: nay, was traduced as a mere phantom with which an unreflecting imagination deludes the entire human race; for the entire human race must indeed be in error if Locke's principle that 'All human knowledge originates from the

senses alone' is true. And so those few philosophers who in times very near our own raised themselves above common sense, and abandoned it to the unsophisticated masses and the numberless philosophical schools, have invented and promulgated a theory so simple, a principle of such vigorous power, that, by attributing to the senses the exclusive right of producing ideas, it condemns as a vain chimera everything which is reasonable, solely because it is not sensistical !

ARTICLE VI.

No portion of a priori knowledge can be explained by means of the senses.

316. It is manifest that Hume was not only not obliged to stop where he did, but that he ought to have carried the consequences of Locke's principle much farther.

The same argument which invalidates the proposition regarded by all men as self-evident, ' Everything that happens must have a cause,' may be employed with equal force to annihilate every other axiom. The general formula of this destruction would be as follows : ' An axiom is a proposition characterised by necessity and universality. But necessity and universality cannot be derived from the senses, because the senses perceive only the contingent and particular ; therefore, no axiom can come from the senses. But we have no knowledge except such as comes from the senses. Therefore there is no real truth in axioms. Therefore we can place no reliance on any of the so-called necessary and universal propositions. In a word, our reasonings have no fixed principle to start from.' [1]

[1] Hume distinguished human cognitions into two classes : (1) those which present to us simple relations of ideas, as, for instance, all reasonings on pure mathematics ; (2) those which descend to facts, as would be the proposition, ' Every effect must have a cause.' He aimed at the destruction of this second species of cognitions, and said nothing against the first. Now, even assuming this distinction to be correct, one part of *a priori* knowledge cannot stand any more than the other. Hume's dialectics, based on the principle of Locke, are a corrosive of such dire efficacy as must infallibly prove fatal, first to the whole, aye to the very shadow of *a priori* knowledge, and then also to that *a posteriori*. The reasoning drawn out in the text proves this conclusively ; and I do not think that any solid reply can be made to it. The above distinction of Hume, even if it were solid, would in no way affect the argument ; both classes of *a priori* knowledge would equally be involved in ruin. Moreover, the proposition ' Every effect must have a cause,' so

Thus the principle of Locke that 'All our knowledge comes from the senses' leads by an inexorable logic to the

long as it is considered in general, expresses nothing but a relation of ideas, just as any proposition of pure mathematics—for example, ' Two things equal to a third, are equal to one another.' But if you apply that proposition to some particular effect or cause, it descends to facts ; precisely as propositions of pure mathematics do, when they are applied to real bodies and give applied mathematics as a result. A proposition which is true in theory is always true in its practical application also, provided proper care is used to take into account all the elements of a nature calculated to modify in practice the result of the purely theoretical proposition. Thus if I, intending to build an arch, wish to calculate its span so that I may know what solidity should be given to its sides, how do I proceed? I start from purely theoretical propositions, from simple relations of ideas about the nature of the arch, the laws of gravitation, of motion, &c., and even before all this, from the abstract rules respecting numbers—in short, from propositions of pure Algebra and pure Geometry. Therefore, between the certitude of those universal and necessary propositions which express *simple relations* of ideas, and the certitude of those which *descend to facts*, there is an intimate connection. If the first exists, the second exists also. They are but one and the same certitude - intrinsic in the first case, applied or communicated in the second. The second certitude, therefore, could not be destroyed without the first being destroyed. Consequently, even assuming, as I have said, the correctness of Hume's distinction, it is manifest that he did not sufficiently examine the *nexus* existing between the series of purely abstract propositions and that of applied ones. He supposed them to be mutually independent, whereas the second are only derivations of the first. What led him into error was the appearance presented by the proposition 'Every effect must have a cause.' By speaking of *effect*, this proposition seems to descend to fact. But on looking at it attentively we see that it speaks, not of this or that real effect in the concrete—in which case

only it would descend to fact—but purely of *effects* in general, ideal effects. In a word, it simply expresses a relation between two ideas, that of *cause* and that of *effect*. Quite a similar relation is expressed by these propositions, ' Two is less than ten,' and ' The three angles of a triangle are equal to two right angles.' The first of them indicates the relation between the ideas of two and ten, and the second that existing between the ideas of the value of three angles in a tri·ngle and of the value of two right angles. If, however, these propositions are applied to real beings—say, to a number of persons and to a particular and material triangle—then they descend to facts, exactly as we have said of the general proposition ' Every effect must have a cause,' when brought to bear on some particular and real effect.

Lastly, Hume's distinction is erroneous.

In all concrete propositions, or those bearing on actual facts, there is always mixed up the universal principle whence they are deduced. Hence they also have some *a priori* element in them. But this element always lies in the theoretical principle itself, and hence in the universal and necessary propositions which express a simple relation of ideas, though applicable to facts. Consequently human cognitions are, indeed, divided into two classes—namely, *a priori* and *a posteriori* ; but the first class cannot be divided, as Hume pretends, into propositions expressive of a simple relation of ideas, and propositions which descend to facts. These latter are not *a priori*, but, although *a posteriori*, they require the *a priori* in order to be deduced according as sensible experience happens to present to us particular facts. To these facts the *a priori* propositions are applicable, and it is thus that they can enable us to judge of them.

In fine, sensible experience, by being found to correspond with the calculations of applied mathematics, bears witness to the truth and efficacy of the theoretical propositions of which the geometrician avails himself in view of making the forces of nature subservient to his purposes.

denial of all *a priori* knowledge, and therefore of the validity of all universal and necessary propositions.

317. Now, in order to understand fully what this denial really imports, we must consider that if universal and necessary propositions are abolished, there is no possibility of our being certain of anything, and *Scepticism* reigns supreme.

In the first place, whatever does not fall under the senses is beyond our experience.

If, then, there are no truly universal and necessary propositions, we have no principle whence to deduce non-sensible truths.

The non-sensible cannot be deduced from the sensible, except through a *principle*. For example, if passing through a lonely place I notice on the ground a number of well-formed geometrical figures, I conclude that some man must have been there, though I do not myself see the man. And why? On the principle that ' Every effect must have an adequate cause.' But if this principle is taken away, I have no means of drawing that inference; and all *principles* are by their nature necessary as well as universal, otherwise they could not induce *necessity* in the consequences.

Whence do I argue the existence of the souls of other men? or the existence of God? From the *effects*; from the *principle of causation*.

Given, therefore, that there is no *a priori* knowledge, no certainty of what does not fall under my senses, and not even the possibility of my obtaining such, what remains to me? Nothing but the *appearances* presented by the senses; the whole world is reduced for me to a huge panorama of appearances; I myself am, to myself, only an appearance. Universal, unlimited, sceptical Idealism—such is the outcome of Hume's line of argument; such the inevitable issue of Locke's principle that ' All our knowledge comes from the senses.'

But I am wrong; not even of sensible appearances will it be possible for me to have any certainty.

To be certain of anything I must always stand on a necessary principle. Certainty is nothing but a just necessity to which my understanding yields assent. I cannot have certainty even about sensible phenomena, if I have not first in my mind the light of a necessary principle to assure me of the authority of such certainty.

Were I to say to myself, ' I am certain of experiencing a modification, of having these and these sensations,' my reason would instantly call me to order by the question, ' Why dost thou presume to claim this certainty ? '   And on my answering, ' Because it is impossible for me not to feel what I do feel,' reason would at once reply, ' This is an *a priori* principle, the principle of contradiction.   How dost thou know that it is true ?   It does not come to thee from the senses, because nothing that comes from the senses has in it either the *necessity* or the *universality* which belongs to this principle. Therefore, to render thy affirmation valid, thou must have recourse to a necessary and universal truth outside the sphere of the senses.   In a word, the senses require to be declared authoritative by me, the Reason.'

318. It is, then, an incontrovertible fact, that all certainty depends entirely on a principle which must be intrinsically necessary, and consequently universal—a principle, therefore, not supplied by the senses, since they can give us only the particular and contingent.   What a strange sort of certainty that would be which did not induce necessity !   ' I am certain that the thing is so, but it may also not be so.'   Is not this a contradiction in terms ?   If, then, we are to yield a rational belief to the depositions of the senses, we must have a *reason* for it ; and this reason cannot come from them, for if it did, we should be thrown upon the absurdidity of being obliged to have recourse to an infinite series of reasons.

Seeing, then, that the *a posteriori* knowledge exists only by virtue of the *a priori*, the destruction of the latter must clearly involve the destruction also of the former.   This is why I have said that the principle 'All human knowledge originates from the senses' issues in absolute and universal doubt.   Doubt, do I say ?   Not even doubt itself could exist without a principle of reason, independent of the senses, to force us to be doubtful.[1]   That Lockian principle, then, leads

---

[1] Doubt always supposes a certainty, for it is a negation of it.   Doubt and certainty are correlative ideas ; the first cannot be conceived without the second.

inevitably to the total extinction of knowledge in its every shape and form. Under a consistent adoption of it certainty becomes impossible, doubt becomes impossible, reason itself becomes impossible ; and thus man is despoiled of his special prerogative, Intelligence. Either, therefore, we must deny so luminous a fact as that man is a rational being, or we must give up the fatal principle that 'All human knowledge comes from the senses.' [1]

319. These last consequences, although not drawn even by Hume himself, are none the less logically necessary. Once admit the principle, and the consequences must inevitably follow. Its fecundity must be entirely exhausted. If the principle is false, this fecundity will end ultimately in the annihilation of all that is true, of all that is, including the principle itself, as well as him who enunciates it.

ARTICLE VII.

How it was attempted to confute the Scepticism of Hume.

320. The existence of true *a priori* knowledge, though admitted by Locke, was denied by Hume, because of its incompatibility with the fundamental principle of Locke's theory, 'All our knowledge comes from sensation and from reflexion on the acts of the soul.'

One could have confuted him by proving the existence of

By saying 'I doubt,' I affirm something. In order to exclude certainty and affirmation altogether, it would be necessary not to think at all. The very act of denying would contain an affirmation, it being impossible to include in that denial the act itself by which it is made.

[1] Des Cartes is therefore inaccurate when he says that 'The senses are nothing but sources of error.' He ought to have said, 'The senses are sources neither of error, nor of truth, nor of doubt.' Taken by themselves alone, they are incapable of producing thought, which always exhibits itself under one or another of these three forms—truth, error, or doubt. These,

I say, are forms of thought, and not of sensations. To say, therefore, that the senses deceive us, is to attribute to them one of the forms of thought.

But if the senses could have one of the forms of thought, they could have all the others as well. It would be absurd to say that the faculty with which we affirm an error differs essentially from that with which we affirm a truth. The senses are no more the sources of error than they are of truth, of knowledge, of ideas. They only furnish to our intelligent spirit the *matter* of cognition ; and the intelligent spirit, with the aid of this matter, makes a judgment, for which it must needs be in possession of some universal.

a priori knowledge in the same way that all facts are proved ; and this was the plan adopted by Reid and Kant.

But determined Sceptics of the stamp of Hume are not so easily brought to own themselves in error. If you were to say to one of these philosophers, ' Please to take note that the *a priori* propositions, such as " There is no effect without a cause," are admitted as absolutely necessary and universal by all men,' he would probably be ready to answer, ' You misunderstand me ; I do not by any means deny the fact which you allege ; on the contrary, I seek to explain it. I say that this fact arises from an error into which the generality of men inadvertently fall by reason of the very close affinity which exists between the idea of *conjunction* of time and that of *connection* as cause and effect. Owing to this affinity it comes to pass that an exceedingly high degree of attention is necessary in order to keep the two ideas separate from each other ; and of this attention the world at large has not proved itself capable thus far. The uneducated in particular, who form the great bulk of our race, cannot long dwell on the first idea without slipping into the second. The same happens to them here as with regard to the motion of the sun. From seeing the sun appear successively in different points of the heavens, they are led to believe that it really goes round, whereas its motion is only apparent. Nothing is easier than to confound appearance with reality, and to rush hastily at erroneous conclusions. So it is with the principle of causation ; men take it as necessary and universal, but they are deceived.'

As against this you could reply, that between the experience of the senses taken by itself, and necessity, there is not even so much as a resemblance. Even were I to see the sun rise every day in my life, I should never conceive that the contrary is intrinsically impossible, as I do in the case of the proposition ' There is no effect without a cause.' This applies to the facts of experience in general. No matter how often or how uniformly a certain event may be seen to happen, and may thereby create in us the impression that it will always continue in the same way, it never can go so far as to make us feel an intimate persuasion that the contrary would be absolutely impossible and absurd. The analysis, therefore, of propositions relating to contingent things, and of those which are called *necessary—e.gr.* ' There is no effect without a cause '—suffices to prove that the supposed universality and necessity of the first has nothing to do with the intrinsic and self-evident universality and necessity of the second.

ARTICLE VIII.

A more effectual way of confuting the Scepticism of Hume.

321. But a shorter and more effectual way of confuting this class of philosophers would be to follow them in their reasonings, and to start from the fact which they themselves admit as past questioning.

This fact is, that all men accept the proposition ' There is no effect without a cause,' and recognise and use it as necessary and universal. What our philosophers deny is, that this proposition is necessary and universal in the true sense of the word : they say that it is so only in appearance.

Now, starting from the fact which they concede, one could argue with them as follows:—

' You say that the proposition " There is no effect without a cause " is necessary and universal only in appearance. Now, I will prove to you that it would not even *appear* such to men unless they had an *a priori* knowledge truly necessary and universal, and therefore not originating from the senses. In fact, let us for argument's sake assume that the said proposition is merely a limited result of experience which, speaking with precision of language, should be formulated thus : " Certain facts are repeatedly followed by certain other facts." I ask—In order that men should have been able with their imagination to transform this empirical proposition into the theoretical one, " Every effect must have a cause," of what ideas must they have been possessed ? It is evident that they could not have made this exchange without having in their minds (1) the idea of *possibility*, (2) the idea of *cause*, (3) the idea of *necessity*, and (4) the idea of *universality*. Now, none of these four ideas can possibly come from the senses, as you yourselves allow—not that of *possibility*, for that which exists only potentially does not fall under the senses; not that of *cause*, for the senses never perceive anything but effects ; not that of *necessity*, for the senses present that which is, and not that which must be ; not that of *universality*, for the experience of the senses is limited to a certain number of things, and is not repeated beyond a certain number of times. You can thus see that the difficulty you find in admitting the principle of causation as *true*, exists also against your admitting it as *apparent*. Given that experience is the only source of human knowledge, men could never have formed to themselves such a principle, or even have supposed or imagined it. And herein lay Hume's great oversight. He forgot to observe that, without drawing on a source wholly outside the sphere of sense, it would be impossible for us to imagine the principle of causation, not only as *necessary*, but even as *possible*—in fact, to conceive it at all. As a consequence, he allowed that men, although erroneously, imagine this principle to be true; and this admission is enough to destroy his whole theory. For me to have the idea of a thing, it is not necessary that the thing should really subsist ; it suffices that I conceive it. Now, men have the conception of *necessity* and *universality*. Whether, therefore, these ideas be applicable to external things or not, they are found in our mind ; and it is the duty of philosophy to explain whence they came there. From the senses they did not come. Therefore, either you must disown the principle that all ideas come from the senses, or you must deny, not only that the principle of causation is true, but also that it is regarded as such by anyone, that anyone has ever thought of it, or imagined, or made mention of it. Now, how will you deny a principle without thinking it, without naming it ? '

Therefore the sceptical argument, based on the Lockian dictum, ' All human knowledge comes from the senses,' is essentially self-contradictory.

ARTICLE IX.

Reid rejects the principle of Locke, and acknowledges the existence of a priori *cognitions.*

322. As we have seen (310), the two propositions conceded by Locke—namely, 'All human knowledge comes from the senses, and from a reflexion devoid of all ideas,' and 'There is an *a priori* knowledge'—clashed with each other, and the first destroyed the second.

The first was the *theory* of a philosopher; the second was a *fact* of nature.

By that destruction Locke's theory had exhausted all its sad fecundity; the philosophers who saw it in this state were in a position to pass judgment on it. Dr. Reid, for instance, did not hesitate to avow his conviction that philosophy had gone wrong inasmuch as it landed men in that absolute *nihilism* from which all beings essentially shrink, and that it was therefore absolutely necessary for it to retrace its steps.

Hence, unlike his countryman Hume, he, with all ages and all the principal philosophers, held to the second of the above propositions as expressing a luminous and undeniable fact, and declared the 'sensation-and-reflexion' principle of Locke to be false, because irreconcilable with that fact.

But it now became necessary to substitute for Locke's principle something which could explain how the *a priori* knowledge was possible.

Reid did not occupy himself much with the question of the possibility of *a priori* knowledge in general; he restricted himself to explaining how we acquire the knowledge of the existence of bodies, which is founded upon some elements of *a priori* knowledge, and had been denounced as illusory by Berkeley and Hume.[1]

---

[1] We have already seen that Hume's mode of classifying the *a priori* cognitions involved the destruction of those *a posteriori* also (315).

Reid applied himself to establish in particular those principles which make us certain of the real existence of external bodies, and which, rather than *principles*, ought to be called *applications of principles* to the real existence of things—applications which take the form of as many *judgments*.

For this end he entered into an analysis of the process by which we form the idea of bodies, and he thought that three several steps should be distinguished in that operation—namely, (1) the *impression* made on our sensitive organs by the external realities; (2) the *sensation* which arises at once in the soul, given that mechanical impression; (3) the *perception* as well of the existence as of the sensible qualities of

Moreover, these *judgments* were considered by Reid as *necessary* and *blind instincts* of our nature.

Hence his philosophy fell short of producing a true defence of the *principles* of reason, and of their unassailable authority; on the contrary, he was obliged to fall into several contradictions. Let us see this.

First contradiction.—As I have remarked (n. to 307), the *universal principles* depend on the knowledge we have of the *essences* of things, so that if this knowledge be denied, the universal principles are destroyed. Reid, not perceiving this, endorsed the pronouncement of Locke that 'the essences of things are unknown to us' (*Essays on the Powers of the Human Mind*, &c., Essay I. ch. i.). But on coming subsequently to speak of the way in which we perceive the existence of bodies, he said that in virtue of a law imposed on our nature by the Creator, we are necessitated to add to the sensible qualities a subject (a substance); but after this he distinctly declared that, of the nature or *essence* of things we have an *obscure notion* (Essay V. ch. ii.). It is the same inconsistency as I have pointed out in Locke.

Second contradiction.—Reid denied ideas; according to him our understanding perceives *external objects* by a direct and immediate act. This imported the destruction, not of universal ideas only, but also of universal conceptions. It reduced the subject-matter of human knowledge to *subsistent individuals* and nothing more. He somewhere expressly affirms that mere *possibilities are nothing*; for, he says, 'That which is merely possible does not exist, and that which does not exist is nothing.' Nor could he speak otherwise after taking away ideas and leaving real things only. If there are

no ideas, there are no possibilities, for the *possible* exists only in idea. But how could he in such a system be consistent with himself? This would have been a more than human feat, for to us men the thought of the *possible* is so necessary that without it we are not able to perform a single intellectual act of any kind. The following passage of the Scottish philosopher is sufficient to show him in open contradiction with all that he had taught elsewhere concerning *essences*, the *possible* and the *objects* of the mind. He writes: 'We know the ESSENCE of a triangle, and from that essence can deduce its properties. It is an UNIVERSAL, and might have been conceived by the human mind, though no individual triangle had ever existed.' (*We are here in the region of the possible.*) He goes on: 'It has only what Mr. Locke calls a *nominal essence*, which is expressed in its definition. But everything that exists has a real essence, which is above our comprehension: and therefore we cannot deduce its properties or attributes from its nature, as we do in the triangle' (*Essays on the Powers of the Human Mind*, Essay V. ch. ii.).

Be it also noted that Locke's *nominal essence* is not understood by Reid as being a mere *word without meaning*; for he says distinctly that 'Words are merely empty sounds unless they express some thought' (*Ibid.*).

He says also that there are such things as *general conceptions*, and that their generality does not consist in the act of the mind, but in the *object* of that act (*Ibid.*).

Thus, according to Reid, there are *universal objects* of the mind, which are not ideas, nor mere possibilities, nor things in real existence, and yet are not *nothing*; what can they be, then?

bodies, which takes place in the soul contemporaneously with the sensation.

Now, although these three things—*impression, sensation,* and *perception*—follow closely the one upon the other, there is no similarity between any two of them ; hence we cannot say that they are connected together as *cause* and *effect.* The *why* of their order of succession is a mystery which no one can fathom.

What can be said is, that since the sensation cannot be the cause of the perception, it is necessary to admit as innate in the soul itself a certain energy or instinct, which, so soon as the sensation is felt, impels us to make that judgment whereby we affirm the existence of bodies. It is this instinctive judgment that causes us to know instantaneously that bodies are something, and that they exist with certain qualities belonging to them.

ARTICLE X.

The theory of Reid does not run clear of Scepticism.

323. Reid considered that by his theory he had effectually disposed of the *Idealism* of Berkeley and the *Scepticism* of Hume ; but in truth he himself did not keep clear of either of these erroneous systems. I will give my reason for thus censuring him.

The Idealists as well as the Sceptics start from this principle : 'We can know nothing beyond what there is in our sensations.' Hence the Idealists conclude : 'Therefore, to say that external bodies exist is a gratuitous assertion ; for our sensations do not contain those bodies.' The Sceptics, with more logic, go further and conclude : 'Therefore, we have no rational ground for affirming that outside of us there is anything, whether corporeal or spiritual.'

Reid, who had the Idealists particularly in view, thinking that if their system were overthrown, Scepticism would also fall with it, said : 'It is an undeniable fact that we are all cognisant of bodies ; but this knowledge cannot come to us from the sensations ; therefore, it must come from a faculty internal to our soul, from an *instinct* which, given the sensations, causes us immediately to have also the perception of bodies.'

But here I would address him thus : Have you not allowed, nay, laid it down as the basis of your system, that between *sensation* and *perception* there is no similarity ? In fact, that these two things have nothing whatever to do with each other ? How, then, can you be certain that your immediate *perception* of bodies tells you the truth ? May you not be deceived in it ? Do not the arguments which you found valid in reference to *sensation* apply with equal force to your *perception* ?

The argument of the Idealists and the Sceptics was this : ' Sensation has nothing to do with the real existence of external bodies, for it is purely a subjective phenomenon, an affection of our own. Therefore the common belief, which attributes a real and objective existence to corporeal substances outside of ourselves, independently of our own modifications, is of no value.'

You reply : ' The existence of *bodies* is cognised by us, not through *sensation*, but through a *perception* which arises within us so soon as the sensations are felt, and these have nothing in common with that perception.'

Well, but have you demonstrated that the immediate perception of which you speak is trustworthy ? Or rather, does it not seem that, instead of confuting your adversaries, you have only helped them to explain better than they had done how the common error originates ? You say that men are made to perceive external bodies, not on any rational ground, but purely by a blind instinct, by a law of their nature, by an inevitable necessity. Your adversaries may therefore rejoin : If such be the case, we can see very plainly how it is that all men come to admit the existence of bodies. They cannot help themselves ; it is not *reason* that guides them, but *nature* that compels them ; and so the common persuasion is nothing but a blind faith, a universal illusion to which they must yield, without knowing by what authority it is imposed.

Therefore, the main objection raised by Idealism and Scepticism is not vanquished by your system, but only removed one step back. From *sensation* it is transferred to immediate *perception*; and the common belief of mankind remains involved in doubt, and devoid of authority all the same.[1]

What Reid said of the immediate perception of bodies, he also meant to apply to some of the principles of reason—for example, that of ' causation.' According to him, we perceive

[1] The animadversion which I here make on Reid is generally admitted to be well founded. See, for instance, what they think of Reid's philosophy in Germany. Bühle writes: 'The principal defect of Reid's philosophy lies in the vagueness and indeterminateness of the idea of *fundamental truth.* According to Reid, a fundamental truth is that in conformity with which man reasons and acts even before having collected together the observations whence to deduce it by abstraction; so that he, without having any clear consciousness of it, acts in most cases in accordance with it, as it were by instinct. As Feder has said in his excellent critique of the theory of Reid, the only rigorous or the only certain notion we can, in this theory, form of *fundamental truth* is, that it consists in a JUDGMENT which springs necessarily from the simple ideas of the subject and the attribute.'

Feder's observation is identical with that on which I have insisted in a former part of this volume (n. 119). Thus thinkers have not been wanting in Germany who noted that Reid did not in any way contribute to the amelioration of the cause of philosophical Dogmatism, or in particular that of *empirical Realism* (Bühle, *History of Modern Philosophy,* Vol. V. c. xii.).

In Italy the excellent Galluppi has proved to demonstration that the system of Reid, far from raising an effectual barrier against Scepticism, tended very materially to promote it. The reason of this, says Galluppi, was because Reid distinguished *sensation* from the *perception of bodies,* and maintained that the two, although contemporaneous, have nothing in common between them, and arise in us each by itself, without our being able to assign any reason for it.

To remedy this defect, Galluppi cancelled that distinction, and transferred to *sensation* all that Reid had said of

perception. Reid had supposed that, by *perception,* our understanding communicates immediately with external things, and thus knows them to exist. Galluppi said that this immediate communication of our understanding with external things is made through the *sensation* itself, without anything else, so that the sensation, far from being purely *subjective,* as Reid had declared, is, like Reid's *perception,* essentially *objective.* Thus Galluppi ascribed to the senses the power of perceiving the existence of bodies—a manifestly sensistic view.

But no such power can be conceded to mere sense. To be convinced of this, it is enough to observe that no one can ever be said to have perceived a body as existing until he has affirmed to himself, 'Such or such a being exists.' Now, it is evident that this affirmation necessarily presupposes in the mind the *universal idea of existence.* I must therefore entirely disagree with Galluppi's opinion that this idea is acquired by us subsequently to the perception through an abstraction exercised on it by our mind. No universal could by any possibility be abstracted from pure particulars. I admit, then, with Galluppi that our soul holds immediate communication with the body—I mean our own body—and also that, by means of our acquired sensations, we experience in ourselves the *action* of external bodies; but I utterly deny that the sensations are sufficient to give us the perception of things as existing in themselves. The *sensations* produced in us by external bodies must not be confounded with *judgments.* We perceive external bodies as existing, through an intellectual operation, whereby to the action received in us from those bodies through the sensations we join the predicate of *existence,* and thus consider them as beings which act on us in a certain mode, determined by the sensations themselves.

these principles by an immediate intuition wholly inexplicable, by a natural instinct which sets them before us and despotically bends our assent to them. He thus succeeded in tracing them to their origin, but left them entirely divested of that reasonableness which alone can justify the free assent of rational beings like ourselves.

ARTICLE XI.

Kant deduces his Scepticism from the fundamental principle of Reid, even as Hume had deduced his from the fundamental principle of Locke.

324. Locke had, without being aware of it, implanted in his theory the deadly germ of Scepticism. That germ developed itself under the hands of Hume.

Reid, wishing to confute the Scepticism thus brought out by Hume, rejected the fundamental principle of Locke; but he, also unconsciously, substituted for it another principle containing an even deeper germ of the same evil. This was likewise to have its development, and it received it at the hands of Kant.

The fact of the existence of '*a priori* knowledge,' denied by Hume and re-asserted by Reid, was admitted by the philosopher of Königsberg.

This fact is attested by the whole human race ; but men, while unanimous in proclaiming its existence, are unable to account for it.   All say : ' We are cognisant of necessary and universal propositions ; ' but they do not say how they have come to know them, or on what ground they give them assent.

Reid had described this assent as an instinctive judgment, natural to man, but for which no reason could be assigned. Man must, therefore, ask no questions, but be satisfied with simply affirming the mysterious fact.

As we have seen, this was the same as to admit an *a priori* knowledge while depriving it of all authority and veracity : and this was the course which Kant decided to pursue.

ARTICLE XII.

*The doctrine of Kant stated: he distinguishes two parts in our cogni-
tions—i.e. form and matter.*

325. The doctrine of Kant may be epitomised as
follows :—

All our knowledge begins with *experience*, but Locke was
wrong in saying that all our knowledge originates from the
senses.

Our knowledge is in part *a priori*—that is, necessary and
universal ; and in part *a posteriori*—that is, contingent and
particular.   It is therefore incumbent on philosophy to
explain how an experience capable of furnishing us with
both these kinds of knowledge is possible.

The *a priori* knowledge has nothing to do with sensations. Therefore, as was said by Reid, it springs up and is
developed within ourselves, from the depths, as it were, of
our spirit, on occasion of the sensations.

It remains, however, to be examined, how it is possible
for this last fact to take place.   Reid contented himself with
noticing the fact : but it is also necessary to analyse it and
investigate the *conditions* which determine its nature.

Here is precisely the point at which the philosophy of
Kant, properly speaking, begins.   This point is the analysis
of the intellectual *perception* in so far as it contains an element
of that *a priori* knowledge which the Scottish philosopher
had admitted, but without fully describing it or distinguishing
it into all its species.

326. Kant, therefore, undertook to show that, although
external beings are perceived by our spirit on occasion of the
sensations, they are not presented to it solely by the sensations—are not, as the Sensists contended, a mere aggregate
of sensations—but each is composed of two distinct elements:
namely, (1) the sensations, and (2) the qualities contributed
by the spirit itself.

To these qualities Kant gave the name of *forms*, and to
the sensations the name of *matter*.

Hence the beings which compose the sensible world are, in so far as perceived by us, made up of *matter* and *form.* The matter is furnished by the senses and constitutes all that is contingent and particular in these beings. The form is furnished by the understanding, and constitutes all that we conceive in them as necessary and universal. In short, the form of our cognitions is posited *a priori* and the matter *a posteriori.*

For example, I perceive a tree : in this perception I am not merely a passive recipient of the modifications produced in my sensitive organs. These modifications, being purely subjective, or sensations of my own, do not posit anything outside of me. I furthermore put forth the activity of my understanding, by admitting that there is something outside of me, something with an existence of its own, independent of me and my modifications.

Now, in order that I may admit this something, this tree, as existing outside of me, that I may represent it to myself— in a word, that I may form it—I must, says Kant, with the activity of my spirit add to the sensations some necessary and universal conceptions.

Of a truth, against this proposition no solid objection could be urged ; for, leaving aside the Kantian *forms* of sense— namely, *space* and *time*—it is necessary that we should add, at least, the universal notion of *existence,* or that of *possibility;* since we could have no intellectual perception of a tree until we have judged that the tree exists, either *actually* or *potentially.*

327. Now, Kant applied himself with great diligence to investigate and describe all the universal notions which enter into the formation of a corporeal being as conceived by us, and he reduced them to fourteen. The first two he designated as the forms of the external and internal sense, and these were, as we have just said, *space* and *time.* The other twelve he termed forms of the understanding or *categories,* meaning thereby twelve universal ideas, under one or other of which it is always necessary to classify the real beings which we intellectually perceive. Nay, to perceive a real being

intellectually is nothing but to place it, by a judgment, in one or other of these classes.

He distributed the twelve forms or categories into four great divisions, each subdivided into three, and they were, *quantity, quality, relation,* and *modality.*

He says, 'It is impossible for anyone to perceive a real being otherwise than as of a certain *quantity* and *quality*; as having some *relation,* such as that of substance or of accident; and likewise as having a distinct *mode* of being—for instance, contingency or necessity.'

Thus the perception of a real being necessitates the placing of it under these four great divisions or classes. Here, then, is one of the *conditions* essential to that *experience* which a philosopher is bound to explain—that is, an experience capable of giving us the cognitions of real beings. Apart from this condition, experience is not possible or even thinkable.

Now, to make this classification is the same as to judge these beings under the above fourfold aspect; and to do this is the same as to furnish them with the four predicates of *quantity, quality, relation,* and *modality.*

But these predicates, being *universal,* cannot be derived from the senses; therefore, they are contributed to the act of perception by the understanding; and it is in virtue of this contribution that beings acquire the nature of *objects.* These predicates may therefore be called the *form,* and the sensations the *matter,* of which the objects perceived by our understanding consist.[1]

---

[1] It must not be supposed that the distinction of our cognitions into *matter* and *form* is a discovery made for the first time by Kant. It is very ancient and well-known in Italy. Genovesi taught it in his letter to Antonio Conti. In it, after discussing the question as to whether *ideas* be the same thing as *perceptions,* he concludes thus: 'By the above reasons we can easily understand that ideas are the *forms of our perceptions,* and that the greater part of such ideas or forms—namely, the primary and simple ones (which are the rudimentary elements of our knowledge) — are received, not created by the mind. Let us not be afraid of accepting this view, which seems to have the stronger weight of argument in its favour.' On this I beg leave to observe, that our intellectual perceptions of bodies are the result of *ideas* united with *sense-perceptions* by means of a *judgment.* Hence we may distinguish three elements in them: (1) pure ideas, or the *simple apprehension* of the thing (*form*); (2) *sense-perceptions* (*matter*); (3) the *judgment* on the

ARTICLE XIII.

How Kant seeks to prevent the charge of Idealism.

328. Kant would have us believe that by his theory he
has refuted the Idealism of Berkeley and the Scepticism of
Hume ; but, in truth, he has done so in one sense only—that
is, by declaring that both the one and the other of these
erroneous systems did not go far enough.

He has transferred Berkeley's Idealism from the senses to
the understanding itself.

Berkeley had said, ' Bodies do not really exist outside of
us ; they are merely our own sensations.' This was a logical
outcome of the theory of Locke. Since, according to that
theory, the whole of our intellectual stock consists of what
we find in the sensations, all that we know of bodies could
only be defined as ' an aggregate of sensations.'

In the system of Kant, bodies are ' A union (a synthesis)
of intellectual forms and of sensations.'

But the forms as well as the sensations issue forth from
our own selves—the first, from the activity of our understanding ; the second, from the receptivity of our senses. Therefore,
we do not know anything truly existent in itself and outside
of us : we have not even the power to know whether such a
thing be possible.

This inference came quite straight from the principle of
Reid. Reid had said, ' The bodies which we perceive do not
consist of sensations alone ; an instinct of our understanding
impels us to add to the sensations an object.' But, seeing
that this instinct was merely a blind force, Kant considered
he had a right to conclude, ' Therefore, the objects which we
perceive are only a product of our spirit.'

Consequently, when our philosopher declares that ' He
is not an Idealist, because he does not, like Berkeley, look

actual existence of the thing (*union of
the form with the matter*), whereby that
which *falls under the senses*, and the

idea are joined into one object. But of
all this I shall speak more at length
later on.

upon bodies as mere aggregates of sensations,' the real drift of his words is, not that he refuses the title, but that he aspires to it in a higher sense than could be claimed by the Irish philosopher. He wants to be a *transcendental* Idealist. It is the same as if he said, 'Take note, that my Idealism reaches much further than that of Berkeley.'[1]

ARTICLE XIV.

How Kant seeks to prevent the charge of Scepticism.

329. Again, Kant says, ' I am not a Sceptic. Scepticism consists in denying the correspondence of our conceptions with the beings outside of us. Now, I do not deny this correspondence ; I analyse the objects perceived by us, and I find that they are the result of two elements, the one empirical (the sensations), and the other rational (the conceptions of the understanding). If these two elements are not united together, we do not think of any object. Now, what can we speak of except of objects present to our thought ? Therefore, the objects perceived by us, and our conceptions of those objects, are not two things about which the question may be raised as to whether they correspond with each other ; they are but one and the same thing, of which our conceptions form one part and our sensations another. Reid said, " There are external onjects, but not *ideas* of them ;" to be consistent, he should rather have said, " There is no object which is not an idea."'

For our understanding to perceive a thing is the same as to see that thing endowed with a certain *quantity*, *quality*, *relation*, and *modality*. Now, the thing could not be seen in this way except through a judgment which places it under each of these four classes—*i.e.* attributes to it each of these four universal conceptions.

But our understanding could not attribute these conceptions unless it took them from itself ; for they do not come to it from the senses. It is, therefore, this faculty which, from

---

[1] *Critique of Pure Reason*, *Elementary Critique*, Part I.; and Part II. 1st division, Book II. ch. ii.

within its own self, creates in part its objects—that is, gives
them the *form*, while the senses supply their *matter*.

In accordance with this, Kant writes: 'Categories are
conceptions which prescribe laws *a priori* to phenomena:
consequently, to nature as the complex of all phenomena
(*natura materialiter spectata*).' [1]

And in another place he says: 'Synthesis, generally
speaking, is, as we shall afterwards see, the mere operation of
the imagination—a *blind* but indispensable function of the
soul, without which we should have no cognition whatever,
but of the working of which we are seldom even conscious.
But to reduce this synthesis to conceptions is a function of
the understanding, by means of which we attain to cognition
in the proper meaning of the term.' [2]

Thus the Sceptical question is entirely eliminated from
the *Critical Philosophy*. For while the Sceptic is made to
ask, 'How can we be certain that external objects correspond
to the conceptions we have of them?' the *Critical Philosophy*
says, 'It is a mistake to think that our conceptions are a
representation of objects; they are a component part of
them—namely, the *formal* part.

330. It seems, however, that Kant by this mode of
justifying himself is making too free with the good-nature of
his readers; for he gravely assumes their implicit acquiescence
in a statement which anyone ever so little acquainted with
the subject must feel to be untrue—a practice which, I am
sorry to observe, is by no means unfrequent in the writings of
this author.

Who does not know that Scepticism consists in denying
the certainty of things considered in themselves, independently of our own modifications? Therefore, to reduce
Scepticism to the question 'Whether the objects perceived
by us correspond to our conceptions' is simply to substitute
one question for another.

To come to the real point: from the moment our
philosopher assures us that *phenomena* are the only things

[1] *Transcendental Logic*, 1st Division, ch. ii. sect. 2, § 22.

[2] *Transcendental Logic*, 1st Division, ch. i. sect. 3.

of which we are certain ; that the objects of our thought emanate, as to their *form*, from our limited understanding ; that our spirit must emit such and such forms and no others ; that of *noumena* or things existent in themselves and outside of us we have not even the idea—indeed, do not even know whether such things be within the range of possibility —is it not clear that he involves us in absolute Idealism, in a state of subjective illusion most profound, in a huge maze of dreams from which we are never permitted to awake so as to be able to get at some reality? True, he does not leave us uncertain of what we know, and therefore cannot in this respect be called a *Sceptic* ; but, on the other hand, he renders the acquisition of any knowledge whatever, in the proper sense of the term, impossible and absurd. Here, indeed, is Scepticism brought to its last perfection under the new name of *Critical Philosophy.* Human nature itself, which exists only in virtue of the faculty of knowing, is annihilated by it, and the work of modern philosophy is completed.

Kant himself avers that his doctrine is essentially of a *negative* kind ; but he compares the philosophy that preceded it to the rash and impossible attempt of Babel's Tower. Such and so great is the humiliation of human reason when abandoned to itself! So wretched are the ultimate results of its wisdom! After so many ages of investigation, so many flattering promises, and so many boastings as to the certainty of its conquest of the truth, when it has arrived at its journey's end, and expects to reap an immense harvest from its labours, it concludes with a confession of its own impotence and nullity, and vaunts this as the grandest, the *ne plus ultra,* of its discoveries!

ARTICLE XV.

The fundamental error of the philosophy of Kant.

331. The fundamental error of the philosophy of Kant consists in his having subjectivised the objects of thought.

These objects, he tells us, are the result of sensations (*matter*) and of intellectual *forms.*

The sensations, being purely modifications of our own sensitivity, do not afford us any sufficient ground for believing that they are produced by a cause external to us, since this conclusion would necessitate the admission of the objective validity of the principle of causation.

But inasmuch as this principle, like all other intellectual *forms*, does not come from sensations, it can only be regarded as an emanation from our own spirit.

Thus, according to Kant, between saying that a cognition, or some element of it, comes from sensations, and saying that it emanates from our own spirit, there is no middle term possible.

Now, an argument based upon such an exclusion is manifestly arbitrary and false, because the enumeration of the alternatives possible in the case is imperfect. Herein lies the fundamental error of this school, and the original sin of all the philosophies which have since arisen in Germany, and taken their inspiration from it.

The supposition upon which Kant built his system, but of the truth of which he did not give the shadow of a proof— namely, that whatever our understanding does not receive through the senses must necessarily be an emanation from our own spirit—arose from his not having considered that being has two modes, the one *subjective*, and the other *objective*; and that it is identical in each of them.

Being in the objective mode is being in so far as it makes itself known ; and it makes itself known as it is, therefore also as subjective. Since in the one mode as well as in the other we have the selfsame being, it follows that the cognition is valid and true.

External things have a subjective existence (to which the extra-subjective also is reduced).[1] This mode of being is cognisable, not through its own self, but only through our uniting to it the objective mode, which is therefore the intelligibility thereof. The subjective existence is supplied to our cognition by the senses ; the objective is not. But owing to the identity of the being in both modes, the intelligibility in no way alters the external thing. It simply illumines it—makes it visible to the eye of the understanding.

332. It is true we perceive external things by means of the idea of existence, as it were by an instrument suited to that purpose; for, whenever we make the judgment, 'Such a reality exists,' we apply the universal predicate of existence to a particular subject—*i.e.* to the term of our sense-perception. But this does not mean that we put universal existence into the thing perceived. By our cognitive act, we simply find (I say *find*, not *create*) in that thing *its own particular existence*; we descry the thing as belonging to the class of existent beings.

If the existence which we perceive in a given real thing by affirming it, were in every respect the same as that which we contemplate in the idea, the result would be that, by perceiving that thing, we should transform it into a universal, for such is the existence seen in that idea. But we do nothing of the sort. We only recognise in the thing an existence particular to it, determined to itself alone. In a word, the objective mode of being enables us to know the subjective.

By overlooking the distinction between the ideal existence—which precedes the perception, and is always universal—and the thing which is perceived by means of it, and is always particular; by confounding the intellectual conception with the real thing responding to it, the author of the Critical Philosophy fell into another error—that of supposing the entire universe to be simply the joint production of the human understanding and the human sensitivity. For him everything was a compound of *matter* and of *form*, the understanding contributing the form, and sensitivity the matter. Had he reflected that the objective form, which shines to the understanding, goes no further than to act as a rule for measuring the sensible and subjective realities, he would have seen that the part taken by the understanding in the perception of these realities consists in *bringing to our cognisance* that which is in them, and nothing more.

333. What I have said of the idea of existence holds equally good in respect of every other idea, and principally

Y 2

of those twelve categories to which Kant imagined he could reduce all universals.

That the truth of this assertion may be better seen, we will apply the reasoning we have just made to one of his four principal ideas or categories—I mean, that of *quantity*.

The quantity of which I have the conception or idea in my mind is not by any means co-extensive with the quantity which, by the aid of my senses, I perceive in a material object —for example, in a building. Both are, indeed, called by the one name of *quantity*, but their respective characteristics differ very widely. The ideal quantity is universal, or applicable to all material objects *ad infinitum*. On the contrary, the quantity which I perceive in the building is wholly determined, is strictly proper to that building, cannot be taken away from it, nor applied to other objects, and is therefore the opposite of the ideal quantity, even as the particular is the opposite of the universal, the ideal of the real, each of which excludes the other.

Although, therefore, the ideal quantity enables me to know the real or concrete quantity, these two modes of quantity are not precisely the same. Hence the Kantian supposition that in the perception of external beings we place in them the ideal or universal quality which is in our understanding, rests on a reasoning similar to that by which Condillac came to conclude that we refer and attribute to external bodies the sensation of colour which is only in ourselves. Whatever may be said about the soundness of the reasoning of Condillac, the Kantian deduction, applied to ideas instead of sensations, is seen to be erroneous so soon as we grasp the distinction between the *universal conception* and the *particular attribute*, or the attribute *particularised* by the sensible determinations of the being perceived by us.

The same kind of reasoning must be made in regard to the ideas of *quality* and of *relation* (of the idea of *modality* I shall speak later), as also in regard to the ideas subordinate to these, and in general to all ideas of which we make use for judging of a real thing by attributing to it the quality, &c., expressed by them. It is always necessary to draw a distinction between the *idea* and the *particular* and *real quality* recognised by us in the thing. The *idea* is the standard by which we form our judgment; the *particular quality* recognised in the external thing is the result of the judgment—*i.e.* what we have come to know by means of it. It is not true, therefore, that our understanding places its idea as such in the thing itself; the understanding simply makes use of that idea for *cognising*, through perception, what there is in the thing whose sensible action we experience in us; it places that real thing in the idea and thus renders it a true and complete *object* of cognition.[1]

334. The truth of this distinction will appear still more manifest by considering what it is that we really do when we pronounce a judgment upon things—for example, when we say, 'This is a large building.'

Let us analyse this proposition: there is nothing in it to indicate either that the building is created by us, or that it is we who place its size in it. Those words signify neither more nor less than an intellectual operation by which we recognise the size belonging to that building.

By examining more closely this operation, we find that it presupposes in us the universal idea of size, which serves us as a means for recognising the size of the building. Therefore, the size taken in the first sense is not the size of the building. The first is ideal, and the second is real. The first is, as it were, an instrument by making use of which we know the second. The particular and real sizes are numberless; the ideal and universal size is one and immutable.

This is what the common sense of mankind deposes. The entire human race, all philosophical schools not less than the multitudes generally, have ever distinguished between a quality considered as an *idea*, and a quality considered as *subsisting* in a particular thing; and they have acknowledged that the

---

[1] Our communication with external realities is effected by means of sensations; and of this fact Kant does not seem to have been aware. Hence he was unable to reconcile together these two truths, (1) that sensible realities are known to us through concepts (ideas); (2) that these realities are different from our knowledge of them. Finding himself placed in this inability, he sacrificed the second truth to the first.

first can be present to our mind even when the second does not exist. Now, since Kant, when conceding an *a priori* knowledge—that is, one characterised by necessity and universality—started from the common sense of mankind, and said to Locke, ' This kind of knowledge cannot be denied, because all men admit it,' why, I would ask, did he not show a similar consideration for the deposition, also of common sense, regarding the distinction of which I speak—namely, between the idea of a quality and the quality as participated by a real thing ?[1] If he undertook to give a theory with the object of explaining a fact certified unanimously by all men, was he not bound to bring into harmony with that theory all the other facts connected with the same subject, and equally attested by the same authority ?

Lastly, if between my idea and the part corresponding to it in the building there were not a true difference, how could I distinguish them from one another ? Why have all men always distinguished them ? What is the foundation of this distinction ? Here, again, comes the ideological question.

ARTICLE XVI.

Another error of the philosophy of Kant.

335. Another error of Kant is this : He gratuitously supposes that as often as we intellectually perceive an external thing, we are obliged distinctly to perceive its *quantity, quality* and *relation* (324). This clearly shows that he did not sufficiently penetrate into the nature of that intellectual act by which we perceive things.

In order that I may intellectually perceive a real thing, it is, indeed, necessary that I should affirm its *existence* ; but as to all the rest—for example, its *quantity, quality* and *relation*— I need not make any pronouncement. On all these points I

---

[1] Reid will be apt to contradict my statement as to this being the deposition of common sense. I am quite willing to leave the decision to the impartial judgment of the reader. This much, however, I may venture to say, that even the difference of opinion concerning what is, or is not, deposed by the common sense, goes to prove that this authority is not always, as some pretend, so self-evident as to secure the assent of all individual men alike.

may very well suspend my judgment, and yet perceive the thing simply by saying to myself, ' It exists.'

The judgment which I make when first perceiving a thing might be formulated thus: ' There is something which acts upon my senses.'

Doubtless, I hereby implicitly admit that the thing must have all the conditions requisite for existence; but, as just said, there is no necessity of my stopping to conceive those *conditions* explicitly. The aggregate of my sensations furnishes me with the means of determining the subject-matter of my judgment sufficiently to make me say, ' It exists'—without my being obliged to think also of the particular mode or determinations of this existence. Nay, I could even abstract in my mind from the particular sensations, in fact from all sensations whatever, as I actually do when thinking of a sensible object in general, or purely and simply of a *being*.

The error, then, which I find here in Kant, lies in his having assumed that the four categories of *quantity, quality, relation* and *modality*, are conditions of the intellectual *perception*, or, as he says, of *experience*; whereas they are only conditions of the *existence* of the external things.

Certainly, no corporeal thing can exist without a certain quantity, some qualities and some relations; but it does not follow that we cannot intellectually perceive or conceive that thing unless, together with its existence, we perceive or conceive each of these attributes also. On the contrary, there are in everything many qualities or properties which always remain hidden from us, or are only discovered in course of time and after long-continued examinations; and yet, without thinking of those qualities or properties, we have been perfectly able to perceive the thing itself.

In short, by examining what are the essentials of the act which we make when intellectually perceiving a corporeal thing we find that they are only two—namely, (1) that the thing should act on our senses; (2) that our understanding should affirm, *i.e.* judge, that it exists.

The judgment affirmatory of the existence of the agent in

so far as it is the producer of our sensations, is precisely the act of intellectual perception.

But, to say it again, the understanding does not require to pronounce so many several judgments on the *quantity*, *qualities* and *relations* of the thing, in order to perceive it, and still less in order to form a simple conception of it. Therefore, it does not require to make use of the ideas of *quantity*, *quality* and *relation*, although it must make use of the idea of *existence*.

When, however, the understanding has perceived a thing presented to it by the senses, it can also examine it and by degrees discover its quantity, qualities and relations. And it is thus that our cognition grows more and more perfect. It exists through the first judgment on the subsistence of things, and it increases through other more particular judgments brought to bear on what has already become an object of the understanding.

336. The error of Kant to which I am here calling attention was inevitable ; because it followed necessarily from the fundamental error of his theory as pointed out in the preceding article.

Not having observed that there were, in the external things themselves, real and particular qualities responding to the four ideas of quantity, quality, relation and modality, he imagined a quantity, quality, relation and modality emanating from within our understanding and going to form part of those very things. Accordingly, the things were mere illusions, for we attributed to them that which belonged only to ourselves ; we took them to be *objects* of our understanding, whereas they were purely creations of our own.

The above distinction once taken away, Kant could no longer distinguish the *conditions of the existence of external things* from the *conditions of our perception* and *ideas* of them.

Hence, as I have said, in his philosophy the external things are not only cognised but also, in great part, created by us ; and, as a result, the conditions necessary for their existence are identified with those necessary for their being intellectually perceived.

The truth, on the contrary, is, that by the act of perceiving things we place nothing of our own *in them*; we merely add to them that which renders them *objects* of our understanding. Therefore, between a *thing* as existing in itself, and the same thing as made an *object* of our understanding, there is a marked difference.

To conclude: there is a quantity and there are qualities existing as particular in things; and there is a *quantity* and there are *qualities* existing as universal in our mind. The first are something *real*, and must be found in the things, else these could not exist; they are conditions of their real existence. The second are something *notional* or *ideal*; they are found in the mind, and constitute the knowableness of the real qualities, the rules by which to judge of things after we have first perceived them; but not the conditions necessary for that first perception. Nevertheless, the real and notional or ideal quantities and qualities are identical as to *being*, different as to the *mode of being*.

ARTICLE XVII.

An objection answered.

337. What I have said on the manner in which the intellectual perception takes place may suggest an objection that I must now solve. And this will lead me to unfold still better the nature of intellectual perception, on the clear knowledge of which depends ultimately the whole question of the origin of ideas.

The objection I speak of is not altogether new; I hinted at it when examining the opinions of Aristotle upon this same question.

I then observed that the intellectual perception of external and material things consists in a judgment by which we say to ourselves, 'There exists a being corresponding to my sensations.' Now, some one might reply, 'Either this judgment is pronounced by the understanding, or it is not. If it is not pronounced, there is no intellectual perception as yet; because the intellectual perception consists in this very judgment. If it is pronounced, then we must perforce admit that the understanding perceives the sensations on which, or at least on occasion of which, that interior judgment is made. Now, if the understanding perceives the sensations, the judgment is not necessary for the perception, since the perception precedes the judgment.'

338. This objection arises simply from a little confusion in one's ideas on the faculties of the soul, as also from a want of distinction in the names which are commonly applied to these faculties by philosophers. It will, therefore, disappear if I can succeed in giving a clear description of the intellectual perception, and an exact enumeration of the faculties which concur in producing it.

Let us recall the definition we have given of the intellectual perception of bodies—namely, ' It is a judgment whereby we affirm as subsistent something which acts on our senses.'

By analysing this judgment we find that, in order that it may be formed—

(1) The body to be perceived must act on our sensories so as to produce sensations in us, for this body is the thing which has to be judged existent.

(2) We must be possessed of the notion of *existence*, which is the universal we apply to the body by saying ' It exists,' and which does not come from the senses.

(3) Lastly, we must make an interior operation wherein the sensible action experienced by us is considered on the side of the agent, and that agent is regarded as existing in itself, outside of us ; in other words, it is placed in the class of existent things. This operation closes the judgment, ' That which acts on my senses exists.'

Thus the judgment called ' the intellectual perception of bodies' is the compound result of the exercise of three distinct faculties, namely—

(1) The faculty of feeling the 'sensible' (*subject*).

(2) The faculty possessed of the notion of *existence*, or the intuition of being in general (*predicate*).

(3) The faculty which joins the *predicate* to the *subject*, and so forms the judgment itself (*copula*).

By whatever names we may choose to designate these faculties, it is always necessary to keep them perfectly distinct one from the other.

If we call the first *corporeal sensitivity*, the second *intellect*, and the third *reason* or the *faculty of judgment*, and never confound together these denominations, then the following reflections will, I think, be found sufficient to solve the above objection completely.

Sensitivity perceives the action of the external body in a purely sensitive and passive way (sensations); the *intellect* has the *notion of existence*—a *sine qua non*, as we have seen, for making the judgment in discussion. Now, it is certain that so long as the sensations or the passion by which our *sensitivity* is affected, and the *existence* contemplated by our *intellect*, remain separate from one another, no judgment takes place. The two elements of the judgment (subject and predicate) are, indeed, there; but the judgment itself does not exist until the synthesis or union is effected between them. Let us now see how this synthesis or union is brought about.

Sensitivity and *Intellect* are two faculties of one and the same perfectly simple subject (the rational soul). This subject unites in the simplicity of its intimate self the two elements supplied to it severally by those faculties. That self, that EGO, which feels affected in its *sensitivity* by an action coming from without, is the very same which has in its *intellect* the notion of existence (knows what *existence* is). This, however, would not be enough, for if these two things— *i.e.* the external agent in so far as operating on sensitivity, and the existence contemplated by the intellect—might be found in a simple subject side by side without being united together, without this subject being made cognisant of their nexus. This simple subject, now possessed of these elements of the judgment—I mean, the ‘sensible’ (*matter*) and the ‘intellectual’ (*form*)—must also be endowed with an energy in virtue of which it can turn its attention to the ‘sensible’ by which it feels affected. Putting forth this energy, therefore, (1) the subject looks simultaneously at that which affects its sensitivity, and at the existence shining to its intellect ; (2) it compares the first with the second ; and (3) it perceives that the first has an existence which is only a particular *realisation* of the existence it previously conceived only in general or as possible to be realised.   These three operations, which I here distinguish for the sake of greater clearness, but which a subject at once sentient and intelligent performs in its inmost self very rapidly (nay, instantaneously), constitute the third of the faculties above named—that is, the faculty of judgment, which is a function of the *Reason.*

To come now to the objection proposed above, I say that, according to the denomination we have given to the said three faculties, the making of judgments does not belong to the *intellect*, and therefore the intellect is not the faculty which perceives individual things.   It simply supplies the *Reason* with the means of perception, or, what comes to the same, with the rule whereby to judge ; such means or rule being precisely that notional existence which serves as a predicate in the formation of the judgment.   Nevertheless, although the perception is not, properly speaking, the work of the *intellect*, it is appropriately called *intellectual*, because the intellect furnishes to it the principal and formal part.

339. From all that we have said thus far, it will not be difficult to make out a more explicit definition of *intellectual perception*, thus : ' To *perceive intellectually* is to cognise a thing which acts sensibly on us, through seeing [1] that thing contained under the universal notion of existence.'

---

[1] The metaphorical use of terms taken from the sense of sight, to signify the operations of other senses, has given rise to numberless ambiguities and errors, as I have often had occasion to remark.   I do not think, however, that the same can be said of the word *seeing* as applied to the mind.   Moreover, it may fairly be said that this word, from being metaphorical at first, has, through established usage, become proper.

ARTICLE XVIII.

Philosophical merit of Kant: he was fully sensible of the fact that to think is nothing but to judge.

340. The principal merit of Kant seems to me to consist in this, that he grasped better than any other modern philosopher the essential difference between the two operations of our soul—*feeling* and *knowing.*[1]

With this distinction clear in his mind, he was in a position accurately to analyse the second of these operations (*i.e. knowing*); which would never have been possible until one had isolated this operation entirely from every other that is akin or adhering to it.

As a result of such analysis, Kant found out a very important truth, which is, that all the operations of our understanding ultimately resolve themselves into *judgments.* 'We can reduce,' he says, 'all acts of the understanding to judgments, so that the *understanding* may be represented as the *faculty of judging.'*[2]

Be it, however, observed, that this applies only to the transient operations which our understanding makes after being constituted *in esse,* not to its *primal intuition.*

ARTICLE XIX.

Kant saw very distinctly the nature of the difficulty to be overcome in accounting for the origin of human cognitions.

341. Having, as we have said, seized upon the fact that every function of our understanding is ultimately reduced to

---

[1] He knew that *knowing* differed essentially from *feeling*, but he did n t reach so far as to seize upon the intimate nature of the cognitive operation. What he saw was, that to *know* is something active, while to *feel* is something passive : 'All intuitions,' he says, 'because sensuous, depend on affections; *conceptions,* therefore, upon functions' (*Critique of Pure Reason, Transcendental Logic, Analytic of Conceptions,* Book I. ch. i. sect. 1).

He called, not without impropriety, by the name of *intuition* whatever is given us by sensitivity ; and this practice, common among philosophers, of applying, in reference to the other senses, words which are proper to that of sight, has been a prolific source of errors.

[2] *Critique of Pure Reason, Transcendental Analytic,* Book I. ch. i. sect. 1.

a *judgment*, Kant was able to see in a fuller and deeper way than any of his modern predecessors, where lay the difficulty of explaining the origin of human cognitions.

He perceived at once that our understanding could not make any *judgment* except on condition of its being possessed of ideas or, as he calls them, *conceptions* ; because a judgment is nothing but the placing of a particular under a universal. Seeing this, he said to himself : 'I can very well understand how the senses can supply us with the representation[1] of a particular ; but I am wholly at a loss to comprehend whence we can obtain the *conceptions*—that is, the universals—which must stand as attribute and predicate to the being represented to us. The difficulty, therefore, can only consist in accounting for the existence of these conceptions, which must be supposed *anterior* to the sensations.'

Hence he concluded that the first thing to be done was to analyse the *function of judgment*, and to indicate all the conceptions of which it stood in need. And this he proposed to do in the part of his *Critique* entitled *Transcendental Analytic*. He writes :—

' Thought is cognition by means of *conceptions*. But conceptions, as predicates of possible judgments, relate to some representation of a yet undetermined object. Thus the conception of *body* indicates something—for example, metal— which can be cognised by means of that conception. It is therefore a conception, for the reason alone that other representations are contained under it, by means of which it can relate to objects. It is therefore the predicate to a possible judgment—for example, "every metal is a body." All the functions of the understanding, therefore, can be discovered when we can completely exhibit the functions of unity in judgments.'[2]

---

[1] In truth, the senses do not represent anything ; they only supply our spirit with terms of sensation.

[2] *Critique of Pure Reason, Transcendental Analytic*, Div. I. Book I. ch. i. sect. I.

ARTICLE XX.

Distinction between analytical and synthetical judgments.

342. Kant, then, had known better than any other modern philosopher, that every operation of the understanding, and therefore intellectual perception, is a judgment.

This luminous truth might have led him straight to a full knowledge of the nature of intellectual perception, had he only examined it carefully, and without that excessive fondness for regularity of form of which his system bears so strong an impress. Let us see, however, what line of thought he pursued instead.

Having firmly laid hold of the principle that 'to *think* is to *judge*,' he took it as his fixed point of departure, and began by investigating the nature of judgment.

He thus found that all possible judgments are reducible to two species. For our understanding operates in two ways —by decomposing an idea into several parts (*analysis*), or by joining several parts into one idea (*synthesis*).[1]

Some judgments, therefore, are analytical, and some synthetical.

The *analytical judgments* are those whereby we attribute to a subject a predicate which is essentially inherent in, or rather makes an identical thing with it, as for instance, 'The triangle is a figure of three sides.' This judgment simply sets forth the meaning of the word *triangle*, by affirming that a triangle is neither more nor less than a figure made of three sides.

The *synthetical judgments*, on the contrary, are those in which the predicate is not contained in the conception or idea

---

[1] Kant says that the distinction between *synthetical* and *analytical judgments* never occurred to any philosopher before him (*Critique of Pure Reason*, Introduction, vi.). To me this seems one of the usual boasts of philosophers, each of whom claims to have been the first to discover the most important truths. Certain it is that the two operations of our understanding here named by Kant (*synthesis* and *analysis*) were excellently described by Aristotle, and, after him, known more or less to all philosophers. And as regards *synthetical a priori* judgments, we find them clearly described in Plato's *Phædo*, although Plato does not call them by that name.

---

of the subject, but is something added thereto. For example, if I say, 'This is a white man,' I add to the subject *man* a predicate (*whiteness*) which is not included in the concept of *man* as such, for there are also men who are black, or of some other colour.

Kant took note of the difference in the property and office of these two kinds of judgments in the following words: 'The former (*i.e.* the analytical) may be called *explicatory*; the latter (the synthetical), *augmentative* judgments; because the former add in the predicate nothing to the concept of the subject, but only analyse it into its constituent parts which were thought already in the subject, although in a confused manner; the latter (*i e.* the synthetical) add to our concept of the subject a predicate which was not contained in it, and which no analysis could have ever discovered therein.[1]

ARTICLE XXI.

The general problem of philosophy as stated by Kant.

343. Having thus distinguished between *analytical* and *synthetical* judgments, Kant proceeded to explain how these judgments can be formed by us, well knowing that if he could give this explanation, the problem of the formation of ideas and of every other intellectual function would be solved.

He therefore began by observing that every *analytical judgment* presupposed a synthetical one; for we cannot decompose except what we have composed. Thus, when I make the *analytical judgment* above mentioned : ' The triangle is a figure of three sides,' I must already know the meaning of the word *triangle*, else I could not define it as I do by this judgment. Now, to know the meaning of the word *triangle*, I must (1) have in my mind the *concept* of triangle, and (2) know that to this *concept* or idea this name has been given.

But how can I have the *concept* of *triangle*,[2] unless I have

[1] *Critique of Pure Reason*, Introduction, iv.
[2] The concept of triangle in general, of which we speak here, must not be confounded with the mere sense-perception of a particular triangle in physical existence.

already joined together in my mind the two concepts, of *figure* in general, and of *three sides*—that is, unless I have first said to myself, 'A figure of three sides is possible'? Now, to say this is nothing but to make a synthetical judgment, because in the *concept* of figure in general, the determination or predicate of *three sides* is not included; for there are figures of various numbers of sides. Therefore, an *analytical judgment* must necessarily be preceded by a synthetical one. A concept (or idea) cannot be divided into its parts, if the mind has not previously seen those parts united in a whole : and this is to make a *synthetical judgment.*

On the other hand, supposing that, through synthetical judgments, I have already become possessed of *concepts*, it is no longer difficult to understand how these *concepts* can be decomposed into their several elements, and *analytical judgments* formed All that I require for this purpose is to fix my attention exclusively now on one of those elements, and then on another, according to the kind of analytical judgment I have occasion to make.[1]

Hence whatever difficulty there may be in explaining the operations of the human understanding, it can only consist in assigning an adequate cause to the *synthetical judgments.*

344. Accordingly, Kant bestows great care on the examination of these judgments ; and first of all he seeks to classify them.

He thinks he has discovered that they are of two species— that is to say, some *empiric*, or founded on sensible experience, and some *a priori*.

The *empiric* are all synthetical.[2]

[1] This is all that our reflection can extend to. Nevertheless, when through analysis I distinguish the several elements of a concept, I must also be able to conceive those elements with that existence and union which they have in themselves, and for this I require to make a synthesis. Therefore, analysis always presupposes synthesis.

[2] *Critique of Pure Reason,* Introduction, iv. Kant calls these empiric judgments *synthetical,* because in them the predicates are supplied by sensible experience, and not contained in the concept of the thing itself. For instance, when I see a white horse, I predicate of him whiteness—a quality which is not included in the concept of *horse*, but furnished to me by the sensation of sight. But if the predicate is in this case supplied to me by experience, how do I come to conceive the *subject* (horse)? *Horse* is an abstract concept, which I never could have unless I had seen real horses. But, on the other hand, this concept, because abstract (universal),

In fact, sensible experience furnishes to us nothing but accidents, which are not necessarily contained in our first concepts of things. For instance, experience shows me that some men are white ; this predicate (*white*) was not included in my first concept of *man*, but I add it thereto from without, and thus make a *synthetical* judgment.

Now, in the formation of this kind of judgments Kant does not find any difficulty, because, he says, we have in them the aid of experience, 'which is already of itself a synthesis of intuitions.'[1] 'But,' he continues, 'to synthetical judgments *a priori*, such aid is entirely wanting. If I go out of and beyond the conception A, in order to recognise another, B, as connected with it, what foundation have I to rest on, whereby to render the synthesis possible? I have here no longer the advantage of looking out in the sphere of experience for what I want.'[2]

Now, it was at this point that Kant found the knot of the question which we are discussing.

345. For the convenience of the reader I will, by recapitulating what I have said, describe the process of Kant's reasoning.

(1) The synthetical judgments are those through which we attribute to a subject a predicate not contained in the concept of the subject itself.

(2) Supposing that we already possess the concept of the subject, the predicate which we wish to add to it cannot be drawn by us from that concept, because it is not contained therein. Consequently, it must be supplied to us from another source.

---

cannot be given me by the senses. Here lies the true gist of the difficulty ; it does not lie in explaining how we obtain the *predicates of subjects we have already conceived*, but in explaining how we form the concepts (ideas) of the subjects themselves.

[1] *Critique of Pure Reason*, Introduction, iv. Leaving aside the impropriety of the word *intuition*, as applied to signify indiscriminately all that our five senses furnish to us of the real world, I shall only observe that Kant ought not to have advanced a proposition like this without proof. It may, however, have

a true sense so long as this 'synthesis of intuitions' is not credited with the power of producing the universal idea of *existence*. But without this idea it is impossible for us to have a synthetical judgment capable of being analysed— nay, to have any judgment at all. Kant, therefore, attributes to corporeal sensitivity more than an accurate examination of its capabilities will allow one to concede to it, showing thereby the weak side of his Philosophy, and its *sensistic* origin.

[2] *Critique of Pure Reason*, Introduction, iv.

(3) This source may be *sensible experience.* When, therefore, the predicate is such that it can be given us by sensible experience, the possibility of our synthetical judgments goes without saying. These are the *empirical synthetic judgments.*

(4) But in this species of judgments there are also certain *predicates* which cannot be given us by the senses.

(5) Therefore, the real difficulty lies in showing whence these *predicates*—neither drawn from experience, nor contained in our concept of the subject to which we attribute them—come to us. Without them the *synthetical a priori judgments* would be impossible. Therefore (concluded Kant), the universal problem of philosophy must be stated thus: ' How are synthetical judgments *a priori* possible ?' [1]

Everyone can see that in the series of the five propositions just enunciated the one which requires to be diligently verified and solidly established is the fourth——namely, that which affirms the existence of *a priori* predicates not contained in the concept of the subject, or, which is the same thing, the existence of synthetical *a priori* judgments.

Do we really make synthetical *a priori* judgments? And if we do, are they of the kind indicated by Kant? This is one of the questions on which the decision regarding the truth or falsehood of the whole Kantian system vitally depends. The thing cannot be granted without clear proof. It is well worth careful attention, since it is, so to speak, the imperceptible point whereon the Critical Philosophy asks permission to rest that lever which is to displace the entire structure of the universe.

ARTICLE XXII.

Is it true that we make synthetical a priori *judgments?*

346. In support of his assertion that we make *synthetical judgments a priori*, Kant has adduced examples ;[2] nor

---

[1] *Critique of Pure Reason,* Introduction, vi.
[2] *Ibid.* v.

could he, in a question of fact such as this is, have taken any other course.

I shall therefore examine all his cases of synthetical *a priori* judgments; and if I succeed in demonstrating that not one of them is what he represents it, the inference will be that synthetical *a priori* judgments have no existence, or that he has wrongly classified them, or misunderstood their nature, and therefore that his system is built on a false basis.

Be it distinctly remembered, then, that the judgments I here impugn are those in which it is asserted that we attribute to a given subject a predicate which is neither contained in the concept already formed of that subject, nor supplied by sensible experience.

In the first place, according to Kant, all judgments relating to Pure Mathematics are synthetical *a priori*; and, as an example, he quotes the proposition, '7 *plus* 5 is equal to 12.'

But what proof does he give of the truth of this proposition?

No other than the following :—The concept of number 12 cannot be drawn from the sum of numbers 7 and 5 except by the aid of some external sign, for instance of our fingers; and this necessity of external signs in order to arrive at sums total is still more clearly seen by trying larger numbers.[1]

Now, this reason concludes nothing to his purpose. The need we have of some external sign for seeing that 7 and 5 make 12 does not prove that the concept of number 12 is not contained in these two numbers taken together; nay, it proves the direct contrary; for unless the former concept were contained in the latter, we could not deduce it even by the aid of external signs. Clearly, these signs make no addition whatever to the concept itself; they only help our mind to see the same thing under two different *forms* or expressions. For we must recollect that the form in which we express a concept is one thing, and the *concept* itself is another. In short, either the aid of the senses is necessary for our conceiving separately each of the two numbers, 7 and 5, or there is no *absolute* necessity for such aid even for summing them

---

[1] *Critique of Pure Reason*, Introduction, v.

up together, and thus obtaining number 12. The concept of 12 units, therefore, is precisely the same as that of 7 units *plus* 5, only that it is differently worded, and is obtained by two different mental acts.[1]

347. In the second place, Pure Geometry, says Kant, abounds in synthetical *a priori* judgments, and the example he gives of this is the proposition, 'A straight line is the shortest between two given points.'

He pretends that in the concept or idea of *straight line* the quality of being *shortest* is not included, and that intuition (sensation) cannot, by itself alone, furnish this proposition.[2]

But I cannot agree with him here. Whether intuition (sensation) be or be not needed by us for deducing the quality of *shortness* from that of straight line, it seems at all events quite evident that the second of these qualities necessarily involves the first. If you only know what *straightness* and what *curvedness* is, you have all that is required for discovering, by examination, that a straight line must be the shortest possible as compared with any curve beginning and ending at the same points with it.[3]

348. In the third place, Kant asserts that even in Physical Science these are synthetical *a priori* judgments; and for an example he refers us to the proposition, ' In all changes of the material world, the quantity of matter remains unchanged.'[4]

---

[1] It is true, however, that in nature there exists no such thing as a *collection*; there are only individuals separate from one another. Hence the concept of any *number* whatever supposes something beyond what is found in nature, or in our sensations ; because a number is always a *collection*, and this shows that in all concepts of *number* there is an element supplied by the understanding—namely, that *unity* in virtue of which the separate individuals are seen as forming a collection. It may justly be said, therefore, that in the concept of a *number* there is always a sort of *synthetical* a priori *judgment*. But the error of Kant consists, as I have said, in placing this synthetical judgment in the summation of the two numbers 5 and 7, instead of placing it in the concept of 5, 7, 12, and of every other number.

[2] Kant's own words are these : 'My conception of *straight* contains no notion of *quantity*, but is merely *qualitative*. The conception of the *shortest* is therefore only an addition, and by no analysis can it be extracted from our conception of a straight line. Intuition (*i.e.* sensation) must therefore here lend its aid, by means of which, and thus only, synthesis is possible.'—*Critique of Pure Reason*, Introduction, v. [TRANSLATORS.]

[3] On the contrary, in the concept of any kind of *line* a synthetical *a priori judgment* can really be discovered ; for to have the concept of a line is to think a possible line, and *possibility* is not found in a physical line, but is a predicate supplied by the understanding.

[4] *Critique of Pure Reason*, Introduction, v.

But this is not an *a priori* proposition except in the
hypothesis that by *changes of the material world* we understand 'changes of forms and of compounds,' as these changes
really are. Now, if we understand the expression in this
sense, the judgment here referred to is, evidently, not synthetical but *analytical*, because the unchangeableness of the
quantity of matter is necessarily involved in that kind of
changes of which the proposition speaks.

349. Lastly, he maintains that even Metaphysics—if,
indeed, there be in his system such a science—'consists
merely of synthetical propositions *a priori*;' and the example
he makes most use of is the celebrated proposition, 'Everything that happens must have a cause.'[1] Now, I think that
here also he is mistaken; but as this proposition deserves
every attention, I shall examine it by itself in the following
article.

ARTICLE XXIII.

*Is the proposition, 'Everything that happens must have a cause,' a
synthetical* a priori *judgment in the Kantian sense?*

350. Kant will have it that 'The conception of a *cause* lies
quite out of the conception of *everything that happens*, and
indicates something entirely different from and consequently
not contained in it.'[2] According to him, therefore, the predicate (*must have a cause*), which in the judgment now under
consideration we add to the subject (*everything that happens*),
is neither derived from sensible experience—because experience does not show us *causes*, but only successive *facts*—
nor contained in the concept of the subject. Whence he
concludes that this is a synthetical *à priori* judgment.

Before accepting such a conclusion, I should like to submit the judgment, 'Everything that happens must have a
cause,' to a more patient analysis than our philosopher seems
to have made of it.

I maintain that in the conception of *everything that happens*
the conception of *cause* is necessarily included; for the two

[1] *Critique of Pure Reason*, Introduction, v.
[2] *Ibid.*, Introduction, iv.

conceptions, of *effect* and of *cause*, seem to me related together in such a manner that it is impossible for us to possess the first without implicitly possessing the second also.

In truth, an *effect* means 'That which is produced by a *cause* ;' and a *cause* means 'That which produces an effect.' Consequently, neither of these things can be properly defined or conceived without the other being implied.

By supposing, then, that I already know what *effect* is (the subject of the judgment) Kant stands pledged to the admission that I know, by implication, what *cause* is (the predicate) ; and *vice versâ.*

Therefore, the judgment which the common sense of mankind makes by saying, 'Every effect must have a cause,' is not synthetical at all, since its predicate (cause) is, by the nature of the case, already contained in its subject (effect).

But here I shall most probably be told that I am changing the question, forasmuch as the judgment proposed by Kant as synthetical *a priori*, was not, ' Every effect must have a cause,' but, 'Everything that happens must have a cause.' And, in fact, men do not generally speak of *effect*, but of *that which happens*, of *events*.

I feel the force of the objection, and proceed to answer it.

When anyone perceives that some new thing has taken place—for instance, when in autumn he notices a fine crop of fruit on the tree which he had seen quite bare in the previous winter—he may look at this new production in two ways : that is, either in its isolated entity and nothing more, or else as a thing which has *begun* to exist. In the first case, he certainly does not think of effect or of cause, since he considers that thing wholly apart from any relations it may have with any other thing. But in the second case he as certainly conceives, somehow or other, the thing as the effect of some cause. It is here only that he applies the general principle of causation, saying, 'This crop of fruit must have had a cause,' must have been produced by something ; and he applies it precisely because he has now conceived the new fruit as an effect. Thus, the conception of *effect* (the subject of the judgment) never precedes, or is never independent of that of *cause* (the predicate of the judgment); but the moment that the first conception is formed, the second is implicitly contained in it.

The difficulty therefore does not, as alleged by Kant consist in explaining how we form the idea of a predicate not contained in that of the subject; but it consists in explaining how we form the idea of the subject itself, in which the idea of the predicate is included.[1]

In other words, the universal and necessary proposition, and therefore the *a priori* judgment, is no other than this, ' Every effect must have a cause,' and this, for the reason I have given, is not a synthetical judgment *a priori* in the Kantian sense.

351. Now, let us apply this *a priori* proposition.

The application is made in the following manner:—

(1) We perceive an event; (2) we recognise that event as an effect; (3) we conclude that it must have a *cause*, for the reason that the idea of *cause* is necessarily called for by that of *effect*.

Now, in which of these three steps does the difficulty requiring explanation lie?

Not in the first; for our perception of the sensible event is adequately accounted for by the use of the senses.

Not, as Kant pretends, in the third, that is, in finding whence we get the *predicate* of our judgment; for, the supposition being that we have already conceived the event as an *effect*, we have thereby implicitly admitted a *cause*. Therefore, the whole difficulty lies in explaining how the second step is possible to us—*i.e.* how it comes to pass that we consider an event as an *effect*, and thus find the *subject* of the judgment, ' Every effect must have a cause,' applied to a particular event.

Independently, however, of the explanation of this difficulty, we may admit as a fact that men 'conceive every event as an effect.' I do not for the present seek to explain it; but the fact is indubitable.

---

[1] Kant could have discovered a synthetical *a priori* judgment, not, indeed, in the proposition, ' Everything that happens must have a cause,' but in the intellectual conception of ' That which happens ' (event).

Now, by means of this fact we are in a position to determine what place among the philosophical propositions regarding *causation* is occupied by that Kantian one, ' Everything
that happens must have a cause.'

This proposition, so enunciated, does not express an *a
priori judgment*, but the *application* of an *a priori* judgment ;
and the application which is generally made of an *a priori*
judgment is, not a principle, but a fact only.

Here, then, is the order in which these diverse propositions
regarding causation stand.

(1) The *a priori principle* : ' Every effect must have a cause.'

(2) The *general fact* : ' Every event is considered by men
as an effect.'

(3) The *general application* of the *a priori* principle :
' Every event must have a cause.'

What remains, therefore, to be explained, to say it once
more, is the *general fact*, 'How it comes to pass that men
conceive every event, not in itself only, but also as being an
effect ;' for if this is explained, we shall also see why it is that
men ascribe that event to a *cause*.

352. Let us, then, briefly analyse this general proposition,
' Every event is an effect.'

When a new event happens, something begins to exist
which did not exist before. We conceive, therefore, two successive times : in the first of them the thing was not, and in
the second the thing is.[1]

Starting from this observation, I argue thus :—

To conceive a thing as *beginning to exist* is to conceive a
change from non-existence to existence.

But to conceive this change is to conceive an *operation*.

Now, the conception of an operation necessarily involves
the conception of a *something* (a being) which does that operation, and is, therefore, antecedent to it.

But a something (a being) which operates in such a manner
as to make a thing pass from non-existence to existence is
precisely what is called a *cause*.

---

[1] It is the unity of my intimate *self*
that enables me to conceive simultaneously and to compare together these
two times.

Therefore, an event is conceived by us as an *effect* when we consider it as *beginning to exist.*

To put the same thing in a different form:

(1) The conception of *cause* is comprised in the conception of something whence an *operation* proceeds.

(2) The conception of *operation* is comprised in the conception of *change.*

(3) The conception of change is comprised in the conception of *beginning to exist* (passing from non-existence to existence).

The whole difficulty, therefore, is ultimately reduced to explaining the way in which we form the conception of *beginning to exist,* or *passing from non-existence to existence.* The explanation once given, the other links of the chain, including the first (the conception of cause), come of themselves.

How, then, do we conceive a thing as beginning to exist, or *passing from non-existence to existence?*

Assuming that we have the power of conceiving the *existence* of the things which fall under our senses, the conception in question no longer presents any difficulty. It is supplied to us by the senses through a judgment.

We see, we touch, in a word, we feel that which we did not and could not touch, see, or feel before; and the comparison of the first of these times with the second gives us the very conception of which I speak.

But, as I have said, this supposes that we are able to conceive the *existence* of that thing (that event); for, if we had sensations only, and not the power of conceiving things as existing outside of (*i.e.* different from) ourselves, the intellectual conception of the passing from non-existence to existence would be impossible to us.

We can see from all this that the only difficulty which remains to be vanquished in explaining the idea or conception of *cause* is expressed by the question, 'How do we perceive things as endowed with *existence,* as *beings?* Whence have we the notion of *existence* or *being?*' Such in very deed is the ideological problem.

ARTICLE XXIV.

The ideological problem was not properly stated by Kant.

353. Kant stated the ideological problem thus: ‘How are *synthetical judgments a priori* possible?’ (Art. XXI.)

Considering the sense he attached to the word *synthetical* (342), the said problem might just as well have been expressed thus: ‘How are those judgments possible in which we attribute to a subject a predicate which is neither given us by sensible experience nor contained in the concept of the subject itself?’

From the problem being presented in this way it would seem that if the *predicate* in question could either be found in the *concept of the subject* or be obtained from *sensible experience*, no difficulty would remain.

But, in the first place, if the *predicate* could be found in the *concept of the subject* that concept would be supposed as already formed by us.

The misfortune, however, is that the difficulty consists precisely in explaining how we can form the *concept of the subject* itself; how we can think of things as *existent*; how we can act so that they become, first, *objects* of our understanding, and then *subjects* of our judgments.

If the concepts of things are supposed as already in our mind, what difficulty can there be in our analysing them, or connecting them together in any way we please? None whatever. The whole knot of the question, therefore, consists in giving a clear and satisfactory account of how the *concepts of things* are formed. They cannot be formed unless things be conceived as existent, which presupposes in us the *notion of existence*; and this notion cannot come to us from mere sensations, because they are particular and the notion is universal, nor from the concepts themselves prior to our having them.

354. In the second place, the Kantian problem, as we have expressed it, supposes that the difficulty would vanish

if the predicate in discussion could be found by means of *sensible experience.*

Now, it is quite true that sensible experience can, in a certain way, furnish a predicate. Thus, when I judge that the wall before me is white, it is by the experience of my eyes that I am induced to apply this predicate of *whiteness.* But before I can do this I must know, or have the concept of, the subject of my judgment (the wall)—*i.e.* I must have thought of it as a thing existent (a being); and so we are thrown back on the difficulty above mentioned, ' How is it possible for me to think of a *being,* to conceive a thing as existent ? ' The notion of existence is always indispensable in the case ; and that notion I cannot draw from the concept itself through abstraction, since I cannot abstract anything from a concept which I have not as yet.

To resume : even if a predicate could be found by means of sensible experience, or by analysing the concept of the subject, the difficulty to be surmounted in explaining the operations of our understanding would nevertheless continue in undiminished force. For there would always remain to be asked, ' How came we to form the concept of the *subject* to which we apply that predicate ? ' And the true answer to this one question would be the true solution of the difficulty. Kant, therefore, by making that difficulty to consist, instead, in pointing out whence we obtain the predicates to be applied to subjects already conceived by us, has completely misrepresented the nature of the ideological problem.

ARTICLE XXV.

The nature of the ideological problem is still more clearly set forth.

355. The problem, then, of which we are treating can be reduced to the question, ' How are those objects of thought produced which we subsequently take for the subject-matter of our judgments ? ' or, more briefly, ' How do we form the concepts of things ? '

Let us analyse it under this new form, even as we have done under others.

To form the concept of a thing we must make a judgment wherein we consider that thing not as a modification of ourselves, but objectively, or in itself—in other words, as belonging to the universal class designated by the term *existence* or *being*.

Now, since in every judgment, when completed, there must be a predicate and a subject, it remains to be seen, in the first place, what, in the judgment just named, is the *predicate*, and what the *subject*; and in the second place, whence the *predicate* and the *subject* are respectively derived.

The *predicate*, here, is nothing but *existence*; for to perceive a thing objectively is nothing but to perceive it in itself, or in the existence belonging to it according to its nature. The *subject*, on the contrary, is that which has fallen under our senses, has acted upon them.

Such being the case, let us consider that the *subject*, anteriorly to the judgment in question, is not as yet anything intellectually perceived by us; because the act of intellectual perception consists in that very judgment. The *subject*, therefore, if we wish so to call it anteriorly to the judgment, is the thing purely in so far as sensitively apprehended, and of which, therefore, we have, not the *concept*, but the *sense-perception* only. It is the term of an act of sense, and nothing more.

We must be very careful to note well this distinction, based on fact—namely, that in our judgments there are subjects of which, antecedently to the judgments themselves, we had not the *concept*, but only the *sense-perception*; for in this observation, simple as it may appear, lies the golden key of all the philosophy of the human spirit.

Should we desire to formulate these judgments—the first which our understanding makes—we should have to say: ' That which I feel exists.' That of which I have sense-perception I perceive intellectually through joining with it the predicate of *existence*. We take, therefore, as the subject of this judgment, what remains after taking away from the formula the word *exists*. And what is this remainder? ' That which I feel'—*i.e.* which affects my senses without my knowing as yet that it is a thing existent in itself, or belonging to the immense class denominated from *existence.*

This analysis of the first judgments we make in the forming of concepts, this purely mental separation of the predicate (*existence*) from the subject (*that which I feel*), will, as I have said, unlock to us the secret of the operations of our intelligent spirit.

By means of such analysis, we come to find, (1) a *subject* (if it is right so to term it while in that separated state), given purely by the senses, and of which we have not as yet any intellectual concept ; and (2) a *predicate*—the idea of *existence* or *being in general*—which cannot by any possibility come from the senses, nor, consequently, be in any way accounted for by those philosophers who pretend to derive all human knowledge from the senses alone.

The ideological problem, therefore, is this : ' Explain how it is possible for us to make those first judgments by which we intellectually perceive the things which act on our senses, and thus form concepts or ideas of them.'

ARTICLE XXVI.

Are the first judgments, through which we form the concepts of things, synthetical in the Kantian sense ?

356. The first judgments whereby we intellectually perceive things, and thus form concepts or ideas of them, are the result of a *synthesis* between the predicate not furnished by the senses (*existence in general*) and the subject given by the senses (terms of *sense-perception*).

Under one aspect, therefore, these primitive judgments are *synthetical,* and it is on them that the possibility of the *analytical* ones depends ; for in the latter we simply decompose the concepts, or ideas which we have formed by means of the said synthesis.

It is not, however, in this legitimate sense that Kant uses the word *synthetical* ; and I must therefore, before proceeding further, point out the germ of the error which lies concealed under the ambiguous meaning of this word.

Synthesis means *union*; hence to say 'Synthetical judgments' is equivalent to saying, 'Judgments wherein we unite to a subject something which is not contained in the subject itself.'[1]

But the words *union* and *to unite*, being metaphorical, or at least apt to raise up before one's mind the image of *physical unions*, it is necessary first of all to explain in what sense these unions may be applicable to express the union of sense-perceptions with concepts or ideas through purely spiritual operations.

By saying, 'I unite a predicate with a subject,' I may understand that I place this predicate in the subject as a diamond is placed in a ring, or as a beam is placed in a building in course of construction, and which is not in the ring or in the building except because it is placed there; and it is in this sense that Kant understands it.

Kant supposes also, as we have seen, that in certain judgments the predicate which we place in and consider as an integrating portion of the subject, neither emanates from the *concept of the subject*, nor is given us by sensible experience.

Hence he concludes that in this class of judgments it is our own spirit that, by an energy intrinsic to it, sends forth from within itself into the subject the predicate which is not therein contained; so that the subject is in part created by ourselves. And if we regard that predicate as a necessary and essential element of the subject itself, that is merely an illusion, a deception, but an illusion and deception which we cannot possibly help, because it is imposed on us by the very constitution of our nature.[2]

Now, all this reasoning would be unimpeachable were it

---

[1] I do not say in the *concept of the subject*, but I say in the *subject itself*; lest anyone should think that we can have the concept of the subject before having made that judgment by which we intellectually perceive, and thus form the concept of it.

[2] How humiliating to man is a doctrine which would fain make him believe that he is always necessarily and essentially deceived, not by his fellow-creatures, but by his very nature, and by the Author of this nature, if, indeed, the existence of a Creator be compatible with such a system! Here is philosophy proclaiming humility with a vengeance! Debasing, not man only, but with man human nature, and therefore God Himself!

not for the damaging fact that it is based on two propositions as gratuitous as they are false.

The first of them is, that the predicate which we attribute to a subject is found neither in sensible experience nor in the *concept* of the subject itself. The truth, on the contrary, is, that whenever the predicate is not furnished to us by sensible experience, or by a reasoning based on that experience, it is invariably found in the *concept* of the subject itself.

The second false supposition is, that when we make a synthetical judgment, we unite the predicate to the subject in such a manner that it forms an integrating part of that *subject*, whereas it forms only an integrating part of the *concept* of the subject.

357. Since, then, the word *synthesis*, as applied to a judgment, cannot be taken in the material sense which Kant ascribes to it, let us see what sense it has when used in reference to spiritual operations. This will serve to explain more clearly how the intellectual perception takes place in us, on the accurate description and analysis of which the whole issue of these inquiries depends.

We have intellectual perception of a body when we attribute existence to it, or, to say better, conceive it *in se*, in its own existence, and not in the relation it has with ourselves.

Now, this perception consists of three elements—

1st *element* : all that our senses supply to us of that body (the term of sense-perception) ;

2nd *element* : existence in general (the idea) ;

3rd *element* : that particular and real existence which we find in that body, and therefore *attribute* to it by a judgment.

Existence considered in general may be called the *predicable*, and the *particular* and *real existence* may be called the *attribute*.

Now, as I have already noted (332–333), Kant confounded the *predicable* with the *attribute* already predicated and affirmed—the ideal existence (and, generally, the ideal quality) which can be predicated of many things, with the *particular* and *real* existence (or other qualities) which we

attribute to the corporeal thing acting on our senses. Thus
he took the two modes of existence (objective and subjective)
for one and the same mode.[1] He did not perceive that the
particular and real existence is proper to one being only, and
cannot be applied to any others, whereas ideal existence,
before being applied, is universal or applicable to all thinkable beings *ad infinitum.* Nor, again, did he perceive that
the *real* existence is as manifold as there are particular
beings existent, for which reason it cannot, with strict propriety, be called purely and simply *existence (existentia)*, but
should be called *being (ens)* ; while, on the contrary, the
ideal is one and immutable, and the only one to which the
name of *existence* properly belongs.

358. But here some one may say : Either the particular
existence of the being of which we have perception is also
perceived, or it is not. If it is not perceived, then we
cannot speak of it ; and if it is perceived, then we have two
ideas—that of existence in general (the predicable), and that
of the particular existence (the attribute).

This objection has already been answered (324–326).
Nevertheless, it is so important to master well its solution
that I deem it advisable to give the same answer again in
another form. This will, I hope, serve to facilitate the knowledge of the true nature of the act called intellectual perception.

Let us begin by fixing with precision the meaning of our
words : this done, the difficulty will soon disappear.

The word *existence*, taken without any adjuncts, indicates
only an idea. A particular being *(ens)* is not said to have
existence for us, until the concept of it has been formed in
our mind. Hence, prior to our conceiving a corporeal being,
this being exists, but we have not any knowledge thereof, and
consequently no word by which to express it.

When this corporeal being acts on our sense—supposing
that our intellectual faculty does not operate at all, and that

---

[1] To distinguish ideal existence
(existence-idea) from particular and real
existence *(existence-thing)*, I am accustomed to call the latter by the name of
subsistence.

we have sensations only—the same corporeal being, through acting on our sensitivity, would begin to have a relation with us. We, on being thus affected by it, might perhaps utter a cry, which would not, however, be a *word*, expressive at once of our affection and its cause. It would not be the sign of a *judgment*; nor indicate a being as it is in itself. It would simply be an *instinctive effect* of the modification or feeling caused in us by that agent. So far, then, there would be no intellectual perception of *a being*.

The only example that I could adduce of this would be the inarticulate cries uttered by animals, or those interjections of pleasure or of pain which, without designating *thought*, as words do, are nevertheless instinctively produced by the feelings experienced by the animal. All the articulate sounds which I could quote—as, for instance, the words *being, body, soul*, &c.—express concepts already formed in the mind, and are quite another thing. In the state of which I speak, therefore, we should not have perceived the *existence* of the being : we should only have felt the passion which the being has produced in us by its action.

But let us now assume that our faculty of judgment (the reason) is also set in motion, and that the agent of which till now we had only a passive sense-perception, is known by us in itself, or made an object of intellectual perception. I ask, what is it that takes place within us in this new operation?

Simply an interior comparison between the particular passion received by our senses, or, to speak more accurately, the *term* of that passion—the thing *felt*—and the idea of existence. Through this comparison we find that the thing felt and the *existence* of an agent different from ourselves are intimately related, and so we say to ourselves, 'That of which I feel the action in me *exists*' (in a given degree and mode determined for me by the nature of that action). Thus the judgment perceptive of that corporeal being is closed. Through this judgment we consider that being as belonging to the immense class of existent things, and therefore see it under a universal aspect, as *existing* in itself, inde-

pendently of us, of our passion, and of all other beings whatsoever.

From this analysis we can see that the intellectual perception is nothing but 'the vision of the relation between a
thing felt (term of sense-perception) and notional or ideal
existence.'

I now come to the solution of the objection proposed
above.

The *Intellect*, defined as the faculty of the intuition of
existence or being in general, is limited to this intuition, has
no idea save this most universal one.

The *Reason*, defined as the faculty which applies the universal idea to the 'sensibles' outside of us, is nothing but the
power we have of seeing the relation between what is supplied to us by the senses, and the *existence* of which the intellect has intuition.

Hence in each intellectual perception of a corporeal being
there are necessarily three elements—

1. A universal seen by the *intellect* (ideal existence);

2. The effect produced by the particular being acting on
the *sense*;

3. The vision of the relation between the said agent and
the universal idea (act of *reason*, perception).

Failing any one of these three elements, the intellectual
perception, and therefore the concept or idea, of a corporeal
being would be impossible to us.[1]

Given, then, that our senses have been affected by the
action of a particular body, or, speaking improperly, of 'the
particular existence' of that body, we should not, by this
alone, have the concept or idea, but only the sense-perception of it. A particular being, or (improperly) a particular
existence, is not, therefore, knowable through itself—*i.e.* is
not an idea; it is merely a sensible element, though necessary for the concrete idea or intellectual perception, which, as

---

[1] Those also who take away the ideal
element, and leave nothing but the real,
make the intellectual perception impossible. Reid excluded the ideal element;
Kant, on the contrary, admitted it, but
denied the real. Both agreed in saying
that our spirit cognises particular beings
by an immediate perception, with this
difference, however, that, for Reid, the
beings so perceived were *real objects*,
while Kant considered them to be, in
part, *concepts*.

I have said, is simply 'the vision of the relation between a particular thing acting on the senses, or (improperly) the particular existence of that thing, and the universal called *existence.*

The outcome of all this is—

(1) That there are not two ideas of existence, the one particular and the other universal, but there is one only—that of existence in general.

(2) That there are many perceptions and concepts of *existent beings,* and they consist, to say it once more, in the vision of the relation between the particulars affecting our senses and the idea of existence.

359. Our difficulty being thus cleared up by a more detailed analysis of the way in which things come to be *understood* by us, it will be easy to see in what sense the name of *synthesis* or union can be legitimately applied to an act which is wholly spiritual—I mean, the act by which we cognise or intellectually conceive a corporeal being.

This act consists in our ' seeing the relation between the particular agent as perceived by the senses, and the universal idea of existence.'

Therefore, we do not by it place this idea in the particular being as though the idea became a component part thereof ; no, we simply conceive (in virtue of the *unity* of our intimate self) the relation which that being has with the existence of which we have the notion or idea.

Evidently, to perceive a relation is not to confound or mix up into one thing the two terms of that relation. This would be a material union, similar to that of two liquids poured into the same vessel, or of two eatables made up into one dish. In the vision of a relation, on the contrary, the two terms are kept distinct ; their union consists simply in this, that the intelligent spirit, by looking simultaneously at both and comparing one with the other, finds them related together, and affirms accordingly. That relation is a purely mental entity, which causes no disturbance or alteration in the terms themselves. It only serves as a light to direct our intellectual act ; or rather, the seeing of it constitutes the act itself—*i.e.*

the intellectual perception, which is at once a cognition and a concept.

In this sense alone do I call *synthetical* and *a priori* those primitive judgments through which our intellectual perceptions of corporeal things are formed ; because in them a spiritual union is effected between that which is given by the senses and becomes the *subject* of the judgment, and that which is no part of the subject in so far as given by the senses, but is found only in the intellect, and goes under the name of *predicate.*

360. Be it carefully noted that, while I say that this predicate does not exist in the subject in so far as given by the senses (the term of sense-perception), I do not say, like Kant, that it does not exist in the *concept* of the subject.

In that *concept* the predicate does undoubtedly exist ; for what is the *concept* already formed of the subject of the judgment but the sensible element (*matter*) with the intelligible *predicate* (*form*) already applied to it ?

It is therefore one thing to say, ' The predicate does not exist in the *concept* of the subject,' and quite another thing to say, ' The predicate does not exist in the *subject.*' The first is the expression of Kant, and in it lie the ambiguity and the error ; the second is the expression which alone I accept and endorse as correct.

In short, the subjects of our judgments may be considered either in so far as given by the senses and nothing more, or they may be considered as already conceived by the understanding. In this latter case, our judgment includes also the *concept* of its *subject*; but it does not in the first case. Then, the subject exists only in a certain way—that is, potentially. It is not yet the subject, and therefore is not yet *conceived* by us, but it *will be* as soon as the predicate is applied to it—*i.e.* as soon as the judgment is made.

Now, it is from these *primitive judgments* which constitute our intellectual perceptions of real beings, that we, later on, abstract the concepts or *determinate ideas* of those beings.

For instance, if I say, 'This man is wise,' my judgment presupposes in me the concept of the subject (this man), and is not, therefore, a primitive judgment. But if I say, 'That which I at this moment feel acting on my senses exists,' then 'that which I at this moment feel acting on my senses' is, indeed, the subject of a judgment already formed ; but it is so, not because of what it has by itself alone as a mere *datum* of the senses, but only because I have ended the proposition by the word 'exists.' Till that moment I had no *concept* of it, for it was only then that my intellectual perception of it began.

In conclusion : the judgments by which we form the concepts or ideas of things are *primitive*—that is, the first that we make upon these things ; they are *synthetical*, because we add to the subject something which is not in it, or, to speak more accurately, we view that subject in relation with an idea (a universal) ; and they may also justly be called *a priori*, because, although we cannot make them without receiving their *matter* from the senses, their *form* is to be found only in our intellect : and in these synthetical *a priori* judgments lies the Ideological problem, the great question of the *Primum Philosophicum.*

ARTICLE XXVII.

The Kantian solution of the ideological problem.

361. Perhaps all the errors of philosophers owe their origin to a wrong way of stating the question. To me it seems easier to solve a question than to present it well, since a question cannot be properly presented unless it be intimately understood, and it cannot be intimately understood unless it has been first solved in one's own mind.

As we have seen, Kant stated the ideological problem thus : 'How are synthetical *a priori* judgments possible ?' meaning by 'synthetical *a priori*' a species of judgments in which the predicate is neither contained in the *concept* of the subject, nor derived from sensible experience, but is placed in the subject by our own selves.

His mistake lay in assuming the existence of these judgments; and having once laid down this wrong foundation, he could only build upon it the *Critical* System of Philosophy, by a process of reasoning which may be summarised as follows:—

Since there are synthetical *a priori* judgments—that is, judgments in which the predicate is not derived from sensible experience, nor contained in the concept of the subject—we must needs admit that we draw this predicate from within ourselves.

There is therefore in the depth of our spirit a portentous energy whence, on occasion of our being affected by sensations, emanate the predicates determinative of the various species of things.

These predicates, not being supplied to us by experience, but existing in us *a priori*, must necessarily be possessed of the two characteristics essential to *a priori* knowledge—namely, *necessity* and *universality*. *Necessity*, because without them. we could not have intellectual perception of any being; *universality*, because all beings which we intellectually perceive must necessarily appear to us possessed of these predicates.

If, then, real beings cannot be perceived by us otherwise than as possessed of the predicates referred to, it follows that such predicates must appear to us as integrating and essential parts of the beings themselves. It is therefore by a display of the energy intrinsic to our spirit that the beings we perceive are, in part, constructed and formed. Our spirit transfuses from within itself into them what is needed for their subsistence. They are not, therefore, in themselves, what they appear to be. In them the spirit sees only its own work, or rather its own self.

These principles once granted, in what was Ideology to occupy itself? Chiefly in two things.

(1) In seeking and enumerating all those *necessary* and *universal* predicates apart from which the beings perceived by us would have no existence: for, on the one hand, owing to their necessity and universality, those predicates cannot come

from experience, which is only contingent and limited,[1] and are therefore *a priori* ; and, on the other hand, not being contained in the concept of the subject,[2] they must belong to synthetical judgments.

(2) In describing the manner in which our spirit applies and transfuses such predicates into the beings perceived, and hence constructs to itself the objects of its cognitions.

The first of these two investigations is called by Kant *Analytic of Conceptions* ; the second, *Analytic of Judgments* ; and both, taken together, form the analytical part of his *Transcendental Logic.*

362. Now, with regard to the first point, Kant thinks he has succeeded in proving that the *conceptions* (or predicates) he was in quest of, and to which he preserves the Aristotelian appellation of *Categories*, are twelve in number. Our understanding, therefore, on occasion of the sensations, emits these twelve predicates or categories from within itself in such a manner that they form part of the external objects. Thus the objects perceived by us are composed of two elements— *i.e.* (1) *pure conceptions* ; (2) sensations, or, as he calls them, empirical *intuitions*, clothed in the forms of space and time.

As regards the second point, or the 'manner in which these two elements come to be joined together, so as to result in one and the same being,' he explains it by having recourse to a third element, intermediate between the categories (wholly pure), and the sensations (wholly empirical), and the effect of which element is to enable the understanding to see the latter

---

[1] This reasoning of Kant is not correct. Not all that is found in *necessary* and *universal* cognitions is *a priori* ; the only thing *a priori* is the *necessity* and *universality* of such cognitions.

[2] Here Kant falls into a contradiction. He maintains that these predicates enter as a component part into the object perceived by us. But how does he describe the object in so far as perceived by us ? He describes it as resulting from two elements—that is, (1) the intellectual concepts ; (2) the empirical intuitions (sensations). His words are : ' Without intuition the whole of our cognition is without objects, and is therefore quite void.' (*Transcendental Logic*, Introduction, iv.) Now, the concepts of which he speaks are pure conceptions : in a word, they are the predicates of the synthetical *a priori* judgments. But if they are such, how can he afterwards affirm that the predicates of the synthetical *a priori* judgments are not contained in the concept of the object perceived ? Can we have this concept without there being in those judgments the pure conceptions, which, according to him, are the conditions of experience and of the formation of our every concept?

in the former. This intermediate element is *time*, and it unites itself to the categories as well as to the sensations.

'Time,' he says, 'unites itself alike to the pure conceptions of the intellect (*categories*), and to the empirical intuitions (sensations). By uniting itself to the former, it produces a kind of conceptions which, although *pure*, come nearer to the sensible things than the simply intellectual only' (*Analytic of Principles*, ch. i.). To this intermediate class of conceptions he gives the name of *Schemata*.

Thus, in the application of the purely intellectual to the sensible part of our cognitions, he distinguishes these three several steps :—

(1) Our understanding supplies from itself the *categories*, or predicates, which are wholly universal.

(2) By considering these *categories* as united with *time* (which is the form of the internal sense, or that by which the action of this sense is conditioned), we obtain the *schemata* which, in substance, are predicates less universal than the categories.

(3) By uniting these *schemata* with the sensations, we produce the real beings cognised by us—*i.e.* the external world.

Such is the solution which Kant gives of the fundamental problem of Ideology and of Philosophy in general, in conformity with the manner in which he had stated that problem —namely, 'How are synthetical *a priori* judgments possible?' or, in other words, 'How do we construct for ourselves the objects of our thoughts?'

ARTICLE XXVIII.

Kant did not understand the nature of intellectual perception.

363. From what we have said of the manner in which Kant proposed the above problem, and of the solution which he accordingly gave of it, we may easily see how inaccurate and materialistic was his view of intellectual perception.

In fact, intellectual perception, according to the analysis we have made of it (357, 358), consists simply in 'the vision of the relation between the idea of existence, and the term of a sense-perception.'

In this operation we do not mix up or confound the idea with the thing sensitively perceived ; nay, we keep it entirely distinct therefrom.   All that we do is, to descry the relation between the idea and that thing ; and, as we shall see better elsewhere, it is by this relation that we are made to cognise sensible beings.

Kant, on the contrary, supposed that the universal ideas (categories) and the things sensitively perceived are mixed up together in such a way as actually to result in the external object of our thought.   This error he owed to his not distinguishing between the *predicate* and the *attribute* (330–332)—*i.e.* between that which really exists as *particular* in the being cognised,[1] and that which exists as universal in the mind, and therefore differs from the particular even as a type differs from its realisations.   For example, *quantity* considered in general— typical quantity—is, most certainly, not the same as the particular quantity found in an individual real being ; although the two quantities have a singular relation of identity, the effect of which is, that the second can be, and is, cognised only through the first.   ' How this relation of identity— between the particular found in the being we cognise, and the universal seen by the mind—is possible,' was the problem that Kant ought to have proposed to himself, but the true nature of which he did not understand.

ARTICLE XXIX.

In what he admits as innate in the human understanding, Kant errs at once by defect and by excess.

364. Kant's theory is nothing but a development of the theory of Reid.[2]

---

[1] That which is particular in a being is not knowable, except by means of a universal present to our mind.   The particular is not by itself an *idea* ; it is simply the term of a judgment which conjoins it with an idea.

[2] The view held by Reid, that our mind has in it no pure ideas, but only *perceptions of beings*, so that our mind perceives the beings themselves by an immediate act, had already been advanced by Arnauld in his book, *Des vraies et fausses idées*.   But in this antagonist of Malebranche the affinity

According to Kant our spirit has in it nothing innate in the sense that the innate precedes sensible experience, but this spirit, when the matter of its cognitions is given it by the senses, is bound to receive that matter according to certain laws, and therefore to vest it with *certain forms.* The *matter* supplied by the senses, and the *forms* which the spirit adds to it, are the two component parts of external objects.

These *forms*, in respect of the understanding, consist of the *twelve categories* or pure conceptions mentioned above. They are predicates which our spirit necessarily and universally conjoins with the data of experience.

As a fitting illustration of the way in which the human spirit operates, Kant proposes to his readers the simile of the prism which we adduced when speaking of Aristotle (256, 257). Even as the light is refracted by the form of the prism into seven different colours, so the sensations, being acted upon by the forms of our spirit, assume all those forms, and are changed into external beings, which afterwards seem to us different from and wholly independent of ourselves.

This manner of considering the human spirit, on the one hand, allows too little of the innate, as we saw when discoursing on Reid ; but, on the other hand, it credits the same spirit with an energy creative of the external world—subject, however, to laws of so dismal a nature that, while continually producing from within itself the universe, it is at the same time inexorably necessitated to involve itself in a profound, horrible illusion, whence it cannot escape except by means of a fresh illusion, also necessary, also fatal—*i.e.* the *Practical Philosophy.*[1]

existing between the system which abolishes ideas, and that of Kant, is perhaps seen even better than in Reid.   For Arnauld, besides maintaining that there are no ideas intermediate between us and external beings, but that we perceive the beings themselves immediately, says also that these our perceptions are of their nature representative, and are, moreover, *modalities* of the soul itself.—But if such is the case, then the soul has in itself the modes (the forms) of all beings.   Everyone can see how near this comes to the Critical Philosophy.

[1] If this ultimate result of Kant's philosophy be taken together with the systems on which I have commented in my 'Essay on Hope' (*Opuscoli Filosofici*, vol. ii.), as well as in 'Short Exposition of the Philosophy of M. Gioja' (*ibid.*), and in which a *state of continual illusion* is made the basis of human happiness, we shall see how very deserving of serious reflection is the history of human wisdom.

ARTICLE XXX.

Conclusion.

365. Although the system of Kant is only a development of that of Reid, I have placed Reid in the number of those

Man starts with an overweening confidence in his own powers, promising to himself the discovery of truth. There shall be no one truth, however recondite, but must reveal itself to his investigations. Meanwhile the passions murmur, dreading lest they may be forbidden the sweet intoxication of the senses. Man reassures them; he promises that the truth which is sure to come to light will sanction all sensible enjoyments. In making this promise, man trusts to a result of which, as yet, he knows nothing, but which he keeps constantly in view, as the one goal to which all his researches must be directed. Truth, however, is not found to bend to the interested views of such a philosophy, and philosophy, therefore, grows indignant. Having tried every means to persuade truth into subserviency to its purpose; having lavished on it caresses and flattery; having threatened to denounce it as inhuman and barbarous if it refuses to be reconciled with the impulses and instincts of a corrupt nature—of a nature not only too degenerate, but also too proud to acknowledge degeneracy; and having found all this to be in vain, what does philosophy do at last? She pauses in order to take counsel. She retraces her steps; she returns to her starting-point. Chagrined at not having been able to subjugate truth, or to corrupt it, or to find a system which would be at once true and indulgent, even to the length of substituting sensuousness for righteousness, she retracts. She no longer vaunts her ability to arrive with certainty at the conquest of truth. She says that her former pretensions in this respect were a blunder —the result of inexperience. But now that, fortunately for herself, her eyes have been opened, she will be wiser, and therefore more cautious. With characteristic modesty, she protests that henceforth *acquiescence in doubt* will be all that men can reasonably expect her to teach them. Thus does she hope to tranquillise the passions which had frowned upon her former undertaking. And it must be confessed that on this new road—the sceptical road—she is more successful. Instead of toiling laboriously in constructing, she has only to clear the ground of all that may ever hinder man in the indulgence of his insatiable desires, and she succeeds only too well. For in proportion as scepticism takes a firmer hold of men's minds, even so increases that spirit of unbridled licence where human concupiscence runs riot. Essentially hesitating and unquiet, like concupiscence, this philosophy tends to nothing so much as to the full attainment of her perfection; and this consists in the passage from the theory of *doubt* to that of *illusion.* In illusion there is none of the uncertainty which invariably attaches itself to doubt. Henceforth, then, it is no longer truth, no longer even doubt, but it is *illusion* that says, man is at liberty to gratify himself to his heart's content. Such must be the true end of this human and all-genial philosophy; and such, we are told, is *progress.* Nevertheless, illusion does not yet satisfy man entirely. Being essentially made for *truth*, man cannot seek to deceive himself without feeling inwardly rebuked. Therefore, philosophy shall *progress* still further, so that this uneasiness also may be removed. *Illusion*, she says, need not cause alarm to anyone; for that it is none of man's own handiwork, but a noble and a happy and an essential effect and property of his very nature. Luckily for itself, this nature is so constituted as necessarily to place its bliss in a universal and absolute illusion. Why show trouble about such an unattainable thing as objective truth? Why stop to ask whether this or that be true or not? *Illusion* —behold the one lofty object of man's intelli-

philosophers who credited the human spirit with too little of the innate, and Kant in the number of those who erred by the opposite extreme.

The reason of this is that, as a matter of fact, Reid never suspected that his solitary admission of an instinct which, on occasion of the sensations blindly impels us to affirm the existence of external bodies, would lead to such consequences as Kant subsequently drew from it. He did not perceive that, this instinct being once conceded, it would be impossible to stop there. Those consequences were a logical necessity of such a premise; and Kant was just the sort of man to dare that necessity unflinchingly. I say *to dare that necessity unflinchingly,* for he must indeed be a daring man who could openly undertake to declare that, in the eyes of reason, the very nature of things stands convicted of a lie!

gence! Be it so, O human philosophy! We now know you fully. You are always proposing to yourself the great problem, 'How man may, by his own self, secure happiness on this earth;' and this is how you solve it. You demand of us to declare that human nature, the nature of everything that exists, is—a lie; and, for this reason, impossible to exist. Yes, one must come to absolute *annihilation* before man's temerity can succeed in fully satisfying, apart from God, the essential wants of his nature. It is a melancholy, an absurd, a mad solution; but before it can take effect in mankind, you will be compelled to recant and change your colours.

CHAPTER IV.

HOW PHILOSOPHY MAY BE SAID TO HAVE PROGRESSED
BY MEANS OF PLATO, LEIBNITZ, AND KANT; AND
WHAT IT STILL REQUIRES IN ORDER TO BE PERFECT.

ARTICLE I.

Recapitulation of the three systems.

366. Plato, better than all other philosophers, and next
to him Leibnitz and Kant, saw, in some part, the difficulty
which is found in explaining the great fact of ideas.

As regards philosophers of less note, who did not see
this difficulty at all, and of whom I have spoken in the
preceding Section, whatever be their merits in regard to
other branches of philosophy, they cannot claim a place
among those who attempted and helped forward the solution
of so important and capital a problem. But in the history of
this solution the three just named, who devoted all the might
of their genius to the noble task of promoting its discovery,
will ever hold a conspicuous place.

It may also be said that this question, in passing successively from one of them to the other, made some progress. I
will explain how.

We have seen that whoever seeks to account for the facts
of experience must not assume more than is necessary for
that purpose, and therefore, when two or more suppositions
present themselves to the mind as equally fit to afford the
explanation, that which is the least and simplest ought to be
regarded as most likely to be the true one (26–28).

Now, all the three philosophers above mentioned, in order
to explain the fact of the origin of ideas, agreed in admitting
something innate in our soul; and so far they were right;

but at the same time they committed the error of making that innate element greater than was demanded by the nature of the case.

Nevertheless, the two last—I mean Leibnitz and Kant—had this merit, that each narrowed somewhat the limits of the superfluous part inherited from his predecessor. This was a distinct gain to philosophy, inasmuch as it brought this science nearer to the golden standard of truth. Everything, in fact, seemed to mark a continuous advance towards perfection, which I have no doubt would have been reached at last if a combination of extraneous adverse circumstances had not arisen to blight these hopes, and to hurry philosophy on to suicide.

Leibnitz admitted less of the innate than Plato, for, whilst Plato held that from the very beginning of our existence all our ideas are in us, complete in themselves, though in a state of oblivion, Leibnitz would have nothing but *traces* of ideas, exceedingly slight, yet endowed with the power of working themselves out into more and more distinctness according to a certain fixed law of harmony (293, 294).

I have already observed that these Leibnitzian traces of ideas do not present any clear meaning, and that all that can be admitted concerning the different states in which ideas are in our mind, is the distinction of *non-reflex* and *reflex* ideas (288, 292). I here of course leave aside the question as to the various degrees of *intuitive force* ; for this belongs to the thinking subject rather than to the object of his intuition—to what he sees in an idea.

Leibnitz, then, by the fact of imagining those little and insensible perceptions, and thus admitting less of the innate than Plato (as also than Des Cartes), showed plainly enough that he felt the necessity of eliminating what was excessive in the theory of the Athenian philosopher. One cannot, however, help regretting that he did not hit upon a better way of decomposing our ideas and descrying in them the part which was innate, than to represent them as, so to speak, ensconced, without light or meaning, in the depth of our soul.

Kant came next, and was more fortunate. He turned to

account a distinction which, though most ancient, had been neglected by modern philosophers—I mean the distinction between the *formal* and the *material* part of our ideas.

Deeply impressed with the importance of this distinction, he limited the innate element exclusively to the *formal part* of our cognitions, leaving to sensible experience the duty of furnishing their *material* part (324–326). The thought was excellent, and, when considered in relation to the spirit of the Platonic philosophy, seems to be the key for penetrating into the inner meaning of Plato, who perhaps did not himself know how to express it distinctly and in precise and thoroughly consistent terms.[1]

By placing the element congenite with the human spirit in the pure *forms* of cognition only, Kant was, clearly, reducing that element to narrower limits than had ever been done by those who had preceded him in comprehending the necessity of assuming as much of it as would be requisite for giving a full and satisfactory account of the fact of ideas and cognitions.[2]

---

[1] In some places Kant assumes the tone of an interpreter of Plato—for instance, where he treats of his three *ideas* or conceptions of the reason, and, with reference to the understanding of the Platonic philosophy, makes the following observation : ' I shall content myself with remarking that it is nothing unusual in common conversation, as well as in written works, by comparing the thoughts which an author has delivered upon a subject, to understand him better than he understood himself, inasmuch as he may not have sufficiently determined his conceptions, and thus have sometimes spoken, nay, even thought in opposition to his own opinions.'—*Critique of Pure Reason, Logic, Transcendental Dialectics,* book i. sec. 1.

[2] The system of *innate forms* (waiving here the historical question as to how Kant understood them, and concerning which I have already expressed my opinion in the chapter where I examined his doctrine) may be considered in two ways—first, in the sense in which Plato or Des Cartes believed ideas to be innate. According

to this, the forms would be as it were so many distinct universal and abstract *ideas* which we carry within us as *ab initio,* and to which the name of *forms* is given to signify the use we make of them for cognising real things ; secondly, in the sense that there is in our soul a radical virtue of such a nature that on occasion of conceiving the beings which act on our senses, the soul emits from within itself the forms which had no existence before, and joins them with the *matter* furnished by sensible experience. Thus our cognitions, and with them the world itself, would spring into existence merely through the energy of our spirit, or rather would be created by it. Now, all I wish to note here is, that by viewing the *forms* in this second way we should be admitting more of the innate than by viewing them in the first, and therefore that the superfluity by which the system of innate *forms* is vitiated would be proportionately greater.

As to this second way of interpreting the system of *innate forms,* I cannot refrain from quoting some remarks of

367. The innate forms assumed by Kant were seventeen —two for the sense (internal and external), twelve for the understanding which he called pure *conceptions* or categories, and three for the reason to which he gave the name of *ideas*.

This number of forms, however, was by far too great. The formal element of the human intelligence is much more simple. Our philosopher did not examine cognitions closely enough to draw the exact line between that which in them is *pure form* and that which belongs only to their *matter*.

The analysis I have endeavoured to make of these Kantian forms satisfies me that they are not the *formal* elements of human knowledge, any more than the four elements of *Empedocles* are the simple substances composing all the various bodies of the universe. But whereas chemical science, in its advance towards perfection, has resolved the elements of the ancients—water, earth, fire and air—into a larger number of principles, metaphysical science, more fortunate, has been able to reverse the process, and to demonstrate that the formal elements of human knowledge are ultimately reducible even to one only—the form at once of the intelligence and of cognition.[1]

Antonio Genovesi in a letter to Conti. From them we shall see that the system of Kant had in substance been thought of and refuted in Italy even before being imported into it from Germany. Genovesi says, 'I willingly concede that this production of the *forms* of things merely possible can be effected by the nature of our soul alone ; but no man will ever be able to understand how the mind, without having any knowledge of existent things, or finding any trace of them in itself, or receiving such trace from external causes, can produce to itself images or forms corresponding to those things. No, this quite surpasses my powers of comprehension. A force like this would be greater than creative force, since, after all, a creator produces only what he understands ; but this force would produce forms of things which it does not understand—of things not merely as possible, but as existent. Say what you will, to me it seems like the case of a painter who should pretend to have made likenesses of objects of which he never had any conception. Nay, more : such a theory would plunge us into the darkest scepticism imaginable about the existence of corporeal things, would involve a complete denial of the evidence of our senses, a betrayal of the clear testimony of our consciousness.'

[1] To say that the human understanding and human knowledge have many *forms* seems to be nothing less than an absurdity, a contradiction in terms. In fact, if it is true that by the word *understanding* I indicate a determinate thing, and do not utter an uncertain sound with no definite meaning, and that by the word *knowledge* I express something with an essence exclusively its own, so that it can be distinguished from everything else, it must also be true that our understanding and our knowledge have one *form* only ; for it is precisely this one *form* that causes them to be what they are. The *form* of a thing is that

Therefore Kant also did admit too much of the innate.
But I must examine a little more at length how this happened,
that I may prepare the way for the following section, in
which, having concluded what I had to say on the utterances
of others, I shall try to fulfil the last part of the promise
made at the beginning of this work (40), by stating clearly
that *theory on the origin of ideas* which seems to me the
true one.

ARTICLE II.

*How the Kantian forms are vitiated by excess, and how they are all
reducible to one only form.*

368. Kant describes and expounds his *forms* with the
most perfect regularity. As I have said, he assigns one to
the external sense, another to the internal ; to the understanding he gives four, but each subdivided into three ; and,
lastly, he bestows three on the reason, neither more nor less.

But this very regularity which the Kantian philosophy
presents in all its parts, so that it seems to have been
drawn out square and plummet in hand, ought to put
cautious readers on the alert, and cause them to inquire all
the more diligently whether an order so symmetrical and
so restricted be in accordance with nature ; for we see that,
in her other works, nature is wont to act with simplicity, and
to display her fecundity on much more liberal and grand a
scale than the puny and presumptuous human imagination
would fain prescribe.

369. I do not pretend here to enter into a minute examination of the *forms* of Kant. He promised to deduce
his categories rigorously from the forms of our judgments
(which is always an excellent thought), but then, instead of

which determines its *essence*, makes it what it is. As, then, a thing cannot have more *essences* than one, so it cannot have more *forms* than one. To assert the contrary would be the same as to maintain that one can be many, that a thing can be itself and not itself. Therefore those which Kant has called by the name of *forms* must be something subordinate to the first and true form of the *understanding* as well as of *knowledge*. They will be partial and derived forms, but not the one we are seeking, which constitutes the nature of our intelligence, and which, being *pure form*, cannot be multiplied except by becoming united with some-thing extraneous and belonging to the real world.

doing so, he presented his 'Table of Categories' ready-formed, with no other voucher for its accuracy than his *ipse dixit.* In no place that I can remember did he undertake to show that the analysis of the forms of our judgments gives as a result his twelve categories, and these adjusted with such nice precision as to make three exactly for each of the four fundamental forms. Having, therefore, failed to justify his symmetrical derivation of the categories, he left us in the same doubt for which he justly found fault with Aristotle,'[1] namely, as to whether these categories have been logically deduced and properly enumerated or not, or whether they give a true and complete classification of the human knowable, so that there cannot be a single item of it which does not necessarily fall under one or other of them. This Kantian partition, therefore, of our most universal ideas is quite as arbitrary as those of the ancients, and consequently the making of a minute criticism of it would be a task no less tedious than inopportune.

370. What we can see at a glance is, that Kant sometimes confounds the outer garb, as it were, which our ideas receive from the various aspects under which the mind considers them, and from the words in which they are expressed, with the ideas themselves ; and thus one and the same idea, merely because worded in a different way, is treated by him as though it were another ; which helps to secure the symmetrical regularity of his division. For example, under the fundamental category of *quality* he invents the subdivision of *infinite judgments,* which, however, do not differ from either the *affirmative* or the *negative* judgments, except in the *verbal* form.[2]

---

[1] In his *Transcendental Analytic,* book i. ch. 1) Kant speaks of the *thread of guidance for the discovery of all the pure conceptions of the understanding,* and places it in the nature of *judgment* ; but then he entirely forgets to deduce these conceptions from our judgments, but exhibits them in a table without more ado ; nor does he condescend to show us how it is that they *must* be twelve, and such precisely as he says, and in that order in which he is pleased to arrange them.

[2] As an instance of *infinite judgments* Kant adduces the proposition, 'The soul is not mortal,' and contends that this judgment differs in its *form* from this other, 'The soul is immortal.' Now if by *form* we understand the mere material wording, I agree with him ; but in themselves the two expressions *immortal* and *not mortal* are

371. In like manner he seems to ignore the existence of ideas which are determinative of distinct species of knowledge, and can therefore be made into new categories, simply from fear lest the number he has fixed upon should be augmented, and the symmetry he is so fond of suffer in consequence. Thus *continuous quantity* and *intensive quantity* ought, by right, to be subdivisions of the fundamental category of *quantity*; but he only places under it *discrete quantity*, because this gives him the opportunity of making out the three nicely-defined classes of *unity, plurality*, and *totality*.

372. Sometimes he strives to secure the predetermined symmetry by doing violence to certain ideas, that he may reduce them to some of those which have had the honour of being elevated to the rank of a *category*—for example, when he pretends to reduce *truth* to *plurality*, and *goodness* to *totality*; as if the abstract idea of the *plural number* could contain the notion of *truth*, and the abstract idea of the *whole* could contain the notion of *goodness*![1]

perfectly synonymous, and therefore do not differ as to that intrinsic or conceptual form of which we here speak. Indeed, the forms arising from the use of words are numberless; but their difference is only apparent, since they are the identical conceptions though clothed in different language. In the above example the denied attribute of *mortal* has but one opposite, *i.e. immortal*, and the case is simple. Not so, however, when the opposites are many, as, for instance, in the matter of colours. If I say 'This body is not green,' I do not by any means imply that it is, therefore, red. This, then, is a complex case, involving double sets of judgments. First set, 'It is not green,' and its contrary, 'It is green;' second set, 'It is red,' and its contrary, 'It is not red,' etc. By reducing, therefore, the complex to simple judgments, we find that there can be no judgments except *affirmative* and *negative*; and this whether the affirmation or the negation be made with probability or with certainty. Consequently the *infinite judgments* of Kant are only a mixture of those

two forms of judgments, and do not exhibit any new or original form.

[1] *Transcendental Analytic*, book i. ch. i. sect. iii. § 8. Hear how Kant attempts to make us believe that the saying of the Schoolmen, *quodlibet ens est unum verum et bonum*, is already contained in his categories of *unity, plurality*, and *totality*. He says, 'These pretended transcendental predicates are in fact nothing else than logical requisites and criteria of all cognition of objects, and they employ as the basis for this cognition the categories of *quantity*, namely, *unity, plurality*, and *totality*. But these, which must be taken as material conditions, that is, as belonging to the possibility of things themselves, they (the Schoolmen) employed merely in a formal signification, as belonging to the logical requisites of all cognition, and yet most unguardedly changed these criteria into properties of objects, as things in themselves.'

In this passage we may notice how Kant himself admits that his categories are not pure *forms*, but have something *material* attached to them.

The reason why he failed in properly

373. Again, in those which he calls *ideas* of reason, and which are his forms of the Absolute, he confounds that which is truly *absolute*, as God, with that which is so only relatively, as the *human soul* and the *universe*; so that all ideas of the Absolute must ultimately be reduced to a thing one and indivisible, namely, to the *Being of beings*, to God.

Thus the three Kantian *ideas* or *forms* of the Reason are in reality one and the same.

374. But the idea itself of God, considered as *form* of the reason, in the way that Kant represents it, remains equivocal.

For either *God* is taken for a subsistent being or He is taken only for a pure idea of our mind which, in order to its own satisfaction, conceives as possible, and also as necessary, a sort of hypothesis of the first cause.

Now this first cause, admitted merely as a vague and abstract hypothesis which our mind feels to be necessary for its own satisfaction, is not, certainly, what mankind generally understand by the term *God*. Therefore Kant, by speaking of God as he does in his *Critique of Pure Reason—i.e.* in a sense different from the universally received one—plays the part of a trickster. He abuses a name held sacred by the

---

dividing the *formal* from the *material* part of thought was because he regarded the objects of thought (considered in general) as things purely *subjective*, and therefore as *modes* of our own spirit, which saw in them nothing more than emanations of itself. With such a view in his mind he very naturally exchanged the *modes* of thought into *forms* of thought ; in the same way that Leibnitz had been deceived, when having made the knowledge both of universals and of real things to emanate from the depth of our spirit, he mixed up and confounded the world of abstractions with that of realities (296-299). Only that Kant committed a much greater error, inasmuch as he confused the objects of thought with its forms, and maintained that not merely our knowledge (to which Leibnitz had restricted his statement), but also the world itself, at least in great part, issued forth from within ourselves.

For the rest, how flimsy is the reasoning with which he tries to prove that the conception of *plurality* contains the conception of *truth !* This is, he says, because ' the more true deductions we have of a given conception, the more criteria we have of its objective truth ' (*Transcendental Analytic*, book i. ch. i. sect. iii.) ; as if the *signs* by which truth becomes known were the same as *truth*, or as if *plurality* could not be found just as well in a number of *false* deductions. *Plurality*, abstractedly considered, is like a container with nothing in it ; whereas *truth* determines and fixes a quality of the thing contained in plurality—for example, among *many* false judgments, the *one* which is true. Again, what an unnatural stretch of logic that is by which he attempts to reduce *goodness* to *totality !* Who ever heard that because I have the *whole* of a thing, therefore that thing must be *good ?* But even if this were the case, the two ideas of *totality* and *goodness* would

human race to deceive his readers and to screen himself from being branded with the opprobrious title of Atheist.[1]

In truth, if God were taken for a real Being, He could not in this present life be a natural form of our intelligence without being at the same time the direct and immediate subject-matter of our thought. But He is no such thing ; for in this life we can only think of Him indirectly, that is to say, by arguing from similitudes drawn from the finite things of which we have experience. The form of our intelligence is *ideal being,* à rule which enables us to arrive, by means of judgments, at the cognition of real beings. Therefore it must be something applicable alike to all the objects of our cognition, and cannot be any one of them.

This being premised, let us see what there is precisely of universal and formal in the idea of a first cause, the Kantian idea of God.

By analysing this idea we find that it is composed of two more elementary ideas, namely (1) the idea of *cause in general,* and (2) the idea of the *cause of all causes,* or the cause of all that exists (the universe).

Now the 'cause of all that exists' is not arrived at by our mind except by applying the idea of *cause in general* to this universe.

The idea of *cause in general* is expressed in the principle : 'Every thing that happens (every event) must have an adequate cause.'

The application of this principle to the whole collection of events, to all things that happen (the universe), imports the proposition, 'The whole aggregate of the finite (the universe) must have an adequate cause.'

Now it is obvious that this proposition, being but a consequence of the principle, that is to say, being contained in the principle as in its germ, presents no new *idea,* specifically different from the idea of 'cause in general.'

always differ as mental conceptions (*entia rationis*), and the one should never be confounded with the other.

[1] In the *Pure Reason* of Kant God is taken only as a type existing in our mind of a most perfect Being ; an ideal, an exemplar from which, however, it is impossible to infer the existence of a real God.

Therefore the idea of a 'first cause' cannot be an original form of the human intelligence different from that of 'cause in general.'

But the idea of 'cause in general' has already been classed by Kant among the twelve categories.

Therefore none of Kant's ideas of reason can be truly called a *form* of our intelligence. He has confounded in these ideas the *material* with the *formal* part of thought.

375. Let us now examine the twelve categories, called by our philosopher *forms of the understanding*, as also his two forms of the internal and external sense; and let us see whether, as he asserts, they are all truly *primitive* and *original* forms of our intelligence.

I have to observe, in the first place, that the twelve Kantian categories cannot all claim an equal rank, in the sense of being each independent of the others, and having a character so exclusively proper as not to admit of being reduced to and placed the one under the other, as minor classes under greater ones.

Let us take the form of *modality*—subdivided by Kant into the three categories of *possibility, existence,* and *necessity*—and compare it with the three other forms of *quantity, quality,* and *relation.*

No one will deny that I can very well think of a being, either *possible* or *really existent,* without being obliged to know precisely the *quantity* of *beingness* there is in it, or what *quality,* or what *relations* it has.

In this case, to use the phraseology of Kant, my understanding is conditioned by the law which binds it to think of that being either as *possible* or as really *existing,* or as *necessary* :[1] but it is by no means obliged, in addition to this, to clothe the same being with the forms of *quantity, quality,* and *relation.*

Since, therefore, a *bonâ fide* intellectual act can take place

[1] The *possible* is always *necessary,* and therefore this threefold division is faulty. The exact division would be (1) the *possible,* (2) the *subsistent,* the latter being subdivided into (a) con-tingent, (b) *necessary.* But this would have entailed the sacrifice of the τριχοτομία with which Kant seemed bent on embellishing his system.

quite irrespectively of the three forms just named, who does not see that they are not the *primitive* and *original forms* we are in search of? For be it understood that by *primitive* and *original* are meant those forms in virtue of which, and not otherwise, the understanding is understanding, and apart from which, therefore, this faculty cannot perform any of the operations proper to its nature. In short, a *primitive* and *original form* constitutes the proximate, essential, necessary term of every intellectual act.

Clearly, then, the form of *modality* is so far independent of those of *quantity*, *quality*, or *relation* that we are able to perform genuine intellectual acts by means of it alone, without having any need of them.

On the other hand, it would be impossible for us to think of the *quantity*, *quality*, or *relations* of a being, unless we had already thought of that being either as *possible* or as *really existent*.

Therefore all these three forms depend on and occupy a place inferior to that of *modality*, so that they are not think-able by us except through and subsequently to it.

Thus we may safely conclude that the three first Kantian forms of *quantity*, *quality*, and *relation* cannot be considered as *original* and *essential* forms of the human intelligence, since its existence and proper operation are conceivable wholly apart from them.

376. The same may be seen also for another reason. I ask, Is it really necessary that every being should have a determinate *quantity* and *quality?*

To affirm this positively, as Kant does, is, to say the least, to make the *Critical Reason* speak with a boldness and temerity more than dogmatical, and to credit it with the power of deciding a question which it is impossible to decide *à priori*.

If Kant had said, ' To declare that every possible being must have a determinate *quantity* and *quality* transcends the capabilities of our reason—because in order to do this we should have to examine all the beings that are possible, and furthermore to penetrate with our investigation into the nature of the Infinite Being, of whom, however, we have not a positive and adequate idea '—he would at least have shown some philosophical modesty, real or certainly apparent. His language would have been consistent with his principles; for he never seems more delighted than when he can seize an opportunity of criticising reason and inveighing against all those whom he contemptuously nicknames *dogmatic philosophers*, because they honestly avow their belief in such a thing as true objective certainty. But by himself speaking in such a peremptory tone on the matter we are discussing, by absolutely laying down the law that *quantity* and *quality* must be primitive and essential forms of the human understanding, so that it cannot think of anything without them, he has given a manifest proof of rashness of judgment, and has incautiously laid bare the hollowness of those pretensions to humility and moderation which the *Critical Philosophy* is never tired of proclaiming.

In conclusion, if among the Kantian forms any can be found worthy of being called *original* in the sense that it is the *informing principle* of the understanding itself as well as of all cognitions proceeding from it—that form can be sought only in *modality*.

Let us see therefore whether *modality* contains anything to our purpose.

377. I shall begin by remarking that when I think or judge that something really exists, I do not thereby necessarily add any perfection to my *idea* of that thing.

Indeed, I may have an *idea* as perfect and determinate as can be desired, without the thing which corresponds to it *existing* in reality.

This shows that the judgment affirmatory of the real existence of the thing of which I have the idea is an act essentially different from that by which my understanding has and contemplates the *idea* itself. My idea, *as idea*, receives no improvement whatever, no new notional element from that judgment.

Consequently the real and external *existence* which is the term of my judgment cannot be an *original form* of my understanding; because in my understanding there is nothing but the *idea* of the thing; and, as just said, this idea remains always perfectly the same, whether the external thing really subsists or not.

Thus the *form* of the understanding can only consist in an *idea*, and not in the *subsistence* of things; and, therefore, of the three Kantian categories or forms—*possibility, existence,*[1] and *necessity*—that of *existence*, considered as a thing apart from the other two, cannot in any way be considered as an *original form*, essential to the nature of our understanding.

378. Let us see, then, if the character of original and essential forms belongs to the other two categories, of *possibility* and *necessity*.

The idea of anything whatever, in so far as not showing any intrinsic contradiction, is what we call the logical *possibility* of the thing.

Now it is certainly impossible to make any intellectual act of any kind without the form of *possibility*.

But when I conceive the *possibility* of a thing, am I obliged also to think explicitly of the absolute *necessity* of the same? No, if there is question of referring this necessity to the thing thought of, and not to the possibility itself; in which latter case the necessity identifies itself with the possibility, from which it is only distinguished by a mental abstraction.

Seeing, therefore, that *necessity* is not universally and immutably the object and term of understanding, we must say that it cannot be one of its *original and essential forms*.

The outcome of all this is, that among the twelve Kantian categories *possibility* is the only one of which the character of *form of the human intelligence* can be predicated. We must, then, strive to penetrate into the nature of this *possibility*.

379. I have said that the *possibility* here spoken of is simply the *idea* of anything whatever. In fact, if we think

---

[1] Kant takes this word *existence* as meaning the particular and real existence of a thing, which mode of being R smini calls *subsistence* (TRANSLATORS).

of possibility at all, it must be the possibility of something ; for we cannot think of the possibility of nothing.

It must, however, be observed that the *something* from the thought of which the possibility (idea) is inseparable need not necessarily be limited to a particular individual, or a particular species, or even a particular genus. It suffices that it be a something, an entity, even perfectly indeterminate.[1]

The necessary inference from this is, that the *idea* (the possibility) of *indeterminate being* is the only original and essential *form* of the human intelligence.

380. We will now see how all the first nine forms ascribed by Kant to the human understanding are reduced to this one as to their formal principle, and how the other two categories placed by him under *modality—i.e. existence* and *necessity*—either have nothing of the *formal* in them or else are elements already contained in *modality* itself. Let us begin with these.

If by *existence* is meant the idea of a thing *in general*, this is included in the idea of *indeterminate being*.

But if it is taken to mean the *actual subsistence* of the thing, then it is nothing but the term of an act of the *faculty of judgment*, and does not therefore add any *form* to our intelligence.

Necessity is found by analysing *possibility*; for what is *possible* is *necessarily* such. In this sense necessity also is comprised in the idea of *indeterminate being*.

But if by *necessity* is meant a *necessary real being*, we must say of this what we have already said of the *actual subsistence* of beings generally.

381. Having thus reduced the three categories of *modality* to the one *idea of indeterminate being*, let us see how this idea includes also the three Kantian categories comprised under the head of *relation*, namely, *substance, causality,* and *action*.

As to the ideas of *substance* and *causality*, I have already demonstrated that whatever intellectual element they contain

---

[1] Even in this wholly indeterminate state it would still present to the under- standing an actual object of thought (TRANSLATORS).

is reduced precisely to the idea of *existence* or being in general
(52, 54, 347, 348). If, then, Kant placed these two ideas
among the original and essential categories or forms of the
human understanding, it was only because he did not carry
the analysis of them far enough to detect and keep separate
in them what is *pure form.*

And as regards the idea of *action,* it must be observed
that *action* is perceived not only by the understanding,
but also, in its own way, by the sense, that is, by its
experiencing it.

Now, the *particular action,* in so far as perceived by the
sense, cannot certainly be placed among the categories ; but
only the action as intellectually conceived, in other words,
the *concept of action.*

But how does it come to pass that the *particular action*
experienced by the sense is *universalised* when made an
object of the understanding ?   Simply in virtue of the power
which the understanding has of considering that particular
action as *possible* to be repeated indefinitely.   It is the
addition of *possibility,* therefore, that renders that action a
universal conception.   The same thing takes place when one
considers the nature of *action* in general, without paying
any attention to the particularities of the diverse species of
action.

The *conception* of *action,* therefore, when submitted to
analysis, is found to be not *pure form,* but composed (1) of a
material element, in so far as the conception has reference to
actions experienced by our senses ; and (2) of a *formal*
element, in so far as our understanding adds the form of
possibility, and thus abstracts and universalises the particular
actions.

Therefore all that there is of purely *formal* in the conception of idea of action is *possibility,* or the idea of *being in
general.*

382. By a similar analysis we can reduce to this same
idea the Kantian forms of *quantity* and *quality.*   When we
have eliminated from these conceptions all their *material*
part, or that supplied by the senses, we find that nothing
remains save the idea of *possibility* or being in general.

In fact, even the term of my sense-perception has a certain *quantity* and a certain *quality*. But the quantity and quality perceived by my senses are in no way a form or informing principle of my understanding. That *quantity*, therefore, and that *quality* of which I have the conception, and which, according to Kant, would also be forms or informing principles of my understanding, are a quantity and quality existing, not as particular, but as universal.

Now, how are universal quantity and universal quality obtained? By the same process which we have described with regard to the conception of *action*. When, through a judgment, I have intellectually perceived a particular quantity or quality, I can abstract from the fact of its real existence, and conceive it purely as *possible*. To conceive it so is to *universalise* it. And if from this conceptual or possible quantity or quality I take away those characteristics which make it a distinct species, I then have *generic* quantity or quality.

Quantity and *quality*, therefore, are not necessary objects of my understanding, as though they were by their own nature its *forms*; but in order to become such forms they require to be themselves *informed* by another form, and this form (added to them by my understanding) is no other than *possibility*.

By themselves alone they are merely a *material part* of thought; it is my understanding which, by adding to them the *formal* part, renders them *conceptions, ideas*.

Thus the analysis of the conceptions of *quantity* and *quality* shows that their only formal element is the idea of *possibility* or *being in general.*

Once more, then, the twelve Kantian forms of the human understanding are seen to be reduced to one only.

383. And here there is no need to speak of those which Kant designates as 'forms of the external and internal sense,' namely, *space* and *time*, because these are not things belonging to the intellectual order. Whatever question, then, may be raised concerning them, can only refer to the conceptions of them.

Now, from what has been said thus far, it will be easy to perceive that the only purely formal part in such conceptions is the idea of *possibility* or being in general, or, which is the same thing, *indeterminate being.*

384. But there is another difference to be noted between the nature of the multitudinous forms of Kant and the nature of that one which has remained in our hands after the disappearance of all the rest. It is, that all the Kantian forms issue from within the thinking subject himself, and are therefore *subjective* ; whereas the one true form is essentially *object.* This diversity of nature, as we shall hereafter see, is of infinite importance. Here I can only forewarn the reader of it.

Let us conclude : the human understanding has not any *determinate* form innate in it ; and the seventeen forms of Kant are not only baseless assumptions, but quite superfluous for explaining the origin of ideas.

The form innate in the human understanding is one only, and that wholly *indeterminate, i.e.* the idea of *being in general.*

This idea is *pure form.* It has no material element of any kind attached to it. It is not subjective, but *per se* object. It is a thing so simple and so small that it would be impossible to simplify it further, or to imagine anything less which could be capable of informing our cognitions. At the same time its fecundity is inexhaustible.

Indeed, it would not be possible to imagine a single intellectual act which does not stand in need of this form, or is not constituted, *i.e.* made what it is, by it ; since if we take away the *idea of being* we annihilate the possibility of human knowledge and of the intellectual faculty itself.

Having thus reduced all that there can be of innate in our intelligence to the *least* possible, it now only remains for me to show how this *minimum* is nevertheless sufficient to account completely for the formation of all our ideas. This I shall endeavour to do in the next volume.

Spottiswoode & Co., Printers, New Street Square, London.

www.ingramcontent.com/pod-product-compliance
Lightning Source LLC
Chambersburg PA
CBHW032306280326
41932CB00009B/712